A Coral Reef Handbook

A guide to the geology,
flora and fauna of
the Great Barrier Reef

A Coral Reef Handbook

A guide to the geology,
flora and fauna of
the Great Barrier Reef

Edited by
Patricia Mather and Isobel Bennett

Published by
Surrey Beatty & Sons Pty Limited

The National Library of Australia
Cataloguing-in-Publication entry:

A Coral Reef Handbook: a guide to the
geology, flora and fauna of
the Great Barrier Reef.

3rd ed.

ISBN 0 949324 47 7.

1. Coral reef biology — Queensland — Great Barrier Reef.
2. Great Barrier Reef (Qld.). I. Mather, Patricia, 1925– .
II. Bennett, Isobel, 1909– . III. Australian Coral Reef Society.
(Series: Handbook series (Australian Coral Reef Society); No. 1).

574.90942

First Edition 1978
Second Edition 1984
Completely revised and expanded
Third Edition 1993

PRINTED AND PUBLISHED IN AUSTRALIA BY
SURREY BEATTY & SONS PTY LIMITED
43 Rickard Road, Chipping Norton, NSW 2170

Acknowledgements

We gratefully acknowledge the generous contribution of the Great Barrier Reef Marine Park Authority, which provided most of the colour photographs used throughout these pages. Other contributors of colour photographs are separately acknowledged in the respective captions. Also, we are especially indebted to Naoko Kikkawa, whose bird paintings are reproduced here in black and white. The illuminations heading the algal, fish, reptile and maritime archaeology sections are by the late R. P. Kenny, committed teacher of marine biology at James Cook University of North Queensland from its inception. They are reproduced here with the kind permission of his widow, Helen. The coral cay and reef at the top of page 7 is by Robert Allen. Roly McKay of the Queensland Museum drew the representative fish silhouettes; E. Cameron drew the skink and gekko; and J. Jeffrey of Sydney University drew the Seagrasses. Mick Fordy and Paul Llewellyn of University College, Swansea, respectively provided the scanning electron micrographs of Bryozoa and the drawings of Zoanthidea. Steve Francis, Vicki Sands and Bronwyn Perkins contributed to the artwork in the coelenterate, worm and echinoderm sections. All other illustrations are the work of each respective author except where expressly acknowledged.

Peta Woodgate typed the final edited manuscript and John Kennedy helped with the final compilation of the figures and their captions. Thora Whitehead and Kevin Lamprell advised on the gastropods and bivalves occurring in the region.

Both Terry Walker and Brian King made their unpublished work available for the article on birds in this handbook. Tragically, toward the end of 1991, Brian King died after a long illness; and only months later, Terry Walker lost his life while monitoring sea birds in the Gulf of Carpentaria.

Preface

Australian Aborigines lived along the coast of northeastern Australia for many thousands of years. Although not great seafaring people, they did visit the near-shore reefs and islands of the Great Barrier Reef. Their middens remain as evidence of the bounty they fished from the sea. Malaysian fishermen, too, who have visited these waters for many centuries, perceive them as a happy hunting ground where clams, trepang and other rich food organisms abound. However, for western European navigators, Chevalier de Bougainville and Captain James Cook of the mid-18th century, and others who followed them, passage through these waters was associated with the ever present fear of imminent shipwreck.

For scientists, perceptions of the Great Barrier Reef are different again. It is a place of mystery and wonder. How the coral grows and the reefs develop have been questions that have excited their imagination and stimulated their enquiries for at least 200 years.

In the Queensland of 1922, Governor Sir Matthew Nathan, and geologist Professor Henry Caselli Richards took steps to have these questions answered. They set up the Great Barrier Reef Committee (originally as part of the Queensland Branch of the Royal Geographical Society) to promote scientific investigation of the Great Barrier Reef.

For 60 years, the Committee sponsored, and sometimes itself conducted, geological and biological research, expeditions and symposia. It founded and operated the Heron Island Research Station, advised governments on use and conservation of the reefs and their resources, and published reports and proceedings.

By 1981, to some extent the result of the Committee's efforts, other institutions had become directly involved in reef research. The University of Sydney, James Cook University and the Australian Museum were operating research stations at One Tree Island, Orpheus Island and Lizard Island, respectively, and the Heron Island Station was by now owned and operated by the University of Queensland. The Australian Government had established the Australian Institute of Marine Science (AIMS) at Cape Townsend near Townsville (to conduct scientific investigation of the Great Barrier Reef); and the Great Barrier Reef Marine Park Authority (to ensure its conservation by regulating its use). Thus, with many of its original aims now achieved, the Great Barrier Reef Committee changed its name and its role, and became the Australian Coral Reef Society.

One of the Committee's last achievements was the publication of the first edition of the Coral Reef Handbook. It was based on field excursion notes prepared when, just after its 50th birthday, the Committee was host to international coral reef scientists at the Second International Coral Reef Symposium (1973) held on board the Dominion Line TSMV *Marco Polo* as it cruised between Lizard and Heron Islands. A slightly expanded edition of the handbook was published by the Committee's successor, the Australian Coral Reef Society (1984). Like the first edition, it referred specifically to the Capricorn and Bunker Groups of islands and reefs at the southern tip of the Great Barrier Reef.

The new Coral Reef Handbook is, as far as it has been possible to make it, a guide to the geology, flora and fauna of the whole of the Great Barrier Reef. As well as having an increased geographic scope it contains sections on marine mammals, sea grasses, maritime archaeology, and the history of the reefs since European settlement in Australia.

The number of taxa treated has been expanded, and all sections have been brought up to date.

The handbook is designed to be a guide for the interested layman, and for teachers and their students at secondary and tertiary level, enabling visitors to the reef to recognize some of the organisms and structures they will encounter, and to understand their significance and role in the coral reef ecosystem, both above and below the high tide mark. A uniform treatment for each section has not been attempted. All the authors are experts in the subject they have treated, and each one has been encouraged to present his or her own unique and original approach to the subject.

It is hoped that this diversity of approach will be stimulating and will help the user of the handbook to an appreciation of the diversity of the reefs, and the complexity of systems which contribute to their growth and development. Nevertheless, in each account, diagnostic notes and drawings are given to assist in identification at least of the commonly occurring organisms and the dominant processes. In a handbook of this size, and in view of its intended use, a detailed and comprehensive account of every species and process is not possible. Instead, references to major works are given and will provide details not available in the handbook. In some cases accounts of one or another part of the Great Barrier Reef are merely an example of the sorts of processes that occur along the 2 000 km of its latitudinal length.

Inevitably the comprehensiveness of any account of the Great Barrier Reef is also limited by what is not yet known. There still remains much that is not understood, many groups of organisms are not yet studied, and some have been studied in only limited areas. Heron Island and One Tree Island and their reefs at the southern end of the Reef, remain perhaps two of the best known reefs and cays, investigated for nearly half a century by generations of student and scientist visitors to the Heron Island Research Station and later, also to the field station on One Tree Island. With the establishment of James Cook University of North Queensland, and its research station on Orpheus Island, followed by the Australian Museum's Lizard Island Research Station, the Australian Institute of Marine Science, the Museum of Tropical Queensland (the northern branch of the Queensland Museum), and the Great Barrier Reef Marine Park Authority, the northern part of the Great Barrier Reef is now subjected to a degree of scientific scrutiny that is setting new international standards in coral reef research.

The reefs and islands of the Great Barrier Reef provide a laboratory in which the natural world can be studied, and knowledge of it increased and used for our long-term benefit. They offer us a rich experience of wilderness and a place for recreation — uses enhanced by their ready accessibility to the cities of the eastern seaboard of Australia.

We hope this handbook will enhance the satisfaction that visitors can derive from a visit to a coral reef through an increased understanding of the processes and organisms that make up these remarkable ecosystems.

Isobel Bennett
Patricia Mather
Editors
August 1992

Contents

CONTENTS

List of Colour Plates

Introduction

The Great Barrier Reef is a chain of coral reefs that stretches for some 2 000 km, almost parallel to the northeastern Australian coastline, on the edge of the Continental Shelf (Fig. 1). Each reef is a thin veneer of living coral that caps a structure composed largely of calcareous debris (sand and rubble) resulting from the breakdown and subsequent consolidation of coral skeletons and those of other organisms. On some of the reefs, coincidence of wind, and tidal and other currents, cause sediments to accumulate, forming coral cays (islands on the top of a reef). Subsequently seeds, dropped by birds or washed ashore by the seas, grow to stablize the coral sands, and provide nesting sites for sea birds and turtles, which in their turn, transfer nutrients from the sea to the land to fertilize the grasses, herbs and forests that create habitats for land-based animals and plants.

As well, continental islands — emergent continental uplands on the drowned continental shelf — provide alternate habitats. The well vegetated cays and islands and extensive reefs (sometimes enclosing deep lagoons), with luxuriant coral growth especially on their seaward slopes, have high natural values, including spectacular seascapes and landscapes both above and below the surface of the sea.

Some of the region's diversity is derived from its great latitudinal length, variety of its habitats, and its proximity to the Australian coast; but some is from its geographic position in the very centre of the vast Indo-West Pacific coralline region. Many of the species of organisms have extensive geographic ranges, from the coral reefs of the Western Indian Ocean through Indonesia and the Malaysian Archipelago to the reefs of the Western Pacific including the Fijian islands and often beyond, to French Polynesia and Hawaii. Although many of the populations probably receive recruits only from neighbouring ones, they are part of a vast interconnected network in which larvae, drifting from reef to reef and island to island, ensure that populations are not isolated.

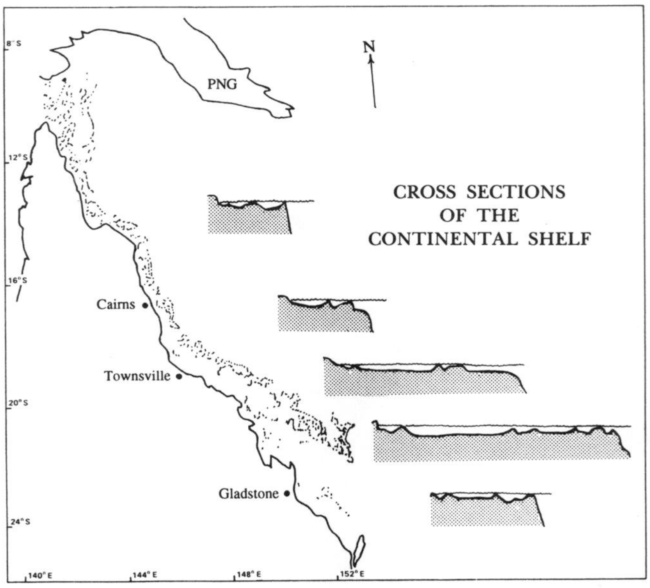

We are beginning to understand some of the fundamental processes common to the whole length of the Great Barrier Reef and to coral reefs wherever they occur. Nevertheless, despite their similarities, there are differences, and those who are lucky enough to visit more than one coral reef location will observe something of the diversity that is one of their most celebrated characteristics.

Fig. 1. Distribution of reefs of the Great Barrier Reef with cross sections of the continental shelf (shelf depth less than 30 m).

Contributors

Phil Alderslade, Museum of the Northern Territory, Darwin, Northern Territory 0801 — **Octocorallia**

Peter Arnold, Museum of Tropical Queensland, Townsville, Queensland 4810 — **Marine Mammals**

Isobel Bennett, Newport, New South Wales 2106 — **Reef Zonation**

Niel Bruce, Queensland Museum, South Brisbane, Queensland 4101 — **Non-Decapod Crustacea**

Lester Cannon, Queensland Museum, South Brisbane, Queensland 4101 — **Worms, Polyclad Turbellaria** (with Leslie Newman), **Coelenterates, Echinodermata**

Alan B. Cribb, Brookfield, Queensland 4069 — **Algae, Terrestrial Plants**

Peter Davie, Queensland Museum, South Brisbane, Queensland 4101 — **Decapod Crustacea**

Valerie Todd Davies, Queensland Museum, South Brisbane, Queensland 4101 — **Spiders**

Stanley J. Edmonds, South Australian Museum, Adelaide, South Australia 5000 — **Echiurida, Sipuncula**

Christer Erséus, Swedish Museum of Natural History, Stockholm, Sweden — **Oligochaeta**

Peter Flood, University of New England, Armidale, New South Wales 2350 — **Geology and Geomorphology**

Peter Gesner, Queensland Museum, South Brisbane, Queensland 4101 — **Maritime Archaeology**

Ray Gibson, Liverpool Polytechnic, Liverpool L3 3AF, England — **Nemertea**

Peter Hayward, University College of Swansea, Swansea SA2 8PP, Wales — **Bryozoa** (with J. Ryland)

Harold Heatwole, North Carolina State University, Raleigh, NC 27695-7617, USA — **Reptilia; Terrestrial Biota of Islands; Terrestrial Arthropods**

John Hooper, Queensland Museum, South Brisbane, Queensland 4101 — **Porifera**

Karen Gowlett Holmes, South Australian Museum, Adelaide, South Australia 5000 — **Polyplacophora**

Kees Hulsman, Griffith University, Brisbane, Queensland 4111 — **Birds** (with J. Kikkawa)

Patricia Hutchings, Australian Museum, Sydney South, New South Wales 2000 — **Polychaeta**

John Jell, University of Queensland, Brisbane, Queensland 4067 — **Foraminiferida** (with V. Palmieri)

Jiro Kikkawa, University of Queensland, Brisbane, Queensland 4067 — **Birds** (with K. Hulsman)

Patricia Kott (Mather), Queensland Museum, South Brisbane, Queensland 4101 — **Ascidiacea**

Anthony Larkum, Sydney University, Sydney, New South Wales 2006 — **Seagrasses**

Colin Limpus, Department of Environment and Heritage, Brisbane, Queensland 4002 — **Turtles**

C. C. Lu, Museum of Victoria, Melbourne, Victoria 3000 — **Cephalopoda**

Helene Marsh, James Cook University of North Queensland, Townsville, Queensland 4810 — **Dugong**

Angus Muirhead, University College of Swansea, Swansea SA2 8PP, Wales — **Zoanthidea** (with J. Ryland)

Vincent Palmieri, Queensland Department of Mines, Brisbane, Queensland 2000 — **Foraminiferida** (with J. Jell)

Darryl Potter, Queensland Museum, South Brisbane, Queensland 4101 — **Gastropoda, Bivalvia** (with J. Stanisic)

William Rudman, Australian Museum, Sydney, New South Wales 2000 — **Opisthobranchia**

Dennis M. Reeves, Brisbane, Queensland 4001 — **Lepidoptera**

Barry C. Russell, Museum of Northern Territory, Darwin, Northern Territory 5794 — **Fish**

John Ryland, University College of Swansea, Swansea SA2 8PP, Wales — **Bryozoa** (with P. Hayward), **Zoanthidea** (with A. Muirhead)

John Stanisic, Queensland Museum, South Brisbane, Queensland 4101 — **Gastropoda, Bivalvia** (with D. Potter)

Christopher Tudge, University of Queensland, Brisbane, Queensland 4067 — **Hermit Crabs**

Carden Wallace, Museum of Tropical Queensland, Townsville, Queensland 4810 — **Scleractinia**

Len Zell, University of New England, Armidale, New South Wales 2350 — **Diversity and Change in Time and Space**

Habitats
Collection
Preservation

Habits and Habitats

The animal and plant communities of a coral reef are rich and diverse and there are few locations or habitats that do not have communities of living organisms, often living in close association with one another. They constitute the complex food webs by which energy is cycled through the system, from the plants that trap it from the sun, through herbivores and filter feeders to the climax carnivores, scavengers and deposit feeders.

As well as organisms that are in open waters *(pelagic)*, floating *(planktonic)* or swimming *(nektonic)* there are those on or in the bottom *(benthic)*, or that burrow into the rock of which the reef is made, and into coral skeletons. The benthic organisms that live on the sea floor *(benthos)* include those that live permanently associated with a particular place *(sessile)*. Sessile animals are either attached to a substrate *(fixed)* or merely live permanently associated with an area *(territorial)*. The term *demersal* is used for fishes that live around a coral reef in contrast to the pelagic species that range the interreefal areas. Still little known because of their small size (less than 1 mm) there also are the minute organisms *(meiofauna)* that live between the sand grains *(interstitial)*. Even smaller organisms *(microfauna)* such as protozoans and bacteria cover surfaces in and on the sediments and hard surfaces, or are suspended in the waters.

Associations between two different organisms that involve actually living together are generally referred to as *symbiotic* relationships. Some of these are so close that the partners are mutually dependant *(mutualism)*. In others, one of the partners exploits the other *(parasitism)*. However, there are other cases of association in which the relationship is less close, the level of dependence is low and the partners do quite well without one another *(commensalism)*.

Collecting

Collecting in the Great Barrier Reef Marine Park requires a permit from the Great Barrier Reef Marine Park Authority and/or from the Queensland Department of the Environment and Heritage.

Many molluscs, worms, and crustaceans can be collected by turning over boulders. Faster moving organisms that retreat back into burrows are best collected by breaking up pieces of reef. Rock or dead coral or calcareous substrates can also be dissolved in acid to release their inhabitants (Hutchings and Weate 1978). Species living in sediments can be sampled with a corer or suction lift bag using compressed air. Some species are easily caught with a dip net.

Meiofaunal organisms (animals that pass through a 1.0 mm sieve or net) can be collected by allowing about 10 litres of sediment to stand in a bucket at a few degrees above the ambient temperature. Surface samples of 20–30 g should be washed in several volumes of sea water and the supernatant quickly decanted through a suitable sieve. This should be repeated with several changes of sea water and then the sieve back-flushed into a petri dish. Other methods, e.g., using anaesthetics or ice to aid in extraction are outlined in Hulings and Gray (1971). Specimens can also be sorted directly from sediments by spreading these out in a flat sorting tray. Small individuals will sometimes float off but larger ones will have to be picked out. They can be seen more easily if they are stained with Rose Bengal.

Care should always be taken when working, or even just walking or swimming on coral reefs. Skin irritations can be caused by stinging coelenterates, polychaete setae, echinoderm spines and sponge spicules. Coral cuts and scratches readily become infected and are difficult to heal.

If possible, colour photographs of living organisms *in situ* should be taken, preferably before collection, for colour, often the shape, and many of the surface features that depend on tissue turgor are lost following preservation.

Fixing and Preserving

Animals should first be narcotized to relax them and prevent distortion by contraction. Fixing is then necessary to kill and stabilize the tissues. The process and the agent used depend on the purpose for which material is being collected. Special agents (such as Bouin's or glutaraldehyde) must be used for histology and electron microscopy. For general purposes the specimen can usually be relaxed by adding a narcotizing agent, such as menthol or magnesium sulphate crystals, to the water it is in; or putting it in a 7% solution of magnesium chloride. It is then killed by adding formalin to the seawater to a strength of 4% — 1 part of 40% formaldehyde to 10 parts (including the specimen itself) of seawater. Formalin is not a good long-term preservative. Unless a buffer is used the formalin reacts with protein in the animal tissues to form an acid. Calcareous particles in the water will buffer it sufficiently for short term preservation (put in a few particles of coral debris) but any organism with calcareous spicules or chitinous exoskeleton (e.g., sponges, crustaceans and echinoderms) should be preserved in 70% ethyl alcohol. Some organisms require special fixing and preserving techniques (see Lincoln and Sheals 1979), some of these are set out below.

Ctenophora — These animals are exceedingly fragile. Nets should not be used and many dissolve completely in formalin. The following formula has been recommended for killing and fixing: 100 cc of 1% chromic acid plus 5 cc of glacial acetic acid. After 15–30 min fixation, specimens are transferred to 70% alcohol by stages, beginning with 30%.

Soft Corals — Fix in 70% alcohol.

Parasitic Worms — These must be carefully handled (see Lincoln and Sheals 1979). It is undesirable either to freeze and thaw the host before examining it for parasites, or to immerse the host whole or dissected into fixative. Ideally worms should be collected from freshly killed hosts and placed in physiological saline. Some, such as flukes and tapeworms, may need to be shaken to remove mucous. Relaxation in freshwater for a few hours often prevents tapeworms from coiling when placed in fixative. Generally, flukes, tapeworms and acanthocephalans should be dropped into or flooded with near boiling 4% (10% by volume) formalin. Nematodes need to be dropped or immersed in 70–80% ethyl alcohol. Flatworms are routinely stained and mounted whole in Canada balsam for identication, but nematodes are merely cleared in beechwood creosote and examined in a temporary mount, then rinsed in acid alcohol before re-storing in alcohol.

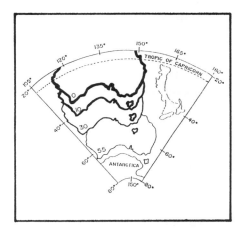

Geological History of the Reef

Drifting Plates and Glaciations

A combination of geological events affecting the northeastern coast of Australia, that began some 53 million years ago, determined the development of the Great Barrier Reef. The first of these was when Australia and New Zealand separated from the supercontinent, Gondwana, and slowly drifted northwards (at a rate of a few centimetres per year). Subsequently the eastern portion of the Australian Plate (now represented by New Zealand and the large continental landmass underlying the tiny Lord Howe Island) separated and moved away from Australia. Simultaneously, spreading produced the Tasman Sea, the margin of the eastern Australian Continental Shelf began to subside, and marine conditions replaced non-marine. Evidence for these events comes from deep seismic studies which show the area underlying the present continental margin dominated by terrestrial sediments from rivers, which eventually gave way to an alternation of deltaic and onlapping marine sediments.

About 30 million years ago the earth began to experience the effects of world-wide temperature fluctuations associated with the great ice ages of the late Tertiary. Falls and rises in sea level varied the depth of water over the continental shelf as the polar ice caps expanded and later contracted. During glacial periods the sea retreated, the continental shelf of northeastern Australia was exposed, and rivers deposited their sediment load along its edge. Each period of glaciation and lower sea level lasted for some hundreds of thousands of years. Then, with each interglacial warming, the ice melted, the sea level rose, and the shoreline moved many kilometres westward across the continental shelf. Depending on the gradient of the shelf, this landward transgression of the sea ranged from 20 km to more than 250 km at the southern end of the Great Barrier Reef.

Meanwhile, irrespective of the rise and fall of the sea, the Australian continental mass continued its northward drift, and the edge of the continent continued its gradual subsidence.

How the Reefs Developed

About 17 million years ago the northern tip of Australia passed into the warm waters of the Tropics, and for the first time the potential for coral reef growth existed. Coral larvae, from the already-flourishing central Pacific coral reefs, were available to colonize the rocky or sandy substrates where the water was shallow. Once established, the coral reefs flourished. The oldest coral reefs include the buried Ashmore-Boot-Portlock reef trend within the Gulf of Papua and others that developed on the tropical platforms of north-east Australia, some persisting until the present day. Though some reefs drowned with rising sea level during interglacial periods, others kept pace with the rise so that the growing coral stayed just below the surface in the clear sunlight. When sea levels fell, and corals were exposed to the air, their hard calcareous skeletons, cemented into large, resistant limestone pinnacles, were left standing on the broad, flat continental shelf (Fig. 2).

The first evidence of the geological history of the Great Barrier Reef came from two deep bores, one on Michaelmas Cay (1926) and one 1 100 km to the south on Heron Island (1937; Fig. 3). In each, similar sequences of coralline material from the surface to depths of 124 and 155 m were encountered. The coralline material rested on poorly consolidated quartz sands. At first it was thought that all the fossils in the bores were similar to present day forms, so it was suggested that there was no firm evidence of any sediment older than Recent (deposited within the past 20 000 years). Further, these fossils appeared to be shallow-water forms, so it was concluded that considerable subsidence, perhaps as much as 200 m, had occurred.

In the early 1970s a major breakthrough in the interpretation of the drill cores showed these proposals to be incorrect. The vertical record is one of superposition of reefs, separated by significant erosion surfaces and sometimes soil development. The reefs are, in fact, composite structures up to 150 m thick, resulting from episodic rather than continuous growth. Only one-fifth of their depth is above the sea floor, the remainder being buried in sand and mud. Researchers demonstrated, in the drill cores, several major solution unconformities or erosion surfaces associated with the reefs exposure at the time of sea level falls.

These features were identified as zones of calcite, formed by recrystallization of the pre-existing aragonitic skeletal material due to exposure to freshwater during subaerial exposure of the limestone. The microfossil content of the bores was also found to include some earlier forms than those originally identified and they indicated that reefs began their growth at Heron Island in the late Pliocene (more than about 2 million years ago).

The latest evidence on the history of the reefs came from the International Ocean Drilling Program in 1990. Investigating the platforms and reefs off the northeastern Australian continental margin it was found that although the oldest reefs are in the north (on platforms in the Gulf of Papua and Coral Sea) where tropical conditions were first encountered, the subsidence of the continental slope off Cairns had not progressed sufficiently for a marine transgression until about a million years ago.

Information about the history of reefs can also be derived from their shape, which often mimics the shape of the substrates on which they developed. Those parts of an exposed

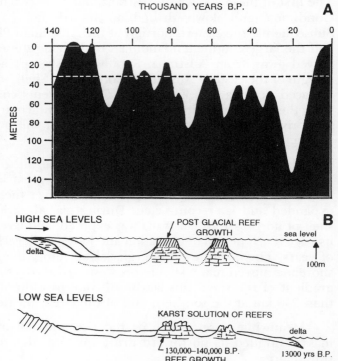

Fig. 2. **A** — Sea Level relative to present sea level for the past 140 000 years (dashed line represents the general level below which the shelf is exposed, reefs are killed and non-marine sedimentation prevailes on the shelf. In addition to the past 10 000 years, coral reef development is generally restricted to the periods 140 000 to 120 000 and 83 000 and 105 000 years before present). **B** — Idealized representation of conditions at times of high and low sea level during the past 2 million years when sea level fluctuated some 150 m in response to glacial events.

4

limestone platform or reef that trap rainwater will eventually be dissolved by that water. Thus central lagoons of exposed reefs become increasingly excavated as water trapped in them dissolves the limestone. The outer margin remains elevated, and when sea levels rise again coral reef organisms re-establish themselves on the limestone substrate of the elevated margin around the central lagoon of the earlier reef — where the water is shallow and where the waves and currents around the outside of the reef circulate the oxygen and nutrients they need for growth and wash them free of the sediments that otherwise might smother them.

Present Reef Morphology

It has been demonstrated by shallow coring of modern reefs that development is closely correlated with the height of the limestone platform relative to the rising sea level. In general the rate of sea level rise (7–10 m per 1 000 years) may outstrip the rate of coral reef growth (7–8 m per 1 000 years). The oldest dated coral reef cores show that growth associated with the recent sea level rise began about 8 500 years ago in water depths ranging from 8 to 20 m below the modern sea level. This means that a water depth in excess of 10 m may have existed during the initial phase of recent reef growth on the pre-existing platforms. Once the sea level stabilized about 6 500 years ago reefs quickly caught up with it, and began to grow laterally.

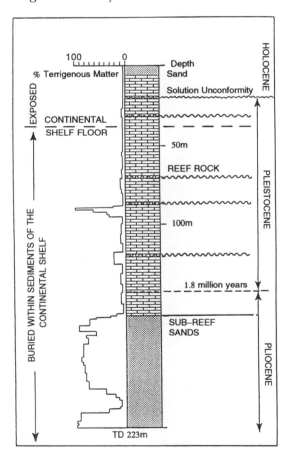

Fig. 3. Heron Island Bore (1937) encountered almost 150 m of shallow water limestone resting on unconsolidated marine sands which contain fossils older than 2 million years. The limestone sequence contains at least six discrete phases of coral reef development separated by solution unconformities.

When observing the present-day morphology of reef types it is important to realize that the reefs are at different stages of development, and that reefs themselves can be described as juvenile, adolescent, mature and senile. Reefs which began to grow on the highest platforms in the shallow water, reached modern sea level before those growing from lower platforms in deeper water, where vertical growth of the coral reef was not able to keep pace with the rising sea level. Thus one tends to observe an across-the-shelf transition of more developed reefs in the shallow water near the shore to less developed reefs in the deeper water near the shelf edge. Once reef growth reaches the level of mean low water, vertical growth ceases and the prevailing hydraulic regime (currents, waves, tides) modifies the growth. Subsequent evolution involves growth primarily to leeward (away from the wind direction), sediment infilling of back-reef lagoons, and replacement of the frame-building organisms which dominated the initial phase of vertical growth by substrate-controlled organisms. It should be noted that the reef framework is only a small part of a mature reef. Most of the reef (as much as 90%) is debris infilling the fore-reef or back-reef (including the lagoon environments on some large platform reefs).

When considering coral growth and reef development it is important to note that growth is the sum of both constructive and destructive processes operating over a time span of several thousand years. Rates of vertical growth of corals of up to 14 m per thousand years have been recorded but such a linear measure of coral growth may be several times greater than the three-dimensional growth of the reef framework. Also it has been shown that different rates of growth occur in different environments in the same reef. Projections of the interplay of reef growth and sediment discharge from the coastal rivers indicate that the Great Barrier Reef could become buried in sand and mud within the next two million years.

Although it is the youngest (reefs in the central Pacific and western Atlantic began to develop 25 million years ago), the Great Barrier Reef is the largest carbonate province in the world today, extending for 2 300 km along the continental shelf from Torres Strait to Lady Elliot Island. Behind the shelf-edge reefs, which in places are 250 km offshore, is the protected lagoon, where waters are never more than 40 m deep.

The northern, central and southern regional divisions of the Great Barrier Reef are based on water depth and type of reef. About 71% of the northern 800 km of the shelf edge has a near continuous line of narrow (ribbon) reefs, separated by small, deep passages. Reefs front only 45% of the 640 km of the central section, most of them being several kilometres landward of the shelf-edge and separated from each other by wide expanses of deep water. Generally reefs are widely dispersed also in the southern section where only 36% of its 800 km of shelf edge has reefs (the Pompey Complex in the northeastern sector).

The Geomorphology of a Coral Reef

Coral reefs and cays are affected by ocean swells and currents, including the strong tidal currents that ebb and flow, usually duirnally, around the reef. Wind also affects the direction of water flow in the surface layers and so affects the direction of sediment and nutrient transport across the reef flat, especially at low tide when the water is shallow. Storms affect reefs by the force of the waves battering at them, breaking coral and disturbing and eroding consolidating sediments; and eroding the shores of coral cays.

The geomorphology of Heron Island, a vegetated coral cay at the southern end of the Great Barrier is discussed in some detail below, and information on other reefs and islands of the Bunker Capricorn Groups is summarized to demonstrate the diversity of reef morphology as well as some of the dynamic forces that persistently shape and change coral reefs and islands.

Heron Island Reef

The Heron Island Reef is an elongate lagoonal platform reef, about 11 km long and 5 km wide at its eastern end. Its sand cay is situated on the leeward side of the western end of the reef.

Ocean swells of 1 to 3 m amplitude predominate from the east-south-east. Waves breaking on the reef rim can exceed 2 m and they retract around the reef. A nett lateral transport of sedimentary particles from windward to leeward occurs across the reef. Sediment is deposited and may accumulate where wave sets converge, e.g., the sand cay area. The water level on the intertidal parts of the reef is sufficiently shallow, even at high tide, to allow wind action to stir up the sand and keep silt in suspension. The tidal range varies from 2 m (springs) to 1 m (neaps). Tidal currents around the reef set westerly on the flood tide and easterly on the ebb tide and rarely exceed 2 km/h. As the water level falls drainage is crudely radial until the reef rim becomes exposed then it flows to leeward past the island. The lagoon experiences slack water for several hours during each tidal cycle. Mean summer (January) water temperatures on the reef flat range between 26°C and 27°C, whereas the mean mid-winter (July) temperature drops to between 20°C and 21°C.

At low water spring tides, a very considerable amount of the reef rim and reef flat lies exposed, water draining off the reef through numerous channels. There is a large lagoon occupying a considerable area of the eastern portion of the reef. From the shore below the Research Station (the southern side of the cay), the following distinct zones are clearly visible, and with slight variation, the same zones are found out from the opposite, northern, side of the cay (see Fig. 4).

The Reef Slope

The reef slope is the subtidal portion of the reef mass extending seaward from the reef rim, and sloping steeply towards the off-reef floor or continental shelf. Its upper 15 m consists of a profusion of living coral forming a strong rigid framework.

On the windward (southeastern, southern and southwestern) edge of the reef, spur-and-groove structure (channels between reef outgrowths) is well developed towards the top of this zone. The spurs carry luxuriant developments of coral and coralline algae, whereas the sandy rubble floors of the grooves support little coral or algal growth apart from occasional *Halimeda* because of the scouring action of waves and tidal run-off through these gullies. The grooves often open out on to a terrace where a fan of rubble and coarse sand accumulates under normal conditions. Sediment is distributed either back to the reef top or down the reef slope during storms or cyclones. The reef slope on the windward side is dominated by large spreading and branching species of the coral *Acropora*, and large heads of massive corals. Coralline algae encrust the coral marginal to the reef rim. On the leeward side spur-the-groove structures are not developed. The slope is less steep, large stands of branching *Acropora* are less common, and a thick sediment wedge develops at the base of the slope.

The Reef Rock Rim

The reef rim is the highest part of the intertidal portion of the reef, being a few centimetres above the upper level of coral growth. It is continuous except for a few places on the western and northeastern margin. Tidal currents are controlled by these breaches, and sometimes modify the sediment distribution on the reef. Coralline algae cement the upper surface of the rim and thereby form a pavement which either slopes gently to seaward or is terraced.

Coral shingle, in places, forms extensive mounds up to 240 m long 15 m wide and 1 m high. Reef blocks (once called niggerheads or negroheads) are also common on the lee side of this zone. To seaward of the reef blocks is a smooth sediment-free platform with

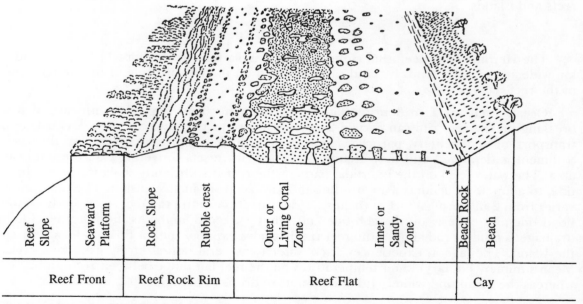

Fig. 4. Cross section (diagrammatic) of a reef in the Capricorn Group, sea to island, not to scale and with vertical distances greatly exaggerated. (*inshore gutter, sometimes present).

corals restricted to the potholes and basin-like pools. *Acropora, Favites, Montipora* and encrusting forms are common, and the pavement may be encrusted also by coralline algae, which in places form low meandering terraces. Low, sand-binding, algal mats, which entrap considerable quantities of sediment including the foraminifers *Calcarina, Baculogypsina,* and *Marginopora* also occur sporadically on these terraces. In places extensive patches of the zoanthid *Palythoa* may occur.

The Reef Flat

The reef flat is the portion of the reef top which extends inward from the inner side of the reef rim. It also is exposed during low tide. Algal encrustation is characteristic of the outer region; living coral cover decreases inwards; and sand predominates on the inner part of the reef flat. Around the eastern and southern margins the large banks of shingle of the reef rim project as tongues across the flat. They form on the windward parts of the reef, in the east-southeasterly direction. At least at the western end of the reef flat the sediment is a veneer over a porous limestone substrate which is cemented by coralline algae and aragonite.

Two subzones with transition zones between are readily defined on the western end of the reef (see Fig. 4). Their differentiation, however, is less obvious to the east. They are:

Outer Reef Flat or Coral-Algal or Living Coral Subzone. Living coral with extensive algal encrustation and sheets of coral shingle are typical of this outermost zone of the reef flat. Sand patches are restricted to coral pools or narrow channels. These average 2.5 m in width and 0.5 m in depth and are aligned perpendicular to the reef rim, giving this zone a radial pattern. The subzone varies in width from 15 to 105 m in the north. The shingle bank on the western end of the reef flat has grown considerably in the past 15 years, and is now 200 m long and 1 m above low tide level. Usually the coral grows 3 to 5 cm above the extreme low-water levels of the reef flat. With the breaches in the harbour wall, the water levels of the reef flat have fallen approximately 10 cm and the upper portion of the corals have been killed. Branching *Acropora* species such as *A. hebes, A. pulchra, A. aspera* and *A. cuneata* are common in this zone. Massive coral genera *Favites, Favia* and *Goniopora* are common while *Platygyra, Seriatopora, Pocillipora, Lobophyllia, Tubipora, Montipora* and *Fungia* occur spasmodically. Echinoids, starfish, molluscs and foraminifers are abundant.

In the transition zone there are fewer strands of living coral, and dead coral is commonly encrusted by algae. Many of the corals common in the zone of living coral are also found in this zone, although some are rare, and those of the sand subzone become more common. The dead coral clumps support a rich growth of macroscopic algae which also support rich faunas of large foraminifers including *Calcarina hispida, C. calcar, Baculogypsina sphaerulata,* and *Elphidium craticulatum.* Molluscan communities flourish in this environment and holothurians are common.

Inner Reef Flat or Sand Subzone. This subzone is typified by broad expanses of sand, with sparse clumps of living coral interspersed with patches of dead coral supporting thick algal growth. Micro-atolls of *Porites andrewsi* and *P. lutea* are common in the deeper waters (e.g., at the eastern end of the cay). Holothurians are prolific inhabitants of this sandy flat and are responsible for the reworking of the bulk of the surface sediment.

To the east of the island on the northwestern flanks of the lagoon there is a transition zone characterized by thick growth of *Acropora, Goniopora, Tubipora* and less commonly by heads of massive corals. Non-encrusting algae including *Halimeda* are common.

The Shallow Lagoon

The Shallow Lagoon is a broad, sandy shelving area in which few frame-building organisms live. Situated between the deeper Blue Lagoon and the southern reef flat, it represents an accumulation of sand derived principally from the reef flat. The marked differences in depth and fauna between it, and the reef flat, and also the Blue Lagoon clearly define it as a major physiographic unit. Well-sorted sand of medium grade composed of equal proportions of coralline algae, *Halimeda*, coral and slightly less molluscan detritus is typical of this zone. There is a noticeable absence of large coral growth. At low tide, water depths range from 0.3 to 1 m. The fauna of the shallow lagoon is sparse and consists of small colonies of corals including *Acropora* and *Goniastraea*, and a wide variety of small molluscs. *Halimeda* is also common as are foraminifers and holothurians. Bioturbation of the sediment is widespread.

The Blue Lagoon

The Blue Lagoon occupies the central part of the reef. It is 4.4 km long and 1.2 km wide and is deeper than the Shallow Lagoon. At low tide it has an average depth of 3.5 m, and its margin is clearly marked by an abrupt increase in depth. The floor of the Blue Lagoon is covered with very fine sediment. Numerous small patch reefs 6 m to 25 m in diameter grow predominantly in the northern and eastern portion where they occupy approximately half of the surface area. In the Blue Lagoon, the patch reefs are composed mainly of species of *Acropora* and other corals common to the reef flat, with some coralline algal encrustations. The fine sediment on the floor of the lagoon contains a rich in-fauna, and bioturbation is extreme.

Sediments

The bulk of the sediment on Heron Reef is composed of skeletal detritus of coralline algae, *Halimeda*, corals, molluscs and foraminifers. These organisms account for more than 90% of the material. Because of their different composition (calcite or aragonite), their different skeletal structures, their different resistances to destructive agencies, and their different areas of intensive growth, the detritus is sorted at the outset rather than being random and heterogeneous. Calcite organisms (coralline algae and foraminifers) appear to be more resistant possibly because of the nature of their skeletal structure. They tend to produce coarser, more durable, less mobile material. By contrast, aragonitic organisms (coral, *Halimeda* and molluscs) provide finer more mobile sediment. Thus the initial tendency for detritus to be sorted persists and is developed further during transportation when suitable physical conditions exist. Complete separation is prevented because of the restricted area over which these factors operate. The resultant sedimentary pattern is one of regions of coarse predominantly calcitic material, other regions of fine aragonitic material and areas of intermediate character. Variations in the pattern depend on the relative influences of physiography, source and mechanical agencies, all of which are interrelated.

Generally there is a gradation in the size composition of sediment particles across the reef. On the Reef Rim and Outer Reef Flat there is coarse poorly sorted material influenced by strongly breaking waves; the Inner Reef Flat and Shallow Lagoon have coarse to medium well-sorted material as a result of translatory waves and tidal currents; and in the Blue Lagoon, a zone of weak wave and current influence, very fine, poorly sorted sediments settle from suspension during slack water periods. It is possible, therefore, to differentiate the zones of the reef on the basis of particle size of the sediments. There is no relationship, however, between the type of organisms that have contributed to the sediments and the physiographic zone in which their particles are found. The skeletal matter that makes up the sediments is derived from a wide range of organisms and is subjected to a variety of biological and mechanical processes both before and after its deposition on any part of the reef.

The Island

Heron Island is a true sand cay composed of calcareous skeletal debris from reef organisms. It is approximately elliptical in outline, 830 m long and 300 m wide, with its long axis aligned approximately ESE–WNW. It rises abruptly from the southern beach to a height of 4.5 m and then slopes gently northwards. The southern margin is constantly subjected to the strong, prevailing south-east winds which carry the finer sand upwards to form a low marginal dune. A sandy beach, 15–30 m wide at low tide, surrounds the island. This in turn is partly surrounded by a belt of beach-rock, 9–21 m wide on the southern shore, 3–6 m wide in the north and west, and outcropping on the eastern shore. It can be divided into three shore-parallel zones based on differing algal assemblages. The rock is composed mainly of algal and coral skeletal debris with lesser percentages of molluscan, foraminiferal, and bryozoan material. Where fine interstitial matrix is completely lacking porosity is high and aragonite needles fringe some of the grains.

The cay is bordered by a shallow moat which is 15–30 m wide and consists of a sandy-floored depression approximately 1 m below the general level of the outer reef rim. The moat represents the plunge line of secondary breaking waves and is caused by wave scour. Its stronger development on the southern flat is related to the narrower reef flat, better development of beachrock, and its position on the windward side where strong currents have augmented the effect of wave scour. The moat is bordered on its landward side by beachrock. This is the channel through which lagoonal water flows as the tide recedes and these currents enter the moat from the east and south-east. The moat is relatively barren of fauna and flora, except for molluscs, occasional coral heads developed on solid substrates and *Porites lutea* occurring as loose heads. On the northeastern side of the cay a large sand flat is developed and usually exhibits ripple marks.

Notes on other Reefs and Islands of the Capricorn and Bunker Groups

Reefs

Reefs may be classified on the basis of morphological differences recognizable in plan view (e.g., symmetrical or linear, the presence or absence of a central lagoon, etc.). Six reef types are represented among the 20 reefs of the Capricorn and Bunker Groups. They are: wall reefs (Lamont and Sykes); platform reefs (North, Tryon, Wilson, Wreck and Erskine); elongate platform reefs (North West, Masthead and Polmaise); lagoonal platform reefs (Heron, Wistari, One Tree and Broomfield); closed ring (platform) reefs (Fitzroy, Llewellyn, Boult and Lady Musgrave); ingrown closed ring reefs (Fairfax and Hoskyn). These reefs are shown in Figures 5–7. They vary in size from the maximum dimension of 1–11 km with corresponding surface area of 1 km² to approximately 40 km². Arranged in increasing order of surface area they are: Wilson (1 km²), Erskine (1.25 km²), Tryon (2 km²), Lamont (2.5 km²), North (2.5 km²), Hoskyn (3 km²), Fairfax (4 km²), Wreck (4 km²), Boult (6 km²), Masthead (7 km²), Sykes (7 km²), Broomfield (9 km²), Lady Musgrave (10 km²), Fitzroy (12 km²), Llewellyn (12 km²), One Tree (14 km²), Wistari (25k m²), Heron (27 km²), and North West (38 km²).

On the northwesterly trend the reef type changes progressively from closed ring or ingrown closed ring to lagoonal platform to elongate platform or platform. This trend which occurs irrespective of the size of individual reefs is accomplished by a shallowing of the lagoonal floor, progressive infilling of the lagoon by a prograding wedge of skeleton carbonate sediment, and by obliteration of the radial pattern of coral growth by a thin cover of sediment and/or by algae veneering the tops of the reef flat corals. It may represent stages in the gradual modification of reef morphology, and it has been occurring on some reefs for the past 5 000 years.

Reefal Shoals

Reefal shoals rise to within approximately 10–20 m of the water surface at low spring tides. They occur as individual mounds (Rock Cod, Irving, Douglas, Haberfield, Guthrie, and Innamincka), as submarine platforms between reefs (North West, Wilson and Broomfield; Heron and Sykes; Wistari and Erskine), or as submarine platforms underlying other reefs (e.g., North, Fitzroy). Their morphology and composition have been examined using scuba, and they appear to be pre-existing reef masses on which coral growth was not able to keep pace with the sea level rise following the Ice Age.

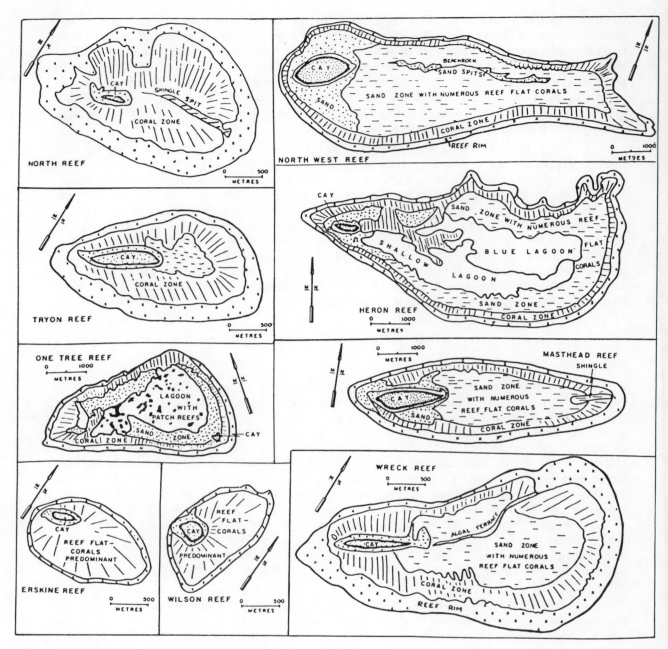

Fig. 5. Reefs with cays, Capricorn Group, showing reef zonation.

Islands

The islands of the Capricorn and Bunker Groups display an extremely interesting variety of sizes, shapes, vegetation, etc. Three varieties may be recognized, namely shingle cays (East Fairfax, East Hoskyn, One Tree); sand cays (West Fairfax, West Hoskyn, Heron, Masthead, North West, Wreck, North, Tyron); and mixed shingle/sand cays (Lady Musgrave, Wilson, Erskine). All cays except for the shingle types are located towards the leeward margin of the reef top. They vary in size, covering from one to 12% of the reef top surface area and arranged in terms of the increasing area occupied on the reef top they are: North, Erskine, One Tree, Wilson, Wreck, Hoskyn, Tryon, Lady Musgrave, Heron, Fairfax, Masthead, and North West. There does not appear to be any correlation between island size, reef size, or stage of reef development.

Some reefs do not have a cay, but have intertidal sand patches on the leeward reef flat (e.g., Boult, Llewellyn, Fitzroy, Wistari, Lamont and Broomfield). Beachrock is exposed on all the islands. Cay rock (supratidally lithified sediment) occurs on Tryon, East Fairfax, Lady Musgrave and North West Islands.

Capricorn Group

North West Island is the largest sand cay of the Group. A sand beach surrounds the cay and beachrock is only exposed at the southwestern and eastern ends. Vegetation is similar to that occurring on Heron Island. Phosphate rock occurs towards the centre of the island.

Masthead Island has beachrock well developed along the southern beach and an occurrence of older beachrock is situated some distance from the beach on the northwestern corner of the cay. Vegetation is similar to that occurring on Heron Island. Prickly Pear, introduced from the mainland, is now well established on the cay.

One Tree Island is a shingle cay. Vegetation consists of scattered *Argusia argentea* and *Scaevola taccada* with several small groves of *Pisonia grandis*. A small pond of brackish water is situated near the centre of the cay. A Field Research Station conducted by Sydney University is located towards the northeastern corner of the cay. An eroding cement pavement consisting mainly of reef-front corals occurs to windward of the present cay; it merges into the beachrock which occurs along the western shore.

Tryon Island has beachrock along the northwestern, northeastern and southeastern beaches. The cay is covered with dense vegetation similar to that occurring on Heron Island. Phosphate rock occurs along the upper beach on the northwestern corner of the island.

Wreck Island has beachrock well developed along the southern and northwestern beaches. Vegetation is similar to that on Tryon Island except that the *Pisonia grandis* forest is less well developed. A shed, presently abandoned, is located towards the centre of the island.

North Island is the smallest cay of the Group. An automatic lighthouse operates on this island. Beachrock occurs along the southeastern beach.

Wilson Island is a mixed shingle/ sand cay. Beachrock is well-developed along the northeastern to southeastern beach.

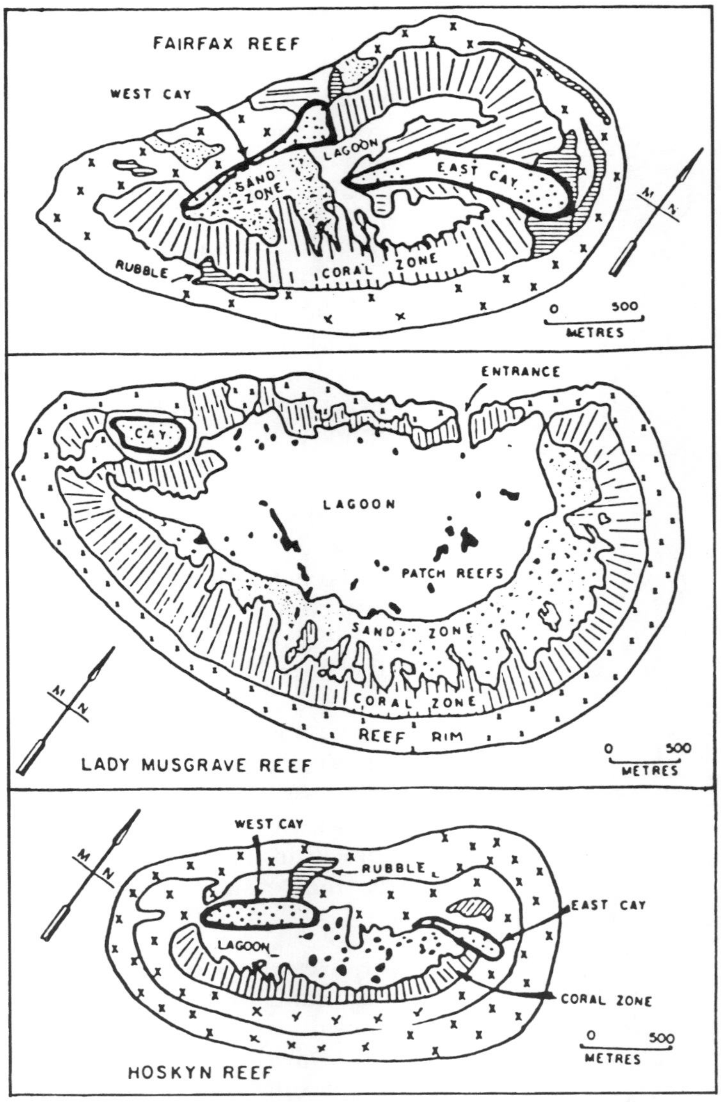

Fig. 6. Reefs with cays, Bunker Group, showing reef zonation.

13.

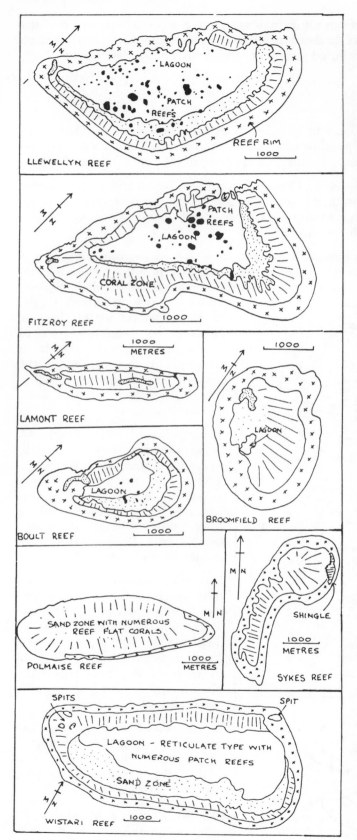

Fig. 7. Reefs (without cays), Capricorn and Bunker Groups, showing reef zonation.

Pandanus tectorius is the dominant vegetation with *Casuarina equisetifolia* restricted to the western side of the cay.

Erskine Island has beachrock well developed on the eastern, southwestern and northwestern beaches. The vegetation differs from that present on the other cays in that *Pandanus tectorius* and *Casuarina equisetifolia* are absent, and the main vegetation consists of *Argusia argentea*, *Scaevola taccada*, and stunted *Pisonia grandis*.

Bunker Group

Lady Musgrave Island is a sand and shingle cay situated on the leeward reef flat. Beachrock is exposed along the northeastern and eastern beaches and an outcrop of lithified coral conglomerate, similar to that (phosphate rock) forming the core of the cay, occurs near the southeastern corner. Vegetation consists of *Pisonia grandis*, *Argusia argentea*, *Casuarina equisetifolia*, and *Pandanus tectorius*. The vegetation is less dense than that of the larger sand cays of the Capricorn Group. A small pond of brackish water is located towards the southern end of the cay.

Fairfax Islands. The eastern cay is composed of shingle and the western of sand and shingle. Interference with the vegetation of the eastern cay occurred as result of phosphate mining and again during the period when the Australian Military Forces used the area as a bombing target. The cay is no longer used for either purpose. Vegetation is dominated by *Pisonia grandis* which is restricted to the north-west part of the island. Two brackish pools are located towards the eastern end of the island.

The western cay features an elongated sand spit that supports vegetation on its western extremity. Cyclone "David" (January, 1976) split the island into two portions. Vegetation is similar to that occurring on the larger sand cays of the Capricorn Group. A galvanized iron shed built by the Navy when the eastern cay was used for bombing practice is located in the centre of the eastern portion.

Hoskyn Islands. The eastern cay is composed of shingle and supports vegetation similar to, although less well-developed than, that of Lady Musgrave Island. The western cay is composed of sand and its vegetation is similar to that of the larger sand cays of the Capricorn Group.

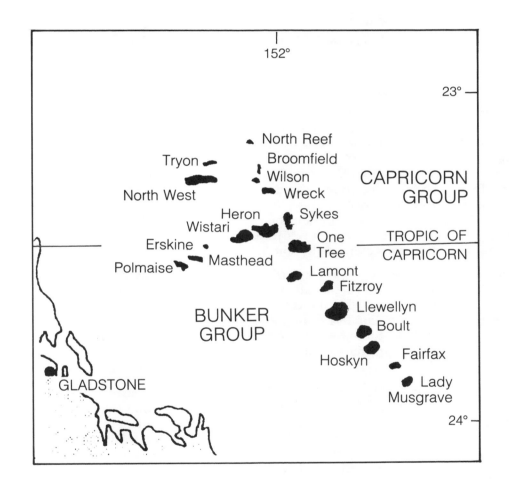

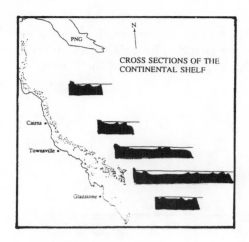

CROSS SECTIONS OF THE CONTINENTAL SHELF

Diversity and Change in Time and Space

There are so many different reef types, communities, sediments, habitats and biological and physical processes within the Great Barrier Reef Province that they defy human description. The Province is a very complex series of coral reefs and veneers of reef life located on a sliding, buckling, growing and eroding continental shelf, and shore line and islands. The growth and shape of each reef is a result of its geomorphological history and many other factors. Thus each has a different exposure to the varied water masses, to air at low tides, to wave action from wind driven seas and reflected waves from nearby reefs and islands. Each reef is affected by its position on the continental shelf — its distance from the coast and the edge of the shelf; and each is affected by latitude — its distance from the equator and from the temperate waters to the south.

In between the reefs, islands and the shelf edge are varied habitats of sand, mud, algae, seagrasses, shingle, rubble and scoured rock. Muddy coastal waters and sand and mud surfaces contrast with the clean outer coral rock slopes and clear water of the shelf edge reefs. Continental islands and coral cays provide further surfaces of rock, mud, sand and rubble for other reef communities, each with unique combinations of boring, cementing and grinding organisms contributing to the growth and erosion of each habitat.

From north to south the average depth of water increases over a progressively wide continental shelf. In the north the outer edge shelf slope tends to be steeper and deeper. Differences in water depth over the continental shelf affect the time that reefs have taken to reach present sea level, and affect their form and maturity. Reef tops have flat algal/coral communities, and shallow to deep lagoons of 1 or 2 m to 10 m depth. Some reefs have "blue holes" — caves which collapsed during the time the reef was dry during the last ice age. Such variations in reef top morphology add to the variability of associated communities.

Climatic variations, seasonal and lunar effects and daily rhythms all play a part in determining reef communities. Variations in them can be detected in coral cores, for instance, fresh water incursions from excessive rainfall and consequent run-off leave tannin stains in coral skeletons and these with changes in calcium carbonate density can be measured. Over the entire region there is a distinct summer monsoonal wet season with much more obvious temperature related seasonal variations in the south. Southeasterly winds (albeit stronger in the central region) affect the whole Province. Extreme low tides coinciding with heavy rain, cold or drying periods have significant kill rates on reef-top life.

Enormous volumes of turbid fresh water flow into the Province from the Fly River in Papua New Guinea and every coastal river and stream of Queensland. Then, from the deep oceanic waters massive tongues of cooler deep water slop up on to the continental shelf and in and around the outer and midshelf reefs under the warmer reef waters. These water masses combine with deep-water oceanic currents, tidal currents, wind driven surface currents and the very large eddies which occur off the east coast of Australia and affect underwater and surface dependent communities (such as sea birds) of the area. Each water mass has a different temperature, salinity, nutrient load, clarity, content and other properties, all of which have an impact on the organisms bathed by it, as well as those which float and swim in it, including the larvae of fish, corals and many other reef organisms which rely on water transport for distribution.

Periods of very heavy rain and river run-off can form surface layers of fresh water which can kill exposed reef areas. Prevailing southeasterly winds build waves which regularly pound the reef fronts while more protected reefs display quite different community patterns and a poorer ability to withstand extremes, especially in those areas of narrow shelf width and limited fetch distances which prevent waves from building to any significant size.

North–south variations are complex. Torres Strait, connecting the Arafura and Coral Seas, has relatively shallow, turbid waters, strong currents and large tidal changes (3.5 m). During equinoxes there is only a single tidal change in this area and that is complicated by the tidal time difference of the two seas. In contrast, are the small tidal variations of the northern/central region (2–3 m), and the larger tides (5–8 m) of the Whitsunday and Cumberland Islands area. In the south (where there is the greater cross-shelf mix of reef types, sizes and shapes) the tides vary by 3 m. High tidal ranges create currents of up to 4 m/sec, e.g., in the Pompey Reef complex in the south, and up to 3 m/sec in the Torres Strait. Areas in between have speeds of 1.5 m/sec or lower. These scouring currents have kept some old fossil reef surfaces free of new growth, and in other areas buried life under sediments.

The arrival of the Aborigines more than 40 000 years ago, and then Europeans 200 years ago, caused increased runoff of silt from loss of vegetation. More recently more serious degradation of coastal and nearshore reef communities (resulting from mining, clearing, agriculture and urbanization of coastal lands) can be detected.

The factors affecting the reef's systems and their evolution are increasing, and anthropogenic pressures are now added to the natural ones. Documentation of the changes that occur will help to determine their causes and contribute to the management of this dynamic system.

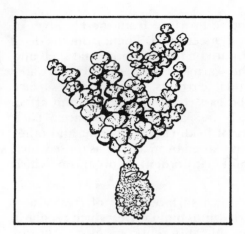

Algae

Seaweeds

Algae are a predominantly aquatic, polyphyletic group of chlorophyll containing plants. Although once it was thought that they were more closely related, the four algal divisions are now believed to be quite separate from one another. A phylogenetic link is possible between one group of green algae and the flowering plants, but otherwise the phylogeny of this group of organisms is not clear.

Four main algal groups as follows comprise the bulk of the attached algal vegetation.

Green Algae (Division Chlorophyta). Chlorophyll is the dominant pigment, and the plants appear green or, if calcified, grey-green.

Brown Algae (Division Phaeophyta). Chlorophyll is masked by the brown pigment fucoxanthin so the plants appear brown.

Red Algae (Division Rhodophyta). The distinctive pigment is phycoerythrin which, in shaded situations, usually masks the chlorophyll giving the plant a pink or red colour. In well-illuminated situations the phycoerthrin content is often much reduced so the plants may be olive, fawn or yellowish and so difficult to assign on the basis of colour.

Blue-green Algae (Division Cyanophyta). The distinctive pigment phycocyanin together with chlorophyll typically gives the algae a blue-green colour. In species occurring in the mid and upper intertidal region, pigments in an extracellular pectin sheath may produce a brownish or almost black appearance. They are prokaryotic (lack a nucleus) and are related to bacteria, sometimes being known as **Cyanobacteria**.

In 1973, a possibly related group, once thought to be a separate division **(Prochlorophyta)** of the Algae, was found in symbiotic association with ascidians (see below). These minute unicellar organisms are also prokaryotic, but differ from the majority of blue-greens in having chlorophyll more like that of nucleated plants, than that of other Cyanophyta.

Common Green Algae

Acetabularia (Mermaid's Wine Glass), has long, slender stalks topped by a ring of wedge-shaped segments united by calcification to form a disc, saucer or cup. Some small, reef-inhabitating species have stalks only a couple of millimetres long, and are obscured by sediment. The species grow only on calcareous substrata.

A. calyculus has usually not more than about 30 segments in the terminal disc.

A. major has usually 60–70 terminal segments (Fig. 8:1).

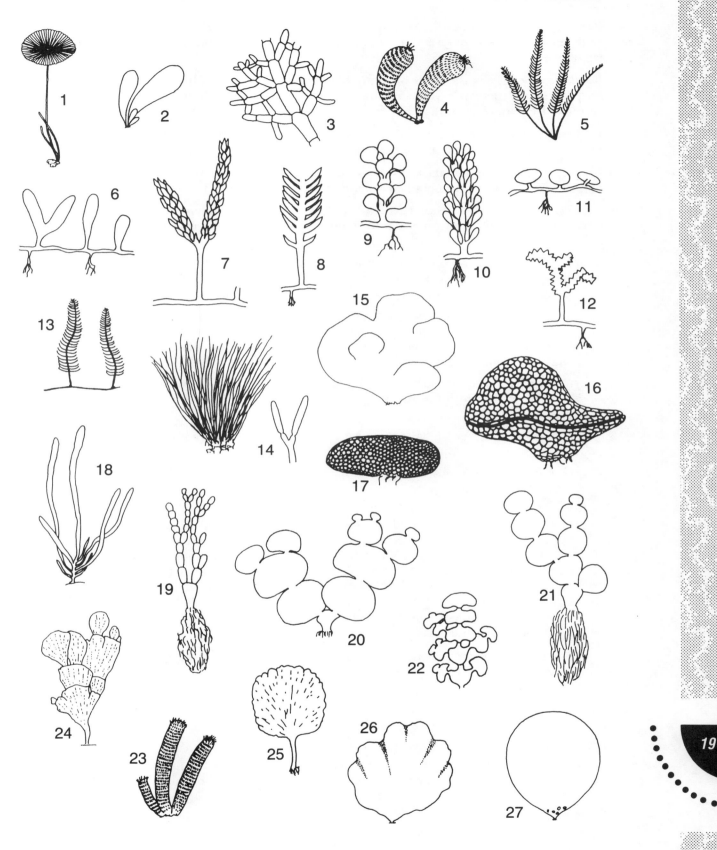

Fig. 8. Some common green Algae.

Boergesenia forbesii occurs singly or as clusters of light green clubs tapered to the base. Each is an enormous cell up to 5 cm long, its firmness due to turgidity rather than to cell wall rigidity (Fig. 8:2).

Boodlea composita has the ends of many filaments attaching to adjacent branches to form a crisp, irregular network which retains its form out of water. It forms light green spongy clumps of extent (Fig. 8:3).

Bornetella nitida is a small grey-green curved club, up to 2.5 cm long, with a tuft of colourless hairs at the apex. With a lens it is possible to detect a fine hexagonal surface pattern (Fig. 8:4).

Bryopsis indica forms lax, dark green clumps of feathery filaments up to a few centimetres high. Each axis bears closely placed slender laterals on one or two sides (Fig. 8:5).

Caulerpa species have a basic structure of prostrate stem attached by rhizoids and erect green branches which vary enormously in form between species. Most grow on rocks or dead coral, a few on sand.

    C. brachypus has two common varieties, both with more or less leaf-like branches. The smaller has simple or once forked erect branches (1–2 cm high). The more robust has green branches up to 5 cm long often well provided with marginal teeth (Fig. 8:6).

    C. cupressoides, one of the relatively few species to grow mainly on sand has the rows of erect branches, often extending for a couple of metres, marking the path of the stem just below the surface. Erect branches are generally densely covered with small sharp-pointed branchlets sometimes arranged in three rows (Fig. 8:7).

    C. lentillifera resembles *C. racemosa* but has almost spherical vesicle-like lateral branches constricted off from the short stalk. Nibbling the turgid vesicles is a pleasant diversion on the shore.

    C. mexicana has erect flattened branch systems with two regularly arranged rows of flattened lateral branchlets (Fig. 8:8).

    C. nummularia is easily recognized by its erect branches in the form of shortly-stalked discs, about 5 mm across, sometimes with marginal teeth. This species often forms grey-green layers of overlapping discs among turf algae.

    C. racemosa with its crowded, vesicle-like branchlets along the erect axes is often the commonest *Caulerpa* on reef flats. A common variety is *C. racemosa* var. *clavifera* (Fig. 8:9) with the ends of the small lateral branchlets suddenly inflated so that there is a sharp distinction between stalk and terminal vesicle. The lateral branchlets of *C. racemosa* var. *orientalis* are gradually inflated (Fig. 8:10). *C. racemosa* var. *peltata* has small stalked discs (Fig. 8:11). Some varieties of *C. racemosa* are edible but others are mildly poisonous. A bitter-peppery taste suggests that *C. racemosa* var. *clavifera* should not be a constituent of the salad.

    C. serrulata has erect branches, sparsely forked, coarsely serrate and often twisted (Fig. 8:12).

    C. sertularioides resembles a fine form of *C. mexicana* with feather-like erect branches, the laterals no more than 0.5 mm across. In some plants the branchlets may be arranged in three rows (Fig. 8:13).

Chlorodesmis fastigiata (Turtle Weed) stands out from the drabness of the majority of reef algae by the brilliant green of its dense tufts of repeatedly forked filaments. The constriction of the branches at uneven distances above each fork distinguishes this species from the less common *C. major* with evenly placed constrictions. The crab *Caphyra rotundifrons* is often associated with clumps of *C. fastigiata* (Fig. 8:14).

Codium spongiosum forms dark bottle-green, irregularly lobed or contorted clumps up to 15 cm diameter, resembling sponge colonies, which sometimes are washed up along the shore in considerable quantities. The crowded, club-shaped filament branches making up the outer layer are not united, but through their turgidity press firmly against each other maintaining the plant's form (Fig. 8:15).

Other species have the form of repeatedly forked cylinders.

Dictyosphaeria plants are made up of large cells, clearly visible to the naked eye.

D. caernosa has a hollow, green or grey-green plant body, up to about 3 cm across, which may break up to form an irregular cup or saucer (Fig. 8:16).

D. versluysii is solid and forms rigid grey-green button-like plants (Fig. 8:17).

Enteromorpha (Green Guts) species grow, in winter in bright green patches on rocks and dead coral in the intertidal region. The plant is a branched tube one cell thick and usually 2–10 cm long, collapsing on emersion. The species may be difficult to identify (Fig. 8:18).

Halimeda plants consist of branched chains of flattened (rarely cylindrical) segments, calcified to varying degrees. The less calcified species are generally brighter green than others.

H. cylindracea generally occurs in groups over a square metre or two. It is easily distinguished from the others on the reef by its cylindrical or barrel-shaped segments, and is one of the few species which grow in sand rather than on dead coral or rocks, its rhizoids penetrating up to 15 cm, forming a sandy tuber (Fig. 8:19).

H. discoidea is the least calcified of the reef species, its bright to dark green discs having no sign of the rigidity due to calcification found in many other species (Fig. 8:20). The generally similar *H. tuna* differs in some anatomical characters; in the field the two can generally be distinguished with a lens by the coarser surface pattern of *H. tuna*.

H. macroloba, like *H. cylindracea*, is an inhabitant of sand and produces a similar sandy tuber. However, its well-calcified segments are disc-like (Fig. 8:21).

H. opuntia is the most heavily calcified of the species and pressure will generally cause the segments to crack rather than bend. The segments of its grey-green clumps vary greatly in outline from round to kidney-shaped or trilobed. Its heavy calcification makes it an important constituent of some reef deposits (Fig. 8:22).

Neomeris plants are small lax cylinders up to 2.5 cm tall, white in the lower part because of calcification but with distinctive lime-green tips. Formation of the calcified reproductive bodies, visible with a lens, proceeds from the base upwards.

N. annulata has reproductive bodies united in transverse rows (Fig. 8:23).

N. vanbosseae has reproductive bodies free from each other.

Udotea has stalked, calcified, fan-shaped plants sometimes irregularly lobed.

U. argentea, a robust species up to 15 cm high, often irregularly lobed and with the surface often finely longitudinally grooved, generally grows in sand and forms a sand tuber (Fig. 8:24).

U. orientalis, a relatively delicate species forming grey-green flexible fans up to 4 cm high is generally attached to dead coral (Fig. 8:25).

Ulvaria oxysperma occurs during winter on beachrock, particularly in shallow pools and shaded crevices. The delicate green membranes, one cell thick and up to several centimetres across appear ruffled and folded in water but at low water are plastered over the rock surface (Fig. 8:26).

Ventricaria ventricosa (Sailor's Eyeballs) is generally found in coral crevices and on the undersides of coral bounders. Its globose or pear-shaped, dark green vesicles up to 3 cm across consist, apart from a few small cells at the base, of a single enormous cell whose remarkable rigidity is due to turgidity. Piercing the vesicle with a pin will release a stream of cell sap like a jet from a water pistol (Fig. 8:27).

Common Red Algae

These include the coralline algae — heavily calcified, jointed or encrusting (lithothamnia).

Amansia glomerata (Red Rosette), mainly a plant of shaded situations such as the underside of coral bounder, consists of rosettes, up to 5 cm broad, of pink, leaf-like blades with marginal flaps (Fig. 9A:1).

Amphiroa is one of the coralline algae forming clumps of mainly forked branches, heavily calcified except at the narrow joints which give the clumps slight flexibility.

> *A. crassa* has more or less cylindrical branches, with joints a little above the points of forking (Fig. 9A:2).

> *A. foliacea* has many of the branches flattened and sharp-edged, with joints at the points of forking (Fig. 9A:3).

Galaxaura rugosa forms pink to dull red clumps, up to 12 cm long, of repeatedly forked, cylindrical branches with little or no tapering. There is some calcification but never enough to prevent crushing of a branch between finger and thumb. Plants vary from hairless, through hairy in lower parts to densely hairy throughout (Fig. 9A:4).

Gelidiella acerosa is a common but inconspicuous alga seldom more than 5 cm high and yellowish, olive or purplish in colour. Its wiry main branches are often arching, and carry one or two rows of short lateral branchlets (Fig. 9A:5).

Gracilaria crassa is a fleshy, rigid alga, either prostrate or erect, its branches 2–3 mm broad and varying from yellowish through olive to purple. There are generally a few irregular forkings, and in some plants prominent constrictions here and there (Fig. 9A:6).

Hypnea pannosa (Spine Weed) forms crips, easily broken, fawn to purplish, intricate clumps or layers between dead coral branches. The main axes, about 1 mm broad, are closely branched and bear numerous short spine-like branchlets (Fig. 9A:7).

Laurencia species have a fleshy branched axis bearing crowded cylindrical or club-shaped branchlets (Fig. 9A:8) each with a tuft of colourless hair from the sunken apex. Among the numerous species present two are fairly easily recognized:

> *L. intricata*, typically green with pink branch tips, forms loose clumps often attached to small pieces of dead coral on the sandy floor of the reef flat. In wave-beaten situations it is more compact.

> *L. majuscula* often accompanies *L. intricata* but can be distinguished by its red-brown to yellow-brown colour and finer branchlets.

Liagora valida consist of dense, lax clumps up to 15 cm high of repeatedly forked branches 0.5–1 mm broad. Loose calcification obscures the red pigment except at the uncalcified tips (Fig. 9A:9).

Lithophyllum kotschyanum is associated with coral in the outermost part of the intertidal reef where it forms stony dome-shaped clumps up to 12 cm across, consisting of irregularly branched processes often united at points of contact (Fig. 9A:10).

Neogoniolithon fosliei is one of several encrusting coralline algae that form a stony pink crust over dead coral surfaces. It often can be recognized in the field by its large shallowly conical reproductive containers, about 1 mm broad, often outlined by a darker ring.

Peyssonnelia species form rounded crusts, red or orange-yellow, and often radially striate. Most are firmly attached over much of their under surface (Fig. 9A:11).

> *P. conchicola*, firmly attached over the whole of its lower surface except for a marginal strip about 1 mm wide, occurs on both immovable substrates and on small pieces of shell and dead coral.

> *P. inamoena* is found in deeply shaded positions, and its brittle crusts are unusual in being often only loosely attached to the substrate.

Fig. 9. **A** — Some common Red Algae; **B** — Some common Brown Algae.

Plocamium hamatum (Hook Weed) inhabits subtidal regions, often hanging in lax tufts from the deeply shaded roofs of overhangs near the outer edge of the intertidal reef. The much-branched clumps of flattened axes have a distinctive arrangement of final branchlets which usually are in alternating groups of three. Sometimes the lowermost branchlet of a group forms a hook (Fig. 9A:12).

Yamadaella cenomyce occurs mainly on coral boulders near the outer part of the intertidal reef where it forms pale pink to dull white clumps up to 4 cm across. Each consists of soft, repeatedly and widely forked branches whose calcification largely obscures the pigmentation (Fig. 9A:13).

Common Brown Algae

Chnoospora implexa (Tangle Bells) with repeatedly forked branches, about 1 mm diameter, forms intricate, springy clumps of mats sometimes 30 cm or more across. On becoming detached they are often rolled on the beach into dark, rusty brown ball-like clumps (Fig. 9B:1).

Colpomenia (Oyster Thief) forms rounded, generally irregularly lobed, easily torn, gas-filled vesicles up to 15 cm across. *C. sinuosa* (Fig. 9B:2) is the more common species and is firmer in texture than *C. peregrina*, which is more "bubbly" in form and papery in texture. In Europe, plants have caused trouble by floating away oysters to which they become attached.

Cystoseira trinodis (Chain Float) has elongate floats commonly in chains of twos or threes. Leaf-like appendages like those of some species of *Sargassum*, but are restricted to the lower strongly roughened part of the branched stem (Fig. 9B:3).

Dictyopteris superficially resembles *Dictyota* in its repeatedly forked, ribbon-like form. The presence of a midrib readily distinguishes it.

> *D. acrostichoides* has a distinctive pungent taste and an unpleasant odour on its rapid decay after removal from the water (Fig. 9B:4).

> *D. australis* is distinguishable from the superficially similar *S. acrostichoides* by the presence of fine lateral veins, visible with a lens.

Dictyota bartayresii, like other species of the genus, is a repeatedly forked ribbon up to about 20 cm long. The branches may be straight or curved outwards to varying degrees. Some plants show a blue-green iridescence when submerged. Several species occur in the area but *D. bartayresii* is the most common (Fig. 9B:5).

Ectocarpus species are delicate, branched filaments forming tufts on larger algae, rocks or dead coral. Plants are sometimes particularly common in some rubble-floored areas of the reef flat where many fragments carry a soft yellow-brown tuft up to 3 cm tall. The name *Ectocarpus* is used here in the old sense to include some species which are often placed in related genera (Fig. 9B:6).

Hormophysa triquetra forms branched plants up to 30 cm high, the stems provided with 2–3 irregularly toothed, leafy and often discontinuous wings. The small floats are 3-angled or 3-winged (Fig. 9B:7).

Hydroclathrus clathratus (Wire-netting Alga, Monkey Feathers) is a net-like alga, with rounded or elliptical perforations, of various sizes even in the one plant. In the more wave-beaten areas it forms firm, compact clumps about 4 cm across but in particularly quiet waters forms lax, weak plants 30 cm or more long (Fig. 9B:8).

Lobophora variegata forms a dark chocolate-brown fan, often lobed, with fine radial striations. It may extend horizontally, attached only at its base; or be loosely attached over much of its under surface (Fig. 9B:9).

Padina (Funnel Weed) is distinctively fan shaped, with inrolled margin and concentric bands of hairs and darker reproductive bodies. When submerged the fans are often curved into a funnel.

P. australis has a band of hairs on both sides of each dark band of reproductive bodies (Fig. 9B:10).

P. tenuis has a band of hairs only below each band of reproductive bodies. Plants sometimes show a light, chalky surface calcification, a condition rare among brown algae.

Ralfsia expansa in the intertidal region forms closely adherent brown-black crusts, round or ring-shaped on regular surfaces but irregular on contorted surfaces such as dead coral. Coral clumps which have been moved so that they project about 15 cm above reef flat low water often become partly blackened by the alga.

Sargassum species, some up to 1 m, are the longest algae in these waters. All have a branched stem bearing "leaves", some with midribs, and globose or ellipsoid floats. At certain stages, one or other of these structures may be absent. Numerous species occur in Queensland and the identity of many of them is uncertain (Fig. 9B:11).

S. crassifolium has relatively short, rigid leaves often much curved (Fig. 9B:12).

S. decurrens, probably the most easily recognized species of the area, has unusual prominent flattening of the branch systems (Fig. 9B:13).

S. polycystum has relatively small leaves usually not over 1 cm long, and leafless prostrate branches from the base (Fig. 9B:14).

Turbinaria ornata (Spiny Tops), usually with an unbranched axis up to 20 cm high, is buoyed up by eventually hollow, closely placed, rigid, top-shaped branches with spiny margins. In spite of its appearance it makes a reasonable vegetable after brief boiling (Fig. 9B:15).

Algal Distribution

The remarkable species diversity of plants in a tropical rainforest and of animals on a coral reef might lead one to expect a comparable tropical richness in the attached algal vegetation of a coral reef. In fact, compared with those of many temperate and cool temperature shores, algae of coral reefs are small in both species number and size. It has been said that the most striking aspect of plant life on a coral reef is how little there is. The tropical region of eastern Australia probably supports no more than half the number of species found along southern Australian shores. Nevertheless attached algae play a vital part in the economy of a coral reef through their productivity and the capacity of some species to become calcified. The low algal mat of the reef rock slope is a highly productive algal meadow heavily grazed by fish, while coralline algae make an important contribution to both stabilizing and building the reef framework.

The Great Barrier Reef, with its true barrier reefs, cay-supporting platform reefs (such as the Heron Island reef), fringing reefs of continental islands, and extensive areas of mangroves (as at Low Isles), includes a wide variety of intertidal and sublittoral algal habitats. However, although the algal vegetation differs from habitat to habitat there is surprising uniformity in species composition in comparable habitats over the Reef's nearly 2 000 km length. This is specially surprising when it is compared with the dramatic change in species composition that occurs in the 2 000 km directly to the south.

Particular habitats are arranged in zones characterized by the dominant organisms in them.

Variations in these zones occur from reef to reef and even from one part of the same reef to another. The account given below is of algal zonation at Heron Island, along a transect from the cay to the sea. A similar, although not necessarily the same pattern can be seen on other reefs and islands along the length of the Great Barrier Reef.

Terrestrial Algae

Coral boulders and shingle on the cay are usually coloured dark grey by blue-green algae, mainly *Anacystis montana* and *Scytonema hofmannii* with sometimes a green stain of *Pseudendoclonium submarinum* on under surfaces.

Shaded sand surfaces are occasionally stained green by small algae, mainly species of *Chlorococcum*, *Klebsormidium* and filamentous blue-green algae, particularly where the surface is partly compacted by bird excreta.

In the outermost band of vegetation, minute colonies of *Nostoc calcicola* sometimes impart a faint blue-green colour and minor stability to subsurface sand to a depth of a few millimetres.

Bark algae are usually poorly developed, but *Anacystis montana* may cause localized dark staining of *Pisonia* trunks. *Schizothrix* spp. form a dark streak on some *Pandanus* trunks where irrigated by seepage from leaf base reservoirs above, and with *Anacystis montana*, may also form black "socks" on the bases of some *Pisonia* trunks.

Marine Algae

The intertidal environment may be divided into four main regions: beach, reef flat, reef rock rim and seaward platform.

One of the most conspicuous differences between Heron Island Reef and others to the north (e.g., Low Island), is that its shallow water vegetation is entirely algal. There are no mangroves or sea grasses.

The Beach

When it is of sand or shingle, it is usually devoid of algae. Shingle in a narrow strip at the base of the beach may be darkened by *Entophysalis deusta* and, particularly in winter, carry green flecks of *Enteromorpha clathrata* and *Ulvaria oxysperma*. Where beachrock (a conglomerate of calcareous fragments) occurs there are usually three algal bands in downshore succession as follows:

1. **Entophysalis deusta Band:** usually brown-black, olive-brown or dark grey and dominated by a thin encrustation of *Entophysalis* often accompanied by *Calothrix crustacea* and by small quantities of other species in pools, pock-marks or shaded crevices, e.g., green flecks of *Ulvaria* and *Enteromorpha*.

2. **Mixed Cyanophyte Band:** usually very pale pink, made up of a thin, smooth layer of various blue-green algae entrapping fine calcareous sediment which largely obscures the algae. Parallel scratch marks of fish teeth can often be seen. The dominant species probably varies from time to time and place to place, but common species are *Schizothrix arenaria*, *S. tenerrima*, *Kyrtuthrix maculans*, *Calothrix crustacea* and *Microcoleus lyngbyaceus*. The small black perithecia of the marine lichen *Arthopyrenia halodytes* are often found in this and the above band particularly in shaded positions. Large chitons (*Acanthopleura gemmata*) and oysters also occur here.

3. **Gelidiella bornetii Band:** usually whitish to pale green, made up of a thin layer of filamentous algae often largely obscured by entrapped sand and sediment which is more loosely held than in the band above. *Gelidiella bornetii* (forming a dull red, sparse fur not over a few millimetres high where not obscured) is usually present and often dominant. It is accompanied by a wide variety of other small algae amongst which *Enteromorpha clathrata* is commonly important, and sometimes dominant and responsible for a distinct green colour during winter.

The Reef Flat

The reef flat is really an enormous tide pool, the water being dammed over it by the reef rock rim. It can be divided into two main regions: inner reef flat (sandy zone) and outer reef flat (living coral zone).

1. **The Inner Reef Flat (Sandy Zone):** an extensive area, usually submerged to a depth of +30 cm at L.W.S., supporting scattered coral, usually the quantity and the proportion of living to dead coral increasing seawards. Coral colonies mostly grow to the same level, usually slightly above the lowest level reached by the water.

    Bordering the southwestern beachrock is a strip up to 4 m wide, relatively bare of algae and coral and with a floor level several centimetres below that of the adjacent part of the reef flat. It has possibly been formed by an enhanced drainage flow, consequent on construction of the boat channel, carrying away sediment disturbed by swash from the beachrock.

    Only those coral surfaces which are dead support algae and consequently algae are often denser in the landward than the seaward part of the inner reef flat. Very numerous algal species occur here, amongst the macroscopic species being *Halimeda tuna*, *H. opuntia*, *Caulerpa racemosa*, *Boodlea composita*, *Chlorodesmis fastigiata*, *Dictyosphaeria cavernosa*, *D. versluysii*, *Padina australis*, *Lobophora variegata*, *Dictyota bartayresii*, *Chnoospora implexa*, *Hydroclathrus clathratus*, *Sargassum* spp., *Turbinaria ornata*, *Gelidiella acerosa*, *Laurencia intricata* and *L. majuscula*. Colonies of *Caulerpa cupressoides* occur creeping over the sand in certain areas. Nearly all dead coral is penetrated by a variety of blue-green and green algae. Common members of this community are *Entophysalis deusta*, *Mastigocoleus testarum*, *Ostreobium reineckei* and *Acetabularia* spp.

    Surfaces projecting above the general upper level of the coral may carry dark chocolate-brown crusts of *Ralfsia expansa*. Undersurfaces of boulders often support species different from those of more exposed surfaces; the large rounded or pear-shaped vesicles of *Ventricaria ventricosa* occur here.

2. **The Outer Reef Flat (Living Coral Zone):** has a depth of up to 75 cm at low water, and well developed coral often forming an even-topped platform dissected here and there by pools and channels. The upper, grill-like surface, is mainly dead, encrusted with pink calcareous algae, and penetrated by microscopic green and blue-green algae. Fleshy algae are usually poorly developed and are mainly restricted to crevices below the uppermost surface. *Halimeda* spp. occur here. Coral branches in the shaded labyrinth below the upper surface support various lithothamnia and *Peyssonnelia* spp.

The Reef Rock Rim

The reef rock rim is a rim of reef rock enclosing the reef flat. It usually is 35–100 m wide and no more than a few centimetres above the reef flat low water level. The reef rock rim is divisible into two parts, the rubble crest and the reef rock slope.

1. **The Rubble Crest** is the crest of the reef rock rim, typically an area of heavy rubble deposition. The extent, composition and position of the rubble varies considerably along the crest. In size it varies from finger-like shingle to reef blocks (negro heads) a metre or more high. In some places along the rubble crest there is a depressed central strip forming a broad, irregular pool 5–30 cm deep, its floor usually strewn with rubble.

    Algal flora of the rubble has something in common with similar levels of beachrock. One of the few macroscopic species commonly present is *Yamadaella cenomyce* which forms small intricate, pale pink clumps of repeatedly forked branches, and is almost entirely restricted to this habitat.

2. **The Reef Rock Slope** is the gentle seawards slope of reef rock, usually 20–80 m wide and 0.5–0.9 m in vertical extent. Reef blocks may occur here as well as on the rubble crest. The slope is smooth or potholed but, typically, it is shallowly and irregularly terraced. These meandering terraces, usually not over 5 cm high, commonly link up to form an irregular reticulum.

    The rock surface is mainly obscured by a dense mat of small, sand-binding algae. Numerous species occur (most of the reef flat species can be found here in stunted condition)

27

but the mat is generally dominated by several dwarf or dwarfed species of *Laurencia*. Other common, macroscopically recognizable species include *Dictyosphaeria* spp. and *Gelidiella acerosa*. Pieces of coral shingle in depressions often support bright orange-red to dull red crusts of *Peyssonnelia conchicola*. Rock surfaces not occupied by the algal mat are usually encrusted with lithothamnia.

The Seaward Platform

This is the outermost part of the inter-tidal reef, a relatively narrow strip, usually 6–30 m wide. Sometimes it slopes gently seawards or is almost horizontal, often with its outer margin elevated 10–20 cm above the general platform level. At its seaward edge it drops precipitously. On some reefs the seaward platform is dissected at right angles to its length by gulches, 2–4 m wide, producing a spur and groove system. In some cases, grooves become isolated as pools through closure of the mouth by coral growth. This spur and groove system is not clearly developed on the Heron Island reef in the vicinity of the cay.

The seaward platform is typically an area of rich coral growth. In some places *Acropora* spp. form an even (easy to walk upon) surface, while in others the separated coral clumps form a much more uneven platform. Encrusting lithothamnia and the branching *Lithophyllum kotschyanum* are common. Along some parts of the platform lithothamnia predominate at the expense of corals.

Fleshy algae are poorly developed, *Chlorodesmis fastigiata* and *Bryopsis indica* usually being the most obvious species. *Codium spongiosum* is common, lining pools in some areas.

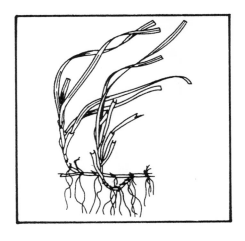

Seagrasses

Seagrasses are the only group of vascular plants that inhabit the open sea. They belong to angiosperms (flowering plants) and although they are not true grasses (they are mono-cotyledons that belong to the Potamogetonaceae and Hydrocharitaceae, families with many freshwater species) they have many features in common with grasses such as creeping stems (rhizomes), short erect stems with grass-like leaves which grow from the base and incon-spicuous flowers. Seagrasses grow mainly on soft substrates (silt or sand) in shallow, sheltered, marine or estuarine situations. On coral reefs they are found on lagoonal sediments and on sandy sites outside reefs: the only exception is *Thalassodendron ciliatum* which can grow on hard coral surfaces by means of a rhizome with specialized roots which allow firm attachment to hard bottoms.

Three *Halophila* species are present in the Bunker-Capricorn Groups at the southern end of the Great Barrier Reef, but further north Seagrasses are more conspicuous, and all species are represented. Further information is available in Lanyon (1986).

Key to the Seagrasses of the Great Barrier Reef

1. Leaves ligulate (i.e., a tongue-like structure at junction of the leaf blade and sheath which attaches to the rhizome) .... **Potamogetonaceae, 8**
   Leaves without ligules .... **Hydrocharitaceae, 2**

2. Leaves strap-shaped, neither compound nor petiolate (stalked) 7
   Leaves compound or petiolate (stalked) .... *Halophila*, 3

3. Erect, lateral shoots bearing a number of compound leaves 4
   Erect, lateral shoots bearing one pair of simple leaves 5

4. 10–20 pairs of opposite leaflets (serrate margins) on an erect shoot .... *Halophila spinulosa*
   2–3 leaflets (serrate margin, no cross-veins), 6–18 nodes per shoot .... *Halophila tricostata*

5. Leaf margin finely serrulate, hairs on leaf surface .... *Halophila decipiens*
   Leaf margin entire, no hairs present 6

6. Leaf blade paddle shaped, < 5 mm long, <10 cross-veins .... *Halophila minor*
   Leaf blade paddle shaped, >5 mm long, >10 cross-veins .... *Halophila ovalis*

7. Rhizome of two forms, scale-bearing and leaf-bearing, short shoots. Root hairs abundant ....
   .... *Thalassia hemprichii*
   Rhizome of only one form, covered with long, black bristles and bearing leaves all over. Root hairs inconspicuous .... *Enhalus acoroides*

8. Leaf blade terete (round) .... *Syringodium isoetifolium*
   Leaf blade flat 9

9. Erect stem long, bearing clusters of leaves at the end; rhizome woody and monopodial ....
   .... *Thalassodendron ciliatum*
   Erect stem short; rhizome neither woody nor monopodial 10

10. Lateral veins less than nine 11
    Lateral veins nine or more .... *Cymodocea*, 13

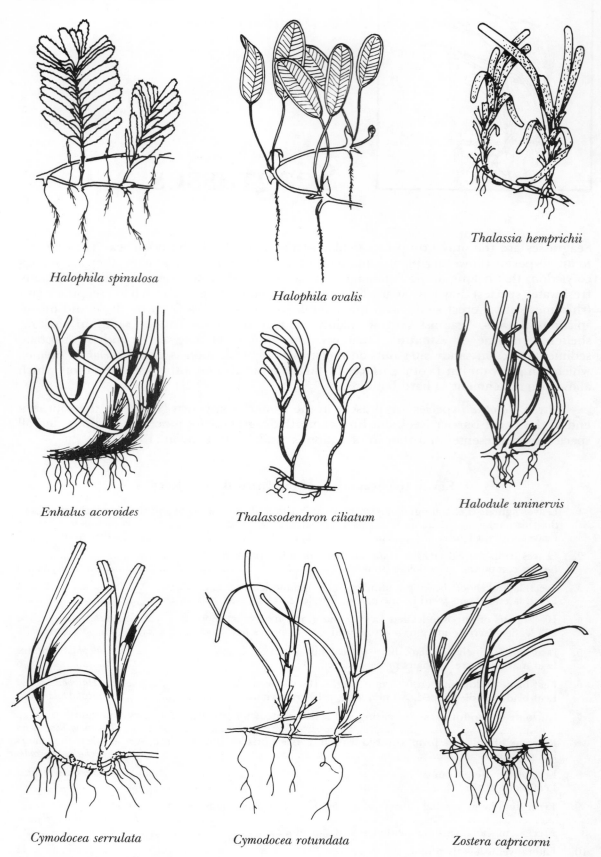

Halophila spinulosa

Halophila ovalis

Thalassia hemprichii

Enhalus acoroides

Thalassodendron ciliatum

Halodule uninervis

Cymodocea serrulata

Cymodocea rotundata

Zostera capricorni

Fig. 10. Seagrasses of the Great Barrier Reef.

Key to the Seagrasses of the Great Barrier Reef — *continued*

11.　Veins five, the middle one (mid-rib) prominent and dilated at tip; leaf 2 mm or more wide ....
.... *Zostera capricorni*
Veins three, the middle one (mid-rib) not prominent and not dilated at the tip; leaf 2 mm or less
wide .... *Halodule*, 12

12.　Tip of leaf with three teeth, the middle one blunt .... *Halodule uninervis*
Tip of leaf with three teeth, the middle one prominent .... *Halodule pinifolia*

13.　Tip of leaf with many teeth, leaf 4 mm or more wide .... *Cymodocea serrulata*
Tip of leaf without obvious teeth, leaf 4 mm or less wide .... *Cymodocea rotundata*

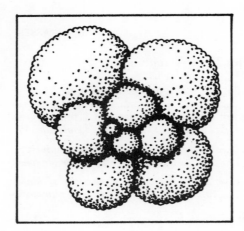

Foraminiferida

Foraminiferida are very small, aquatic (mostly marine), single celled organisms of the phylum Sarcomastigophora in the sub-kingdom Protozoa. They are usually from 0.1 to 2 mm in diameter, only a few reaching greater dimensions. The majority live on the sea floor (benthic) where they are either free-living, moving about very slowly over the bottom, or they are attached to algae or other organisms.

Most foraminifers secrete a simple to complex shell, or test of mineral material, commonly calcium carbonate. The test may consist of only one chamber (unilocular) or several (multilocular). In the multilocular forms, an initial chamber (proloculus) is formed first and other chambers are added systematically according to patterns that are characteristic of each species. The tests contribute significantly to reef sedimentation. On the reef flat of Wreck Reef, they constitute up to 90% of the sediment.

The body of a foraminifer consists of a mass of protoplasm inside the test and a layer around the outside. The layer has many elongate projections called pseudopods that are used mainly for respiration, capture of food, and explusion of waste as well as for locomotion and attachment. Foraminifers usually feed on minute organisms, larvae and eggs. Digestion takes place in the protoplasm either inside or outside the test.

On the reef flat around Heron Island, clumps of algae such as *Chlorodesmis fastigiata* (Turtleweed), *Halimeda macroloba* and *Turbinaria ornata* are the hosts for numerous foraminifers such as *Calcarina hispida* (Fig. 11:25), *Baculogypsina sphaerulata* (Fig. 11:21) and *Marginopora vertebralis* (Fig. 11:10). A few species like *Planorbulina mediterranensis* (Fig. 11:13), are cemented on to hard substrate. Some species such as *Globigerina dutertrei* (Fig. 11:22) and *Globigerinoides conglobatus* (Fig. 11:24), are planktonic and float or swim about in the oceans.

Several assemblages of foraminifers can be recognized in the Great Barrier Reef. In the Capricorn-Bunker Groups, the reef flat assemblage is characterized by *Calcarina hispida* (Fig. 11:25), *Baculogypsina sphaerulata* (Fig. 11:21), *Marginopora vertebralis* (Fig. 11:10), *Pararotalia calcar* (Fig. 11:18), and *Peneroplis planatus*. The lagoons support an assemblage dominated by small miliolids such as *Quinqueloculina* and *Spiroloculina*, except around the patch reefs where the assemblage resembles that of the reef flat. The deeper waters between reefs have an association of larger forms with *Operculina bartschi, O. ammonoides, Heterostegina depressa* (Fig. 11:8), *Amphistegina lessoni* (Fig. 11:17) and *Alveolinella quoyi* (Fig. 11:9) as indicative forms. A similar assemblage represents the fore-reef environment.

Fig. 11. Foraminiferida of the Capricorn-Bunker Groups: **1**, *Siphogenerina raphanus*, ×50; **2**, *Amphicoryna separans*, ×50; **3**, *Spiroloculina foveolata*, ×17; **4**, *Spiroloculina angulata*, ×25; **5**, *Quinqueloculina costata*, ×42; **6**, *Textularia pseudogramen*, ×20; **7**, *Brizalina alata*, ×25; **8**, *Heterostegina depressa*, ×10; **9**, *Alveolinella quoyi*, ×6; **10**, *Marginopora vertebralis*, ×10; **11**, *Guttulina problema*, ×30; **12**, *Peneroplis pertusus*, ×12; **13a,b**, *Planorbulina mediterranensis*, ×25; **14**, *Marginulinopsis aculeatus*, ×9; **15**, *Elphidium craticulatum*, ×20; **16**, *Mississippina concentrica*, ×20; **17a,b**, *Amphistegina lessonii*, ×18; **18**, *Pararotalia calcar*, ×35; **19**, *Elphidium macellum*, ×65; **20**, *Epistomaroides polystomelloides*, ×25; **21**, *Baculogypsina sphaerulata*, ×8; **22**, *Globigerina dutertrei*, ×50; **23**, *Globigerina calida*, ×50; **24**, *Globigerinoides conglobatus*, ×50; **25**, *Calcarina hispida*, ×10.

The classification of the Foraminiferida is based primarily on the test. Characters used are its composition and microstructure, unilocular or multilocular nature, mode of chamber and septal addition, chamber form and arrangement, and apertures. Some of the more conspicuous foraminifers in the Capricorn-Bunker Groups are set out below:

Suborder Textulariina: Characterized by tests composed of foreign material such as sand grains cemented together by various cements. *Textularia* is a typical form in which the test is free, biserial, compressed in the plane of biseriality and composed of numerous chambers. (*T. pseudogramen* Fig. 11:6).

Suborder Miliolina: Represented by numerous genera all with calcareous porcellaneous (appearance like porcelain), imperforate tests. *Spiroloculina* and *Quinqueloculina* are representative of a large group of forms which have the chambers added two per whorl in varying planes about a longitudinal axis (*S. foveolata* Fig. 11:3; *S. angulata* Fig. 11:4; *Q. costata* Fig. 11:5). *Peneroplis* is a typical planispiral form in which the later whorls may become uncoiled (*P. pertusus* Fig. 11:12). *Marginopora*, a conspicuous form in the beach sediments, is discoidal, biconcave and up to 2 cm in diameter; usually the initial chambers are lost leaving a central hole in the disc: they are often threaded to make necklaces (*M. vertebralis* Fig. 11:10). *Alveolinella* has a large test, up to 3 cm in length, coiled about an elongate axis so that it is cigar-shaped (*A. quoyi* Fig. 11:9).

Suborder Lagenina: Characterized by forms with calcareous shells which usually appear glassy and are perforate. *Amphicoryna* and *Marginulinopsis* are nodosariids with the chambers arranged in a straight single series (*A. separans* Fig. 11:2; *M. aculeatus* Fig. 11:14). *Guttulina* has its chambers arranged in a spiral series about a long axis (*G. problema* Fig. 11:11).

Suborder Rotaliina: Comprises a great variety of forms of which those figured represent but a few groups. *Brizalina* is a biserial, compressed and carinate form of bolivitinid (*B. alata* Fig. 11:7). *Siphogenerina* is a biserial form in early stages becoming uniserial in later stages (*S. raphanus* Fig. 11:1). *Epistomaroides* is trochospiral but nearly equally biconvex with beautifully sculptured chambers (*E. polystomelloides* Fig. 11:20). *Pararotalia* is also trochospiral, usually plano-convex to biconvex with umbilicus filled with a plug of calcite (*P. calcar*, formerly known as *Calcarina*, Fig. 11:18). *Calcarina* and *Baculogypsina* are very common on the reef top and are usually pink to orange; the former is very spinose whereas the latter has only a few lateral spines (*C. hispida* Fig. 11:25; *B. sphaerulata* Fig. 11:21). *Elphidium* is a very common form throughout the area (*E. craticulatum* Fig. 11:15; *E. macellum* Fig. 11:19). *Heterostegina* is planispiral with a raised central area and outer chambers divided into rectangular chamberlets (*H. depressa* Fig. 11:8). *Amphistegina* and *Planorbulina* are both planoconvex forms (*A. lessonii* Fig. 11:17; *P. mediterranensis* Fig. 11:13).

Suborder Robertinina: *Mississippina* is a foraminifer with a shell of aragonite, a polymorph of calcium carbonate (*M. concentrica* Fig. 11:16).

Suborder Globigerinina: *Globigerina* and *Globigerinoides* are planktonic forms with small spherical chambers (*Globigerina dutertrei* Fig. 11:24).

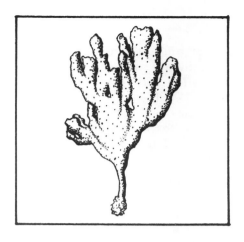

Phylum Porifera

Sponges

In the Beginning

Sometime early in the history of life, single-celled Protozoa-like animals with whip-like flagellae, used for swimming, joined together to form colonies, and eventually became the group of animals we know today as sponges. Sponge-like animals were around during the Precambrian, about 650–700 million years ago (MYA). By the Middle Cambrian (500 MYA) the Demospongiae, the largest extant class of sponges (representing about 95% of presently living species), was well established.

A massive radiation of these animals occurred about 460 MYA, during the Ordovician, when many of the families we recognize today, as well as many now extinct, originated. For the next 100 million years extensive barrier and fringing reefs, similar in structure to today's coral reefs but composed of sponges rather than corals, grew around the ancient continents.

Sponges declined as the primary reef-building organisms at the end of the Devonian (350 MYA), probably due to their inability to compete with the faster growing zooxanthella-bearing corals. Until relatively recently reef-building sponges were thought to have completely died out by the end of the Cretaceous, but their living relics have been found on deep slopes of the Great Barrier Reef and other coral reefs. Previously referred to as classes and orders (stromatoporoids, chaetetids and sphinctozoans), they are now considered merely to be grades of construction or ecological adaptation within the classes Demospongiae and Calcarea. These relic sponges (such as *Acanthochaetetes wellsii* and *Astrosclera willeyana* from the Great Barrier Reef) have solid calcareous skeletons (Fig. 14:10) analogous to the skeletons of modern hermatypic reef-building corals, as well as the discrete (or secondarily fused) spicules characteristic of modern sponges (e.g., Fig. 14:12).

Sponges Today

Sponges have colonized most aquatic habitats, marine and freshwater. They are diverse and common, ranging from polar to tropical seas, and from intertidal to abyssal depths. It is estimated that there may be about 5 000 extant species in Australia, although less than one-quarter of these have been described. Around northeastern Australia, including the Great Barrier Reef, 374 known species (of a probable 1 000) are known to occur (see Wiedenmayer *et al.* 1992).

Sponges and Coral Reefs

Sponges now are perceived to have only a minor structural role in living coral reefs. However, they are considered to be of some importance in accreting coral skeletons in deeper waters where light is limiting and coral growth rudimentary.

Coral reefs have other important and ecologically adapted sponge communities of which the most visible are the autotrophic ones, living mostly off the photosynthetic products of the resident symbiotic cyanobacteria. These communities, significant contributors to the net primary productivity of reef systems, are found predominantly on reef flats and in lagoons. They belong primarily in the two orders Dictyoceratida and Haplosclerida (the latter including the "order" Petrosiida) of the Demospongiae. A different, predominantly heterotrophic sponge fauna, feeding on food particles and waste products filtering down from the coral reef above, is found on the reef slope and towards the base of coral reefs. Sometimes, particularly near the shore, these are large, crowded populations of several hundreds of species.

"Boring" and "burrowing" sponges, found on most coral reefs, chemically dissolve (etch) calcitic and aragonitic substrates including live corals, cause the phenomenon of "coral bleaching", and sometimes result in the destruction of large tracts of coral reef. These sponges (notably genera in the order Hadromerida — *Terpios*, *Spirastrella*, *Cliona* and *Chondrilla* — but also species in other taxa), are substantial contributors to the whole dynamic process of reef bioerosion and consolidation. Some of the etching chemicals are also toxic to humans, denaturing proteins.

Along the northeastern coast of Australia the sponge fauna can be divided into three main groups.

A. Coral reef sponges are the most conspicuous of these three groups, but the least diverse. Many have phototrophic nutrition (autotrophic), living in relatively clean waters off the coast. They are sometimes in large local populations, or they are on live coral substrates on the reef slope, under coral boulders and coral rubble on the reef flat, or in the shallow lagoons adjacent to reefs. It is estimated that less than one half of these species have been described. The species in this group appear to be largely the same on both sides of the continent, ranging from the Rowley Shoals, Western Australia, around the continent to the Wessel Island, Northern Territory, across to Heron Island, Queensland.

B. Inter-reef sponges living in relatively nutrient rich waters near the coast, on mangroves, river mouths, at the base of coral reef slopes and on the sea bed between reefs, are more diverse than those directly associated with coral reefs. Recent sampling of the soft and hard benthos between reefs of the Great Barrier Reef yielded more than 200 species, but few are yet described. Most live on hard substrates, such as coral rubble or rock reefs scattered over the sea bed, but a small number are restricted to particular habitats (such as soft sediments, *Halimeda* beds, mangroves, etc.). What little is known about the Queensland inter-reef sponge fauna suggests that it is quite different from the fauna at similar latitudes on the west coast of the continent.

C. Deeper-water sponges, living on the edge of the Queensland shelf and continental slope, are relatively well known in comparison to inter-reef sponges. Many were discovered by the great exploring expeditions of the late 19th—early 20th century. They include species that occur throughout the world's oceans, and some at least are thought to be remnants of an ancient Tethys fauna. That they have changed little from that time illustrates their conservative morphology. Nevertheless, these known relics may represent only a small proportion of the deeper-water fauna, as indicated by the recent discovery of many new species of ancient, hard-bodied, "lithistid" sponges from the Norfolk Rise (off the Australian continental shelf). Only one such deep-water "lithistid" has been described so far from the Queensland continental slope.

Morphology and Classification

Sponges are primitive multicellular animals (Metazoa) with a layer of unique collar cells (*choanocytes*), partially lining the internal water-filled system of canals. These canals are used for feeding, breathing and excretion. Motile amoeboid secretory cells, such as spicule-secreting (*sclerocytes*), collagen-secreting (*spongocytes*) and feeding/transport *archaeocytes* lie within an intercellular matrix (*mesohyl*; comparable to the mesenchyme of higher metazoans). Sponge cells do not form tissues, nor are they organized into organs for particular functions as they are in higher metazoans, but in two classes the cells are arranged in two layers.

Many sponges are morphologically plastic, their growth form and colour sometimes being affected by local conditions and habitats. In some cases there are substantial morphological and biochemical differences between individuals with only small changes in environmental conditions.

Demospongiae and Calcarea have two cell layers, a layer of collar cells embedded within a cellular matrix, each with a central *flagellum* and collar of smaller *microvilli* lining the internal chambers (Fig. 12A), and a layer of flattened *pinacocyte* cells forms the external surface and continues into the openings of the inhalant canals *(ostia)*, where the pinacocytes become elongated *porocyte cells* (Fig. 12A). The Hexactinellida has the epithelial layer *(pinacoderm)* not covered by pinacocytes but composed merely of an acellular *(syncytial)* matrix (Fig. 15B). It also has its collar cells (called collar bodies in this class) embedded within a syncytial protoplasm *(trabeculae)*, which is stretched across the rigid, fused mineral skeleton (or *dictyonine framework*) (Fig. 15A).

Structurally the sponge can be divided into three major regions, based on the distribution of epithelial cells and secreted inorganic *(spicule)* and organic *(spongin fibre)* skeletons, both produced by nonepithelial sponge cells. Both the spicules (constructed either of opaline silica or calcite) and the spongin fibres (composed of collagen, usually forming strands) are currently the most important characters for taxonomy of the phylum. In the Demospongiae and Calcarea the *ectosome* (or *dermis* or *cortex*) is an outer layer of epithelial cells, covering the external surface *(exopinacocytes)* and basal surface *(basopinacocytes)* (Fig. 12A). An ectosomal skeleton is the inorganic and/or organic skeleton which is associated with this region (Fig. 12B). The *choanosome* includes the internal region containing choanocytes, bounded by the pinacocytes at the surface. The choanosomal skeleton includes mineral (siliceous and/or calcitic) spicules, organic spongin fibres and the organic intercellular region (mesohyl) (Fig. 12A,B). The *subectosomal* region lies between the ectosome and the choanosomal skeleton (Fig. 12B), often represented only by free spicules dispersed between (not associated with) spongin fibres, but sometimes consisting of special categories of fibres. This component of the skeleton varies considerably in its development between different groups of sponges. In the Hexactinellida the choanosome has two sections: one associated with the interior membraneous acellular *(syncytial)* body wall, and the other associated with the membrane bounding the internal gastral cavity (Fig. 15B).

Spicules often occur as two forms, *megascleres* and *microscleres*, differentiated both by their relative sizes and morphology. Both have a diverse geometry (Fig. 13A,B), and in several orders are lost (Table 1). Similarly, the distribution of spicules within the skeleton, the development and form of the organic skeleton and general skeletal structures vary considerably between groups (Fig. 14), and these features figure prominently in the classification.

The classes of sponges presently recognized are *Demospongiae, Calcarea* and *Hexactinellida*, distinguished by the chemical composition of the mineral skeleton (siliceous or calcitic spicules), and certain cytological characters. The class Sclerospongiae, containing the living, relic, hypercalcified, reef-building species, was found to be polyphyletic, its components now being assigned either to the Demospongiae or Calcarea. More than 100 families of living sponges are recognized, with many more extinct groups. There are various publications that provide useful definitions to identify sponges to order and family levels (e.g., Lévi 1973; Bergquist 1978; Hartman 1982). However, the validity of many existing groups is not yet established, and classification of the Porifera is still unstable. Tables 1–3 summarize the major characters used to distinguish classes, subclasses and orders of sponges. The species referred to are some of those known to occur on (or in the vicinity of) the Great Barrier Reef.

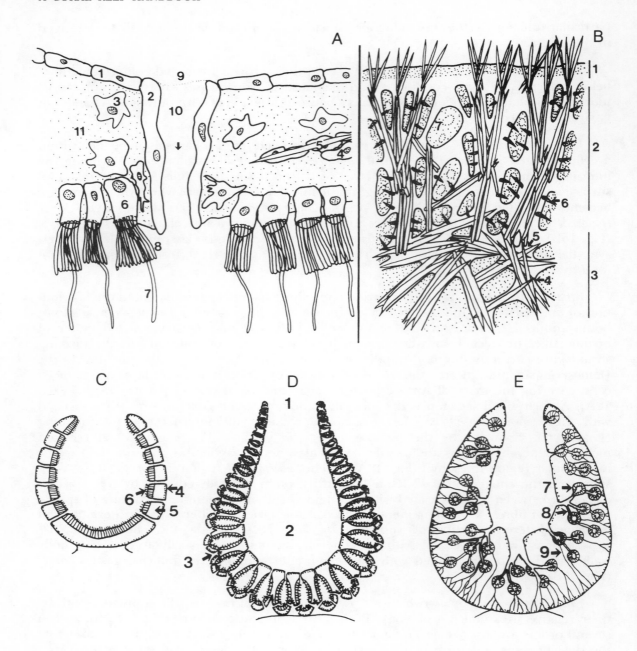

Fig. 12. **A — Cytological organization of generalized sponge** (after Rigby and Stearn 1983), **1**, exopinacocyte on ecto-some; **2**, porocyte; **3**, archaeocyte in mesohyl; **4**, sclerocyte; **5**, spicule secreted by sclerocyte; **6**, choanocyte in choanosome; **7**, choanocyte flagellum; **8**, choanocyte microvillae; **9**, ostium; **10**, inhalant canal = prosopyl; **11**, collagenous fibrils in mesohyl. **B — Skeletal structure of generalized demosponge**, **1**, ectosomal skeleton — cortex or dermis; **2**, subectosomal skeleton — extra-axis; **3**, choanosomal skeleton — axis or core; **4**, spongin fibres; **5**, spicules coring fibres; **6**, spicules echinating fibres; **7**, fibre meshes containing collagenous fibrils and choanocyte chambers — leuconoid aquiferous system. **C–E — Body plans of sponges** (not to be confused with growth forms; after Kukenthal), **C**, asconoid construction, the simplest form of aquiferous system (in many Calcarea and a few demosponges in Homoscleromorpha) with simple tubular construction, without folding of the body wall. **D**, syconoid (in many Calcarea) with choanocyte chambers in direct contact with pinacocytes ("aphodal" condition), folding of both the exterior (pinacoderm) and interior (choanoderm) walls producing choanocyte chambers lying within the body wall rather than only lining the central atrium, and with chambers opening directly on to atrium. **E**, leuconoid (in some Calcarea, most Demospongiae, all Hexactinellida), with canals leading to and from choano-cyte chambers ("diplodal" condition), choanocyte chambers becoming oval, isolated in a maze of canals within body wall, and chambers open on to branching and complex excurrent canals. (Key: **1**, osculum — exhalant pore; **2**, atrium — gastral cavity; **3**, ostia — inhalant pores; **4**, ectosome — zone of pinacocytes; **5**, mesohyl — area with ground substance and mobile cells; **6**, choanosome — choanocytes; **7**, choanocyte chamber; **8**, exhalant canal — apopyle; **9**, inhalant canal — prosopyl).

Table 1. Keys to the orders of Calcarea.

"Calcareous sponges." Mineral skeleton exclusively calcitic, with both discrete spicules (Fig. 13A: 44–51) and fused crystalline calcite skeletons; three grades of construction frequent (Fig. 12C–E): asconoid, syconoid or leuconoid.

Class Calcarea

Subclass Calcinia

Free triradiate spicules (Fig. 13A: 44) with rays and angles between rays being equal, with or without monactinal or diactinal free spicules.

Order Clathrinida

(1 family) spicules only triradiates (Fig. 13A: 44) with arms of equal length and at equal angles to each other: body plan asconoid (Fig. 12C); *Clathrina clathrata*.

Order Leucettida

(3 families) spicules both triradiate and quadriradiate (Fig. 13A: 45, 51); periphery of skeleton has distinct cortex; 4 species, including *Leucaltis clathria* and *Pericharax heteroraphis*.

Subclass Pharetronida

Massive reinforced calcitic skeleton, together with randomly distributed tuning fork spicules (Fig. 13A: 50) and quadriradiate spicules (Fig. 13A: 45) around each osculum.

Order Inozoida

(5 families) diagnosis as for subclass; not yet recorded from this region.

Subclass Calcaronia

Spicules free, triradiate (Fig. 13A: 44) and sagittal (two rays paired and third ray longer than others; Fig. 13A: 46), as well as free monaxonic (monactinal or diactinal) forms (Fig. 13A: 47–49).

Order Leucosolenida

(1 family) spicules triradiate (Fig. 13A: 44), sagittal with unequal angles (Fig. 13A: 46); body plan asconoid (Fig. 12C). *Leucosolenia challengeri*.

Order Sycettida

(5 families) ectosomal cortex usually continuous, and sagittal triradiate spicules always present (Fig. 13A: 46); body plan syconoid or leuconoid (Fig. 12D,E); 8 species, including *Leucilla uter* and *Sycon arboreum*.

Table 2. Keys to the orders of Hexactinellida.

"Glass sponges." Mineral skeleton composed of six-rayed spicules (hexacts), typically forming rigid lattice-like skeletons and also occurring as discrete spicules.

Class Hexactinellida.

Subclass Amphidiscophora

Birotulate microscleres present (Fig. 13B:143), hexaster microscleres absent, sponges embedded within soft sediments by one or more long basal prostal spicule (Fig. 13A: 59, Fig. 15A).

Order Amphidiscosida

(3 families) diagnosis as for subclass. *Hyalonema (Leptonema) aculiferum*; several other unpublished species are also known, including a species of the giant "fishing rod" sponge *Monorhaphis*.

Subclass Hexasterophora

Hexaster microscleres present (Fig. 13B: 127–135), birotulate microscleres absent; sponges usually fixed to substrate with basal attachment, basal prostal spicules pentactines (e.g., Fig. 13A: 54) or anisodiactines (e.g., Fig. 13A: 62) in tufts.

Order Hexactinosida

(6 families) parenchymal skeleton rigid, fused hexactine spicules (Fig. 13A: 55); dermal and gastral spicules (Fig. 15) usually pentactines Fig. 13A: 54) with unpaired ray directed inwards, sometimes stauractines (Fig. 13A: 56); not yet recorded from this region.

Order Lyssacinosida

(4 families) parenchymal spicules range from hexactines to rhabdodiactines (Fig. 13A: 55), usually free within the syncytial (acellular) matrix, or sometimes secondarily fused to form rigid framework; a specialized, single layer of ectosomal spicules present (hexactines or pentactines; Fig. 13A: 54–55), with the single, longest, proximal ray pointing inwards, or with a layer of small dermal spicules overlying larger hypodermal pentactines, with unpaired ray extending inwards; *Holascus undulatus*.

Order Lychniscosida

(3 families, parenchymal spicules lychniscs or derivatives (Fig. 13A: 64) united together in rigid framework (Fig. 13A: 63), with the hollow centre of each spicule framed by 12 struts; sponges firmly attached to substrate; not yet recorded from this region.

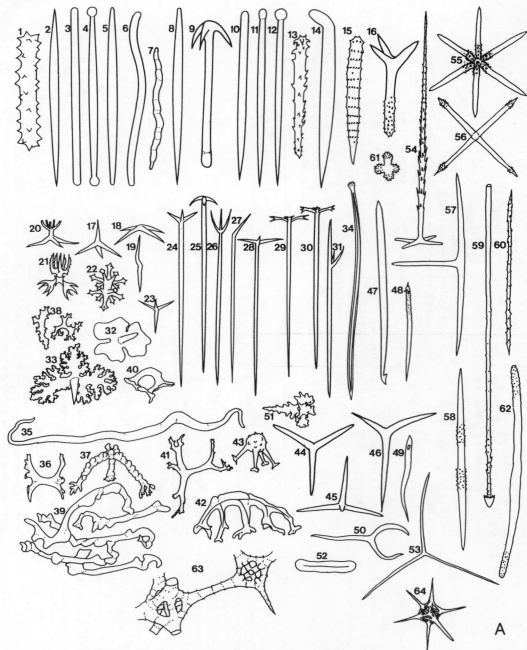

Fig. 13. **A — Range of geometric forms of sponge megascleres and calthrops** (after various authors) 1–9, **Diactinal (monaxonic) megascleres** (1, acanthotylostrongyle; 2, oxea; 3, strongyle; 4, tylote; 5, strongyloxea; 6, sinuous strongyle; 7, tuberculate vermiform strongyle; 8, anisoxea; 9, cladotylote). 10–16, **Monactinal (monaxonic) megascleres** (10, style; 11, subtylostyle; 12, tylostyle; 13, acanthostyle; 14, rhabdostyle; 15, verticillate acanthostyle; 16, sagittal triact — acanthoplagiotriaene). 17– 22, **Calthrops and derivatives** (17, undifferentiated calthrops; 18, tetrapod calthrops; 19, centrangulate diact; 20, monoloph (lophotetractine); 21, candelabrum; 22, amphimesodichotriaene). 23–34, **Tetractinal (tetraxonic) megascleres** (23, short shaft triaene; 24, plagiotriaene; 25, anatriaene; 26, protriaene; 27, promonaene; 28, orthotriaene; 29, dichotriaene; 30, trichotriaene; 31, trichodal or heterocladal protriaene; 32, discotriaene; 33, phyllotriaene; 34, oxytylote — diact). 35–43, **Desmas** (35, ophirhabd — monocrepidial; 36, dendroclone; 37, tricranoclone — tricrepidial; 38, rhizoclones — monocrepidial; 39, fused heloclones — monocrepidial; 40, megaclone — monocrepidial; 41, tetraclone — tetracrepidial; 42, rhabocrepid — monocrepidial; 43, sphaeroclone — tetracrepidial). 44–51, **Calcareous megascleres** (44, triradiate; 45, quadriradiate; 46, sagittal triradiate; 47, "oxea"; 48, acanthose "microxea"; 49, "needle-eye" microxea; 50, "tuning fork" spicule; 51, acanthose quadriradiate). 52–53, **Collagenous spongin spicules** (52, tylotiform; 53 triaeniform). 54–64, **Hexactinellid megascleres** (54, pentactinal pinule; 55, hexactin; 56, stauractin; 57, triactin; 58, diactinal rhabd; 59, terminal end of basal bidentate with anchor; 60, uncinate; 61, tetractinal acanthophore; 62, diactinal acanthophore; 63, part of dictyonal mesh, with two lychniscs joined, the younger still unconnected; 64, young lychnisc).

Fig. 13. **B — Range of geometric forms of sponge microscleres** (after various authors), 65–85, **Meniscoid microscleres** (65, palmate isochelae; 66, arcuate isochelae; 67, anchorate isochelae; 68, unguiferous isochelae; 69, birotulate isochelae; 70, bipocilla; 71, palmate anisochela; 72, placochela; 73, sphaerancora; 74, canonochela; 75, clavidisc — compound diancistra; 76, diancistra; 77, c-sigma; 78, s-sigma; 79, serrate sigma; 80, croca; 81, centrangulate sigma; 82, tetrapocilla; 83, cleistochela; 84, spined isancora; 85, spined chela). 86–112, **Monaxonic microscleres** (86, toxa; 87, spined toxa; 88, forceps; 89, discorhabd — didiscus; 90, anthosigma; 91, sanidastoid discorhabd — *Latrunculia*; 92, sanidastoid discorhabd — *Sigmosceptrella*; 93, anisodiscrohabd; 94, spiraster; 95, spinispira; 96, spirula; 97, toxaspire; 98, sigmaspire; 99, selenaster; 100, microxea; 101, microstrongyle; 102, centrotylote microxea; 103, microtylostyle; 104, comma; 105, raphide; 106, trichite — bundle of raphides; 107, onychaete; 108, spined centrotylote rod; 109, spear-shaped microstyle; 110, thraustoxea; 111, sanidaster; 112, "ecailles" — monocrepidial disc). 113–126, **Astrose microscleres**, (113, plesiaster streptaster; 114, amphiaster streptaster; 115, metaster streptaster; 116, spiraster streptaster; 117, oxyaster euaster; 118, oxyspheraster euaster; 119, pycnaster euaster; 120, strongylaster euaster; 121, tylaster euaster; 122, anthaster euaster; 123, anthospheraster euaster; 124, sterrospheraster euaster; 125, sterraster euaster; 126, aspidaster euaster). 127–152, **Hexactinellid microscleres** (127, onychohexaster; 128, strongylhexaster; 129, oxydiaster; 130, oxyhexaster; 131, discohexaster; 132, discoctaster; 133, spherical discohexaster — discospiraster; 134, tylohexaster; 135, codonhexaster; 136, graphiocome; 137, floricome; 138, plumicome; 139, discocome; 140, strobiloplumicome; 141, amphidisc; 142, hexadisc; 143, birotulate amphidisc; 144, scopule (sceptule); 145, disc-ended clavule (sceptule); 146, spino-anchorate clavule (sceptule); 147, pilate clavule (sceptule); 148, sarule (sceptule); 149, lonchiole (sceptule); 150, centrotylote rhabd; 151, sphere; 152, ring "sigma").

Table 3. Key to the Orders of Demospongiae.

Class Demospongiae

"Siliceous or true sponges." Mineral skeleton composed of silica spicules and/or spongin fibres; collagenous filaments (or fibrils) always present in ground substance of the intercellular mesohyl.

Subclass Tetractinomorpha

Tetraxonid (Fig. 13A: 24–34) and monaxonid megascleres (Fig. 13A: 1–9, 10–16), various asterose microscleres common (Fig. 12B: 113–126); skeleton usually radial or axially compressed.

Subclass Homoscleromorpha

Tetraxonid spicules with equal rays (Fig. 13A: 23); megascleres and microscleres undifferentiated; spicules may be lost completely.

Order Homoscierophorida

(2 families) diagnosis as for subclass; *Oscarella tenuis* (with only collagenous fibrils), and *Corticium candelabrum* (with lophotetractines. Fig. 13A: 20).

Subclass Ceractinomorpha

Monaxonic megascleres (Fig. 13A: 2–6, 10–12) either monactinal (styles) or diactinal (oxeas to strongyles), never tetractinal (although modifications to the ends of some of these spicules do occur (e.g., Fig. 13A: 9)); great diversity of microscleres (meniscoid, oxeote, toxote, spheres; Fig. 13B: 65–90), never asterose forms; usually with well developed organic skeleton; spicules have been secondarily lost in 3 orders.

Order Hadromerida

(11 families) uniform monaxonic spicules only (styles, oxeas; Fig. 13A: 2–6, 10–12), never tetractinal forms; with radially arranged skeleton obvious at least at surface if not in choanosome; ectosomal spicules typically smaller than choanosomal spicules, usually standing perpendicular to surface; microscleres include asterose forms (euasters, streptasters and derivatives; Fig. 13B: 113–126) and monaxonic forms (microxeas, spirasters; Fig. 13B: 100, 116) may be absent; 37 species including the common *Spirastrella vagabunda*, the "axinellid" *Axos flabelliformis*, and the hypercalcified "sclerosponge" *Acanthochaetetes wellsii* (Fig. 14: 10).

Order Axinellida

(3 families) only monaxonic megascleres present (styles, strongyles, oxeas in various combinations; Fig. 13A: 1–16); skeletal tracts often localized in particular regions of the sponge, with condensed axial skeleton and a plumose or plumo-reticulate extra-axial skeleton typical (Fig. 14: 5–6); microscleres usually absent, sometimes raphides, singly or in bundles (trichodragmata) (Fig. 13B: 105–106); 21 species, including *Phakellia flabellata*, *Auletta constricta* and *Reniochalina stalagmitis* (Fig. 14: 3).

Order Agelasida

(2 families) well developed spongin-fibre skeleton, forming regular or irregular reticulation, superficially resembling commercial bath sponges (Spongiidae); rarely only a solid calcitic basal skeleton; fibres echinated by short styles and/or oxeas with verticillate spines (Fig. 13A: 15); microscleres absent; *Agelas mauritiana* and the hypercalcified "sclerosponge" *Astrosclera willeyana*.

Order Dictyoceratida

(3 families) mineral spicules lost (although detritus and contaminating spicules often found inside fibres and on surface); main skeleton reticulate spongin fibres, frequently with primary, secondary and sometimes tertiary networks; fibres homogenous or lightly laminated in cross-section, with or without central pith, and collagenous filaments sometimes scattered in mesohyl; 85 species including *Fascaplysinopsis reticulata*, *Carteriospongia foliascens*, *Luffariella variabilis*, and *Spongia officinalis* (Fig. 14: 9).

Order Halichondrida

(2 families) main skeleton disorganized criss-cross (Fig. 14: 8) of styles (Fig. 13A: 10), oxcas (Fig. 13A: 2) or both intermixed, usually with more organization at surface than in choanosome; fibres absent; typically with large subdermal cavities; microscleres usually absent, occasionally raphides (Fig. 13B: 105) or microxeas (Fig. 13B: 100); 11 species including *Ciocalypta penicillus* and *Halichondria frutex*.

Order Verongiida

(3 families) mineral spicules lost; spongin fibres form large, widely spaced reticulate skeleton, without differentiated primary or secondary elements; fibres aggregated (fasciculated) into bundles, laminated, and with distinct pith of fine fibrils; collagenous consistency; mesohyl with abundant collagenous fibrils; typically with pigment that oxidises to a purple colour on contact with air; 9 species including the more common fans *Ianthella basta* and clubs *Pseudoceratina durissima*.

Order Haploscierida

(3 families of probably polyphyletic freshwater sponges, 5 families of marine sponges) main skeleton usually very regular reticulation (=isodictyal), with uni, pauci or multispicular tracts of spicules forming triangular, rectangular or polygonal meshes; megascleres consist exclusively of oxeas (Fig. 13A: 2) or strongyles (Fig. 13A: 3, 6), bonded together with sparse collagenous spongin or enclosed entirely within spongin fibres; microscleres not diverse, but may include centrangulate sigmas (Fig. 13B: 81), toxas (Fig. 13B: 86) or microxeas (Fig. 13B: 100); 84 species including *Gelliodes fibulata*, numerous species of *Callyspongia* and *Amphimedon*, and the barrel sponge *Xestospongia testudinaria*.

Order Poecilosclerida

(16 families) microscleres include meniscoid forms (in 11 families) such as chelae (unique to this order; Fig. 13B: 65–74, 82–85) and (in all families) other diverse forms (sigmas, toxas, raphides, etc.; Fig. 13B: 75–81, 86–88, 90); megascleres often localized in distinct regions (e.g., inside fibres); sand/detritus may replace megascleres; 95 species (about 70% of total known for this region) including *Amphinomia sulphurea* (Fig. 14: 2), *Echinodictyum mesenterinum* (Fig. 14: 4), *Raspailia vestigifera* (Fig. 14: 6), *R. phakellopis* (Fig. 14: 11), *Hemectyonilla involutum* (Fig. 14: 12), *Clathria tuberosa* (Fig. 14: 7), *C. cactiformis*, *C. toxifera* (Fig. 14: 1), and *Biemna saucia* (Fig. 14: 8).

Order Astrophorida

(7 families) large oxeas (Fig. 13A: 2) always present, sometimes with triaenes (Fig. 13A: 23–31); radial skeleton may be visible at surface only; microscleres commonly asterose forms (sometimes lost) (Fig. 13B: 113–126), microxeas and microrhabds (Fig. 13B: 100–101); 10 species including *Jaspis stellifera* and *Disyringia dissimilis*.

Order Lithistida

(polyphyletic) articulated siliceous desma megascleres (Fig. 13A: 35–43) produce a rigid skeletal structure; desmas classified by number of secondarily silicified rays (crepis); 1 (monocrepid; Fig. 13A: 35, 38–40, 42) to 4 (tetracrepidal; Fig. 13A: 41, 43); secondary skeleton of free spicules present or absent; 3 suborders:

Suborder Rhabdosina

(3 families) ectosome without megascleres but with minutely spined microstrongyles (Fig. 13B: 111), microspined sigma-like microscleres (cf. Fig. 13B: 77) or monocrepidal (one-rayed) disks (Fig. 13A: 40); (affinities with Hadromerida and Axinellida; not recorded yet from this region).

Suborder Anoplina

(3 families) neither ectosomal megascleres nor microscleres present; (affinities uncertain); not recorded yet from this region, although the neighbouring Norfolk Rise has a rich, lithistid fauna.

Suborder Triaenosina

(3 families), peripheral skeleton radially arranged triaenes (Fig. 13A: 23–34); microscleres amphiasters, spirasters or microrhabds (Fig. 13B: 114, 116); (obvious affinities with Astrophorida); *Theonella*

Order Spirophorida

(1 family) spherical growth form; megascleres triaenes (Fig. 13A: 23–31) and oxeas (Fig. 13A: 2) in radiate arrangement, microscleres contorted sigmaspires (Fig. 13B: 98); 5 species including *Cinachyra australiensis* and *Raphidotethya enigmatica*.

Feeding

All sponges are able to efficiently irrigate themselves by drawing in water, and to select or reject food particles (according to particle size) from that water. This process is an active one whereby a water current is set up from the beating of flagella on the collar cells. Water enters the sponge through inhalant pores *(ostia)*, and is subsequently filtered by a series of sieves of diminishing mesh size. Water enters the sponge itself — into the mesohyl with its mobile cell population — through small pores *(prosopyles)* located around the base of the collar cells and passing through even smaller spaces between the microvilli on the collar cells. Here the food particles are ingested by the amoeboid cells (archaeocytes) within the mesohyl, and waste products are returned to the exterior via the water vascular system and exhalant pores *(oscula)* in an excurrent stream of water (Fig. 12).

Interactions

The ability to digest and modify the waste products and chemicals produced by other organisms which live in, on or near them may also partly explain the unusual biochemistry of many species, and why sponges are usually unpalatable, and often even toxic. There is now some good evidence to suggest that they use their extensive arsenal of secondarily metabolized chemicals as both offensive and defensive weapons — to repel predators or parasites, and to compete for space.

Sponges are unappetising by human standards, but some are eaten by molluscs, echinoderms, fishes and turtles. On the Great Barrier Reef and in northwestern Australia some sea cucumbers (*Synaptula* species) are frequently seen congregating on branching and fan sponges (*Axos* and *Ianthella* species), presumably feeding on the mucus exudate. Nudibranchs (such as *Rostanga*) are active feeders on sponge mucus and collagen, and these molluscs are quite specific as to the species or genus of sponge upon which they prey (in this case the poecilosclerid family Microcionidae). Nudibranchs also ingest the sponge's toxic chemicals, concentrating them and reusing them for their own chemical protection. The predators are usually the same colour as the sponge, having ingested the sponge's characteristically brightly coloured carotenoid pigments. Other documented predators of sponges on the Great Barrier Reef include Hawksbill turtles and several species of grazing fishes.

Reproduction

Sponges reproduce both sexually and by replication. They probably are sequentially hermaphrodite, one individual containing either only male or only female cells at one time. Often sex cells are absent altogether: their occurrence is thought to be ephemeral. Sequential hermaphroditism is a means of ensuring that individuals are not self-fertilized — the cells of one sex maturing before those of the other. Sexual reproduction involves the development of free-swimming larvae (*amphiblastulae, parenchymellae, coeloblastulae,* depending on which group of sponges), which ensures that populations receive new recruits, preventing their isolation from one another. Fertilization is internal, with larvae being brooded by the parent (viviparous), or it is external, male and female gametes being released together (oviparous). There is evidence of synchronous release of gametes in species of *Xestospongia* in the Great Barrier Reef, but few other species have been investigated and the extent of synchronous spawning in sponges is not yet well understood.

Replication is very common in this phylum. In more severe habitats, such as tropical intertidal zones, areas of high wave action, current scours, etc. sponges fragment to form replicates or clones of themselves, as do corals and many other sedentary colonial organisms in the tropics.

Longevity of sponges varies considerably, although growth rates and life span are poorly understood. Some species reproduce and die in less than one year, whereas others are thought to live for centuries.

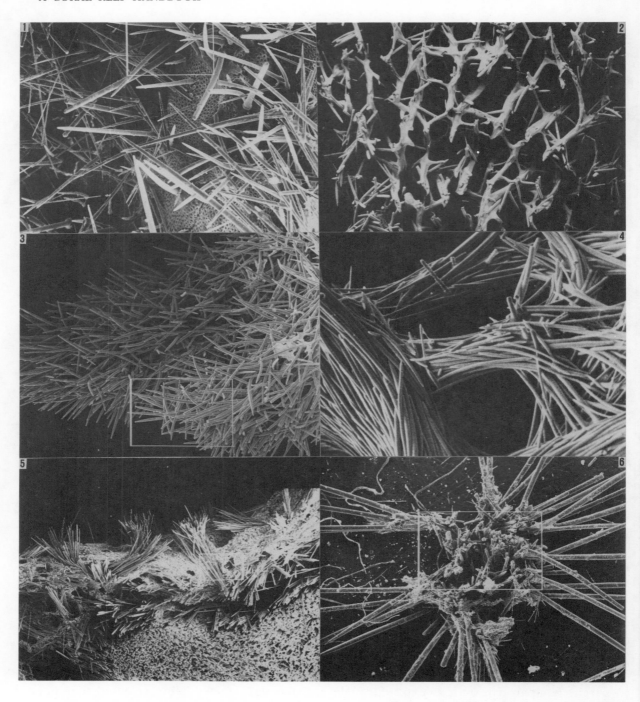

Fig. 14. Examples of skeletal structures in demosponges (A, 1–6): 1, hymedesmoid (*Clathria toxifera*; Microcionidae); 2, subrenieroid (*Amphinomia sulphurea*; Raspailiidae); 3, plumoreticulate (*Reniochalina stalagmitis*; Axinellidae); 4, reticulate (*Echinodictyum mesenterinum;* Raspailiidae); 5, compressed radial (*Axos flabelliformis*; Hemiasterellidae); 6, differentiated axial and extra-axial skeletons (*Raspailia vestigifera*; Raspailiidae).

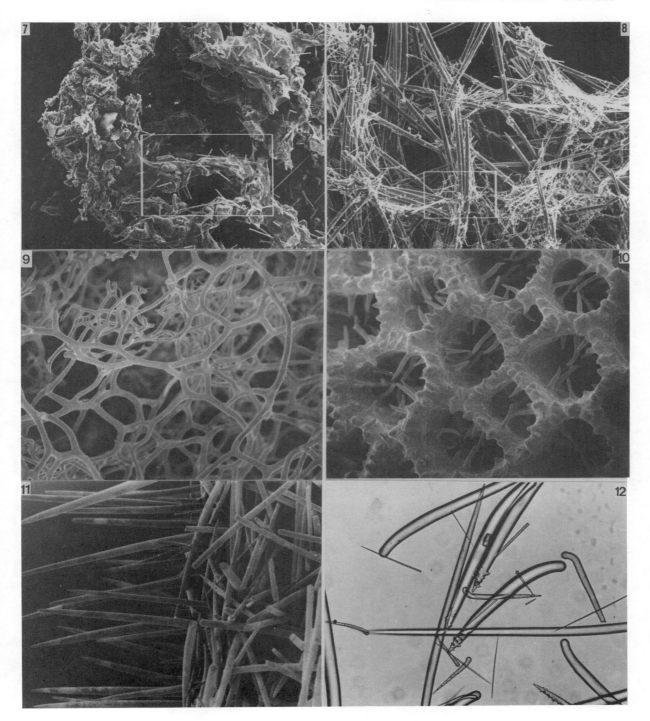

Fig. 14. Examples of skeletal structures in demosponges (**B**, 7–12): **7**, arenaceous (*Clathria tuberosa*; Microcionidae); **8**, halichondroid reticulate (*Biemna saucia*; Desmacellidae); **9**, reticulate spongin fibres only (commercial bath sponge *Spongia officinalis*; Spongiidae); **10**, solid calcitic basal skeleton and free spicules ("hypercalcified" *Acanthochaetetes wellsii*; Spirastrellidae); **11**, compressed axial, plumose radial skeleton (*Raspailia phakellopsis;* Raspailiidae); **12**, loose spicules of *Hemectyonilla involutum* (Raspailiidae).

Sponge Identification

The higher taxa of sponges are set out in Tables 1–3, together with the number of families known, the number of known species and the common ones known from the Great Barrier Reef. Full species citations for common species are given in Wiedenmayer *et al.* 1992.

Sponge identification depends on histological preparations to determine spicule geometry, skeletal structure and structure of the aquiferous system. Calcareous sponge spicules are obtained from bleach-soaked (sodium hypochlorite) sections of sponge tissue (including ectosomal and choanosomal regions), in a flask or directly on a slide. Siliceous sponge spicule preparations can also be made in this manner, or more simply by using a method involving nitric acid digestion of tissue directly on a slide gently heated over a flame.

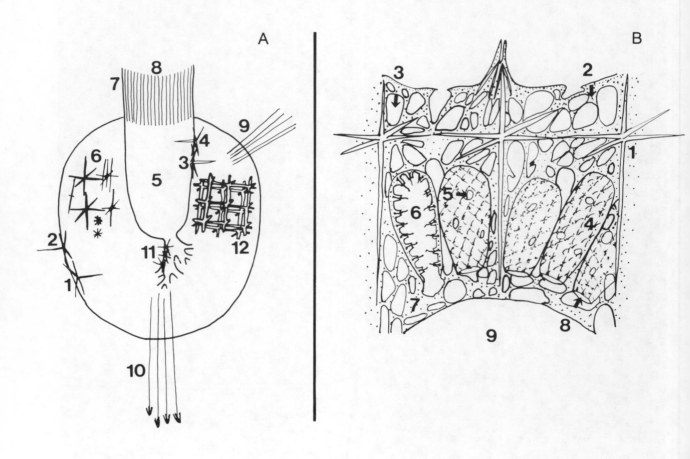

Fig. 15. Localization and terminology of spicules found in the Hexactinellida: **A — Cross Section Through Whole Specimen** (after Schulze 1887). (Key to symbols — **1–2, dermal region:** 1, hypodermal spicules; 2, hyperdermal spicules; **3–8, gastral region:** 3, hypogastral spicules; 4, hypergastral spicules; 5, gastral cavity or atrium; 6, parenchymal spicules; 7, marginal prostals; 8, osculum (exhalant pore); **9–12, parenchymal region:** 9, pleural (or lateral) prostals; 10, basal prostals; 11, canalaria spicules; 12, portion of the rigid parenchymal skeleton, forming a dictyonine framework). **B — Internal Organization Section Through Body Wall** (after Bergquist 1978) (Key to symbols — 1, structural hexactine spicule forming non-rigid part of skeleton; 2, subdermal trabeculae (indicated by arrow = mesh-like soft "tissue"); 3, subdermal cavities or lacunae (indicated by arrow); 4, choanocyte chamber; 5, inhalant aperture (prosopyle) on exterior of choanocyte chamber (indicated by arrow); 6, section through chamber, showing individual collar body units; 7, inner trabecular "tissue"; 8, exhalant aperture (apopyle); 9, gastral cavity).

Coelenterates

Coelenterates (an old term) are simple, radially symmetrical animals with cup-shaped bodies formed of two cell layers — an outer layer (ectoderm) and an inner layer (endoderm) — around the gastric cavity *(coelenteron)*. Sometimes a complex, thick, jelly-like matrix *(coenenchyme)* is between the cell layers but there never is a middle layer of cells (mesoderm) characteristic of all higher animals. Coelenterates consist of the comb jellies (Phylum Ctenophora), and the anemones, corals and jellyfishes (Phylum Cnidaria): both are found on the Great Barrier Reef. The figures (pp. 48, 50) provide an introduction to the groups.

Phylum Ctenophora — Comb Jellies

Comb jellies are delicate, mostly planktonic, with eight longitudinal bands of cilia on the outside of the body, but without stinging cells. They are all, at times, intensely bioluminescent. Many are bell-like, or spherical, others flat and ribbon-like. Often they are seen floating near the surface of the sea. Most are so fragile that they disintegrate when caught. A common reef species is the Sea Gooseberry *(Pleurobrachia pileus)*. An introduction to the group is provided by Harbison and Madin (1982).

Phylum Cnidaria — Stinging Coelenterates

These are the most commonly encountered stinging coelenterates, with the stinging cells *(cnidocysts* or *nematocysts)* usually on tentacles around the mouth — using them to trap or kill prey. Some have extremely potent, even deadly venom.

Cnidarians are solitary or colonial, and many have a complex life cycle involving both sedentary and free-floating generations. The sedentary polyps or *hydroid* form has the tentacle-rimmed mouth facing up. In the free-living medusoid form (also known as a *medusa* or jellyfish), the tentacles hand down from an inverted saucer or bell-shaped animal. Many sedentary cnidarians secrete a hard skeleton to support and protect the animal or, more usually, the colony.

Although most groups of cnidarians are well represented in reef waters, not all are equally well known. The hard corals, because of their dominance, have been well studied. In contrast, the anemones and relatives have been largely neglected.

Class Hydrozoa

Complex life cycles with alternation of generations between sessile hydroid and planktonic medusoid forms characterize this group. Sometimes one or other generation is suppressed. Hydroid and medusoid generations often are studied independently, and each has its own separate classification. Most sessile hydroid colonies have a fine, scleroprotein skeleton. Those that incorporate calcium to become heavier and more robust are the hydrocorallines. These are often treated with the true or stony corals.

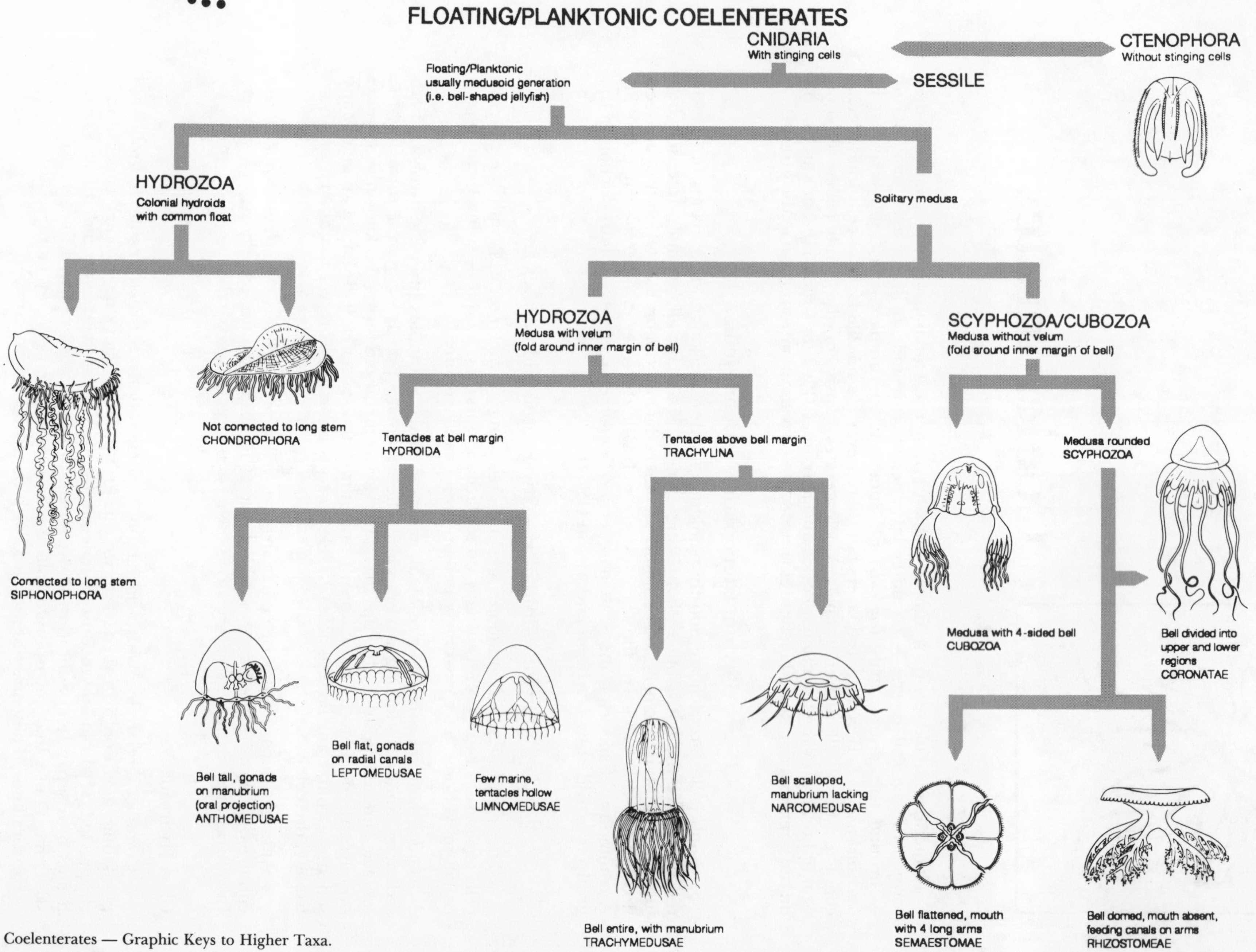

FLOATING/PLANKTONIC COELENTERATES

CTENOPHORA
Without stinging cells

CNIDARIA
With stinging cells

SESSILE
Floating/Planktonic
usually medusoid generation
(i.e. bell-shaped jellyfish)

HYDROZOA
Colonial hydroids
with common float

Solitary medusa

SCYPHOZOA/CUBOZOA
Medusa without velum
(fold around inner margin of bell)

HYDROZOA
Medusa with velum
(fold around inner margin of bell)

Medusa rounded
SCYPHOZOA

Bell divided into
upper and lower
regions
CORONATAE

Bell domed, mouth absent,
feeding canals on arms
RHIZOSTOMEAE

Medusa with 4-sided bell
CUBOZOA

Bell flattened, mouth
with 4 long arms
SEMAESTOMEAE

Tentacles above bell margin
TRACHYLINA

Bell scalloped,
manubrium lacking
NARCOMEDUSAE

Bell entire, with manubrium
TRACHYMEDUSAE

Tentacles at bell margin
HYDROIDA

Few marine,
tentacles hollow
LIMNOMEDUSAE

Bell flat, gonads
on radial canals
LEPTOMEDUSAE

Bell tall, gonads
on manubrium
(oral projection)
ANTHOMEDUSAE

Not connected to long stem
CHONDROPHORA

Connected to long stem
SIPHONOPHORA

Coelenterates — Graphic Keys to Higher Taxa.

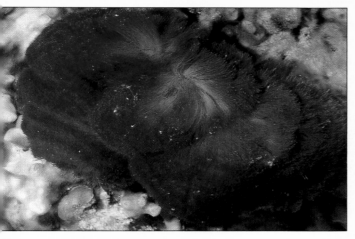

Chlorodesmis fastigiata, Turtle weed.

Halimeda discoides.

Callyspongia (Spinosella) sp. (Haplosclerida, Callyspongiidae) Heron I.
(Photo courtesy of Neville Coleman.)

Auletta constricta (Axinellida, Axinellidae) Heron I.
(Photo courtesy of Neville Coleman.)

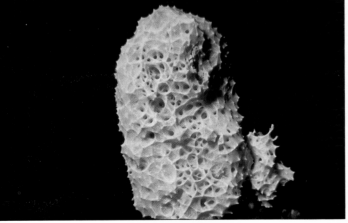

Luffariella variabilis (Dictyoceratida, Ircinidae) Swain Reefs.
(Photo courtesy of Neville Coleman.)

The fan sponge *Phakellia flabellata* (Axinellida, Axinellidae)
Lizard I. (Photo courtesy of Neville Coleman.)

Sea cucumbers (the holothurians *Synaptula*) feeding on the
mucous exudate of the sponge *Axos flabelliformis* (Hadromerida,
Hemiasterellidae) Cockburn I. (Photo courtesy of John Hooper.)

Phototrophic foliose sponge *Carteriospongia foliascens*
(Dityoceratida, Spongiidae) Nomad Reef.
(Photo courtesy of John Hooper.)

PLATE 2

Unless otherwise stated photos courtesy of
Great Barrier Reef Marine Park Authority

Aglaophenia cupressina (Hydrozoa, Hydroida).

Cassiopeia andromeda (Scyphozoa).

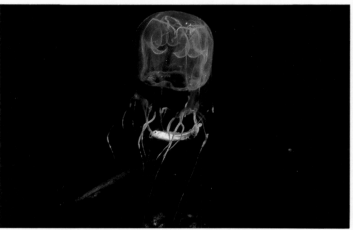

Chironex fleckeri (Cubozoa), the Box Jellyfish; its stings are fatal to man.

Anemone tentacles (Anthozoa, Actinaria).

Parazoanthus axinellae (Anthozoa, Zoanthidea).

Protopalythoa (Anthozoa, Zoanthidea) (left) mixed with *Zoanthus mantoni*. (Photo courtesy of J. Ryland.)

Zoanthus vietnamensis (Anthozoa, Zoanthidea). (Photo courtesy of J. Ryland.)

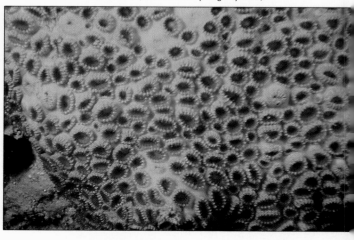

Palythoa caesia (Anthozoa, Zoanthidea).

Among the floating hydrozoans, the biggest group, HYDROIDA, includes the **Anthomedusae** and **Leptomedusae** (each with a sessile stage), and the **Limnomedusae** (sometimes with a sessile stage).

TRACHYLINA includes the **Trachymedusae**, **Narcomedusae** and **Laingiomedusae** (rarely encrusted).

Kramp (1953) listed the medusoid forms from the Great Barrier Reef. No comprehensive guide to local sessile species exists, and the best introduction to the sessile hydroids is Millard's (1975) work on South African forms. On the Great Barrier Reef, Pennycuik (1959) reported 28 sessile hydroid species from Heron Island. Most of these (25) were the sessile colonial generations of Leptomedusae (thecate hydroids with polyps of the colony protected by a cup into which they can withdraw). Only three of the small athecate species (medusoid generation of Anthomedusae) were found. Representatives of several additional thecate genera have been trawled from between the reefs.

Of particular significance to divers are the stinging hydroids or "fire weed". The large, brown, fern-like fronds of *Aglaophenia cupressina* and the more wispy, white fronds of *Lytocarpus* spp. can deliver severe stings. Also capable of stinging is "fire coral" MILLEPORINA (*Millepora* spp.) a hydrocoralline. The other hydrocoralline group is the STYLASTERINA with usually small, often purple, fragile colonies.

Two groups of floating colonial hydrozoans are found in the plankton of the Great Barrier Reef, the **Siphonophora** containing the familiar Portuguese Man-o'-war *Physalia* which buds from a stem; and the **Chondrophora**, containing *Velella* and *Porpita* which lack the stem, the polyps budding off a central float.

Classes Scyphozoa and Cubozoa — Jellyfish

The medusa or jellyfish are the dominant forms in these groups. Most are cosmopolitan. **Coronatae** have the bell divided into upper and lower regions; **Semaeostomae** have a mouth and four broad flounced oral arms; and **Rhizostomae** lack a distinct mouth, filtering food drawn in through canals in eight oral arms. The sessile **Stauromedusae**, usually found in cold water, are not reported from reef and adjacent waters. Kramp (1961) provides an invaluable introduction to world records.

Best known of the jellyfish are the big blubbers *Cyanea* (Semaestomeae) which can grow up to 1 m across and are found in open waters, and the peculiar, upside down *Cassiopea andromeda* (Rhizostomeae) found on sheltered reef flats. Its tissues are filled with symbiotic algae similar to those found in corals.

Relatively recently the Cubozoa (which contains the highly venomous, square-belled jellyfish) were separated from other Scyphozoa. Inshore, especially in sheltered bays in summer are the deadly sea-wasps *Chironex fleckeri*. Details of this important species are found in Hartwick (1987). The minute *Carukia barnesi* (Carybdeidae) which is responsible for the Irukandji Syndrome (see Fenner, Williamson, Callinan and Audley 1986) is found off shore.

Class Anthozoa

Anthozoa completely lack any medusoid form. The hydroids also differ from those of Hydrozoa in having partitions (mesenteries) within the polyp. Two groups are recognized — those with six tentacles and mesenteries (or multiples of six), the Hexacorallia or Zoantharia; and those with eight, the Octocorallia or Alcyonaria.

Alcyonaria (Octocorallia), with pinnate tentacles are all colonial and build a skeleton. In the blue coral *Heliopora* it is non-spicular aragonite, the soft corals (**Alcyonacea**) have a skeleton of calcite spicules, the sea fans (**Gorgonacea**) have a branched scleroprotein axis and the sea pens (**Pennatulacea**) an unbranched one.

49

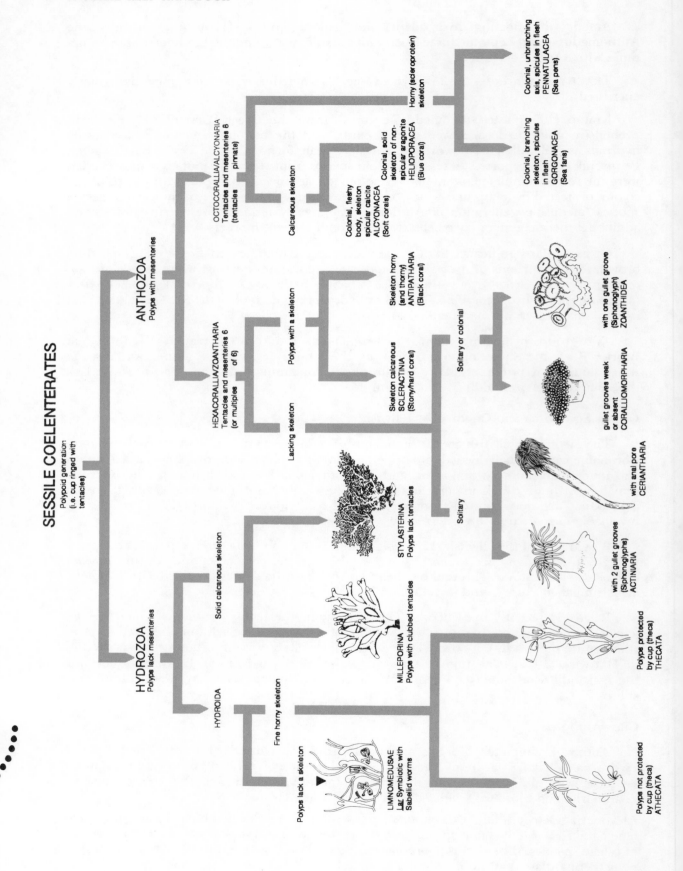

SESSILE COELENTERATES
Polypoid generation (i.e. cup ringed with tentacles)

HYDROZOA Polyps lack mesenteries

HYDROIDA

Solid calcareous skeleton

Fine horny skeleton

Polyps lack a skeleton

LIMNOMEDUSAE Lar. Symbiotic with Sabellid worms

MILLEPORINA Polyp with clubbed tentacles

STYLASTERINA Polyps lack tentacles

Polyps protected by cup (theca) THECATA

Polyps not protected by cup (theca) ATHECATA

ANTHOZOA Polyps with mesenteries

HEXACORALLIA/ZOANTHARIA Tentacles and mesenteries 6 (or multiples of 6)

OCTOCORALLIA/ALCYONARIA Tentacles and mesenteries 8 pinnate

Polyps with a skeleton

Lacking skeleton

Calcareous skeleton

Skeleton horny (and thorny) ANTIPATHARIA (Black coral)

Skeleton calcareous SCLERACTINIA (Stony/hard coral)

Solitary or colonial

Solitary

with one gullet groove (Siphonoglyph) ZOANTHIDEA

gullet grooves weak or absent CORALLIMORPHARIA

with anal pore CERIANTHARIA

with 2 gullet grooves (Siphonoglypha) ACTINIARIA

Colonial, fleshy body, skeleton spicular calcite ALCYONACEA (Soft corals)

Colonial, solid skeleton of non-spicular aragonite HELIOPORACEA (Blue coral)

Horny (scleroprotein) skeleton

Colonial, branching skeleton, spicules in flesh GORGONACEA (Sea fans)

Colonial, unbranching axis, spicules in flesh PENNATULACEA (Sea pens)

Zoantharia (Hexacorallia) are both solitary and colonial. The true or stony corals **(Scler-actinia)** have a skeleton of calcium, most are colonial. Black corals **(Antipatharia)** have a horny skeleton, all are colonial. The remaining groups all lack a skeleton:

Actiniaria (anemones) are never colonial. May appear not especially diverse in reef waters. Some particularly large ones, e.g., *Stichodactyla* are found in rubble areas (Dunn 1981). These are often home to one or more pairs of clown fish *Amphiprion* spp. For a comprehensive account of Actiniaria refer to Calgren (1949).

Ceriantharia (tube anemones) are never colonial. They have an anal pore and lie embedded in the sediments, their long tenacles spilling out of the tube. Some species have small lophophorate worms, *Phoronis*, which live symbiotically around the anterior end of the tube. Calgren (1937) reported *Arachnathus* and *Anthoactis* from the Great Barrier Reef.

Coralliomorpharia are represented by solitary *Rhodactis* spp., recorded from the Great Barrier Reef by Calgren (1950). These animals are intermediate between anemones and stony corals. **Zoanthidea** and **Coralliomorpharia** sometimes are colonial. Only the Zoanthidea are relatively well known (see below).

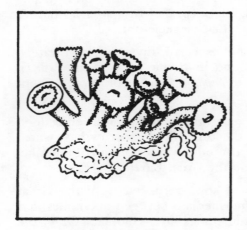

Order Zoanthidea

(Class Anthozoa, Zoantharia)

The Zoanthidea, an order of Zoantharia (Hexacorallia), are solitary or colonial anemone-like anthozoans. Like actinians, zoanthids (with the exception of the imperfectly known *Gerardia*) do not secrete a skeleton but many of them incorporate sediments into the mesogloea during growth, giving support and protection to the zooids (Fig. 16:1,2). Alternatively the mesogloea sometimes is significantly thickened. In *Palythoa* the polyps are almost immersed in the well developed, particle impregnated coenenchyme (Fig. 16:6).

Zoanthids are abundant in the tropics, usually occurring in distinct zones such as back-reef flats, lagoon floors, reef crests and the shallow sublittoral. Many species have symbiotic zooxanthellae in the endoderm and/or the ectoderm, but it is not clear how important are these photosynthesising commensals in satisfying the host energy requirements (autotrophy) in comparison with the contribution of ingested food (heterotrophy). Some *(Isaurus, Sphenopus)*, are known to feed actively at night whereas others (e.g., some *Protopalythoa*) seem to open in response to light.

Asexual replication is normal among reef-dwelling species and can result in colonies being up to 1 m across, or extensive areas can be dominated by a single clone. So far the only study of sexual reproduction of zoanthids from the Great Barrier Reef is of *Protopalythoa* at Orpheus Island, which spawns simultaneously with scleractinian corals, externally fertilized eggs developing into zooanthella larvae (Babcock and Ryland 1990; Ryland and Babcock 1991). Deeper water species of *Epizoanthus* (Fig. 18:23) are always of one sex (gonochoric) and have very high fecundity. In shallow water, zoanthid colonies with hermaphrodite zooids have been found, mesenteries bearing testes and ovarian tissue either at the same or different times. Hermaphrodite colonies within which some individual zooids are male and others female have also been found.

Synopsis of Families and Genera

The actinopharynx has one siphonoglyph (conventionally ventral) and the mesenteries conform to one or other of two bilaterally symmetrical arrangements (macrocnemic and brachycnemic). The ventral directive mesenteries are perfect (reaching the actinopharynx), the dorsal ones imperfect (Fig. 16:2,3). In macrocnemic zoanthids the fifth couple (i.e., the equivalent mesenteries on opposite sides starting from the dorsal directives) are perfect; in the brachycnemic condition they are imperfect. The remaining mesenteries are alternatively imperfect and perfect. New mesenteries are added in the ventrolateral exocoels, perfect and imperfect alternately. Taxa marked * are not discussed here.

I. Mesenteries brachycnemic (see above); imperfect mesenteries comparatively well developed (Fig. 16:3) .... **BRACHYCNEMINA**

   A. With mesogloeal sphincter .... ZOANTHIDAE

      1. Solitary; siphonoglyph developed into a hyposulcus (Fig. 16:3); no zooxanthellae .. **Sphenopus**

      2. Colonial or grouped (rarely solitary); no hyposulcus; with zooxanthellae

         a. Sphincter muscle in two parts (Fig. 16:4); zooids not sand encrusted .... **Zoanthus**

         b. Sphincter muscle single (Fig. 16:1,5); zooids sand encrusted or not

            i. Mesenteries meeting in basal part of column as meshwork; not sand encrusted; sphincter muscle well developed, more than 75% width of mesogloea (Fig. 16:5); usually 40–42 mesenteries; mesogloea with endodermal involutions; zooids markedly asymmetric when contracted .... **Isaurus**

           ii. Mesenteries not meeting as meshwork; sand encrusted

               a. Zooids embedded in well developed coenenchyme (Figs 16:6, 17:16,17); mesenteries few (frequently 15–20) .... **Palythoa**

               b. Zooids more or less separated (Fig. 17:11–15); mesenteries numerous (often 60 or more) .... **Protopalythoa**

   B. With endodermal sphincter .... NEOZOANTHIDAE, *__Neozoanthus__

II. Mesenteries macrocnemic; imperfect mesenteries very small (Fig. 16:2); mostly without zooxanthellae .... **MACROCNEMINA**

   A. With mesogloeal sphincter .... EPIZOANTHIDAE

      1. With canals and lacunae in the mesogloea; often epizoic on pagurids, hydroids or sponges .... **Epizoanthus**

      2. No canals and lacunae .... *__Thoracactus__

   B. With endodermal sphincter .... PARAZOANTHIDAE

      1. Without axial skeleton

         a. With well developed canal system including "ring canal"; zooids often vivid yellow; often epizoic on gorgonians .... **Parazoanthus**

         b. Poorly developed canal system and no "ring canal" .... *__Isozoanthus__

      2. With an axial skeleton .... *__Gerardia__

Two other genera, *Acrozoanthus* and *Platyzoanthus*, were described by Saville-Kent (1893). The former, created for *A. australiae* and thought to be of erect habit, was later shown to be based on a *Zoanthus* growing on polychaete tubes (Haddon 1895). The latter is clearly not a zoanthid at all.

Most recent (but unpublished) information on Great Barrier Reef zoanthids relates either to Heron Island or to the Townsville-Port Douglas sector. Earlier, Haddon and Shackleton (1891) and Haddon (1898) described species of *Zoanthus*, *Isaurus*, *Protopalythoa* (as *Gemmaria*), *Palythoa* and *Parazoanthus* from the Torres Straits, whilst Carlgren (1937, 1951) described several species of *Palythoa*, *Protopalythoa* (as *Palythoa*) and *Zoanthus* from New South Wales and Queensland. Unfortunately these accounts included very few field data or observations. They often omitted cnidom values, making subsequent identification very difficult. The following notes and the key are intended as a guide to the usual appearance and areas of occurrence of the main zoanthid genera in western South Pacific coral reef ecosystems. A few species can be named and may be identified from the descriptive notes and photographic illustrations.

Key to Zoanthid Genera Common in Tropical Waters

1. Polyps heavily impregnated and encrusted with sand 2
     Polyps without sand 3

2. Polyps immersed in coenenchyme; colonies in the form of flat lumps .... **Palythoa**
     Polyps separate or joined basally by coenenchyme .... **Protopalythoa**

3. Polyps erect, open underwater by day; colonies often extensive .... **Zoanthus**
     Polyps recumbent, never open by day; colonies small .... **Isaurus**

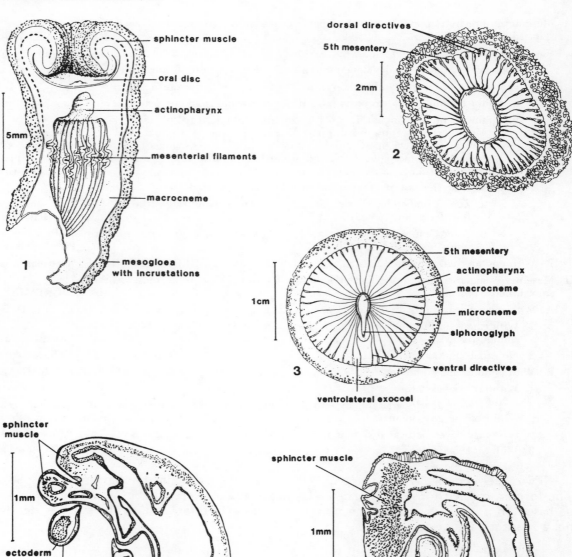

1. — sphincter muscle — oral disc — actinopharynx — mesenterial filaments — macrocneme — mesogloea with incrustations — 5mm

2. — dorsal directives — 5th mesentery — 2mm

3. — 5th mesentery — actinopharynx — macrocneme — microcneme — siphonoglyph — ventral directives — ventrolateral exocoel — 1cm

4. — sphincter muscle — ectoderm — tentacle — oral disc — endoderm — mesogloea — 1mm

5. — sphincter muscle — tentacles — 1mm

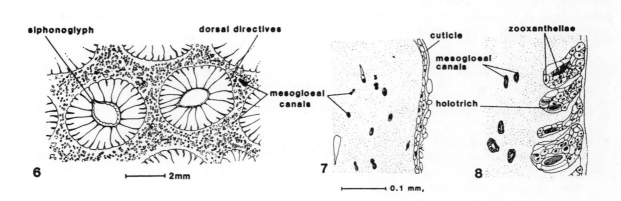

6. — siphonoglyph — dorsal directives — mesogloeal canals — 2mm

7. — 0.1 mm

8. — cuticle — zooxanthellae — mesogloeal canals — holotrich

Zoanthid species identification is difficult owing to the plasticity of colony morphology, the lack of a skeleton, and paucity of studies on the group. Histological sectioning of material is necessary to determine taxonomically significant characters.

Palythoa colonies often dominate the reef flat area immediately behind the reef crest. They occur also in permanently submerged areas such as the lagoon floor or in the spur and groove channels of the reef slope. Polyps are embedded in particle impregnated coenenchyme (Fig. 17:16,17) giving an overall buff or pale yellow appearance, although the polyps themselves are often darker. Colonies often convex, rarely exceeding 30 cm diameter. Decalcification is essential before histological examination can be made. The commonest species, in which colonies divide into blobs a few square centimetres in size, is *P. caesia* (Fig. 17:16,17), but a sheet-like species with smaller polyps is present in places.

Protopalythoa (formerly *Gemmaria*), sometimes merged with *Palythoa*, occurs most often as crowded clones of non-embedded or separate polyps in shallow fore-reef, reef crest or outer reef flat areas (Fig. 17:11,14,15). Substantial shallow-water reef areas are sometimes dominated by this genus and cover may exceed 90%. Other species occur as small clumps of polyps or separate individuals (Fig. 17:12,13) sublittorally in inter-reef situations. The polyps are particle-incrusted and the colour is usually that of the oral disc, often brown or dark green under water; the tentacles often are very short. Decalcification is essential for histological examination. Mesenteries usually numerous, often exceeding 60. Individual polyps are sometimes incapable of closing completely, owing to width of oral disc. No species can be named at present.

Zoanthus species also replicate prolifically, sometimes forming large colonies (to 1 m diameter) found in back reef areas to the shallow sub-littoral. Zonation is evident. *Zoanthus* spp. are usually brightly coloured, disc and tentacles often strongly contrasted (Fig. 18:19,20). Several colour morphs often are found in close proximity. Sediment is not incorporated and generic identification can be confirmed histologically by the presence of a divided sphincter muscle (Fig. 16:4). Some back-reef forms are attached below the level of the sand and only the oral disc protrudes when the polyp is open (Fig. 18:18,19).

Zoanthus mantoni occurs in low energy situations, such as shallow parts of reef lagoons and intertidal flats. It frequently spreads over large areas of shore, in clonal patches distinguished by colour, often intermingled with a species of *Protopalythoa*. It is tolerant of sediment, growing up through 1 cm or more of accumulated silt. Oral discs then spread on the sediment surface (Fig. 18:19). Fully expanded discs are about 4 mm across and tentacle length slightly exceeds half the disc diameter. The column is only 3 mm in thickness but grows to 15 mm high through silt. Colour varies from dark brown through olive to bright green and blue-grey. Disc and tentacles often contrast, and the former may be patterned with a whitish ring, cross or star. Up to about 38 tentacles. Present on the shore and reefs in the Cairns-Port Douglas area and it (or a similar species) is abundant in the Townsville area; also Fiji.

Z. pacificus has variable colony morphology, forming small to extensive patches or small clumps of zooids in rather exposed sites, often intermingled with a species of *Protopalythoa*. Polyps 9–20 mm high, shortest in strong exposure; tentacles short, less than one-quarter of

---

Fig. 16. Zoanthidea: 1, Semidiagrammatic longitudinal section through polyp of *Protopalythoa australiensis* to show basic zoanthid structure; 2, Transverse section through a typical macrocnemic zoanthid; 3, T.S. through *Sphenopus marsupialis* showing the brachycnemic arrangement of mesenteries and the large siphonoglyph; 4, L.S. through part of crown of *Zoanthus pacificus*, showing the characteristic, divided mesogloeal sphincter; 5, L.S. through part of crown of *Isaurus tuberculatus* showing the well developed, undivided mesogloeal sphincter; 6, T.S. through *Palythoa caesia*. The polyps are sectioned at the level of the actinopharynx and show the brachycnemic arrangement of mesenteries. Mesogloeal canals are distributed throughout the common mesogloea; 7, Section through the continuous ectoderm of *Zoanthus pacificus*, showing the outer cuticle with adherent foreign particles; 8, Section through the divided ectoderm of *Isaurus tuberculatus*, showing pigmented peripheral cells, zooxanthellae and nematocysts (holotrichs) within each unit of the ectoderm.

Mesogloea is indicated by light stipple. Scale lines refer to fixed material.

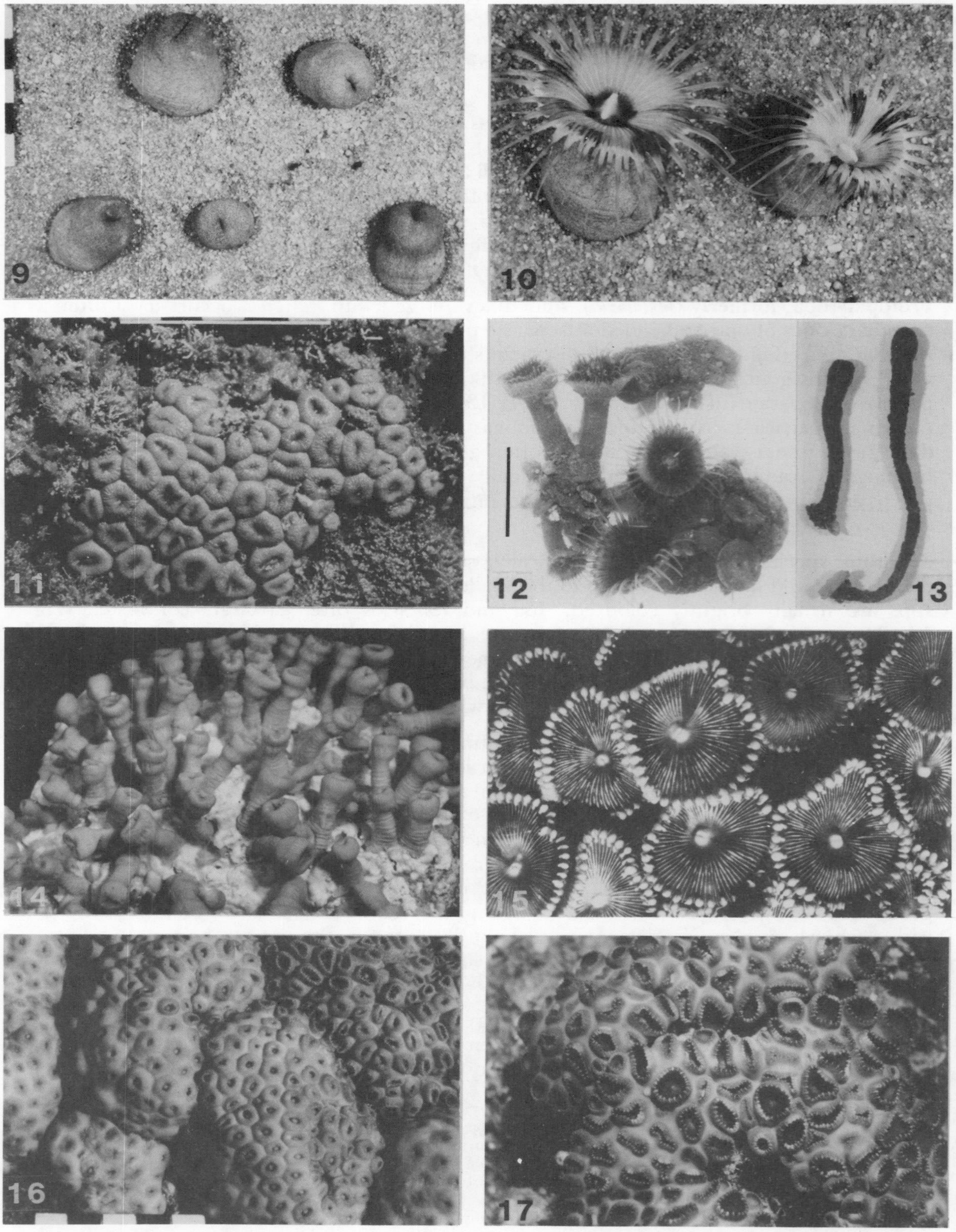

Fig. 17. **9**, *Sphenopus marsupialis;* scale = 5 cm; from off Magnetic Island; **10**, *Sphenopus*, upper two from 9, open at night; **11**, *Protopalythoa australiensis*; scale = 5 cm; intertidal, Cape Ferguson; **12**, *Protopalythoa* sp. clusters on forams *Marginopora*; scale = 25 mm; off Magnetic Island; **13**, *Protopalythoa* sp.; length of shorter zooid — 25 mm; from off Magnetic Island; **14**, *Protopalythoa* sp., clone with polyps contracted; photo width = 85 mm; Tomberua Passage, Fiji; **15**, *Protopalythoa* as 14, polyps open under water; Makuluva, Fiji; **16**, *Palythoa caesia; scale* = 5 cm; Tangangge fringing reef, Fiji; **17**, *Palythoa caesia*; as 16, polyps open underwater; Suva, Fiji.

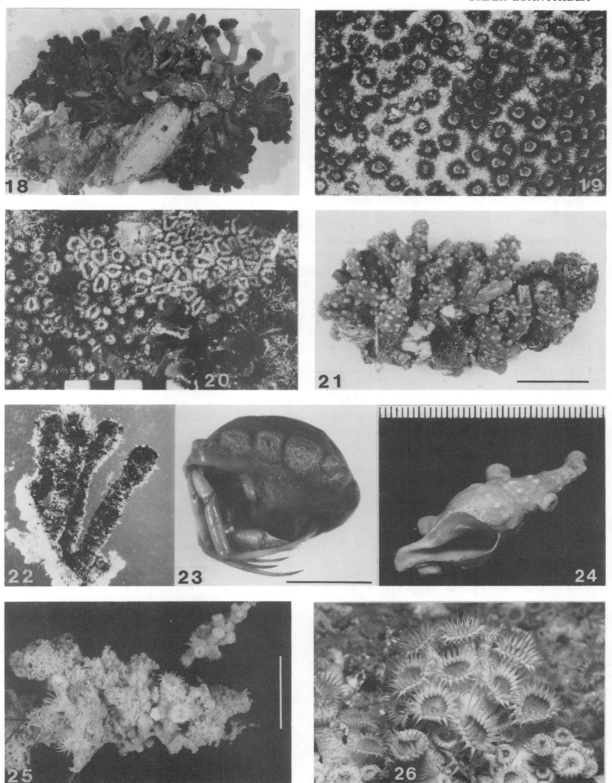

Fig. 18. 18, *Zoanthus mantoni* as 19, on coral rock; 19, *Zoanthus mantoni* as 18, discs opening through intertidal sand; Thangilai, Fiji; 20, *Zoanthus pacificus*; scale bar = 5 cm; intertidal reef crest, Malevu, Fiji; 21, *Isaurus tuberculatus*, Malevu fringing reef, Fiji; scale bar = 25 mm; 22, *Epizoanthus* sp. on intertidal sponge; length of R zooid = 11 mm; Cape Ferguson; 23, *Epizoanthus* sp. carcinoecium with *Parapagurus pilosimanus*; from off Danger Pt., Queensland, 500 m; scale bar = 20 mm; 24, *Epizoanthus* sp. on neogastropod shell; 25, *Epizoanthus* on *Lytocarpus philippinus*, from off Magnetic Island; scale bar = 10 mm; 26, *Parazoanthus* sp. Carnac Island, Wesern Australia (Photo Western Australian Museum).

disc diameter. Most variable in colour: disc green, emerald, olive, brown, dull grey or mauve, its centre often lighter, more vivid or contrasting; e.g., olive or grey-green on brown; tentacles greyish to brown, matching the disc or centre, or contrasting with both. Commonest near the seaward edge or reefs. Capricorn Group and probably elsewhere; also Fiji.

Z. vietnamensis a distinctive species forming extensive bluish sheets in the intertidal wavebreak zone (where it occurs with *Palythoa* spp.), has a colony about 4 mm thick with small (3–6 mm diam.), closely packed polyps completely embedded in coenenchyme when contracted, emergent to about 3 mm. When living in wave exposed situations it often forms rubbery mats with thick coenenchyme between polyps, though this is obscured when they are open. The light blue discs contrast with the general mauve-blue-grey background, and the short tentacles (about 50) are grey, beige or (at least in Fiji) brown. Common along the north edge of Heron and Wistari reefs; also Fiji.

Isaurus is another genus known from the Great Barrier Reef. As in *Zoanthus*, the polyps do not incorporate sand particles. The most common species, *Isaurus tuberculatus* (Fig. 18:21), is pantropical in distribution and has many synonyms (Muirhead and Ryland 1985). It occurs as small clumps of polyps in exposed areas in the vicinity of the reef crest, and also extends into the sublittoral where the body form becomes more elongate. In its usual reef crest habitat, polyps open only at night (Larson and Larson 1982); during the day the small (1–4 cm) asymmetric polyps lie close to the substratum. These characters provide a ready means of distinction from the much commoner non-embedded species of *Zoanthus*.

Epizoanthus species usually found encrusting sponges and hydroids (Fig. 18:22,25), occasionally bare rock, from the intertidal or reef slope areas. In such cases the colonies are stoloniferous and the individual polyps frequently small. In deeper water, when hard substrata become less common, *Epizoanthus* usually live commensally with pagurids (Fig. 18:23,24) and form characteristic, easily recognizable carcinoecia. These are known from depths of 20–4300 m and may be taken by dredging.

The remaining zoanthid genera are less obvious in reef areas and consequently records are scarce. **Sphenopus** (Fig. 17:9,10) is a truly solitary form and is known from sandy inter-reef areas near Magnetic Island (and also from Moreton Bay). It seems likely that it will be present throughout much of the Great Barrier Reef Province. **Parazoanthus** species, some well-known to scuba divers on account of their vivid yellow colour, are known from tropical areas but the polyps and entire colonies are small, occurring mainly on sublittoral sponges and gorgonians (Fig. 18:26).

Order Scleractinia

Stony Corals
(Class Anthozoa, Zoantharia)

Stony corals are responsible for the very existence of the reef. In life they form its living veneer and provide shelter for many other organisms. Breakdown of their skeletons after death provides material for redistribution and consolidation into the reef framework. These corals are the vegetative phase of coelenterates of the order Scleractinia. A few members of other groups have hard skeletons but their contribution to the reef structure is relatively small.

The reef-building corals are colonies of replicated polyps, each with a structure similar to that of an anemone, but with two important additions: they build a hard skeleton of calcium carbonate and their tissues contain single celled symbiotic plants called zooxanthellae. These, in sunlight, synthesize organic material that is passed to the coral. Corals obtaining most of their nutriment in this way are *autotrophic*, others are *heterotrophic*.

The polyp (Fig. 19) has a mouth at the top, and this opens into a central gut cavity (*coelenteron*). The mouth is surrounded by tentacles. Fleshy plates (*mesenteries*) radiate in from the wall of the body column towards the central axis of the polyp. Within these mesenteries the sex cells (gonads) develop. In many corals on the Great Barrier Reef, each polyp contains both male and female gonads. Other coral species have the sexes separate, with all the polyps of the one colony being the same sex — either male or female. Gonads usually develop over a period of some months and release their eggs and sperm once a year. For many species this once a year event coincides in the "coral mass spawning event" which occurs after a full moon in late spring or early summer on the Great Barrier Reef.

The skeleton of the polyp is called a *corallite*. It has a basal plate, from which arise partitions called *septa*. The septa alternate in position with the fleshy mesenteries. From the centre of the plate a structure called the *columella* may extend up into the corallite. The skeletal walls support the polyp, and they are variously formed by the outer edges of the septa or by extensions between the septa. New polyps are budded off by division of a mature polyp or separately from between the polyps. In some corals, the polyps move upwards in the corallites and lay down new basal plates as the colony matures: the old basal plates are known as *dissepiments*. The skeletal material between the corallites is called the *coenosteum*, and this may bear outside extensions of the septa called *costae*.

Corals are best identified using features of the dried skeleton. However, for most of the common genera, it is quite easy to become familiar with the characteristics of living colonies.

It is these features (rather than those used for taxonomic separation) which are indicated in the account (below) of the families of the Scleractinia, together with commonly occurring genera and species. The numbers in parenthesis relate to Figures 19–25.

Those who wish to carry their identifications further should consult the relevant volumes of "Scleractinia of Eastern Australia" (Veron and Pichon 1976, 1979, 1983; Veron *et al.* 1977; Veron and Wallace 1984), or Deas and Domm (1976), Bennett (1984), Talbot (1984) or Veron (1985).

Astrocoeniidae

Only one living genus occurs in the Indo-Pacific.

Stylocoeniella — small encrusting colonies usually found in crevices or on the dead lower parts of the other coral colonies. The corallites are round to square in outline, separated by coenosteum which bears pillar-like structures. *S. armata* (20:8), *S. guentheri*.

Pocilloporidae

Branching corals with small corallites, poorly developed septa and a rodlike columella. They are commonest on reef flats and lagoons. *Pocillopora* is often regarded as a "weedy" genus, which settles in great numbers on most parts of the reef.

Pocillopora (brown coral) — with corallites grouped into small hillocks, called *verrucae*. The common species, *P. damicornis,* occurs as round clumps with club-like clusters of short branchlets. Others have more plate-like branches, studded by the verrucae. Bases of some colonies are a rusty brown colour, even in cleaned skeletons. Living colonies bright pink, green or dull brown. *P. damicornis* (20:3,4), *P. verrucosa* (20:7), *P. eydouxi, P. meandrina, P. woodjonesi.*

Stylophora — round clumps of thick, slightly laterally flattened branches, feeling slightly prickly to the touch because of a "hood" which arches over the upper edge of the corallite. Colour bright purple, pink, green or brown. Found on the reef flat, slopes and lagoon. *S. pistillata* (20:5,6).

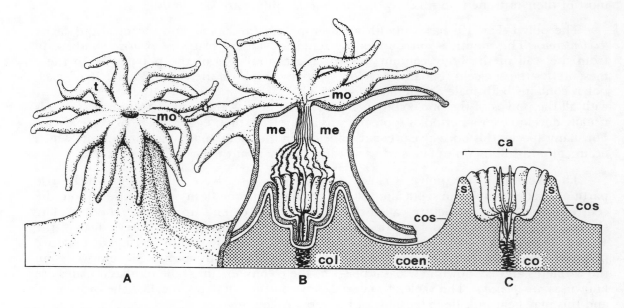

Fig. 19. Coral morphology (diagrammatic): **A**, entire polyp; **B**, section through polyp and skeleton; **C**, tissues removed to show polyp skeleton (corallite). Symbols: **ca**, calice; **coe**, coenosteum; **col**, columella; **cos**, costa (extension of septum); **me**, mesentery; **mo**, mouth; **s**, septa; **t**, tentacle.

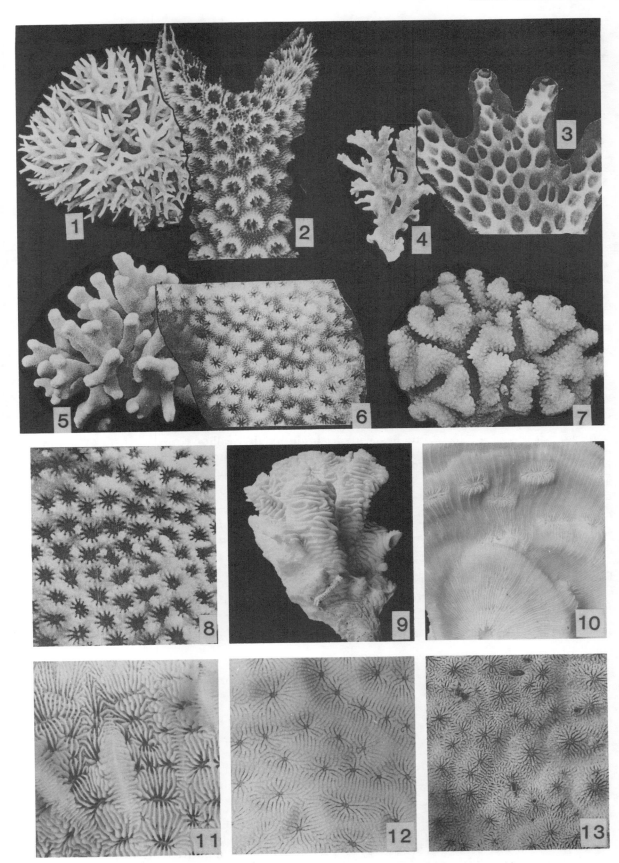

Fig. 20. Scleractinia: **1–7**, Pocilloporidae; **8**, Astrocoeniidae; **9–11**, Agariciidae; **12, 13**, Siderastreidae.

Seriatopora (needle coral) — small round clumps (occasionally large thickets) with sharp needle-like branches, corallites more or less in rows, usually pink and cream. Found on the reef flat and lagoon. *S. hystrix* (20:1,2) *S. caliendrum.*

Palauastrea — colonies resemble branching *Porites* (see below). Corallites are like those of *Stylophora.* This rare genus is found on sand in turbid conditions, *P. ramosa.*

Madracis — cryptic small colonies look like *Stylocoeniella* under water — rare, *M. kirbyae.*

Acroporidae

A family with few genera but many species; with small corallites, coenosteum with spongy appearance, and simple corallites without a columella and up to 12 simple septa.

Montipora — usually thin, often layered, plates or incrustations, but occasionally branching. Corallites tiny, separated by coenosteum (unlike *Porites* with corallites close together). Some species have elaborate projections on the coenosteum, making it rough to the touch. Species cannot be identified with certainty in the field. *M. tuberculosa, M. hoffmeisteri, M. floweri, M. millepora* (21:6), *M. turgescens, M. foveolata* (21:9), *M. danae, M. verrucosa* (21:8), *M. incrassata, M. venosa, M. digitata, M. hispida, M. nodosa* (21:3), *M. informis, M. foliosa* (21:7), *M. aequituberculosa, M. crassituberculata, M. spongodes* (21:2), *M. undata* (21:5), *M. australiensis* (21:4), *M. monasteriata* and others.

Astreopora — dome shaped, with round corallites, slightly protuberant (much larger than those of *Montipora*), appearing cavernous because of short septa. Commonest colour whitish-blue. Uncommon, occurs on reef flat and slope. *A. myriophthalma* (21:1), *A. moretonensis, A. cucullata, A. ocellata.*

Acropora (staghorn corals) — a very large subgenus of branching forms, and a small subgenus of encrusting to branching forms.

Acropora (Acropora) — has branches with a single axial corallite running through them, opening at their tip. Numerous radial corallites surround the axial. The radial corallites have various shapes, but the axial is always a cylinder. Since the colonies grow by extending and adding branches, their shapes can be quite variable. They are here grouped into their most familiar shapes:

Open branching species — *A. aspera* (21:10), *A. pulchra, A. formosa, A. nobilis* (21:12), *A. yongei, A. grandis* (21:14), *A. valenciennesi, A. horrida, A. acuminata.*

Sturdy branching species — *A. robusta, A. danai.*

Rounded or flat-topped clumps — *A. humilis* (21:12), *A. digitifera, A. millepora* (21:13), *A. valida* (21:11), *A. nasuta, A. cerealis, A. secale, A. latistella, A. aculeus, A. nana, A. tenuis, A. divaricata, A. dendrum, A. verweyi, A. busheyensis, A. willisae.*

Table or plate-like colonies — *A. hyacinthus* (21:12), *A. cytherea, A. clathrata, A. donei.*

Small plates in deep water — *A. granulosa.*

Bottlebrush or shrubby forms — *A. longicyathus, A. florida, A. loripes, A. sarmentosa, A. austera, A. lutkeni,* sometimes *A. horrida.*

The most common species of *Acropora (Acropora)* on the Great Barrier Reef are:

A. aspera and *A. pulchra* — occur as thickets on reef flats. *A. aspera* has thick-walled and prominent axial corallites, and is commonly greyish blue. *A. pulchra* has less obvious axial corallites, and is either cream (sometimes with blue tips), brown, or bright blue. Both species have two sizes of radial corallites on the branches, and they are very difficult to tell apart.

A. formosa — common staghorn of reef slope and deeper reef flat areas, with tubular radial corallites, is brown or bright blue. It may occur with two other common staghorns, *A. nobilis,* whose branches are sturdy and have an obvious mixture of very tall and very short radial corallites, and *A. yongei,* whose radial corallites have very wide openings.

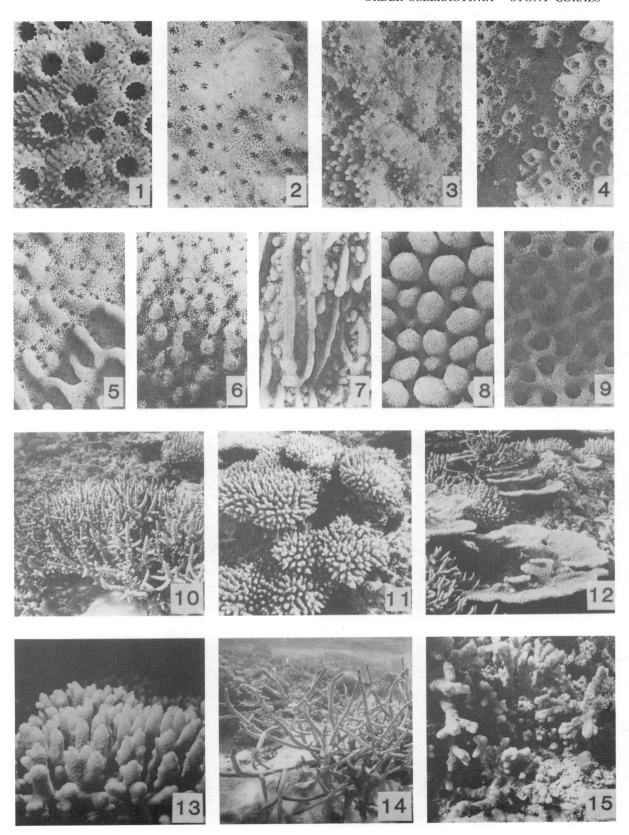

Fig. 21. Scleractinia: Acroporidae.

A. hyacinthus — large flat-topped tables or side-attached plates, particularly on the upper reef slope, is often a pinkish brown with a pale blue rim. It is easily confused with *A. cytherea*, a similar species with more crumbly texture.

A. humilis — sturdy cone-shaped branches arise from a growing area that is anything from a stalk to a wide encrustation. A common coral on the outer reef flat, it is cream, brown, or vivid purple. Related species *A. gemmifera* and *A. monticulosa* have similar shape and colouring.

A. digitifera — abundant on the outer reef crest sometimes with *A. nasuta* and *A. valida*, two similar species. Its narrow cone-shaped branches are cream or brown with blue tips. *A. valida* is usually bright purple with yellow radials; *A. nasuta* cream with blue tips.

A. millepora — low branched colonies, usually from a central growing point, with smooth branches covered by neatly arranged scale-like corallites. It occurs with *A. aspera* on the inner reef flat and is commonly green with orange branch tips or a mixture of pink and blue.

Acropora (Isopora) — is the smaller of the two subgenera of *Acropora*. It has species with several axial corallites, or no truly axial corallites. Branches are thick, irregular in cross-section, or keel-like. Two of the three common species are difficult to distinguish in the field. Their growth form differs from one part of the reef to another, and in some localities both species have the same form. Both are either brown or green:

A. cuneata has the smaller corallites of the two. Corallites are conical, not closely packed together, and the branch surface has an irregular appearance.

A. palifera (21:15) has very large corallites with a horseshoe-shaped opening. These are crowded, and the branch surface is smooth.

A. brueggemanii the third species, has thick rounded branches and is often whitish green.

Anacropora — slender, branching colonies with *Montipora*-like corallites, simple coenosteum and no axial corallite. Seen mostly in turbid conditions. *A. forbesi, A. puertogalerae, A. reticulata, A. matthai.*

Agariciidae

The septa extend beyond the corallite wall as costae, some of which continue between adjacent corallites, giving a distinctive linked pattern.

Pavona — either encrusting or forming numerous small to large leafy vertical plates, with corallites on both sides. *P. cactus, P. decussata* (20:11), *P. explanulata, P. clavus, P. minuta, P. varians, P. venosa, P. maldivensis.*

Pachyseris — with a series of concentric ridges running between rows of corallites. It occurs as horizontal plates or grouped two-sided vertical plates, usually coloured brown, in areas such as the edges of surge channels. *P. rugosa* (20:9), *P. speciosa.*

Leptoseris — found in shaded parts of the reef, such as overhangs and caves, this species occurs as thin plates, or plate-like branches, usually with a central corallite and others scattered around it united by costae. Sometimes gentle concentric ridges are developed. *L. scabra, L. yabei, L. hawaiiensis, L. mycetoseroides, L. explanata* (20:10), *L. papyracea, L. gardineri, L. foliosa.*

Gardineroseris — encrustations or moulds, in which corallites occur as groups of one to five, surrounded by angular ridges. *G. ponderosa.*

Corloseris — This genus has only one species, *C. mayeri* which looks superficially like *Goniastrea* (see below), but corallites have an empty appearance lacking a columella. Colour yellowish brown, massive colonies in lagoons or reef-slopes.

Siderastreidae

With small corallites which, under magnification, seem to be crowded with septae.

Psammocora — small round clumps of lumpy or keel-shaped short branches, brown or wine-coloured. Corallites are minute, almost invisible to the naked eye, and lack walls. Between them run lines of costae. The surface of colonies has a grainy texture. Occurs on reef flat and slope. *P. contigua, P. digitata, P. profundacella, P. haimeana* (20:13). Rare species: *P. merstraszi, P. explanulata.*

Coscinarea — resembles *Psammocora*, but the corallites are easily visible to the naked eye, and have numerous fine-toothed septa, and groups of corallites separated by low ridges. *C. columna* (20:12), *C. exesa.* Rare species: *C. wellsi, C. crassa.*

Fungiidae

The "mushroom" corals, mainly non-attached, either solitary or colonies of a small number of individuals, with distinctive prominent septa. Young individuals attached to the reef by a stalk.

Cycloseris — small solitary mushroom-shaped (around 2 cm diameter), occurs on sandy bottom areas of the reef. *C. cyclolites* (22:1). Some other, very rare, species.

Diaseris — another small mushroom coral from sandy bottom areas. Individuals flat, and divided into wedge-shaped, easily separated portions (usually 2–4), which will survive and grow. *D. distorta* (22:2), *D. fragilis.*

Heliofungia — large, solitary, with long fleshy tentacles which are extended during the day. *H. actiniformis.*

Fungia — large, solitary, with small tentacles, not usually extended during the day. There are several subgenera (not discussed here). *F. fungites, F. concinna* (22:5). *F. scutaria* (22:3), *F. paumotensis* (22:7).

Herpolitha (slipper coral) — looks like an elongated *Fungia* with a groove running through its centre, and corallite openings recognizable over its surface. *H. limax* (22:6).

Polyphyllia — elongate, free-living, but colonial, with daisy-shaped corallite all over surface and on axial furrow. Corallites extended during the day, *P. talpina.*

Sandalolitha — large, domed, colonial, without a central groove. Corallite openings are scattered over its surface. *S. robusta* (22.4).

Halomitra — large, dome-shaped free-living colonies, *H. pileus.*

Poritidae

Colonies with numerous round corallites, close together, and with a porous fine structure.

Goniopora — occurs on the reef flat and in the lagoon, polyps have a very long body and 24 short tentacles and are almost always extended. The skeleton has a very granular appearance, and the septa come up from the floor of the corallite (in *Alveopora* they come out from the wall). *G. lobata* (22:12), *G. stokesi, G. columna, G. minor, G. stutchburyi, G. tenuidens* (22:8), *G. norfolkensis.*

Porites — corallites are so tiny in this genus that the colony surface often appears solid. There are several species, some of them difficult to separate. Colonies may be massive domes, encrusting plates, or branching or nodular clumps. When magnified, the septa can be seen to be a complex combination of fine granular points. Colours can be bright purple, brown, light greenish brown, or grey:

Massive species: *P. lutea, P. australiensis, P. lobata, P. murrayensis* (22:9), *P. vaughani, P. mayeri* (22:11), *P. solida* (22:14).

Branching species: *P. cylindrica* (22:10), *P. nigrescens.*

65

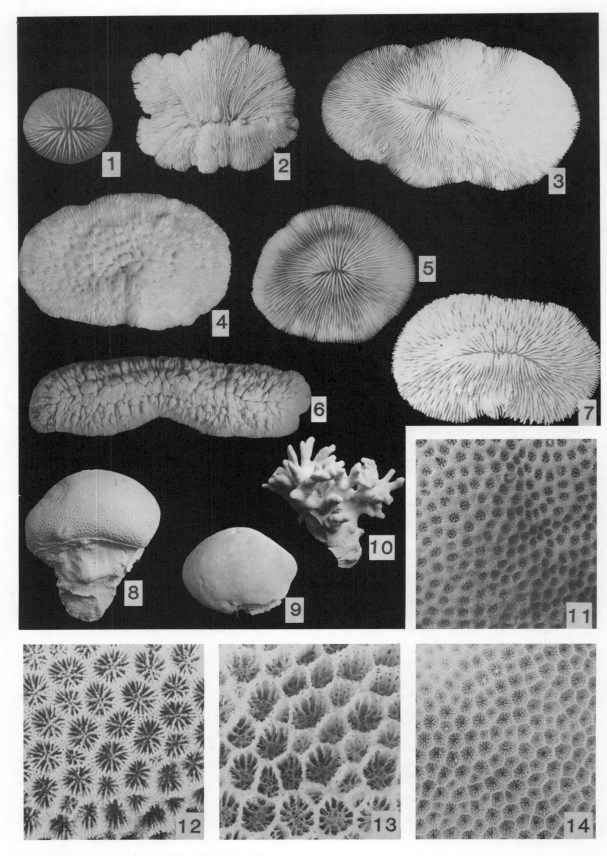

Fig. 22. Scleractinia: 1–7, Fungiidae; 8–14, Poritidae.

Lobed species: *P. lichen.*

Alveopora — small mounds or thick plates, with corallites like those of *Goniopora*, except for a very open lace-like structure. As in *Goniopora*, polyps are often extended, but they have only 12 tentacles. *A. allingi* (22:13), *A. spongiosa, A. tizardi.*

Faviidae

This family includes the "brain corals". Colonies are usually domed or encrusting, less often they have thin plates or branches. The corallites are large and easily visible to the naked eye, with sturdy walls and septa. The genera are widely distributed on the reef, and the commonest colours are greens and browns.

Caulastrea — Corallites are large and connected only by stalks. Usually found in sandy areas. *C. furata, C. curvata.*

Favia — corallites large, more or less rounded, and separated from one another (a few exceptions are easily confused with *Favites* species). Usually some of the corallites in the colony can be seen in the process of dividing. *F. pallida, F. stelligera* (23:1), *F. speciosa* (23:2) *F. laxa, F. helianthoides, F. maxima, F. favus, F. lizardensis, F. matthaii, F. rotumana, F. rotundata, F. maritima, F. veroni.*

Favites — similar to *Favia*, except the corallites are not separated, so that adjacent corallites share a common wall. *F. abdita* (23:3), *F. flexuosa, F. halicora, F. chinensis, F. complanata, F. pentagona, F. russelli.*

Barabattoia — like *Favia*, but corallites are raised out from the colony surface. *B. amicorum.*

Goniastrea — adjacent corallites share a common wall. The corallites are smaller and neater than those of *Favites*, and in most species several corallites are linked in series without internal walls. The individual corallite openings can be recognized in these series, as they are surrounded by strong lobes on the inside edge of the septa. *G. aspersa, G. australensis, G. benhami, G. pectinata, G. favulus* (23:4), *G. retiformis, G. edwardsi, G. palauensis.*

Platygyra — adjacent corallites share a common wall and are linked in series, but individual corallite openings are not as marked as in *Goniastrea*. The columella is a continuous tangle of spines. *P. daedalea, P. lamellina* (23:5), *P. sinensis, P. pini.*

Leptoria — adjacent corallites share a common wall and are linked in series. The appearance is similar to that of *Platygyra*, but the surface is more regular, and the columella is a broken plate. Only one species. *L. phrygia* (23:6).

Oulophylla — corallites linked in series as in *Platygyra* and *Leptoria*, but the valleys are broad, deep, and very open. *O. crispa* (23:7), *O. bennettae.*

Montastrea — corallites round and separate from each other and slightly raised from the surface. Septa drop deep into the corallite. New corallites are budded off from the skeleton between the corallites, and costae are visible. *M. curta* (23:8), *M. valenciennesi, M. annuligera, M. magnistellata.*

Plesiastrea — similar to *Montastrea*, but corallites are smaller, and septa do not drop deep into the corallite. They also form a central "crown" of obvious lobes. *P. versipora* (23:9).

Diploastrea — with large, round, domed corallites on very large mound-like colonies. Usually green. Only one species *D. heliopora.*

Leptastrea — corallites slightly separated from each other, with an angular, rather than rounded, appearance. They are smaller than corallites of *Montastrea* — otherwise the genera are quite similar. *L. purpurea* (23:10), *L. transversa, L. inequalis, L. pruinosa.* Rare: *L. bewickensis.*

Cyphastrea — small, round corallites, raised from the surface, well separated from each other by coenosteum which appears blistered and has a granular surface. *C. chalcidicum, C. serailis* (23:11), *C. microphthalma* and a branching species, *C. japonica.*

67

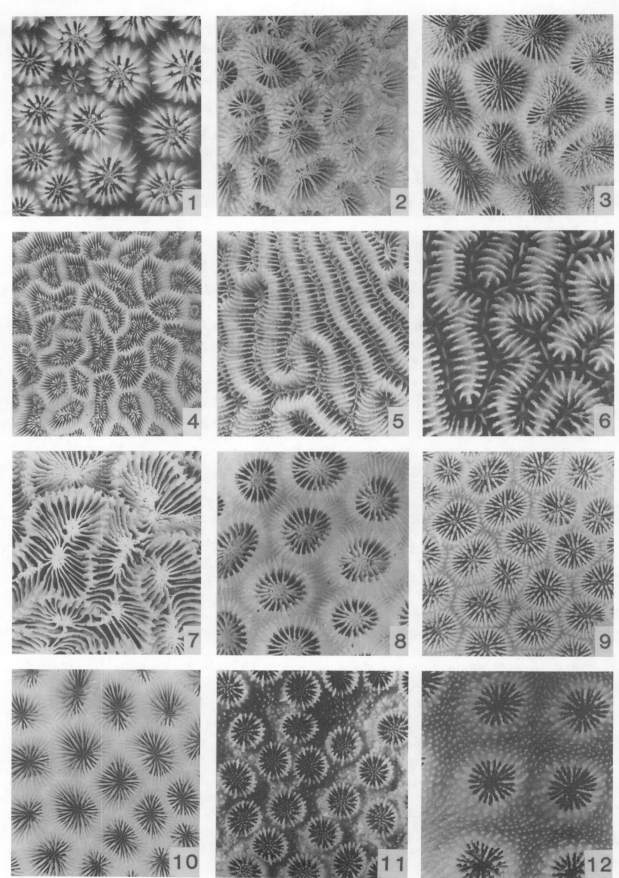

Fig. 23. Scleractinia: Faviidae.

Echinopora — round, raised corallites are well separated, and there may be costae or granules between them. The different species occur as plates or branching colonies. *E. lamellosa* (23:12), *E. horrida*, *E. gemmacea*, *E. hirsutissima*, *E. mammiformis*.

Moseleya — small, domed colonies with a central very large corallite surrounded by large, then small corallites. Only one species: *M. latistellata*.

Trachyphylliidae

The genus *Trachyphyllia* in the family has small free-living colonies of very large meandering corallites. *T. geoffroyi*.

Oculinidae

The two genera in this family are easily recognized by their spiky appearance, due to the septa extending above the corallite, and their solid, though light and fragile, walls.

Galaxea — corallites separated by deep spaces with septa projecting upward and outward. The material between corallites is light and spongy. Colonies are domed or encrusting, and colours are green, grey or brown. *G. fascicularis*, *G. astreata* (24:1).

Acrhelia — branching, with scattered, spiky corallites projecting from the branches. Colours are brown, pinkish brown or grey. Only one species, *A. horrescens* (24:2).

Merulinidae

A small family, in which corallites are joined in series, with high walls separating them.

Merulina — thin plates, or plates and branches mixed. Lines of corallites fan out towards the edges of plates. Usually lavender or brown, found on the reef slope. *M. ampliata* (24:3), *M. scabricula*.

Hydnophora — previously regarded as a faviid, this genus has an unusual appearance, as the shared corallite walls project as discontinuous cones with the corallite openings at their bases. *H. exesa*, *H. microconos* (24:4), *H. rigida* (branching).

Mussidae

In this family the corallites are very large and have a very spiky appearance, due to the presence of long projections called teeth along the blade of the septa, which are very thick.

Acanthastrea — rounded with round corallites. This genus looks superficially like *Favia*, but has the characteristic mussid teeth on the septa and very fleshy polyps. *A. echinata* (24:5), *A. bowerbanki*, *A. hillae*.

Lobophyllia — corallites large, and may be single or joined in series, without internal walls. The single corallites or series are born on stem-like bases, hence are well separated from each other. *L. corymbosa*, *L. hemprichii* (24:7), *L. pachysepta*, *L. hataii*.

Symphyllia — like *Lobophyllia*, except the walls of adjacent corallite groups are joined together. *S. recta*, *S. agaricia*, *S. valenciennesii*, *S. radians* (24:6).

Scolymia — like *Lobophyllia*, but only a solitary corallite, occurring in deeper or more shaded parts of the reef, commonly around 15 cm diameter and often with vivid green or orange colouring. *S. vitiensis* (24:8).

Cynarina — solitary corallite, commonly 3–4 cm diameter, with pale brown colouring, occurring in deep or shaded areas. Septa are very thick, with large teeth. *S. lacrymalis* (24:9).

Pectiniidae

In this family, the corallites are always visible to the naked eye, and may be very large. They do not have definite walls, and adjacent corallites are linked. All genera occur mainly on the reef slope and off-reef floor.

69

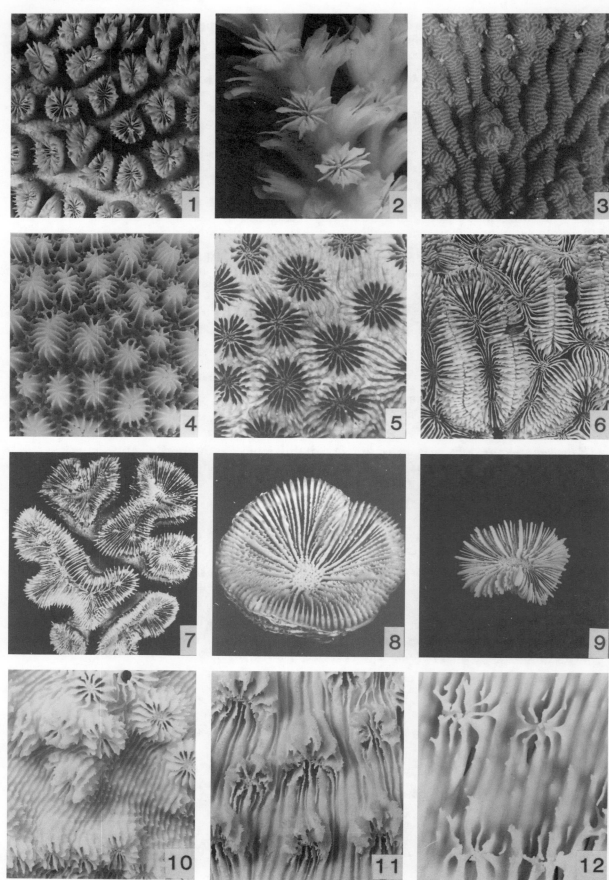

Fig. 24. Scleractinia: 1–2, Oculinidae; 3–4, Merulinidae; 5–9, Mussidae; 10–12, Pectiniidae.

Echinophyllia — large thin plates with corallites scattered in a pattern of concentric rows, with costae between them. *E. aspera* (24:10), *E. orpheensis*, *E. echinata*, *E. echinoporoides*.

Mycedium — large thin plates, on which the corallites are well separated. They are raised slightly from the surface and are connected by costae; they usually face outwards to the edge of the plate. *M. elephantotus* (24:11).

Oxypora — large thin plates, on which the spider-like corallites are well separated, and perforations of the plate can be seen between them. *O. lacera* (24:12), *O. glabra*.

Pectinia — rows of corallites are separated by tall, delicate, fluted walls. *P. lactuca*, *P. paeonia*, *P. alcicornis*.

Caryophyllidae

A large family includes many solitary, non reef-building corals, which range into temperate waters. The colonial forms which occur on reefs have very large corallites with large fleshy polyps, and they are not common at Heron Island. They have smooth, plate-like septa, and the coenosteum may be covered by a chalky material (epitheca).

Euphyllia — corallites very tall (up to 15 cm) and either single or in rows, which are separate even at their bases. Polyps usually at least partly extended, so that masses of tentacles project from the surface of the colony. The polyps are brown or wine coloured, with cream tips. The various species have variously shaped — round, horseshoe-shaped, or branching — tips to the tentacles. *E. glabrescens*, *E. cristata* (25:5,6), *E. ancora*, *E. divisa*.

Catalaphyllia — although its skeleton can only be distinguished with great difficulty from a *Euphyllia* with rows of corallites, this genus is distinguished by the polyps, which have a wide fleshy central area (usually pale green), fringed by tentacles (usually cream or brown). Only one species *C. jardinei* (25:4,7).

Physogyra — corallites united at the tops of the walls, with only septa projecting. The polyp tissues are swollen, and appear to completely cover the surface with pale bubbles. *P. lichtensteini* (25:1,2).

Plerogyra — with the same swollen tissues as *Physogyra*, but corallites or corallite rows are united only at the base. *P. sinuosa* (25:3).

Heterocyathus — small and solitary, juveniles fix to the shell of a gastropod, which is subsequently covered by the growing coral. There is also a commensal sipunculan enclosed in the base of the coral. *H. aequicostatus*.

Dendrophylliidae

Mainly ahermatypic. The polyp tissues do not contain symbiotic algae and the skeletons do not contribute in any appreciable way to the construction of the reef. Corallites are prominent and usually well separated. Colonies occur on shaded parts of the reef.

Heteropsammia — small, usually with only two corallites, occurring on the sandy off-reef floor. Like *Heterocyathus*, it has an association with a sipunculan and a mollusc shell. *H. cochlea* (25:8).

Tubastrea ("daisy coral") — occurs in clumps on the sides of reef patches and in caves and underhangs. It is usually brilliant orange in colour, but can be black or grey. *T. aurea*, *T. faulkneri*, *T. coccina* and a tall branching species *T. micrantha*.

Dendrophyllia — like *Tubastrea*, and can only be separated by a skeletal character called "Pourtales Plan", where secondary septa are joined into a wishbone formation. *D. gracilis*.

Turbinaria — a hermatypic genus. It usually occurs as tables, vases, or convoluted plates, in which neatly rounded corallites are separated by smooth coenosteum. One species

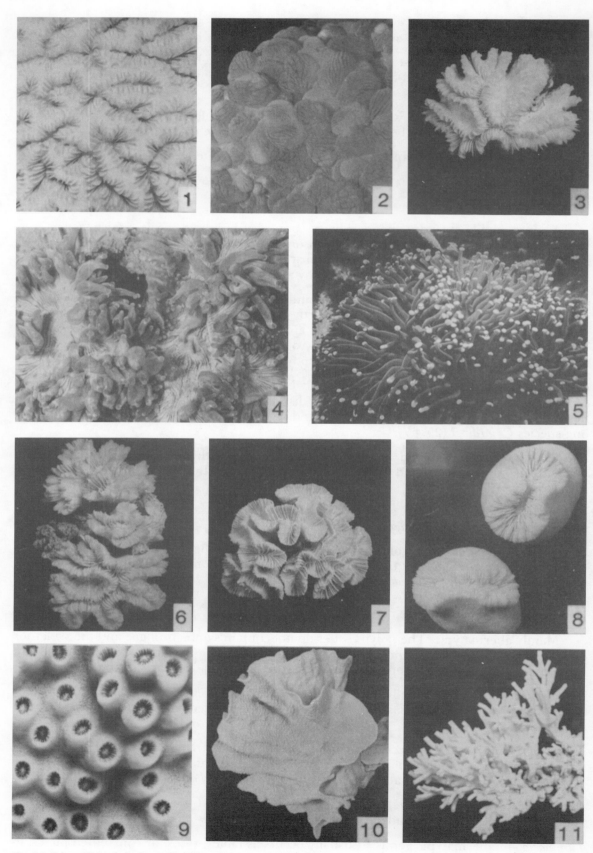

Fig. 25. Scleractinia: 1–7, Caryophyllidae; 8–11, Dendrophyllidae.

(T. heronensis) is branching. Tends to occur in deeper or silty locations, and colour is commonly brown, green or acid yellow. *T. peltata* (25:9), *T. patula, T. frondens, T. mesenterina* (25:10), *T. stellulata, T. bifrons, T. heronensis* (25:11), *T. reniformis, T. radicalis.*

Duncanopsammia — a rare genus found on the northern Great Barrier Reef. Colonies consist of long tubular corallites arranged as diverging branches. Only one species, *D. axifuga.*

Order Antipatharia — Black Corals
(Class Anthozoa, Zoantharia)

The highly polished black coral jewellery sold around the world is made from the dense horn-like material of the axial skeleton of members of the Order Antipatharia. Black corals are colonial animals whose non-retractile polyps, usually with only six simple tentacles, are united in a thin membrane-like coenenchyme, and nestle among the thorns of the flexible proteinaceous axis (Fig. 26). The erect axis can be very bushy or unbranched and whip like. Whips are often spirally coiled and may grow to 5 m in length.

Antipatharians are not very common at depths of less than 20 m. Colonies can be male, female or hermaphrodite. The only black part of black corals is their skeleton. Whips are commonly yellow or brown, while bushy forms may be yellow, orange, or white like frost covered trees.

Branched colonies with rounded or elliptical polyps and crowded tentacles are *Antipathes.* Unbranched flagellate colonies are *Cirrhipathes.* See Faulkner and Chesher (1979) for photographs and Opresko (1972) for a review of the literature.

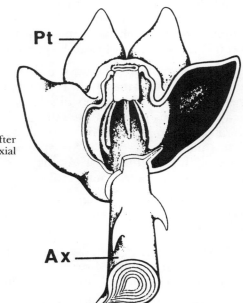

Fig. 26. Antipatharian morphology (after Graffhoff 1981a): Ax, thorny axial skeleton; Pt, polyp tentacle.

Subclass Alcyonaria Octocorals

(Class Anthozoa)

Occurring in all oceans, from the equator to the poles, at all depths, intertidal to abyssal, octocorals are, however most abundant in the warm, shallow waters of the tropics.

Of the octocorals the soft corals (**Order Alcyonacea**) and the gorgonians (**Order Gorgonacea**) make up a major part of the reef fauna and in some areas, soft corals in particular, dominate the underwater scene. This abundance is in marked contrast to the amount of research performed on this group. Very little is known concerning which taxa occur on the reef and even less about their habits.

Octocorals are sedentary and are usually cemented to a hard substrate. They all possess polyps with eight mesenteries and eight pinnate tentacles (Fig. 27). Animals with expanded polyps are therefore readily distinguished from other polypoid groups. Another distinguishing feature of this group is the nature of the skeletal material. With very few exceptions octocorals possess within their tissue calcareous particles called sclerites. Sclerite shape, ornamentation (tubercles, warts, thorns, spines) and size (0.01 mm–10 mm) are characteristic of each species and are the most important diagnostic features. Sclerite location is also important and portions of base, stalk and polypary should be examined for identification.

Although small solitary polyp forms do occur, most species are colonial and formed by vegetative budding. Gorgonian fans 1 m high or encrusting soft corals 5 m across are not uncommon.

Many colonies contain enormous quantities of symbiotic zooxanthellae to which they owe their green and brown colourations. Others are more brilliantly coloured by the pigments incorporated in their sclerites.

Feeding behaviour includes capturing zooplankton, digesting symbiotic zooxanthellae and taking up dissolved organic matter from the sea water. Gonads occur on the mesenteries and reproduction involves the release of gametes into the surrounding water. Fertilization may occur externally or within the polyp cavity. A free living planktonic larval stage is produced which metamorphoses to polyp form upon settling.

Bayer *et al.* (1983) should be consulted for terminology and Bayer (1981) for a key to genera. See Deas and Domm (1976) and Faulkner and Chesher (1979) for photographs.

Genera likely to be encountered in the Great Barrier Reef are set out below. Symbols in parenthesis relate to Figures 28–29, and numerals to Figure 30.

74

Order Alcyonacea — Soft Corals

Colonies usually fleshy, stolonate, membraneous, encrusting, or erect with tree-like branching. Skeleton (primarily of sclerites, occasionally fused) usually present. Some genera with dimorphic polyps —- autozooids and tentacle-less siphonozooids.

Clavularia (Aa) Individual polyps (2–40 mm) united by ribbon-like stolons. Polyp anthocodia completely retractile into the anthostele which is stiffened by spindle-shaped sclerites (11). Brownish.

Carijoa (Ab) Bushy colonies of tall, thick-walled axial polyps which bud off small daughter polyps. Axial polyps joined by stolons. Polyps retractile. Sclerites, slender branched rods (3) sometimes fused or locked in clumps. Colonies often covered in red sponge.

Pachyclavularia (Ac) Colonies and sclerites violet. Polyps retractile into calyces arising from thin sheets, often layered. Spindle shaped (4) and multiradiate sclerites sometimes fused in clumps (5).

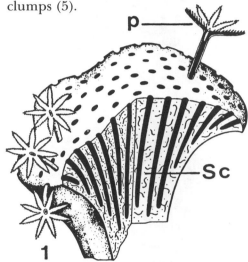

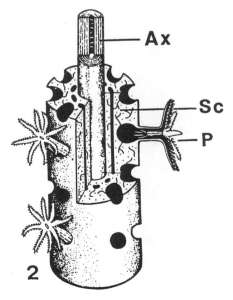

Fig. 27. Octocoral morphology: 1, soft coral; 2, gorgonian. Ax, horny axial skeleton; P, polyp; Sc, scleritic coenenchyme. (After Grasshoff 1981.)

Tubipora (Organ-pipe coral) Large solid multitubular skeleton of fused red sclerites. Tubes connected by many levels of stolonic platforms.

Alcyonium (Ad) Small to large, often fleshy, lobate colonies. Polyps retractile. Coenenchymal sclerites (<1 mm) often spindles (6) and tending to be homogeneous throughout. Brownish.

Cladiella (Ae) Colonies similar to *Alcyonium* but with smaller lobes. Coenenchymal sclerites are small spikey dumbells (27).

Asterospicularia (Af) Small lobed colonies. Polyps retractile. Sclerites are spiny balls (22). Greeny-brown.

Sarcophyton (Ag) Colonies often large. A distinct stalk and a rounded capitulum, marginally folded and bearing abundant dimorphic retractile polyps. Interior sclerites spindle shaped (7), surface ones include clubs (21). Brown to green.

Lobophytum (Ah) Colonies encrusting, often large. Upper surface lobate, digitate or with high ridges, covered in abundant dimorphic retractile polyps. Sclerites of the interior spindle to barrel-shaped with warting often in girdles (25). Surface sclerites includes clubs (21). Brown to green.

Sinularia (Ai) Encrusting colonies, often very large, with simple or branched lobes. Polyps retractile. Interior sclerites large warty spindles (12). Surface sclerites nearly all clubs (21). Brown to green.

Parerythropodium Encrusting membranes 1–3 mm thick. Polyps retractile. Sclerites usually spindle-shaped (12). Brown to yellow.

Nephthea (Aj) Arborescent. Polyps with supporting bundle of sclerites, non retractile and arranged in lobes. Sclerites irregular (23), spindle or caterpillar-like (8). Brown to bright colours.

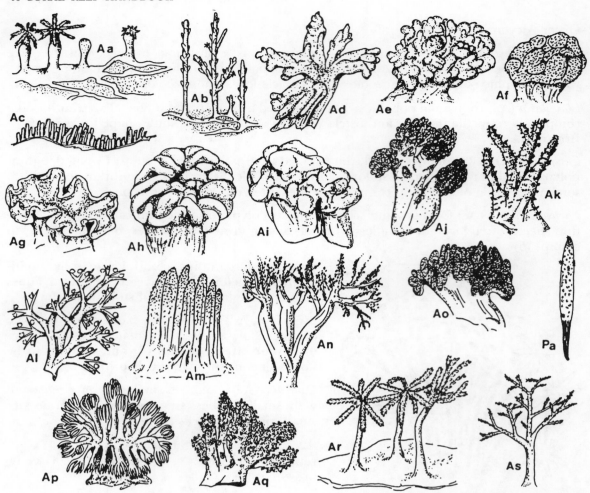

Fig. 28. Representatives of soft corals and sea pens likely to be found in the Great Barrier Reef: Aa, *Clavularia*; Ab, *Carijoa*; Ac, *Pachyclavularia*; Ad, *Alcyonium*; Ae, *Cladiella*; Af, *Asterospicularia*; Ag, *Sarcophyton*; Ah, *Lobophytum*; Ai, *Sinularia*; Aj, *Nephthea*; Ak, *Stereonephthya*; Al, *Dendronephthya*; Am, *Paralemnalia*; An, *Lemnalia*; Ao, *Capnella*; Ap, *Xenia*; Aq, *Cespitularia*; Ar, *Anthelia*; As, *Siphonogorgia*; Pa, *Cavernularia*.

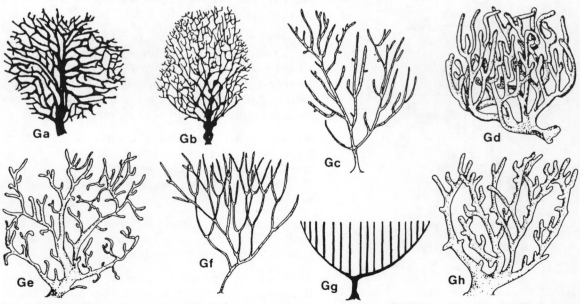

Fig. 29. Representatives of gorgonians likely to be encountered in the Great Barrier Reef: Ga, *Subergorgia*; Gb, *Melitella*; Gc, *Echinogorgia*; Gd, *Rumphella*; Ge, *Euplexaura*; Gf, *Ellisella*; Gg, *Ctenocella*; Gh, *Isis*.

Stereonephthya (Ak) Stiff and arborescent. Non-retractile polyps, with supporting bundles, in small groups all over the stem and branches. Sclerites like *Nephthea*. White to highly coloured.

Dendronephthya (Al) Colonies arborescent and glomerate, umbellate or divaricate. Non-retractile polyps, with large supporting bundles, in small groups on the twigs. Sclerites like *Nephthea*. Colonies highly coloured.

Paralemnalia (Am) Digitate. Polyps retractile. Interior sclerites thin needles (20). Surface forms needles (20), spindles (30) and crescents (28). Brown to green.

Lemnalia (An) Arborescent. Non-retractile polyps isolated on twigs. Interior sclerites long thin needles (20). Surface forms include capstans (19), crescents (28) and brackets (29). Brownish.

Capnella (Ao) Colonies small, arborescent to lobed. Lobes crowded with incurved polyps that are covered in club-like sclerites (9). Interior sclerites often globular (10), surface ones leafy to spikey capstans (19). Grey.

Xenia (Ap) Small and sparsely branched. Non-retractile polyps on domed branch ends. Sclerites minute platelets (13). Pale grey to brown.

Heteroxenia Like *Xenia* but has siphonozooids between the autozooids. Pale grey to brown.

Cespitularia (Aq) Small branched colonies with non-retractile polyps on stem and branches. Platelet sclerites (13). White to coloured.

Efflatournaria Like *Cespitularia* but with retractile polyps. White to coloured.

Anthelia (Ar) Individual non-retractile polyps united by a thin membrane. Sclerites finger-biscuit-like (14). Brownish.

Sympodium Thin membrane with small retracile polyps. Platelet sclerites (13). Blue-White.

Siphonogorgia (As) Rigid arborescent gorgonian-like colonies. Branches, formed from packed spindles (12), having no central axis. Polyps retractile into calyces. White to coloured.

Order Gorgonacea — Gorgonians

Colonies erect, whip-like to branched, bushy or fan-like. Axial skeleton of horn-like gorgonin which may incorporate sclerites or calcareous sections.

Subergorgia (Ga) Large colonies, bushy, or reticulate fans. Axial skeleton of gorgonin and partially fused sclerites (32). Sclerites of cortex double discs (15) and/or spindles (31). Brown, red or yellow.

Melitella (Gb) Small to large fans. Sometimes reticulate. Axial skeleton of alternate nodes of gorgonin combined with small red-like sclerites (33) and internodes of fused sclerites. Cortical sclerites include birotulates (16) and clubs (34). Red/yellow.

Mopsella Like *Melitella*. Sclerites include abundant leaf clubs (24). Red/yellow.

Acabaria Like *Melitella* but may be bushy. Sclerites mostly spindles (1). White to coloured.

Echinogorgia (Gc). Fans, sometimes reticulate. Continuous sclerite-free axis. Sclerites of calyces rooted leaves and rooted heads (2). White to coloured.

Euplexaura (Ge) Planar colonies with continuous gorgonin axis. Sclerites plump spindles and spheroids (35). White, grey, brown.

Rumphella (Gd) Bushy. Continuous axis. Sclerites symmetrical clubs (36) and spindles (37). Brown.

Ellisella (Gf) Sparsely branched to whip-like. Continuous axis. Sclerites double heads (17). White, orange, red.

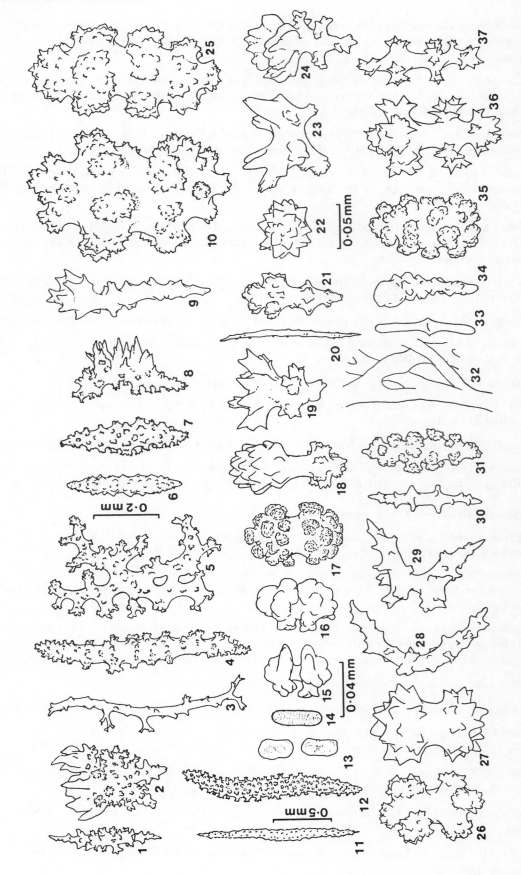

Fig. 30. Octocoral sclerites: see text for types and their occurrence. 1–10, scale line 0.5 mm; 11–12, scale line 0.2 mm; 13–20, scale line 0.04 mm; 21–37, scale line 0.05 mm.

Junceella Like *Ellisella* with double heads and characteristic pineapple-like clubs (18). White, orange, red.

Ctenocella (Gg) Colony lyrate. Sclerites like *Ellisella*. Brown red.

Isis (Gh) Planar to bushy. Axial skeleton of alternating horny nodes and non-spicular solid calcium carbonate internodes. Sclerites include abundant capstans (26). Yellow-brown.

Order Pennatulacea — Sea Pens

Colonies unbranched. Primary polyp forming a muscular peduncle, for anchorage, and a distal rachis with budded autozooids which may be on leaf-like processes. Siphonozooids and mesozooids often present. Heavily calcified central axis. Sclerites usually smooth needles or plates.

Cavernularia (Pa) Soft clavate colonies. Axis often reduced. Sclerites angular plates.

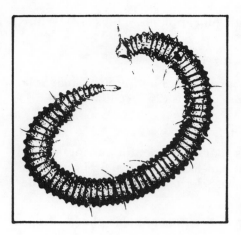

Worms

Worms are creeping, gliding or burrowing creatures usually of simple attenuated form. They lack a body skeleton, but sometimes have a firm external cuticle. Some are large and conspicuous members of the marine macrofauna, many are microscopic, living free among the sediments (meiofaunal), while the majority of the known species live in associations with the other organisms (as symbionts). "Worms", although they may look similar superficially, belong to many different, unrelated, phyla.

In the sea, worms are in the acoelomate phyla Mesozoa, Gnathostomulida (Jaw worms), Platyhelminthes (Flat worms and Tapeworms), Nemertea (Ribbon worms); in the pseudocoelmate Nematoda (Round worms), Nematomorpha (Gordian worms), Gastrotricha, Rotifera, Kinorhyncha, Loricifera, Acanthocephala (Spiny-headed worms); and in coelomate Annelida (Segmented worms), Echiura (Spoon worms), Sipuncula (Peanut worms), Phoronida (Lophophore worms), Chaetognatha (Arrow worms) and Hemichordata (Tongue worms).

Macrofaunal Worms

These are usually the more complex coelomate groups Annelida, Echiurida, Sipuncula, Phoronida, Chaetognatha and Hemichordata, though some acoelomate Platyhelminthes and Nemertea have large free living representatives.

Meiofaunal Worms

Small free-living interstitial worms, <1 mm long, in the little studied meiofauna are sometimes acoelomate, viz. Platyhelminthes (Turbellaria), Gnathastomulida and Nemertea; many are pseudocoelomate, *viz.* Nematoda and related phyla Gastrotricha, Rotifera, Kinorhyncha, and the new phylum Loricifera; and some are small representatives of coelomate polychaete and oligochaete Annelida.

In the Great Barrier Reef region meiofaunal turbellarians are known to be diverse (Dittman 1991), but few have been described (Winsor 1990). Similarly Nematoda have been little studied, and the other pseudocoelomates are unrecorded as yet. The new phylum Loricifera Kristensen, 1983 has been recorded from the Chesterfield Rise to the east of the Great Barrier Reef.

Meiobenthic Oligochaeta have been reported. Some families of exclusively meiofaunal polychaetes also are known, but most belong to groups also known from the macrobenthos (see below).

For a comprehensive guide to the collection and taxonomy of meiobenthic organisms see Higgins and Theil (1988).

SYMBIOTIC WORMS

Aspidogastrea

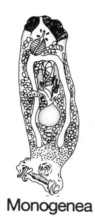

Monogenea

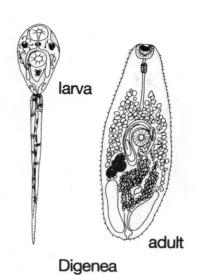

larva

adult

Digenea

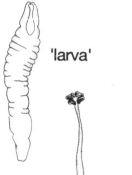

'larva'

adult

Cestoda

Acanthocephala

Nematoda

Myzostomida

Hirudinea

MEIOFAUNAL WORMS

Turbellarian

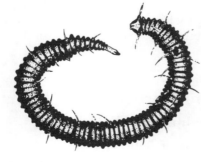

Nematoda

Oligochaeta

Symbiotic Worms

Some symbiotic relationships are mutualistic, the partners being physiologically inter-dependent as are small, acoel turbellarians and their contained algal symbionts (Winsor 1988, 1990). More often the relationship is less defined and seemingly benign, i.e., commensalism, as between polynoid polychaetes and echinoderms (Gibbs 1969).

Most symbiotic relationships are parasitic, with one of the partners being entirely dependent on the other, its host. It is in certain groups of parasitic worms (Acanthocephala, Nematoda, Nematomorpha and Platyhelminthes — collectively known as *Helminthes*) that life histories often are complex, involving several body forms and several host organisms.

Among the smaller parasitic groups the acoelomate, radially symmetrical Mesozoa are yet to be recorded from Queensland waters. They may be present, however, as one group (Dycemida) is known from the urinary bladder of cephalopods in New Zealand (Short and Hochberg 1969) and the other (Orthonectida) parasitize a variety of invertebrates (Kozloff 1969). Nematomorpha are also unrecorded, but can be expected as parasites of crustaceans.

Parasitic worms known to be abundant and diverse in the Great Barrier Reef are Nematoda and Platyhelminthes. The pseudocoelomate Acanthocephala (Edmund 1964) are present, but are uncommon. Annelida are represented by Myzostomida which are known to associate with many reef invertebrates, especially echinoderms (Grygier 1990).

While free living nematodes in the meiofauna are very small, parasitic nematodes can be large (several centimetres). As adults they are found in all vertebrates, usually in the gut. Their complex life cycles often involve a variety of hosts both invertebrate and vertebrate. They are particularly common in reef fishes: the larvae of *Anisakis*, a worm which matures in dolphin, can invade the flesh of such fish as Coral Trout and Red Emperor. If the flesh is not cooked larval worms can invade stomach and intestine and form inflamed nodules, i.e., cause anisakiasis in man.

Among the Platyhelminthes, Turbellaria (although predominantly free-living, see below) has several groups that are parasites of invertebrates (especially molluscs and echinoderms) and fishes. All the remaining flatworms (Aspidogastrea, Monogenea, Digenea, Cestoda) are exclusively parasitic. The Aspidogastrea, represented by *Lobatosoma manteri*, parasitizes alternately beachrock snails and *Trachinotus blochii* a small trevally (Rhode 1973). Monogenea live on the gills and skin of fishes. Digenea are found especially in the gut of birds and fishes with developmental stages in molluscs. Cestoda (tapeworms) are found in the gut of vertebrates and developmental stages in invertebrates. The large black cysts so often seen in coral trout are intermediate stages of tapeworms which mature in the gut of sharks.

For identification the best general guides for the helminthes are — Nematoda (Yamaguti 1961). Acanthocephala (Yamaguti 1963b), Monogenea (Yamaguti 1963a), Digenea (Yamaguti 1971), Cestoda (Schmidt 1986), Turbellaria (Cannon 1986). Lester and Sewell (1989) provide a comprehensive list of parasites for Heron Island, the area most studied.

Polyclad Turbellarian Worms
(Phylum Platyhelminthes)

Polyclads are among the largest of flatworms. They are mostly leaf-like and almost exclusively marine. Many are white or brown, but in tropical seas they often are brightly coloured. The most comprehensive recent account is by Prudhoe (1985).

Mostly, polyclads are predators, although a few are symbionts. They crawl over and engulf their prey with a large tubular or ruffled pharynx. Food is distributed into many blind arms of the gut. "Polyclad" means many gut pockets. They sometimes swim through the water with delicate undulations and ruffling of their leaf-like bodies, but generally they creep over the bottom on their cilia. Because of their extremely thin and flexible body they can disappear into tiny holes and cracks. Their delicacy makes them hard to capture and to study.

These worms are hermaphrodites and lay eggs (often in gelatinous plaques) from which small juveniles emerge. A few have planktonic larvae and some lead a planktonic life (though none of these are recorded from Australia).

Although many kinds have been recognized by divers only a few have been described from the Great Barrier Reef: and nearly all of these are in the genus *Pseudoceros*. These are brilliantly marked and coloured worms, usually about 3–4 cm long and 2 cm wide but sometimes larger. They often are mistaken for nudibranch molluscs, but are of much simpler construction, and lack the conspicuous opisthobranch tuft of gills.

A list of species from the Great Barrier Reef and adjacent waters follows:

Acotylea — without ventral adhesive disc

Family Stylochidae — pharynx ruffled
   Stylochus vigilax Thursday Island; *Idioplana australiensis* Hope Island

Family Apidioplanidae — pharynx tubular
   Apidioplana apluda Milln Reef — on gorgonians (Cannon 1990)

Cotylea — with a ventral adhesive disc

Family Euryleptidae — pharynx anterior tubular
   Prostheceraeus flavomaculatus GBR

Family Pseudocerotidae — pharynx anterior ruffled
   Pseudoceros bedfordi Heron Island; *P. corallophilus* Heron Island; *P. dimidiatus* GBR; *P. ferrugineus* GBR; *P. flavomarginatus* Barren Island; *P. fuscopunctatus* GBR; *P. haddoni* Mer Reef; *P. kenti* GBR; *P. limbatus* Masthead I.; *P. regalis* Mer Reef.

Family Diposthidae — pharynx posterior ruffled
   Diposthus corallicola Hope Island

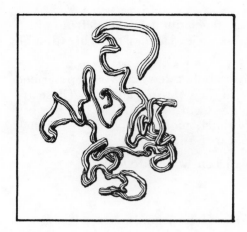

Phylum Nemertea

Ribbon Worms

As their common name implies, nemerteans are typically elongate, flattened and bilaterally symmetrical worms. Their most characteristic feature is an eversible proboscis housed in a fluid-filled chamber (rhynchocoel) extending above the gut, but they are also unsegmented, acoelomate and have both a closed blood system and gut with separate mouth and anus.

Most species are small and slender, never becoming more than 10–30 mm long, but several species reach 50–100 cm in length and a few grow even longer. Individuals of one species (*Lineus longissimus* from the northern Atlantic and Baltic) have been recorded with lengths of 30 m long or more.

Nemerteans are found under stones or boulders, in rock crevices, amongst algal fronds or the branches of holdfasts, or in sand, mud or algal turf. A few are parasites or commensals of other organisms and one group (about 100 species) is entirely pelagic. Mostly nemerteans are carnivores or scavengers, feeding upon other invertebrates or their eggs. They are typically members of the marine benthos, found at all depths from the intertidal to 2 500 m or more, but estuarine, freshwater and terrestrial forms are also known. Often they are locally abundant. Some species able to tolerate high levels of heavy metal contamination may be useful indicators of pollution. Others as parasites affect commercial crab and lobster fisheries. Because their soft bodies would otherwise be vulnerable to predators, they synthesize protective chemicals, some of which may be useful in medicine.

Fig. 31. 1, *Carinoma patriciae* anterior, dorsal view. 2, *Hubrechtella queenslandica* A, whole worm; B, cephalic lobe, dorsal view; C, anterior, lateral view. 3, *Aetheorhynchus actites* A, whole worm; B, dorsal cephalic colour pattern. 4, *Baseodiscus delineatus*, strongly contracted worm. 5, *Baseodiscus hemprichii* AD, dorsal view; ad, ventral view (corresponding upper and lower figures of one individual); E, whole worm (CF, cephalic furrow; CO, cerebral organ aperture; MT, mouth). 6, *Baseodiscus quinquelineatus* whole worm. 7, *Bennettiella insularis* whole worm, proboscis partly everted. 8, *Cerebratulus magneticus* anterior, dorsal view. 9, *Colemaniella albulus* anterior, dorsal view. 10, *Gorgonorhynchus repens* contracted worm, proboscis everted. 11, *Lineus tricuspidatus* A, whole worm; B,C, cephalic region (B, living and C, preserved appearance). 12, *Micrura tridacnae* living worms A, whole worm; B, head lateral view; C, anterior, dorsal view; D, midbody, ventral view; E, small caudal cirrus at posterior tip. 13, *Parborlasia hutchingsae* anterior end preserved worm A, dorsal and B, ventral views. 14, *Quasilineus pulcherrimus* A, whole animal; B, dorsal cephalic markings. 15, *Valencinina albula* ventral view of anterior end showing minute mouth. 16, *Nemertes hermaphroditicus* A, whole worm; B, lateral view of cephalic region showing eyes. 17, *Pantinonemertes enalios*, anterior end A, dorsal view; B, lateral view (CF, cephalic furrow; MT, mouth; PP, proboscis pore). 18, *Pantinonemertes mooreae* A, whole worm; B, C, head showing eyes and cephalic furrow B, dorsal view; C, lateral view. 19, *Poseidonemertes bothwellae* whole worm dorsal view. 20, *Urichonemertes pilorhynchus* A, whole worm; B, dorsal cephalic lobe and eyes. 21, *Xenonemertes rhamphocephalus* head and anterior body showing distinct cephalic "beak" and eyes and cephalic furrows A, dorsal view; B, lateral view, with part of everted proboscis.

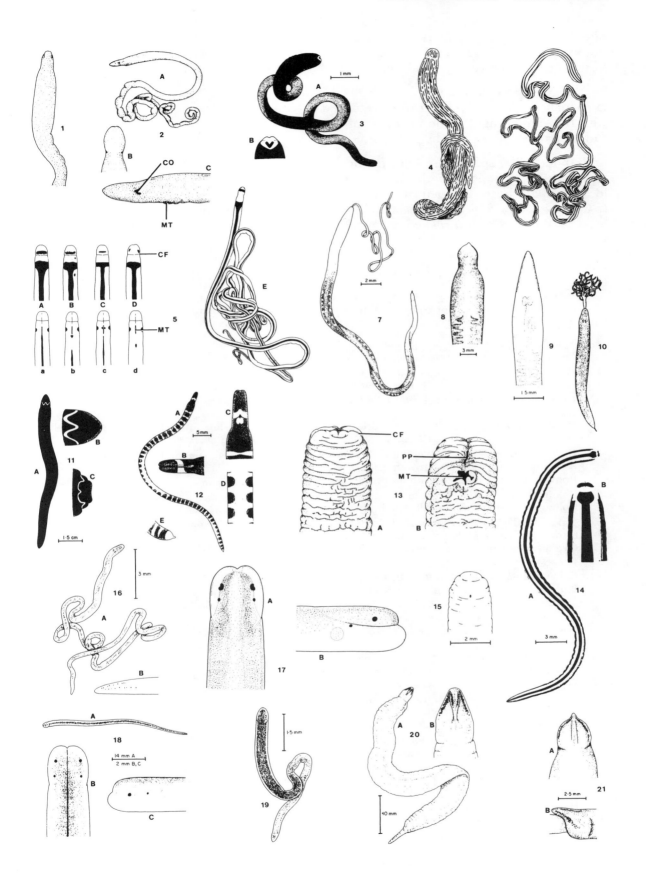

Many species, including those from coral reefs, are brightly and strikingly coloured, often with distinctive patterns of longitudinal stripes or transverse bands. Colour alone, however, is not always useful as a taxonomic character and species identification is based on histological studies coupled with internal and external anatomical features.

Magnesium chloride (0.3 N in distilled water) can be used to narcotize specimens for examination; they will recover when returned to seawater. Internal organs can often be seen with transmitted light if the worm is flattened carefully under a cover slip. The proboscis can sometimes be everted by gently squeezing the posterior tip of the body.

About 1 200 species are known world wide, but only a small number is known from Australia; of these, 22 species, most known from one or a few specimens from single localities, have been recorded from the Great Barrier Reef region. Only *Basediscus delineatus* (pan tropical-subtropical), *B. hemprichii*, *Gorgonorhynchus repens* and *Lineus tricuspidatus* (Indo-West Pacific) and *Baseodiscus quinquelineatus* (western Pacific) have a wider known geographic range.

Key to the Nemertea of the Great Barrier Reef

The following key is based on features distinguishable in living specimens and its use requires neither a knowledge of nemerteans nor equipment more elaborate than a good hand lens or low-power binocular microscope. The species marked with an asterisk are inadequately known.

1. Mouth and proboscis pore separate .... Class **ANOPLA** — 2
   Mouth and proboscis pore not separate .... Class **ENOPLA** — 17
2. With neither eyes nor lateral head furrows .... Order **Palaeonemertea** — 4
   With lateral head furrows or, if without furrows, with eyes .... Order **Heteronemertea** — 3
3. Head rounded, with distinct dorsal epidermal lobe, colour uniformly creamish white ....
   .... *Carinoma patriciae* (Fig. 31:1)
   Head bluntly pointed, without dorsal lobe, colour translucent white anteriorly, rich creamy-yellow posteriorly .... *Hubrechtella queenslandica* (Fig. 31:2)
4. Distinct colour pattern of longitudinal stripes or transverse bands extending full length of body, or body uniformly coloured but with distinct pattern on head 5
   Body uniformly coloured, without distinct pattern 11
5. Colour pattern confined to head 6
   Colour pattern extending full length of body 7
6. Tip of head white with dorsal chevron of blackish brown pigment, remainder of body dark chocolate brown dorsally, slightly paler ventrally .... *Aetheorhynchus actites* (Fig. 31:3)
   Overall colour dark green, head with distinct looped white collar W-shaped dorsally ....
   .... *Lineus tricuspidatus* (Fig. 31:11)
7. Colour pattern of longitudinal stripes, with or without additional markings on head 8
   Wide but ventrally incomplete transverse bands of bright pea-green alternating with narrower bands of translucent white .... *Micrura tridacnae* (Fig. 31:12)
8. Longitudinal stripes on both dorsal and ventral surfaces 9
   Ventral surface off-white, dorsal surface with median longitudinal black stripe with, on each side, a pale yellowish lime-green, slender black stripe and outer narrow stripe of bright orange. Mid-dorsal stripe expands anteriorly to roughly pentagonal black patch on rear of head surrounded on three sides by white, tip of head with bilobed transverse patch of vivid orange ....
   .... *Quasilineus pulcherrimus* (Fig. 31:14)
9. Longitudinal stripes, dark, not more than seven; body colour white to cream 10
   Longitudinal stripes irregular, brown; numerous, sometimes merging; body colour fawn to reddish brown .... *Baseodiscus delineatus* (Fig. 31:4)
10. Median dorsal and ventral longitudinal stripes of black, purplish black, dark brown or maroon; dorsal stripe at rear of head expands to transverse collar and dorsal anterior surface of head with pigment patch of same colour .... *Baseodiscus hemprichii* (Fig. 31:5)
    Longitudinal stripes black or dark brown, three or five dorsal and two ventral sometimes irregularly interrupted .... *Baseodiscus quinquelineatus* (Fig. 31:6)
11. Head distinctly pointed 12
    Head blunt or bluntly rounded 13
12. Constriction separating head from trunk, body brick red, head orange
    .... *Cerebratulus magneticus* (Fig. 31:8)
    No constriction between head and trunk, overall translucent white ... *Colemaniella albulus* (Fig. 31:9)

Key to the Nemertea of the Great Barrier Reef — *continued*

13. Proboscis branched, body bright orange, posterior tip with short caudal cirrus ....
.... *Gorgonorhynchus repens* (Fig. 31:10)
Proboscis not branched, colour whitish, pink brown or dull olive-brown 14

14. Caudal cirrus present, body translucent white anteriorly, mid-body dark pinkish brown fading to cream posteriorly, mouth small .... *Bennettiella insularis* (Fig. 31:7)
Caudal cirrus not present and/or mouth large 15

15. Lateral head furrows deep, distinct, mouth large 16
Lateral head furrows shallow, mouth small, uniformly creamish white..*Valencinina albula* (Fig. 31:15)

16. Body bulky, not dorsoventrally compressed .... *Parborlasia hutchingsae* (Fig. 31.13)
Body distinctly compressed dorsoventrally .... *Cerebratulus haddoni*

17. Head bluntly rounded or with distinct anterior notch and bilobed in lateral view, eyes four (may be masked in life by pigment) or numerous and small; proboscis armed with single central stylet on cylindrical basis .... Order **Hoplonemertea**, Suborder **Monostilifera** 18
Head distinctly triangular in shape, with median dorsal lobe, eyes large and numerous; proboscis armed with several minute stylets on paddle-shaped basis ....
.... Order **Hoplonemertea**, Suborder **Polystilifera** 21

18. Eyes four, either large and distinct or small and masked by pigment so that animal in life may appear eyeless 19
Eyes about 20 in two longitudinal rows each side of head, body dusky pink with transparent margins, ovaries in sexually mature individuals show as white spots in intestinal region ....
.... *Nemertes hermaphroditicus* (Fig. 31:16)

19. Eyes conspicuous in rectangle, head with anterior notch and distinctly bilobed when viewed laterally, not dark brown 20
Eyes inconspicuous in life, head bluntly rounded, without anterior notch and not bilobed in lateral view, dark brown with distinctly transparent body margins ..... *Poseidonemertes bothwellae* (Fig. 31:19)

20. Dorsal body surface slate grey with median longitudinal stripe of dark grey or black ....
.... *Pantinonemertes mooreae* (Fig. 31:18)
Dorsal body surface fawn-brown, orange-brown or orange, without median longitudinal stripe but with crescent of darker pigment over anterior pair of eyes .... *Pantinonemertes enalios* (Fig. 31:17)

21. Head with median dorsal lobe, eyes in four longitudinal rows, body distinctly flattened dorsoventrally in intestinal region, overall dull light grey .... *Urichonemertes pilorhynchus* (Fig. 31:20)
Head produced into a "beak", eyes from a dark greyish pigment band along each cephalic margin, body uniformly pale yellowish tan .... *Xenonemertes rhamphocephalus* (Fig. 31:21)

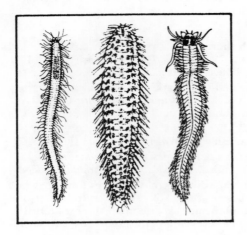

Phylum Annelida

Segmented Worms

Annelids, bilaterally symmetrical worms with a body cavity, are divided into four classes. The Polychaeta (aquatic, primarily marine or estuarine), the largest class with over 10 000 described species, is well represented in the waters around coral reefs. The other classes, Oligochaeta (terrestrial and aquatic earthworms), Hirudinea (leeches) and Myzostomida are less common in the Great Barrier Reef area, although they all occur there. Myzostomids are small dorsally flattened individuals which live in the feeding grooves of the arms of certain echinoderms — crinoids (feather stars). Marine leeches are known from some fishes on the reef (Mann 1962) but are poorly studied in Australia.

Class Polychaeta

The basic characteristic of the more mobile worms in this class is the pair of fleshy, paddle-like vertical flaps *(parapodia)* on each segment, one projecting from each side. Each flap is divided into a dorsal lobe *(notopodium)* and a ventral lobe *(neuropodium)*, each containing bundles of bristles *(setae)* which act as a supporting skeleton. However, in many less mobile, usually tubiculous or burrowing forms, the parapodia are variously modified and reduced. Parapodia are not on the two head segments, respectively a *peristomium* around the mouth and a *prostomium* in front of it. The latter has sensory organs *(palps, tentacles, cirri)* or, in sessile forms, is modified for feeding and respiration.

Polychaetes are long and narrow to short and compact. Some live in burrows with or without tubes, or underneath boulders or in crevices or in weed, or sand, or rock. Tubes may be of consolidated sand grains or mud, and in a couple of families each worm secretes its own calcareous tube. Some burrowing species living in sediments secrete a fine protective mucous sheath around their bodies, which tend to be streamlined with reduced parapodia and without head appendages. Modifications of the anterior end of worms living in permanent tubes involve the development of a *branchial crown* (with ciliated, mucus secreting cells) which extracts food and oxygen from the water it filters; or the development of feeding tentacles which are spread over the substrate to collect sediments for ingestion and tube building. In contrast species that actively move have parapodia for walking or swimming, and numerous sensory appendages on their prostomium for detecting food, avoiding predators, and finding suitable substrates to move to or settle in. Many of these mobile carnivores (such as Nereididae and Eunicidae) have a well developed muscular everting pharynx, with hard pincer-like jaws and row of denticles which may be used to catch and macerate prey. However, not all species with well developed jaws are carnivores, e.g., some use jaws for catching drift algae.

Some polychaetes are carnivores, others herbivores or scavengers and some are opportunistic omnivores eating whatever comes their way. Some are filter feeders straining the water column for food particles, and some are deposit feeders ingesting sediments to obtain nutrients from algal and bacterial films that cover them. Deposit feeders living deep inside the coral substrate extend their tentacles or palps up on to the surface where they collect sheets of mucus (produced by the coral) together with the trapped sediment. These worms living inside coral got there by either chemically dissolving it, or mechanically grinding it, or they live in the vacated burrows of other boring organisms such as sponges or bivalve molluscs. Polychaetes are diverse in coral rocks, as evidenced by the 1 400 worms representing 103 species found in one sample (Grassle 1973).

Many species of polychaetes living on coral reefs are small (less than 2 cm long), cryptic and not often seen. By living in cryptic habitats they are protected from predators, for they have few defence mechanisms. Sometimes their bristles may discourage predators, as in fire worms, which have numerous brittle bristles. If they penetrate human skin they are hard to dislodge and they cause a burning sensation, hence their common name. The long tentacles of some deposit feeders that spread out to enmesh food-containing sediments are particularly vulnerable to predation, and certain species that feed in this way have protective toxins in their tentacles.

Although polychaetes are abundant on coral reefs, little is known of the role that they play in the coral reef ecosystem. As with all organisms in the ecosystem they undoubtedly contribute to the cycling of energy through it. They probably are important in recycling many of the sediments and mucus they ingest and some that bore into dead coral initiate the breakdown of the coral skeleton. Some species are prey for carnivorous gastropods, and the larvae of many species that reach maturity within a few months and breed prolifically, may be an important food item for many other organisms.

Most species have separate males and females although some are hermaphrodites and a few change sex during their life. Many shed their gametes into the water where fertilization occurs. Others mate within their tubes and either lay their fertilized eggs in capsules, brood them in their tubes, or deposit them on the body of the female on which they develop. Embryos usually develop into a pelagic larval stage. After varying times in the plankton they settle as juvenile worms, some into particular habitats on the same reef, although some may be dispersed and recruited to other reefs.

In some families asexual reproduction also occurs. During asexual reproduction the worms may split in half, one half growing a new head and the other a new tail (F. Cirratulidae); or the worm partitions into sections, each section developing a new head and tail before separating from its fellows and swimming off as a new individual (F. Syllidae).

Nearly 80 families of polychaetes are known and probably most are represented in Great Barrier Reef waters, they are collected by such techniques as washing and seiving sand and rubble, turning over boulders or breaking up dead coral. The following are the most commonly seen families (Fig. 32):

Polynoidae (Scale worms): Large, often brightly coloured, overlapping scales originating from each segment to cover the dorsal surface. Polynoids are often found beneath ledges or at the base of coral colonies. They actively hunt for food, using their eversible proboscis to catch small crustaceans, worms and other prey. Some are territorial, living alone, and forming pairs only at breeding time when the male mounts the female to fertilize the eggs as they are released. In some species embryos are brooded to planktonic larvae beneath the dorsal scales. In others, eggs and sperm are released into the sea where fertilization and development occurs. Some scale worms, such as the pairs commonly found on the under-surface of certain holothurians, and others in the burrows of terebellid polychaetes, live in close association with other animals. *Harmothoe* and *Lepidonotus* are the most common genera on coral reefs.

Amphinomidae (Fire or Bristle worms): Stout, dorso-ventrally flattened and of variable length with dense protective bundles of setae, often with poison glands at the base. In at

89

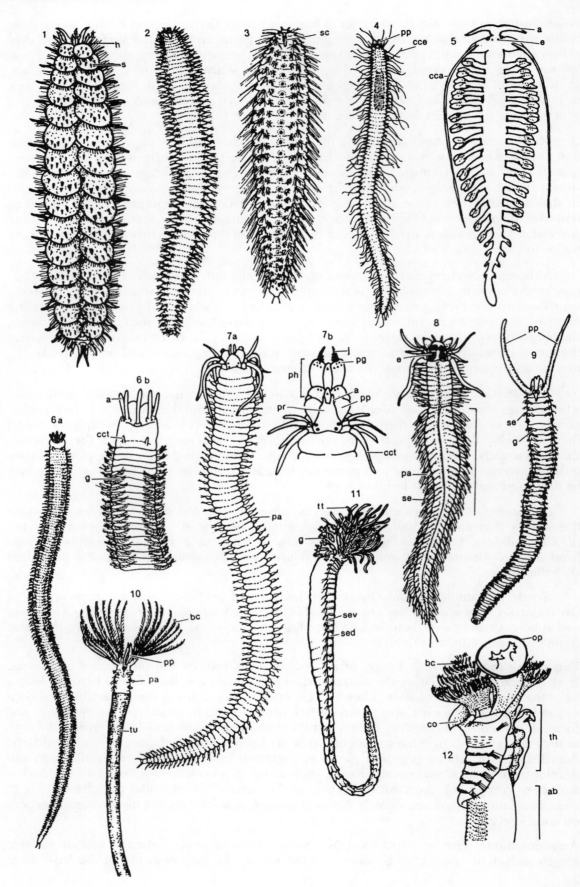

least one species of amphinomid, swarms of mature individuals move off the bottom into the water column at night. They swim in tight circles just below the surface where they simultaneously release their gametes. It is likely that the spent worms then die.

Amphinome rostrata and other species are often found on floating driftwood or pumice. *Eurythoe complanata* is greyish brown and often occurs under intertidal boulders. *Chloeia flava*, up to 10 cm long and 4 cm wide, has masses of long golden setae and distinct black spots on its head.

Tomopteridae: transparent planktonic worms which live in the top few centimetres of the sea, and feed on other planktonic organisms. They have long setae (which help them to float) on the two anterior segments.

Nereididae (Rag worms): Long, narrow, slightly flattened worms with well developed parapodia are common in sand, mud and rubble and probably are one of the most numerous families on the reef. At breeding time the individuals of many species become heteronereids or epitokes with expanded parapodia, lengthened setae, enlarged eyes, often luminescent bodies, and their body cavities full of ripe gametes. Just after dusk they swarm to the surface, probably in response to some cue such as phase of the moon or change in water temperature. They then perform a spectacular nuptial dance, and males release a hormone (pheromone) that stimulates males and females of the same species to release their gametes by the splitting of their body walls. This simultaneous release of eggs and sperm, which separately are viable only for a short time, increases the chances of successful fertilization. In the northern Great Barrier Reef spawning has been observed on many nights during the summer, whereas in the southern part of the Reef spawning has been reported only in early summer. This could be a reflection of lack of sampling. Several species may spawn on the one night but hormonal cues are recognized only by the same species and a species spawns only once a year. Spent worms die, and are dispersed, washed up on to the beaches during the night, and often eaten by predators.

Many genera of nereids are represented on the Reef, the common ones include: *Perinereis, Leonnates, Ceratonereis, Nereis,* and *Neanthes*.

Eunicidae: long almost cylindrical worms, up to 2 cm in diameter. Their parapodia have branched gills on the dorsal lobe but otherwise are not especially well developed. Eunicids are abundant and diverse on reefs, under boulders and commonly found boring into dead coral substrates. They are carnivores, scavengers or herbivores. Many are brightly coloured (e.g., *Marphysa* spp. iridescent black with red branched gills, or species of *Eunice* that are pink marbled colour with a white band). Like nereids (and possibly in response to similar cues such as temperature change or moon phase) a few species of *Eunice* in the northern Great Barrier Reef swarm just after dusk in early summer. On Samoan reefs, the locals recognize the cues, and capture these worms for food as they swarm above the reef.

Syllidae: small, narrow, dorso-ventrally flattened worms. Their parapodia are single-lobed with a long dorsal cirrus (a narrow tentacular projection). They are abundant in sediments and in reef rock communities. They are carnivores and some feed exclusively on hydroids, using their muscular pharynx to suck out the polyps.

Fig. 32. Polychaeta: 1, *Harmothoe* sp. showing well developed head (h) and dorsal scales or elytrae (s). 2, *Eurythoe complanata.* 3, *Chloeia flava* showing sensory caruncle (sc). 4, Syllid showing the simple palps (pp) and elongate beaded dorsal cirri (cce). 5, *Tomopteris* sp. showing the antennae (a), well developed eyes (e) and cirriform appendages (cca). 6, *Eunice* sp.: a, whole body; b, head and anterior end of body showing antennae (a), tentacular cirri (cct) and gills (g). 7, *Nereis* sp.: a, whole body with parapodia (pa); b, head with everted pharynx (ph) showing jaws (j), chitinous denticles or paragnaths (pg), biarticulate palps (pp), tentacular cirri (cct), prostomium (pr) and antennae (a). 8, heteronereid showing enlarged eyes (e), unmodified anterior segments and modified posterior segments with elongate setae (se) and extended parapodia (pa). 9, *Polydora* sp. showing grooved ciliated palps for feeding (pp), gills (g) and modified setae (se). 10, Sabellid showing branchial crown (bc), palps (pp), reduced parapodia (pa) and muddy sandy tube (tu). 11, Terebellid showing grooved buccal tentacles for feeding (tt), branched gills (g), notosetae (sed) and neurosetae (sev). 12, *Spirobranchus giganteus* showing calcareous operculum (op), branchial crown (bc), well developed collar for secreting calcareous tube, thorax (th) and the anterior part of the abdomen (ab).

Spionidae: small worms, some living in semi-permanent tubes, and some efficient borers living in coral substrate or in mollusc shells. They have short, fine white tentacle-like food collecting palps visible on the surface of sediments. Sometimes these are used for filter feeding and sometimes for deposit feeding.

Cirratulidae: range considerably in size and have numerous gills and feeding tentacles along part of the body. Typically they are well buried in the sediment, but sometimes the dark feeding tentacles can be seen moving just above the sand. The worm retracts deep into the sand when the tentacles are touched.

Capitellidae: microscopic to large (up to 15 cm long) cylindrical worms like earthworms. Their bodies are bright red as a result of the blood pigment (haemoglobin) they contain. They feed on the algal and bacterial film on the sediments which are ingested through the proboscis. They live in semi-permanent mucous tubes and burrow rapidly through the sediments by peristaltic contractions of longitudinal and circular muscles in the body wall.

Terebellidae: sedentary, tubicolous worms with numerous long tentacles seen spread like spaghetti over the surface of sediments, feed on the algal and bacterial film on the sediments they ingest. Tiny hairs (cilia) create currents that draw particles into a groove along the tentacles. Here it is wrapped in mucus and moved along to the mouth where glandular lips sort the particles. Small particles are used as food and medium sized particles are mixed with mucus to form the tube in which they live. Larger particles are rejected by the animal coughing and the particles are shot out.

Reteterebella queenslandia, a conspicuous, large worm, has masses of long (up to 1.5 m) white tentacles that, when touched, are withdrawn into a tube deep in the reef rock.

Serpulidae and **Sabellidae:** families of sedentary, tubicolous worms, probably the most conspicuous polychaetes in these waters. Both have a branchial crown of ciliated filaments that can be expanded to a V-shaped structure. The ciliated cells on these filaments secrete mucus to enmesh particles filtered by the cilia from the feeding current they create by their activity. Mucous packages so created are then moved down the branchial filaments by other cilia to the mouth at the base of the crown. The worm selects suitable food particles from these packages. Sabellids use the larger particles for tube construction whereas serpulids secrete their own calcareous tube. Eye spots often are present on the branchial crown, which retracts rapidly into the tube when a shadow passes over it. However, branchial crowns regularly found in the guts of small reef fishes indicate that some organisms are faster than the worms. Worms deprived of their branchial crown cannot feed. Fortunately it usually regenerates rapidly. In serpulids one of the branchial filaments is calcified to form a calcareous (sometimes ornamented) plug to close the top of the calcareous tube.

Spirobranchus giganteus, a common species with a branchial crown that resembles a small Christmas tree is brilliant red, purple, yellow, blue or green. Many different coloured individuals are often found in crowded colonies on live coral (especially *Porites*). The species is now known to be a complex of several morphologically similar species all of which exhibit the same colour patterns and range. Off Townsville, this species complex breeds at slack water in the first lunar quarter in October. After a brief planktonic larval stage the larvae settle on live coral colonies probably where a coral polyp has been damaged (perhaps by a grazing fish) thus minimizing the chances of being eaten by the carnivorous coral polyps. The larvae metamorphose and secrete a calcareous tube which grows continuously as the coral grows, thus ensuring that the entrance to the worm tube is always open and the worm can feed. The oldest parts of the tube of large individuals are thus embedded deep in the coral colony. Living *Spirobranchus* is rarely found on dead coral. Other serpulids occur on the surface of reef rock. *Filograna implexa* forms dense colonies of fine white tubes, each with a red branchial crown. A passing shadow causes all the worms to retract simultaneously. Sabellids have soft tubes of mud and sand and are often found in sediments at the base of coral boulders.

Class Oligochaeta

The best known of the oligochaetes are the earthworms. However, during the last 25 years it has been recognized that there also are substantial numbers of oligochaetes in the marine environment. Oligochaetes are readily distinguished by their cylindrical bodies with only few and simple bristles (setae) projecting along each side. The sensory and external feeding organs at the anterior end of the body are only poorly developed and inconspicuous. Their body form suits their habit — either burrowing through sand, or living in the spaces between sand grains.

That these worms are present on coral reefs was first demonstrated at Heron Island in the Great Barrier Reef about 15 years ago, when they were found in a coral head off the reef crest. Since then they have been found in various kinds of intertidal and subtidal coral sands all over the world.

The marine oligochaetes are small and generally confined to, and move about in, the space between the sand grains. This habitat is known as "interstitial". On the reef flat at Heron Island, these worms are more numerous under clumps of coral than in exposed sandy areas. This may be partly because the coral protects them from predators.

All the oligochaetes described so far from the Great Barrier Reef (Heron Island and Lizard Island) are in two families, the Tubificidae and the Enchytraeidae. The former family has been most extensively studied and 38 new species including several new genera have been described (Jamieson 1977; Erséus and Davis 1989; Erséus and Jamieson 1981).

On Heron Island reef, the marine sediments are largely composed of coralline particles that provide porous, often well sorted sands suitable for interstitial fauna. Therefore oligochaetes occur virtually everywhere. The worms appear to be particularly common in the coarse sand on the reef flat immediately off the beaches.

On the other hand, Lizard Island, a continental island, has sediments that generally are a mixture of mineral and coralline particles. The mineral particles are coarse and seem to grind the coral debris into very fine sand and silt. Consequently the sands near the island are poorly sorted with limited space available for interstitial fauna, including oligochaetes. In contrast, the sediments around the true coral reefs and cays at some distance from Lizard Island are characterized by large populations of oligochaetes.

Some of the tubificid worms that are particularly common in poorly oxygenated sand in tropical seas and very common in the Great Barrier Reef are of particular interest because they have no gut (genera *Inanidrilus* and *Olavius*). Instead, their nutritional needs are provided by symbiotic bacteria that live in their body wall making them conspicuously white and opaque. These bacteria are able to assimilate organic matter dissolved in the sediment water.

Marine oligochaete species described from the Great Barrier Reef are:

Enchytraeidae: *Grania macrochaeta* subsp. *trichaeta* Jamieson, 1977; probably a good species, separate from *G. macrochaeta* (Pierantoni).

Tubificidae: *Heronidrilus fastigatus* Erséus and Jamieson, 1981; *H. bihamis* Erséus and Jamieson, 1981; *H. heronae* (Erséus and Jamieson, 1981); *Heterodrilus queenslandicus* (Jamieson, 1977); *H. scitus* Erséus, 1981b; *H. keenani* Erséus, 1981b; *H. claviatriatus* Erséus, 1981b; *H. jamiesoni* Erséus, 1981b; *H. inermis* (Erséus, 1981b); *Aktedrilus parviprostatus* Erséus, 1980; *Bathydrilus rohdei* (Jamieson, 1977); *B. superiovasatus* Erséus, 1981a; *Coralliodrilus atriobifidus* Erséus, 1981a; *C. oviatriatus* Erséus, 1981a; *C. parvigenitalis* Erséus, 1981a; *Duridrilus pastoralis* Erséus, 1990; *Inanidrilus carterensis* Erséus, 1984; *I. wasseri* Erséus, 1984; *Jamiesoniella athecata* Erséus, 1981a; *Olavius albidus* (Jamieson, 1977); *O. geniculatus* (Erséus, 1981a); *O. filithecatus* (Erséus, 1981a); *O. clavatus* (Erséus, 1981a); *O. (Coralliodriloides) avisceralis* (Erséus, 1981a); *O. (Coralliodriloides) loisae* Erséus, 1984; *Pectinodrilus heronensis* (Erséus, 1981a); *Pacifidrilus aquilinus* (Erséus and Davis, 1989); *Limnodriloides australis* Erséus, 1982; *L. armatus* Erséus,

1982; *L. tenuiductus* Erséus, 1982; *L. uniampullatus* Erséus, 1982; *Smithsonidrilus grandiculus* (Erséus, 1983); *S. minusculus* (Erséus, 1983); *S. capricornae* (Erséus, 1983); *S. sacculatus* Erséus, 1983; *S. irregularis* (Erséus, 1983).

Phylum Sipuncula — Peanut Worms

Like so many other worms on the Great Barrier Reef, the unsegmented worms of the small phylum Sipuncula commonly known as Peanut worms live in sand, under rocks, in crevices, in coral and in encrusting corallines. They are marine invertebrates with a cylindrical, subcylindrical, sac, flask or spindle-shaped, fluid-filled muscular trunk, and an anterior, extensible introvert that can be partly or completely withdrawn into the trunk. The mouth is at the anterior extremity of the introvert where there usually is a group of tentacles. The anus is at the anterior end of the trunk near the base of the introvert. The antero-dorsal position of the anus distinguished sipunculans from other groups of marine worms.

Most sipunculans are burrowers or borers, and detritus or algal feeders. By their boring action (believed to be partly mechanical and partly chemical) some help to break down coral skeletons into fragments that are subsequently incorporated in the consolidated reef. Sipunculans are eaten by fishes and some molluscs, especially the carnivorous gastropod *Mitra* spp.. So far 23 species are known from the Great Barrier Reef.

Sand Burrowers

Sipunculus sp. (Fig. 33:1) and *Siphonosoma* spp. (Fig. 33:2) are stout, cylindrical, up to 260 mm long. They make unlined, and non-permanent burrows. Longitudinal and circular muscle bands are prominent in *Sipunculus* but *Siphonosoma* has only longitudinal ones. Numerous small, posteriorly-directed, triangular papillae are on the introvert of *Sipunculus* but not *Siphonosoma*. *Sipunculus robustus*, *Siphonosoma cumanense*, *S. vastum*, *S. boholense* and *S. rotumanum* have so far been recorded.

Borers in Coral and Calcareous Substrates

This group includes species sometimes found under rocks, boulders and in crevices.

Themiste lageniformis (Fig. 33:3) and *T. huttoni* have a pear to globular trunk and smooth body-wall. Tentacles branch from four to eight stems.

Phascolosoma spp. (Fig. 33:4) have a trunk (up to 35 mm long), usually with prominent longitudinal muscle bands, and prominent and pigmented papillae on the body wall. *Phascolosoma scolops*, *P. stephensoni*, *P. perlucens*, *P. nigrescens*, *P. pacificum* and *P. albolineatum* are commonly recorded. *Aspidosiphon* (Fig. 33:5) resembles *Phascolosoma* but possess a hardened shield or disc at each end of the trunk. The introvert arises ventral to the anterior shield and not from the centre of the trunk as in *Phascolosoma*.

Aspidosiphon elegans, *A. gracilis*, *A. cumingii*, *A. steenstrupii*, *A. klunzingeri* and *A. inquilinis* are frequently found. *A. jukesi* lives commensally in the base of the solitary corals *Heteropsammia* and *Heterocyathus*.

Cloeosiphon aspergillus (Fig. 33.6) has its trunk crowned with a white, pineapple-like, calcareous cap, and the introvert arises from the centre of the cap. *Lithacrosiphon cristatus* has a white, conical cap at the anterior extremity of the trunk and introvert arises ventral to the cap and not from its centre. Both *Lithacrosiphon* and *Cloeosiphon* are found in coral.

Golfingia herdmani, the only representative of its genus known from the Great Barrier Reef, has been found in sandy substrates at Heron Island. The body wall of *Golfingia*, like *Themiste*, is smooth and lacks bands of longitudinal muscle. In *Themiste*, however, the tentacles are branching and sometimes even dendritic or tree-like while in *Golfingia* they are simple and do not branch.

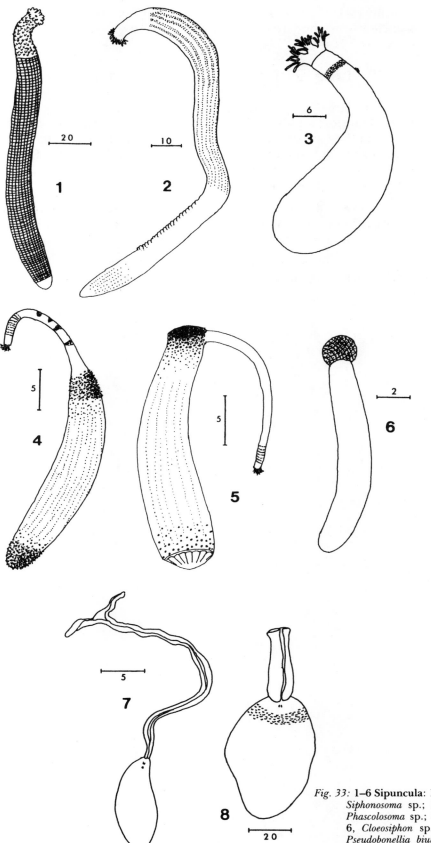

Fig. 33: **1–6 Sipuncula:** 1, *Sipunculus* sp.; 2, *Siphonosoma* sp.; 3, *Themiste* sp.; 4, *Phascolosoma* sp.; 5, *Aspidosiphon sp.*; 6, *Cloeosiphon* sp. **7,8, Echiura:** 7, *Pseudobonellia biuterina*; 8, *Anelassorhynchus porcellus.*

95

Strangely, the genus *Phascolion*, which normally lives in the empty shells of molluscs, has not yet been reported from the Great Barrier Reef.

Phylum Echiura — Spoon Worms

Echiurans are small to large-sized, unsegmented, marine worms, with a subcylindrical to sac-like trunk and an anterior, highly extensible proboscis that cannot be withdrawn into the trunk. The mouth is at the base of the proboscis and the anus at the posterior extremity of the body. Two hook-like setae usually are present just behind the mouth. Echiurans are often light to dark green. They are found in burrows in sand, mud or rock and are detritus feeders. Two species are known from the Great Barrier Reef:

Pseudobonellia biuterina (Fig. 33:7) has a sub-elliptical to oval dark green trunk 5-20 mm long and a slender, forked proboscis. A very small male is carried by the female in a small sac. They live in fissures, cracks, and tubes in coral rock and under stones and boulders.

Anelassorhynchus porcellus (Fig. 33:8) has a sac-shaped to elliptical trunk 30-50 mm long and an undivided fleshy proboscis that is easily detached. It lives in sand and under rocks.

PLATE 3

Anthozoa, Scleractinia — a diverse array of stony corals on the reef slope, their colonies spreading out to catch the light.

Staghorn coral with butterfly fish. (Photo courtesy of P. Harrison.)

Favites abdita, green brain coral spawning.
(Photo courtesy of P. Harrison.)

Favites abdita, green brain coral polyps. (Photo courtesy of P. Harrison.)

Galaxea fascicularis spawning egg sperm bundles.
(Photo courtesy of P. Harrison.)

Acropora tenuis spawning. (Photo courtesy of P. Harrison.)

Favites pentagona, brain coral polyps expanded at night.
(Photo courtesy of P. Harrison.)

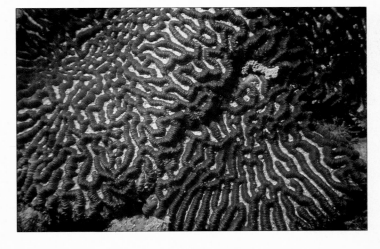

Platygyra daedalea, brain coral. (Photo courtesy of P. Harrison.)

PLATE 4

Unless otherwise stated photos courtesy of
Great Barrier Reef Marine Park Authority

Xenia sp. (Anthozoa, Alcyonacea).

Nepthea sp. (Anthozoa, Alcyonacea).

Pseudoceras ferrugineus (Polycladida, Turbellaria).
(Photo courtesy of L. Newman and A. Flowers.)

Pseudoceros corallophilus (Polycladida, Turbellaria).
(Photo courtesy of L. Newman and A. Flowers.)

Protula magnifica (Annelida, Polychaeta).

Filograna implexa (Annelida, Polychaeta).

Reteterebella queenslandia (Annelida, Polychaeta). Feeding tentacles.

Spirobranchus giganteus (Annelida, Polychaeta).

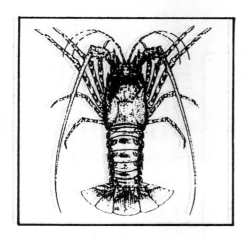

Phylum Crustacea

Members of this large group of principally aquatic animals (both freshwater and marine), are characterized by their chitinous exoskeleton and jointed biramous limbs that serve locomotory, sensory, respiratory and feeding functions. Once classified as a sub-phylum of the Arthropoda, the group is now regarded as a phylum in its own right (Manton 1977). Crustaceans range in size from minute parasitic and planktonic organisms to large free living lobsters and crabs.

Only a few groups of crustaceans have been studied in any detail, and there are many that are relatively unknown.

Only the most conspicuous elements of the fauna are referred to in this account, and full species lists of recorded species are not given. Works containing more detailed information are set out in the reference list at the end of this volume.

Their bodies are divided into a head *(cephalon)*, thorax *(pereon)* and abdomen *(pleon)* each with similar, sometimes fused, segments. The head, which is at the front of the animal, has the sense organs *(eyes* and *antennae)*; and the eating organs (mouth parts, such as *mandibles*, *maxillae)* which are adapted from the characteristic crustacean biramous, segmental appendages. In the centre of the body, on the thorax, the segmented appendages often are adapted for walking *(pereopods)* and defence; and on the abdomen the appendages are usually for swimming *(swimmerets* or *pleopods)*. At the posterior end of the body there often is a tail with *uropods* and a *telson*. The chitinous exoskeleton on the upper half of the anterior segments is often fused into a particularly hard shell *(carapace)*, which can be produced forwards into a pointed rostrum. As crustaceans grow, they discard their hard chitinous exoskeleton (shell) for a new one, just as insects do. Crustaceans usually have larvae that pass through many different stages in the plankton before they reach their adult form; and in the plankton they are dispersed around the seas to be recruited into new populations of their own species. Some crustaceans, however, brood their embryos, holding them to their bodies by one or more special appendages *(oostegites)*. Embryos develop directly to young adults, resembling the parent, without an intervening planktonic stage.

Crustaceans are carnivores, herbivores or filter feeders, and in their turn, are the food of other carnivores (including *Homo sapiens*) or even filter feeders (such as whales).

The small planktonic cladocerans and ostracods, many species of copepods, mysids and larvae of most other groups occur in the waters that bathe the reefs. Many arrive in these waters in the oceanic currents that move along the edge of the continent. Most groups have their representatives in weed, under rocks, in crevices, and in the interstices of the rocks and the sediments that lie on the reef flat, in the lagoon and on the sea floor between the

MAJOR GROUPS OF CRUSTACEA
(After Bowman and Abele, 1982)

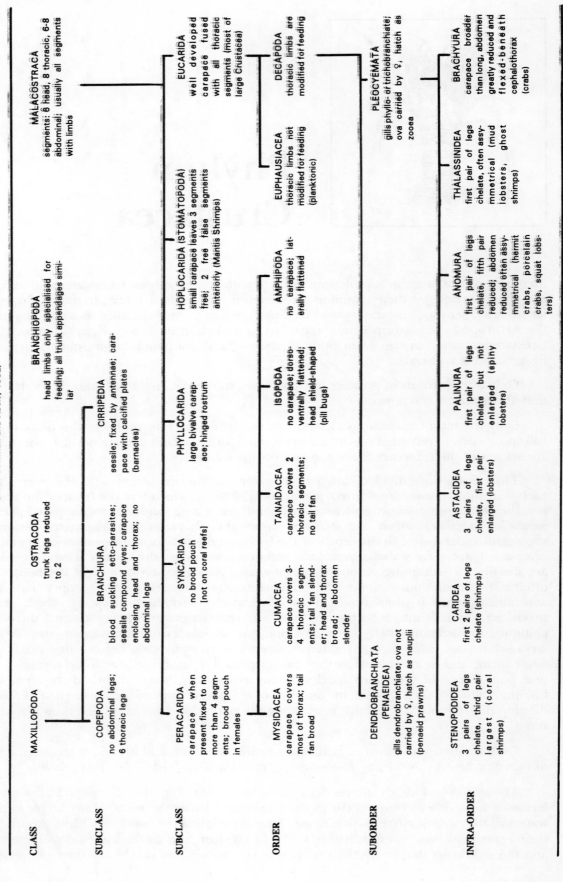

CLASS

MALACOSTRACA
segments: 6 head, 8 thoracic, 6-8 abdominal; usually all segments with limbs

BRANCHIOPODA
head limbs only specialised for feeding; all trunk appendages similar

SUBCLASS

OSTRACODA
trunk legs reduced to 2

EUCARIDA
well developed carapace fused with all thoracic segments (most of large Crustacea)

BRANCHIURA
blood sucking ecto-parasites; sessile compound eyes; carapace enclosing head and thorax; no abdominal legs

CIRRIPEDIA
sessile; fixed by antennae; carapace with calcified plates (barnacles)

SUBCLASS

PERACARIDA
carapace when present fixed to no more than 4 segments; brood pouch in females

DECAPODA
thoracic limbs are modified for feeding

HOPLOCARIDA (STOMATOPODA)
small carapace leaves 3 segments free; 2 free false segments anteriorly (Mantis Shrimps)

SYNCARIDA
no brood pouch [not on coral reefs]

PHYLLOCARIDA
large bivalve carapace; hinged rostrum

ORDER

EUPHAUSIACEA
thoracic limbs not modified for feeding (planktonic)

AMPHIPODA
no carapace; laterally flattened

ISOPODA
no carapace; dorso-ventrally flattened; head shield-shaped (pill bugs)

TANAIDACEA
carapace covers 2 thoracic segments; no tail fan

CUMACEA
carapace covers 3-4 thoracic segments; tail fan slender; head and thorax broad; abdomen slender

MYSIDACEA
carapace covers most of thorax; tail fan broad

SUBORDER

PLEOCYEMATA
gills phyllo- or trichobranchiate; ova carried by ♀, hatch as zooea

DENDROBRANCHIATA (PENAEIDEA)
gills dendrobranchiate; ova not carried by ♀, hatch as nauplii (penaeid prawns)

INFRA-ORDER

BRACHYURA
carapace broader than long, abdomen greatly reduced and flexed beneath cephalothorax (crabs)

THALASSINIDEA
first pair of legs chelate, often assymmetrical (mud lobsters, ghost shrimps)

ANOMURA
first pair of legs chelate, fifth pair reduced; abdomen reduced often assymmetrical (hermit crabs, porcelain crabs, squat lobsters)

PALINURA
first pair of legs chelate but not enlarged (spiny lobsters)

ASTACIDEA
3 pairs of legs chelate, first pair enlarged (lobsters)

CARIDEA
first 2 pairs of legs chelate (shrimps)

STENOPODIDEA
3 pairs of legs chelate, third pair largest (coral shrimps)

reefs, and on and in sponges, corals, worms, echinoderms, ascidians, fishes and other crustaceans.

Class Ostracoda

Ostracods are small (usually 3–10 mm) crustaceans whose outstanding character is a bivalved, often ornate and sculptured, carapace. They are found in most marine habitats, but in the Great Barrier Reef are predominantly benthic although a few are planktonic, and some are commensals on echinoderms. Over 8 000 species are known world-wide, most marine taxa belonging to the suborders Myodocopa and Podocopa. The majority are suspension feeders or detritivores, but a few are known to be carnivorous scavengers.

Class Maxillopoda

Subclass Copepoda

Copepods, a diverse, abundant and ubiquitous group of mostly small (0.3–10 mm) crustaceans, show a diversity of body shapes from worm-like parasites to compact harpacticoids. Most have a distinct head shield, a thorax of six segments and an abdomen of five segments. Many free-living copepods have a single dorsal eye, while parasitic forms often lack eyes altogether. There are over 9 000 named species, and many more are as yet undescribed. Currently there are eight orders (Schram 1986) with about 177 families. The principal free living copepods are the Calanoida, the Cyclopoida and the benthic Harpacticoida. Copepods are also commonly encountered as commensals or parasites of other marine animals — corals, echinoderms, sponges and fish all commonly acting as hosts to copepod symbionts. The major symbiotic orders are the Poecilostomatoida, the Siphonostomatoida and the Monstrilloida. Some species of parasitic copepod have such highly modified morphology that they are scarcely recognizable as crustacean.

Subclass Cirripedia

Barnacles are well known to everyone who visits the seashore. For a long time these unusual crustaceans were thought to be molluscs, but inside the interlocking shellplates is a true crustacean similar to an upside down shrimp. Also, barnacle larvae are unmistakeably like their other crustacean relatives. Barnacles are anchored to the substrate so their larvae must find suitable sites — they test environmental properties such as surface textures, water quality, wave action and current flow before settling down for life. The typical adult barnacle filter feeds by opening the top plates of the shell and protruding the feathery legs (cirri) which catch micro-organisms in the water flowing past. Species are present in most habitats and also are common living in commensal and parasitic relationships. The most conspicuous groups are: the "acorn" barnacles, named after the superficial resemblance of some species to the conical shape of an acorn; and the "goose" or stalked barnacles (see Fig. 34).

Forty-three species in 23 genera are known from the Great Barrier Reef, with even more from coastal waters. For more information, Jones *et al.* (1990) have provided a checklist of species, and references to papers on the general biology of Australian species.

Order Thoracica

Suborder Balanomorpha (Acorn Barnacles). Common intertidal and shallow sub-tidal species, attached to boulders and reef blocks on the reef flat, and on beach rock, are *Tetraclita vitiata, T. coerulescens, Tetraclitella purpurascens, Tesseropora rosea, Balanus amphitrite, B. trigonus, Megabalanus tintinabulum*. Some species live attached to other animals: *Chelonibia patula* on the shells of crabs and molluscs; *C. testudinaria* on the carapace of turtles; and *Platylepas hexastylos* embedded in the skin of turtles and dugong; *Acasta* spp. embed in sponges; and several species, like *Creusia spinulosa*, burrow into corals.

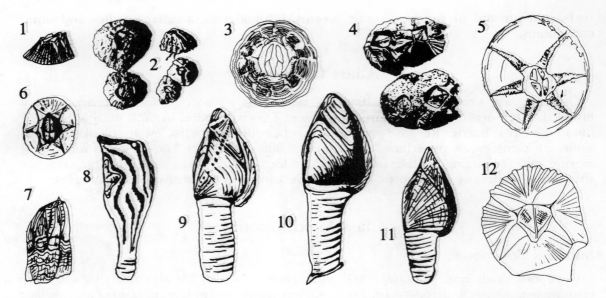

Fig. 34. Representatives of the Cirripedia: **1**, *Balanus amphitrite* (15 mm diameter); **2**, *Tesseropora rosea* (20 mm diam.); **3**, *Platylepas hexastylos* (15 mm diam.); **4**, *Tetraclitella purpurascens* (15 mm diam.); **5**, *Chelonibia testudinaria* (to 60 mm diam.); **6**, *Chelonibia patula* (to 30 mm diam.); **7**, *Megabalanus tintinabulum* (to 60 mm diam.); **8**, *Conchoderma virgatum* (to 40 mm long); **9**, *Lepas anatifera* (to 50 mm long); **10**, *Lepas hilli* (to 50 mm long); **11**, *Lepas anserifera* (to 50 mm long); **12**, *Balanus trigonus* (18 mm diam.).

Suborder Lepadomorpha (Goose or Stalked Barnacles). "Goose" barnacles are usually found attached to floating objects that get washed ashore. Like "acorn" barnacles they often attach to other organisms. Common species are: *Lepas anatifera, L. anserifera, L. hilli* and *Conchoderma virgatum. Ibla cummingi* is a small species living on the underside of coral rocks.

Order Acrothoracica

These are the "burrowing" barnacles, burrowing into calcareous rocks or shells of other animals. They are similar to the thoracicans in adult body form but differ in their soft carapace, and reduction or absence of calcareous plates. The burrows are visible from outside as small slits. The brilliantly purple *Berndtia fossata* occurs in coral on the reef.

Order Rhizocephala — Parasitic Barnacles

Sacculina spp. are very odd barnacles that have become internal parasites of crabs — they are recognized by the large, leathery, egg producing *sac* that they produce under the crabs abdomen.

Class Malacostraca

Subclass Hoplocarida

Order Stomatopoda

Mantis Shrimps form a small group of highly successful predators that feed mainly on fish and molluscs. They live in a variety of habitats. Commonly encountered species such as *Gonodactylus chiragra* (Fig. 35:I) and *G. smithii* live in cavities in live or dead coral where the females guard the eggs. They are an ancient lineage that split off from other Crustacea around 400 million years ago. World-wide, 15 families, 80 genera and over 400 species are known. Sixty-one species are known from New Caledonia and the Chesterfield Reefs, and although 21 species are known from the reef around Lizard Island, the total number for the entire Reef will be much greater. Manning (1980) and Moosa (1991) can be used as a good introduction to the literature.

Odontodactylus spp., such as *O. cultrifer,* and the large (18 cm), very beautiful, *O. scyllarus,* occur amongst the corals on the reef slope.

Subclass Phyllocarida

Order Leptostraca

These are mostly small (4–10 mm), usually transparent, and are easily recognized by the prominent bivalved carapace with a hinged rostrum and stalked red or black eyes (Fig. 35A). Although they are not uncommon under coral rocks or in coarse subtidal sediments, the group has not been studied in the Great Barrier Reef and none has been positively identified.

The most recent revisionary study on the group is that of Dahl (1985). Twenty species in five genera are recognized at present.

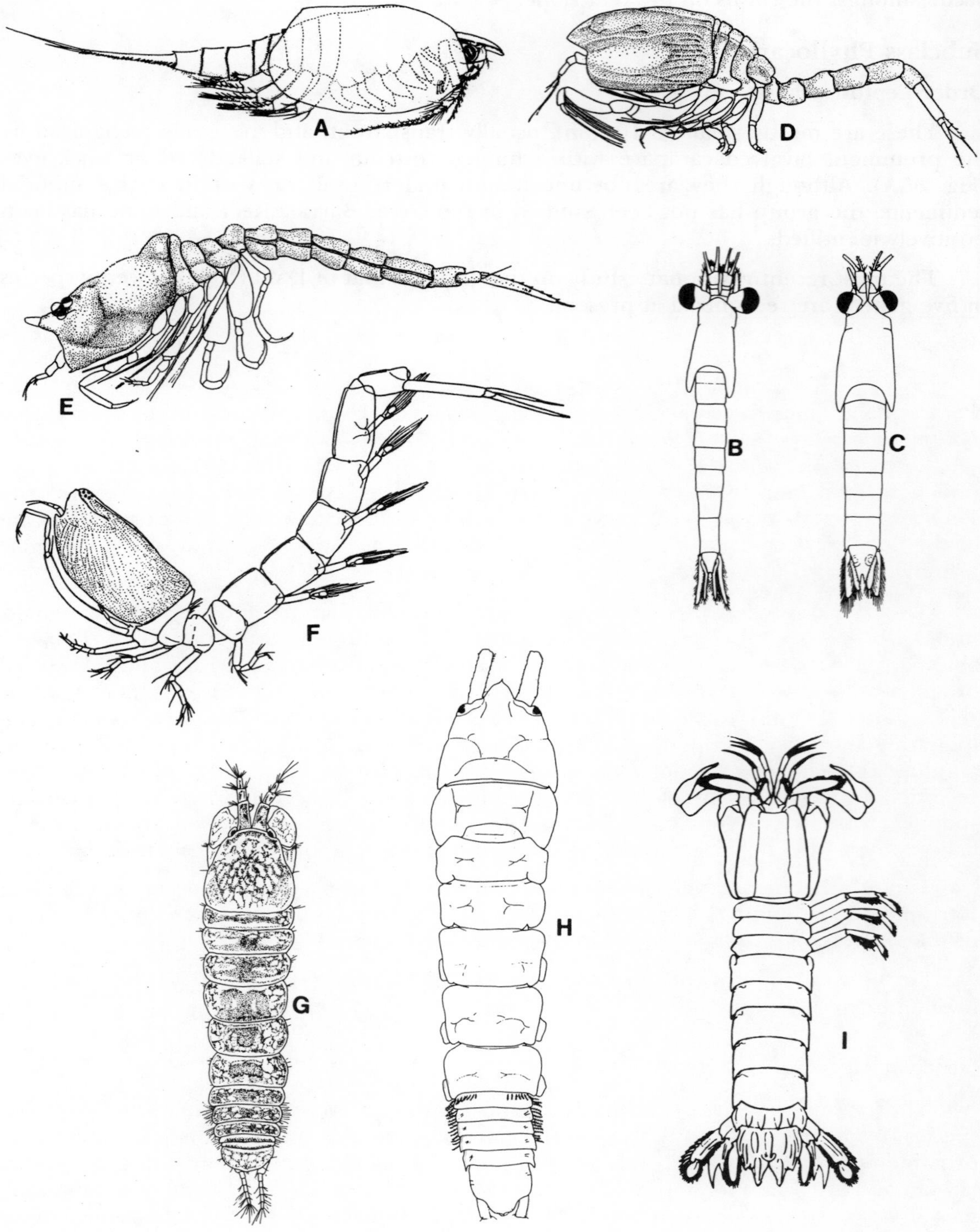

Fig. 35. **Leptostraca** — **A**, *Nebalia marerubri,* Wägele 1933 (Red Sea). **Mysidacea** — **B**, *Anisomysis mullini,* Murano 1987; **C**, *Heteromysis gracillis,* Murano 1988 (Darwin). **Cumacea** — **D**, *Gynodiastylis lata,* Hale 1946 (Moreton Bay); **E**, *Nannastacus inflatus,* Hale 1945 (Moreton Bay); **F**, *Cyclaspis strigilis,* Hale 1945 (Fraser Island). **Tanaidacea**: *Tanais littoralis,* Shiino 1978 (Macquarie Island); **H**, *Apseudes caeruleus,* Boesch 1973 (Stradbroke Island); **Stomatopoda** — **17**, *Gonodactylus chiragra* (60 mm). (Illustrations not to scale; figures from authors as indicated.)

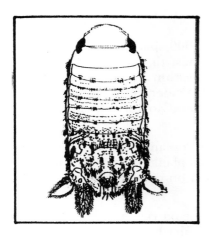

Subclass Peracarida

(Class Malacostraca)

Peracarida are mostly small (1–20 mm), but occasionally larger (40 cm as in the giant isopod *Bathynomus*) crustaceans, characterized principally by the blade-like process (*lacinia mobilis*) on the mandible, and direct development of the young which usually are brooded in a pouch formed from *öostegites* (brood plates). Characters commonly associated with the Peracarida, but not present in every order include reduction or lack of a carapace, fusion of the first body segment to the head, uniramous thoracic appendages, eyes usually sessile, terminal uropods and a simple telson.

The Great Barrier Reef has a diverse peracarid fauna, much of which remains undescribed. All of the orders known from marine environments are represented. The most abundant are the amphipods and isopods, followed by tanaids, cumaceans and mysids. All orders are likely to be represented in dead coral, coral rubble, reef flat sediments and off reef sediments. Coral rubble samples have fewer mysids. Pelagic samples contain nocturnally migrating amphipods, isopods and cumaceans as well as zooplanktonic taxa such as hyperiid amphipods. Symbiotic relationships are not common in the Peracarida. These have been recorded for some mysids (with sponges and hermit crabs) amphipods (with hydroids, sponges, tunicates, hermit crabs). Several families of flabelliferan isopod are parasites of fishes, others are known symbionts of sponges, crinoid echinoderms and hermit crabs.

Unless otherwise stated, illustrations used here are of species that occur on the Great Barrier Reef, although the figured specimen may be from a different location. The source of the illustration is acknowledged in the figure caption.

For general accounts of the Peracarida consult Schram (1986) and Parker (1982) and the literature cited therein.

Order Mysidacea

The mysids (possum shrimps) are a small order of about 120 genera and over 800 species (from Bowman and Abele 1982) commonly arranged into six families. They have a prominent carapace, stalked eyes, antennal scale, an elongate abdomen with a prawn-like tail-fan and are 3 mm to 10 mm long (Fig. 35B,C). On coral reefs they are most commonly seen in dense schools between bommies or in depressions in the reef, but are also common in the nocturnal plankton. Some are known to be associates of corals (e.g., *Heteromysis australica* Bacescu and Bruce, on *Porites andrewsii*), others of hermit crabs (*Heteromysis harpaxoides* Bacescu and Bruce, on *Dardanus megistos*).

The first and only comprehensive treatment of the Great Barrier Reef Mysidacea is that of Tattersall (1936). Murano (1988) gives a key to the Australian species of *Heteromysis* from Australian waters. The total number of species known from the Great Barrier Reef is about 50.

Order Cumacea

The Cumacea consist of about 110 genera with about 1 000 species placed into eight families. These small (3 mm–20 mm) crustaceans have a most distinctive "tadpole-like" appearance. Anteriorly the body is dilated and contained within a carapace while the posterior part of the thorax and the abdomen are long and slender, terminating in a pair of prominent styliform uropods. The eyes generally are fused to form a single dorsal anteromedian eye lobe on the carapace (Fig. 35D–F).

Cumaceans are commonly found in the bottom sediments on and around reefs, as well as in deeper shelf and slope habitats. They swim into nocturnal plankton to moult and mate. Little is known of their biology but they are believed to feed on detritus and the organic films on sand grains.

There have been no studies on cumaceans from the Great Barrier Reef itself, and few records exist from tropical Australia. Herbert M. Hale published a series of papers (culminating in 1951) on cumaceans from the southern half of Australia, which included about 20 species from Queensland.

Order Tanaidacea

The Tanaidacea, currently with about 600 species and 100 genera, is divided into four suborders. Typically tanaids are more or less cylindrical, with an anterior carapace covering the first two pereonites. The first pereopod is chelate; the pleon usually has short cylindrical segments; the uropods are generally filiforme; eyes, when present, are on lobes (Fig. 35G,H).

The Tanaidacea, both in Australia and on a world-wide basis, are the most poorly documented of the peracarid orders. In Australia knowledge of the Tanaidacea dates back to the early carcinologists Whitelegge, Chilton and Haswell, around 1902. There has been only one later publication on Australian tanaidaceans (Boesch 1973) and none dealing with species from the Great Barrier Reef, although there are some works on species from the Western Pacific (Shiino 1963, 1965).

Order Amphipoda

Amphipoda ("sea fleas, scuds, sandhoppers") usually are recognized by being the only bilaterally compressed peracarids. Morphological features that distinguish them from the other orders are the presence of biramous antennules, pereopods two and three subchelate and three pairs of uropods.

The Amphipoda is the largest of the peracarid orders and contains in excess of 1 100 genera and over 6 000 species. The dominant suborder is the Gammaridea, its members having a remarkably uniform appearance in spite of the very large number of families (91), genera (1 055) and species (5 733) (Barnard and Karaman 1991). The other suborders represented in the Great Barrier Reef are the Hyperiidea and Caprellidea. Caprellids are elongate, typically with small eyes; the anterior two legs are chelate or sub-chelate while the posterior three are used to secure the animal to the substratum; the abdomen is very small and without prominent appendages (Fig. 36). This suborder is not abundant in reefal habitats.

Hyperiids are oceanic pelagic animals, and are not commonly found in nearshore waters. Many species are associates of jellyfish and siphonophores, some feeding on their "host". While typically amphipod in appearance they are often more globose in shape and frequently have very large united eyes which occupy most of the head.

The gammarideans occur as free living algal browsers, scavengers, and also symbionts of ascidians, sponges and hydroids. Others live in association with algae. About one-third of the Indo-Pacific amphipods belong to the families that form tubes. In contrast to the Isopoda, few amphipods are truly parasitic (although in many cases the trophic relationship is not known). The Cyamidae are traditionally considered parasites of cetaceans, and are

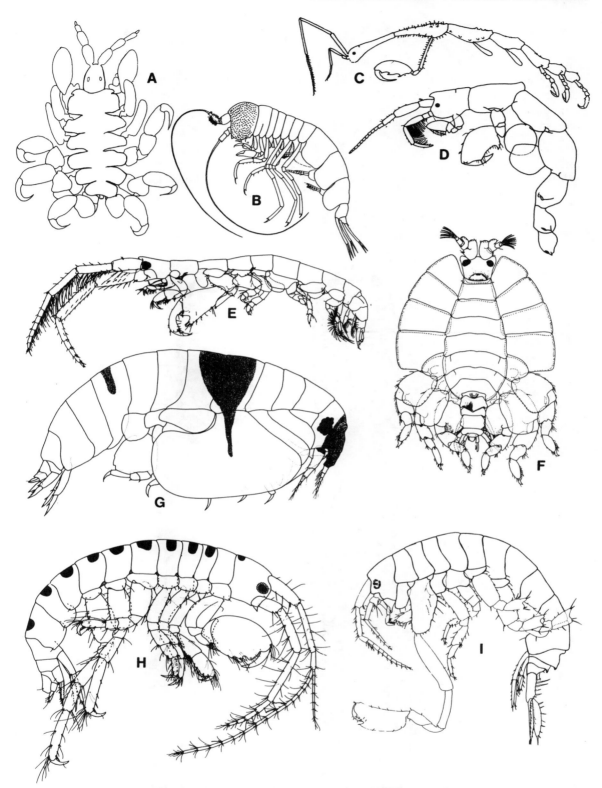

Fig. 36. **Amphipoda: Cyamida A**, *Isocyamus delphini*, Weinstein-Sedlack 1990. **Hyperiidea B**, *Phronimopsis* sp., Bowman and Gruner 1973. **Caprellida: C**, *Caprella mutica*, Arimoto 1976 (Japan); **D**, *Caprella penantis*, Laubitz 1972 ("Australia"). **Gammaridea, Ischyroceridae E**, *Baracuma alquirta*, Barnard and Drummond 1981 (Victoria); **Philiantidae F**, *Iphiplateia whiteleggei*, Barnard 1981; **Wandinidae G**, *Wandin griffini*, Lowry and Stoddart 1990; **Aoridae H**, *Bemlos ephippium*, Myers 1988. **Melphidippoidea I**, *Jebarnia stocki* Thomas and Barnard, 1990. Illustrations not to scale; figures from authors as indicated).

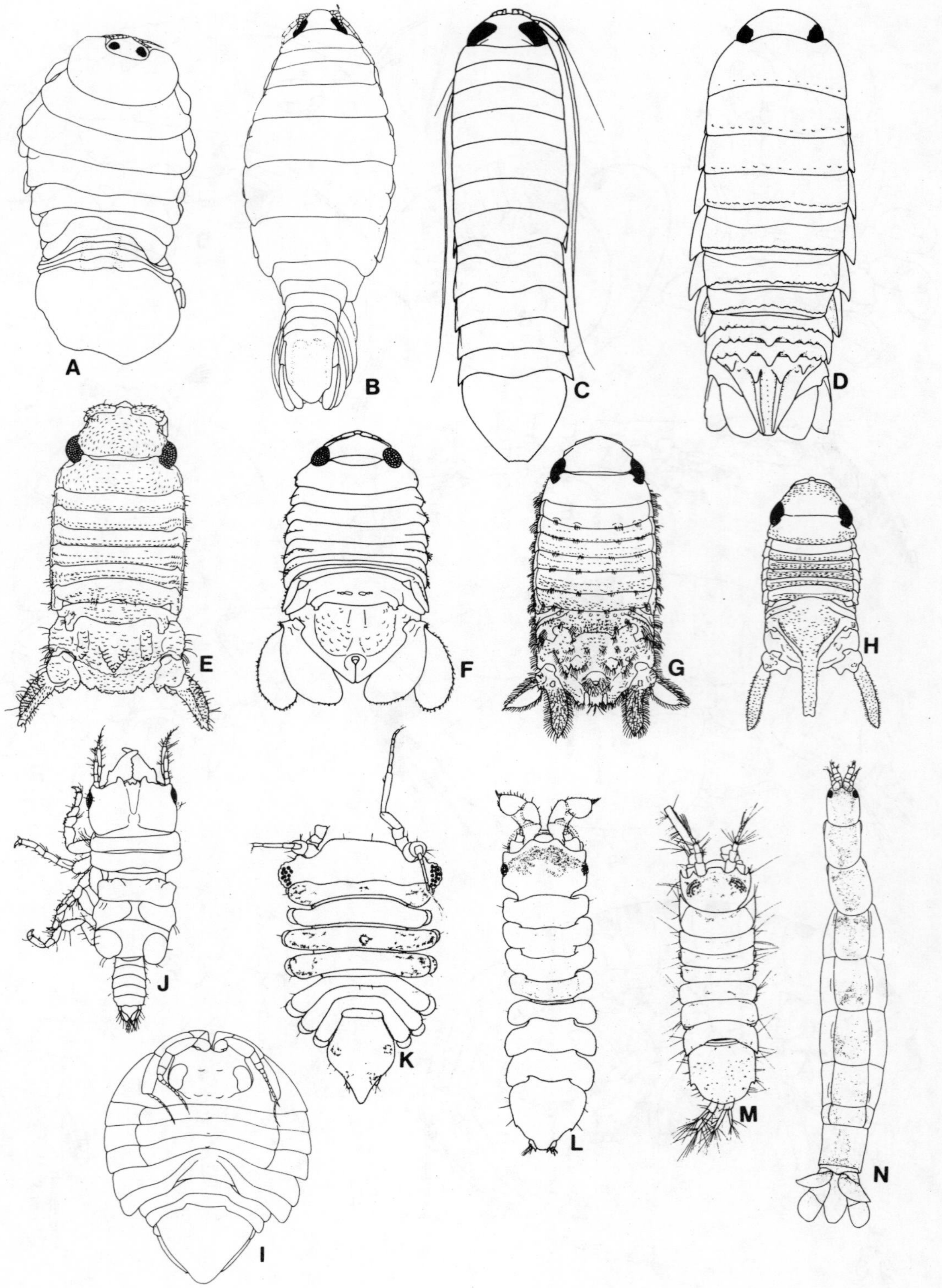

Fig. 37. **Isopoda: Flabellifera, Cymothoidae A**, *Elthusa myripristae*, Bruce 1987; **B**, *Anilocra apogonae*, Bruce 1987. **Cirolanidae C**, *Eurydice woka*, Bruce 1986; **D**, *Cirolana tuberculosa*, Bruce 1986. **Sphaeromatidae E**, *Neonaesa rugosa*, Harrison and Holdich 1982; **F**, *Dynamenella ptychura*, Harrison and Holdich 1982; **G**, *Cymodoce pelsarti*, Harrison and Holdich 1984; **H**, *Cilicaeopsis whiteleggi*, Harrison and Holdich 1984. **Serolidae I**, *Serolina holia*, Poore 1987. **Gnathiidea J**, *Gnathia calmani*, Holdich and Harrison 1981. **Asellota K**, *Salvatiella polynesica*, Müller 1990 (Bora Bora); **L**, *Jaeropsis gertrudae*, Müller 1989 (Moora); **M**, *Stenetrium hanseni*, Müller 1991 (Moora). **Anthuridea N**, *Chelanthura ajuga*, Poore and Lew Ton 1990. (Illustrations not to scale; figures from authors as indicated).

certainly obligate symbionts, but again, the trophic interaction has not been clearly determined. Lyssianassoideans, including an *Ichnopus* species common near beach rock at Heron Island, are carnivorous scavengers.

Only two major papers are devoted to amphipods of the Great Barrier Reef: Barnard (1931) and Berents (1983). In view of the vast literature and a large number of taxa, identification of amphipods is daunting. In contrast to the Isopoda, there are no "field guides" or handbooks dealing with common species or higher taxon groupings of any region. Essential literature for the Australian region is to be found in Barnard and Karaman (1991).

Order Isopoda

Isopods ("fish lice, slaters, pillbugs") present the greatest morphological diversity of any crustacean group, and certainly amongst the Peracarida. Generally isopods are characterized as being dorsoventrally compressed, lacking a carapace, with sessile eyes, antennae uniramous, pereopods with coxae fused to the body, a single pair of uropods and the telson fused to one or more pleonites. The typical marine isopod shape is presented by valviferans or flabelliferans such as *Cirolana* or *Sphaeroma*. Other shapes (Fig. 37) include extreme dorso-ventral flattening (serolids), cylindrical to vermiform (anthurideans), extreme mandible development and extreme sexual dimorphism (gnathiids) or the extreme reduction and modification of appendages (epicarids).

The Isopoda with over 4 000 species and over 700 genera are second in size only to the Amphipods and are well represented in reefal habitats. Almost any sample of coral rubble or similar substrate will yield examples of the suborders Flabellifera, Anthuridea, Gnathiidea and Asellota. The reefal and off reefal sediments are similarly rich in isopods. Some particularly common flabelliferans that occur throughout the region are *Cirolana erodiae, C. capricornica* and on mainland beaches *Exicirolana orientalis* (Family Cirolanidae). The sphaeromatid *Neonaesa rugosa* is virtually ubiquitous, while the corallanid *Argathona macronema* is found in the nasal passages of coral trout and sweetlip emperors. Most are free living, although a few are planktonic. The Cirolanidae are carnivorous and include some voracious predators. Several species have been reported as biting bathers or even attacking divers. A significant number of families occur as temporary or obligate parasites of fishes (principally the flabelliferan family Cymothoidae) and other crustaceans (the Epicaridae). Immature gnathiideans (called "pranizas") also parasitize fishes. Isopods are the only peracarids to have a significant terrestrial presence, with one suborder, the Oniscoidea being strictly terrestrial.

The marine isopods of the Great Barrier Reef have been well documented in comparison to other peracarid orders. Currently about 154 species are known but there probably are as many still unrecorded. No convenient reference to the taxonomy of Great Barrier Reef isopods is available. Kensley and Schotte (1989) is the most useful guide to the major families and many genera are also represented. Bruce (1986) revised the cirolanids, and Holdich and Harrison (1984) reviewed the literature on sphaeromatids. The large suborder Asellota remains effectively unstudied in Queensland waters although well represented in reefal habitats with Pacific species having been recently described by Müller (e.g., 1990, 1991).

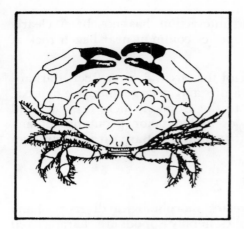

Order Decapoda

(Class Malacostraca, Eucarida)

The decapods are the shrimps, lobsters and crabs, so named because they all have 10 legs arranged in five pairs. They are the most conspicuous crustaceans because many are quite large; there are however many small and inconspicuous species. Often they are cryptic in colour and in habit, hiding in weed, under rocks, and commensal with other organisms.

On the Great Barrier Reef, the portunid and xanthid crabs have been studied by Stephenson *et al.* (1957–61), Patton (1966) and Ward (1936), the pontonine shrimps by Bruce (1976, 1983) and the alpheid shrimps by Banner and Banner (1973, 1975, 1981) most of the other major groups of Decapoda still await the attention of zoologists.

Suborder Dendrobranchiata

Infraorder Penaeidea — Prawns

The penaeid prawns, the group to which most of the commercially important species belong, are poorly represented in the reef fauna. *Penaeus longistylus* juveniles are common on sandy substrates. *Metapenaeopsis lamellata* (small, red and white; Fig. 38:14) and *Heteropenaeus longimanus* (first pair of thoracic limbs very elongate) both occur in lagoons. *Acetes* spp. occur in the night plankton. The penaeids of the region are well illustrated and described by Grey *et al.* (1983).

Suborder Pleocyemata

Infraorder Stenopodidea — Coral Shrimps

Stenopus hispidus (the Banded Coral shrimp) is red, white and blue (Fig. 38:2) and well known to underwater photographers and aquarists. Two other species are known from the Reef, *S. cyanoscelis*, and *S. chrysexanthus*, distinguished by differences in colour pattern (see Goy 1992). *Microprosthema validum* (white with orange lines; Fig. 38:1) occurs beneath dead coral masses on the inner reef flat.

Infraorder Caridea — Shrimps

In the vicinity of 200 species are known from the Great Barrier Reef, many beautifully coloured and patterned, but small and easily overlooked (Fig. 38:3–16). Species of Alpheidae and Pontoniinae (along with stomatopods) are responsible for many of the night-time snapping noises made by the fingers of the chelae snapping shut. Holthuis (1955) is the best guide to the many genera of carids. So far the Capricorn-Bunker groups have been the most intensively explored for caridean reef shrimps. The reef Caridea are divided into the following families:

Palaemonidae — *Leandrites cyrtorhynchus* (a fish cleaner) is one of the few representatives of the subfamily Palaemoninae. The majority of shrimps recorded in this family (about 90 species) are in the sub-family Pontoniinae. A few are free living micropredators but most are commensals of sponges, anemones, hydroids and other coelenterates, bivalve molluscs, nudibranchs, echinoderms (excepting only ophiurids) and ascidians. Species associated with corals are particularly well represented. *Jocaste* spp., and *Coralliocaris graminea* (a common bright green species) are found mostly associated with *Acropora* corals, whereas *Harpiliopsis beaupresii* and *Fennera chacei* live in *Pocillopora* and *Stylophora* colonies. The genus *Periclimenes* is represented by many species both free living and commensal, on a variety of hosts. It includes the common and very beautiful *P. brevicarpalis* found living with anemones. Gorgonian, echinoid and bivalve molluscan commensals are quite rare, except for giant clams (*Tridacna* spp.) which play host to the large *Paranchistus ornatus*, and other *Anchistus* species. (See Bruce 1983 and Patton 1966, for a fuller account of the species).

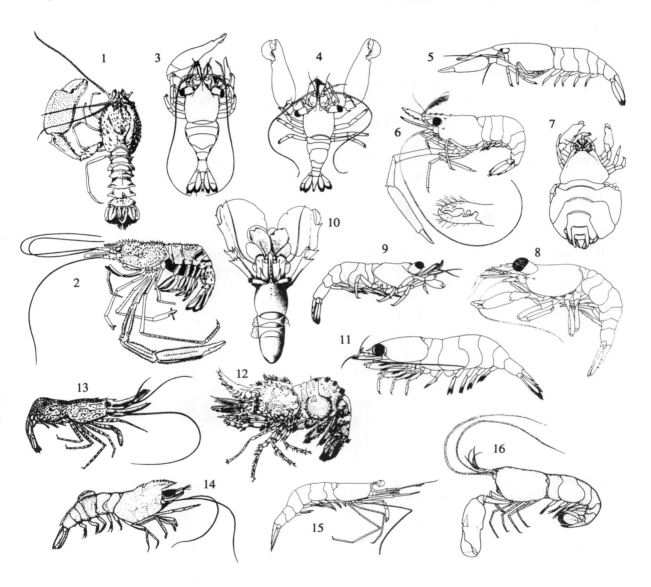

Fig. 38. Representatives of Stenopodidea, Caridea, Penaeidea: **Stenopodidea** 1, *Microprosthema validum* (10 mm); 2, *Stenopus hispidus* (60 mm). **Caridea** 3, *Jocaste lucina* (15 mm, Palaemonidae); 4, *Coralliocaris graminea* (20 mm, Palaemonidae); 5, *Anchistus custos* (20 mm, Palaemonidae); 6, *Periclimenes* sp. (25 mm, Palaemonidae); 7, *Paratypton* sp. (20 mm, Palaemonidae); 8, *Harpiliopsis* sp. (10 mm, Palaemonidae); 9, *Fennera chacei* (5 mm, Palaemonidae); 10, *Hymenocera* sp. (25 mm, Gnathophyllidae); 11, *Discias* sp. (8 mm, Bresiliidae); 12, *Saron marmoratus* (30 mm, Hippolytidae); 13, *Thynchocinetes* sp. (45 mm, Rhynchocinetidae); 15, *Nikoides multispinatus* (20 mm, Processidae); 16, *Alpheus edwardsi* (50 mm, Alpheidae). **Penaeidea** 14, *Metapenaeopsis lamellata* (75 mm). Figs 1, 2, 3, 5, 10, 11, 13 from Holthius 1955; total body length for each species indicated.

Alpheidae — About 52 species of these shrimps are known from the Great Barrier Reef. Many are free living but others are commensal on crinoids (*Synalpheus* spp.) and in sponges. Several conspicuous species live on the reef flat. *Alpheopsis yaldwyni* (red and white banded) lives under coral colonies. Living in the same habitats is the olive green *Alpheus strenuus*, one of the largest alpheids on the reef reaching 80 mm in length. *Alpheus frontalis* occurs in pairs, in long tubes of felted green algae intertwined amongst branches of coral colonies. Several species of *Alpheus* have a remarkable association with gobies, excavating and sharing the burrow with the fish. (See Banner and Banner 1973, 1975, 1981, for identification keys).

Hippolytidae — Species are less common than alpheids, but *Saron marmoratus* (found under coral colonies) is the largest shrimp on the reef. In the same habitat is the smaller *S. neglectus*, with "eye spots" on its tail. *Lysmata amboinensis* (orange, red and white body, white antennae), a fish cleaner, lives in caves. *Gelastocaris paronae* is an unusual sponge commensal. *Thor amboinensis*, a small, dark brown shrimp with large white opalescent spots, lives on anemones, corals or other coelenterates. There are also two other species of *Thor*, two species of *Latreutes* and three species of *Hippolyte*.

Pasiphaeidae — In the Capricorn-Bunker Groups at least, is represented by two species of *Leptochela* (one buried in sand, and one in the nocturnal plankton).

Bresiliidae — A single species of *Discias* has been found commensal in a sponge (*Jaspis stellifera*).

Rhynchocinetidae — the beautiful little striped and spotted "hinge-beak prawn", *Rhynchocinetes rugulosus*, is remarkable in having its rostrum hinged so that it can move up and down.

Thalassocarididae (with light producing organs), Processidae (nocturnal, soft substrate burrowers, e.g., *Nikoides* spp.), Crangonidae (true shrimps, found in sand pools) are represented by a few species each.

Gnathophyllidae — the Painted Shrimp, *Hymenocera picta*, with its enormous flattened plate-like claws, and vibrant colour pattern, and the rare, *Phyllognathia ceratophthalma*, are both asteroid predators.

Infraorder Thalassinidea — Ghost Shrimps

These are sparsely represented and difficult to catch. All are expert burrowers and rarely seen unless disturbed. Poore and Griffin (1979) have reviewed the Australian genera and species. The following are the main families represented on the reef flats of the Great Barrier Reef.

Axiidae — *Axius plectorynchus* is common in vertical burrows just beyond the edge of the beach rock. *Scytoleptus serratipes* is found under coral rubble boulders.

Callianassidae — *Callianassa* spp. (yabbies) are found in sand or fine gravel on the reef flat or under dead coral (Fig. 39:10).

Upogebidae — *Upogebia* spp. are commonly found in male-female pairs, but sometimes also in larger numbers, in a wide variety of sponges.

Infraorder Palinura — Spiny Lobsters

Palinuridae — *Panulirus versicolor* (the Painted Crayfish); *P. longipes femoristriga* (Tropical Crayfish), and *P. ornatus* (the Coral or Ornate Crayfish) often are encountered on coral reefs in the region. *Panulirus ornatus* is one of the largest species, growing to 50 cm body length. All species are readily distinguished by their distinctive colour patterns (Fig. 39:1–3). Holthuis (1991) gives good accounts of all the species.

Scyllaridae — The nocturnal *Scyllarides squammosus* (Slipper Lobster; Fig. 39:4) is most common on reefs and rocky areas in depths of 20–50 m, but can also be found in shallower water. *Parribacus caledonicus* (Mitten Lobster; Fig. 39:5) is found in shallow water, usually on the exposed side of reefs in surge channels, and in crevices or caves.

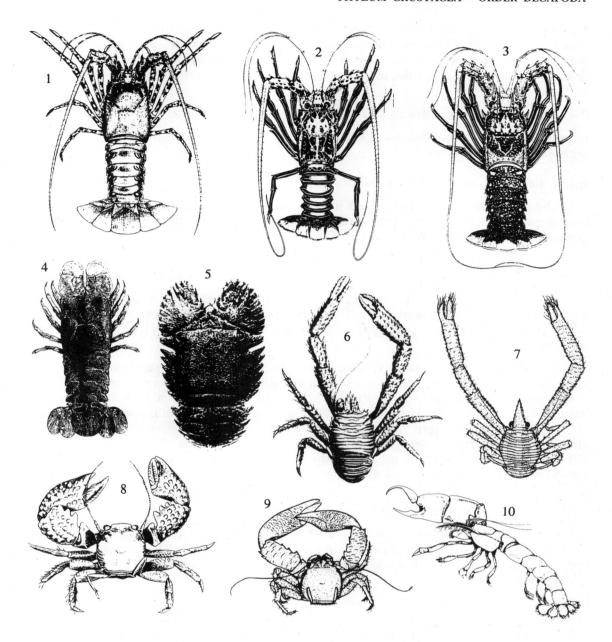

Fig. 39. Representatives of Palinura, Anomura, Thalassinidea: **Palinura** 1, *Panulirus ornatus* (50 cm, Palinuridae); 2, *Panulirus versicolor* (40 cm, Palinuridae); 3, *Panulirus longipes femoristriga* (30 cm, Palinuridae); 4, *Scyllarides squammosus* (40 cm, Scyllaridae); 5, *Parribacus caledonicus* (18 cm, Scyllaridae). **Anomura** 6, *Galathea australiensis* (7 mm, Galatheidae); **7**, *Allogalathea elegans* (10 mm, Galatheidae); 8, *Pachycheles sculptus* (5 mm, Porcellanidae); 9, *Petrolisthes lamarckii* (16 mm, Porcellanidae). **Thalassinidea** 10, *Callianassa australiensis* (60 mm, Callianassidae). Figs 1–5 and 10 from Holthuis 1991; 6 and 8 from Grant and McCulloch 1906; total body length indicated for each species.

Infraorder Anomura — Hermit Crabs and Related Groups

Porcellanidae — are represented by free living (under dead corals) and species commensal with sponges and corals. At present 12 species of seven genera are known. The dark red *Petrolisthes lamarckii* is very common in shingle areas (Fig. 39:9). *Pachycheles sculptus* (Fig. 39:8), *Pisidia gordoni*, *P. dispar*, and *Polyonyx obesulus* are all common in the cavities in the bases of live and dead coral. *Neopetrolisthes oshimai*, a pretty and distinctive, finely spotted species, lives commensely with a variety of anemones, usually in pairs.

Galatheidae (Squat Lobsters) — *Galathea* species, although often small and inconspicuous, sometimes are abundant in and around live and dead coral (Fig. 39:6,7). *Galathea subsquamata, G. magnifica* and *G. corallicola* are all known to be associated with coral. The distinctively striped *Allogalathea elegans* is common on many crinoids. Haig (1973) gives a key to species.

Paguridae, Diogenidae, Coenobitidae (Hermit Crabs) — See chapter on Hermit Crabs below.

Hippidae — *Hippa adactyla* lives in sand on the reef flat. It is often found on the beach on night high tides.

Infraorder Brachyura — True Crabs

The crabs are diverse and varied in appearance and the most conspicuous of all the crustaceans on the reef (Fig. 40). Many families are represented. Sakai (1976) is the best general modern guide to Indo-West Pacific crabs.

Leucosiidae (Pebble Crabs) — are probably common but not often seen as they bury in the substrate by day. *Philyra* and *Leucosia* species are the most likely to be encountered.

Hymenosomatidae — are spider-like, mostly very tiny species. The most common reef representive, *Trigonoplax spathulifera,* found beneath dead coral blocks on the reef flat, is usually dark brown with a pale body, and about 1 cm across. Lucas (1980) has revised the Australian species.

Majidae (Spider Crabs) — an incredibly diverse group on the reef, are usually slow moving and inconspicuous, often with a covering of added material, such as sponges, ascidians or anemones, on the carapace or limbs. *Hyastenus* spp. (on coral or algae), *Camposcia retusa* (large, often found under coral blocks) and *Oncinopus araneus* (small, among algae) are all easily recognized. The spiny *Schizophrys aspera* is a relatively large species that commonly inhabits the branches of *Acropora* corals. The small "snub-nosed" *Micippa* species are also distinctive and unusual majids inhabiting the reef. Griffin and Tranter (1986) have provided a good account of the species of this family.

Raninidae (Frog or Spanner Crabs) — *Ranina ranina* is sometimes found on the reef, but is more common on sandy bottoms away from the reef.

Dromiidae (Sponge Crabs) — have the posterior legs modified for grasping and are used for holding a live sponge or ascidian colony over the carapace. The protective colony is shaped to exactly fit and hide the body of the crab. They sometimes are found beneath coral blocks on the reef flats.

Calappidae (Box Crabs) — are represented on the beaches by the burrowing species of *Matuta,* which usually disappear rapidly into the sand when disturbed. In deeper water on the reef flat, *Calappa* are commonly found, buried in the sand by day, and feeding actively on molluscs at night.

Fig. 40. Representatives of Brachyura: 1, *Trigonoplax spathulifera* (14 mm, Hymenosomatidae); 2, *Philyra platycheira* (17 mm, Leucosiidae); 3, *Hyastenus diacanthus* (35 mm, Majidae); 4, *Camposcia retusa* (40 mm, Majidae); 5, *Micippa* sp. (25 mm, Majidae); 6, *Xenocarcinus depressus* (10 mm, Majidae); 7, *Schizophrys aspera* (50 mm, Majidae); 8, *Ranina ranina* (100 mm, Raninidae); 9, *Petalomera lateralis* (20 mm, Dromiidae); 10, *Matuta planipes* (55 mm, Calappidae); 11, *Calappa hepatica* (80 mm, Calappidae); 12, *Xanthasia murigera* (14 mm, Pinnotheridae); 13, *Hapalocarcinus marsupialis,* ♀ (4 mm, Cryptochiridae); 14, *Daldorfia horrida* (100 mm, Parthenopidae); 15, *Kraussia nitida* (20 mm, Cancridae); 16, *Harrovia elegans* (13 mm, Eumedonidae); 17, *Echinoecus pentagonus* (8 mm, Eumedonidae); 18, *Lissocarcinus orbicularis* (10 mm, Portunidae); 19, *Thalamita stimpsoni* (35 mm, Portunidae); 20, *Portunus granulatus* (30 mm, Portunidae); 21, *Pilumnus spinicarpus* (11 mm, Pilumnidae); 22, *Glabropilumnus dispar* (15 mm, Pilumnidae); 23, *Trapezia cymodoce* (20 mm, Trapeziidae); 24, *Carpilius maculatus* (115 mm, Carpiliidae); 25, *Chlorodiella nigra* (20 mm, Xanthidae); 26, *Etisus laevimanus* (50 mm, Xanthidae); 27, *Phymodius ungulatus* (30 mm, Xanthidae); 28, *Lophozozymus pictor* (120 mm, Xanthidae); 29, *Actaeodes tomentosus* (35 mm, Xanthidae); 30, *Atergatis floridus* (60 mm, Xanthidae); 31, *Eriphia sebana* (60 mm, Menippidae); 32, *Ocypode ceratophthalma* (45 mm, Ocypodidae); 33, *Ocypode cordimana* (30 mm, Ocypodidae); 34, *Grapsus strigosus* (70 mm, Grapsidae); 35, *Pachygrapsus minutus* (10 mm, Grapsidae). Figs 4 and 7 from Tirmizi and Kazmi 1988, 21 from Grant and McCulloch 1906; maximum carapace width for each species indicated.

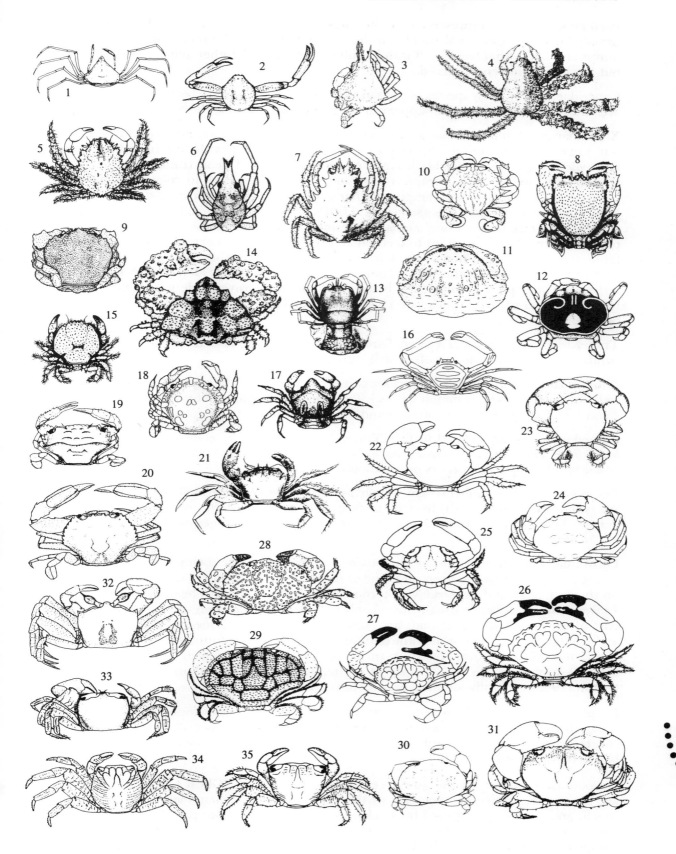

Parthenopidae — is represented by the large, grotesque, slow moving, *Daldorfia horrida*, usually burrowed into coral rubble on the reef flat or below the reef slope. It is a mass of lumps and knobs that blend well with its rubbly background. Other genera are also present but less commonly encountered.

Cancridae — only a few species of the sand burrowing *Kraussia* have been recorded, but more are undoubtedly present. They appear to live in the coarse sand at the base of coral clumps.

Xanthidae are dominant amongst the reef flat crab fauna. Most are herbivores or browsers, but some are commensals. Species of *Cymo* are associated with live branching corals. *Chlorodiella nigra* is a small black crab common in live and dead corals. Another closely related, common species, *Phymodius ungulatus,* is also often dark in colour but has many strong rounded lobes on the carapace. Other genera such as *Liomera* sp., *Actaea* sp., *Atergatis floridus, Leptodius exaratus, L. sanguineus* and *Eriphia sebana* are found amongst dead coral and rubble. The dark brown *Etisus laevimanus* is one of the largest crabs on the reef flat; it can often be seen when it emerges to feed on an evening low tide. *Carpilius maculatus*, also of a large size, is distinguished from *Carpilius convexus* by the big red spots on its shell. *Lophozozymus pictor* is another large, common species that is easily identified by being bright red with white spots. Serne (1984) is the most comprehensive guide to this family. Ward (1936) has recorded 30 species of 17 genera from Heron Island but many more species occur there.

Trapeziidae — species of *Trapezia, Tetralia,* and *Domecia* are associated with live branching corals (Patton 1966), and are often strikingly coloured.

Pilumnidae — there are many representatives of these "small hairy crabs", but they are not well known. The most common genus is *Pilumnus. Glabropilumnus dispar* is unusual in being smooth and shiny; it is most often found around the base of living coral.

Eumedonidae — are related to the Pilumnidae and many are commensals. *Ceratocarcinus longimanus* and *Harrovia elegans* have been found associated with crinoids. *Echinoecus pentagonus* (dull purple) occurs on echinoids.

Pinnotheridae (Pea Crabs) — are usually associated with bivalve molluscs. A small *Pinnixa* sp. (whitish and pea-sized), lives in pairs in the branchial cavity of the abalone *Haliotis asinina*. The unusually ornate *Xanthasia murigera* (with raised ridges on the carapace) occurs in *Tridacna* spp.

Portunidae (Swimming crabs) — are conspicuous on the reef flat, being aggressive predators and scavengers. *Thalamita stimpsoni* is one of the most abundant species, *T. admete* is common on the reef crest, and *T. coerulipes* is a common inhabitant of coral heads. A related species *Thalamitoides quadridens* is usually found only in living coral. *Portunus* spp. occur on the sandy part of the reef. Other portunids are "commensals", such as *Lissocarcinus orbicularis* (black and white) which occurs on holothurians and *Caphyra laevis* is found on *Xenia* (a soft coral) and *C. rotundifrons* is found on green turtle-weed (*Chlorodesmis comosa*). Portunids are one of the best known groups with the works of Stephenson and co-authors (various dates) and Griffin (1969) generally allowing easy identification.

Grapsidae — *Grapsus albolineatus* is a large greenish-brown species found on or under slabs of beach rock. *Pachygrapsus minutus* is a tiny intertidal species especially common on oyster covered rocks. The elusive and vibrantly coloured *Percnon planissimum* is found under coral blocks on the reef flat.

Ocypodidae — occur on the inner reef flat and beach. The "Ghost Crabs" (*Ocypode* spp.) are the most conspicuous members of this family. *Ocypode ceratophthalma* is found on the beach, and is easily recognized by its elongated, stalked, eyes and the characteristic brown patch on the shell. The other common species, *O. cordimana*, is usually found behind the frontal dunes and often well back onto land. Two species of *Macrophthalmus* are known. The very small and inconspicuous *M. boscii* lives intertidally on coral flats, burrowing into the fine white sand exposed near the beach. *M. telescopicus* lives subtidally in burrows on the floor of the lagoon.

Cryptochiridae — consists of a small number of genera which are obligatory associates of a variety of corals. *Hapalocarcinus marsupialis* is a common and widespread species in *Stylophora* and *Seriatopora* colonies, occupying a small gall formed by the coral branches. The female is imprisoned in the gall, where it is found and fertilized by the minute free-living male.

Hermit Crabs

(Order Decapoda, Infraorder Anomura)

Hermit crabs are a colourful and conspicuous part of the Great Barrier Reef fauna. They are generally scavengers or detrital feeders which are active both at night and during the daytime and can be seen scuttling across all areas of the reef. Being harmless, relatively shy creatures, they can be easily handled and are commonly picked up by reef visitors. The hermit crabs of the Great Barrier Reef vary in size from small individuals, less than 1 cm in length, to much larger ones which may reach nearly 30 cm. They also range from land or terrestrial hermit crabs which live above the high tide level on some coral cays, to large, deepwater dwelling specimens such as *Dardanus megistos*. All the other reef habitats from beach to crest have hermit crabs associated with them (Fig. 41).

On the Great Barrier Reef, all the species of hermit crab (except *Paguritta harmsi* which squats in serpulid polychaete worm tubes in massive corals) live in abandoned gastropod mollusc shells. Any mollusc shell, including old and damaged ones, is a potential home for a hermit crab; although certain species have particular shell preferences.

The following common species are known from the Great Barrier Reef:

Coenobitidae

Coenobita perlatus, the only coenobitid or terrestiral hermit crab on Heron Island is typically nocturnal. Adults with striking pale to a vivid red carapace and legs. Juveniles generally creamy-white with red bands on chelae and legs. Commonly found in sun-bleached *Turbo* shells. A small population is above the high tide level on the northern shore of Heron Island, amongst a large stand of *Casuarina* trees. Widely distributed in the Indo-Pacific. Great Barrier Reef records only from the Swains and Capricorn-Bunker Groups.

Diogenidae

Aniculus aniculus distinctly scutellate chelipeds and walking legs, setose eyestalks and stout chelipeds. Carapace olive green with red lines and spots, the lateral edge coarsely hirsute, the branchial region with reticulate brown and white markings. Eyestalks olive green dorsally, cream ventrally, with a dorsal red patch proximally and a thin yellow band adjacent to the corneas. Brown corneas have a conspicuous, horizontal white stripe in life. Basal segments of both antennae olive green with blue markings, flagellae of smaller set orange, larger set pale green. Chelipeds and walking legs hirsute, tuberculous and scutellate. Each scute olive green with a setose, vividly red coloured frontal margin. Chelae and dactyli black-tipped. Chelipeds stout, subequal in size. All body setae coarse and yellow. Uncommon, generally found on the reef flat. Recorded in *Turbo* shells.

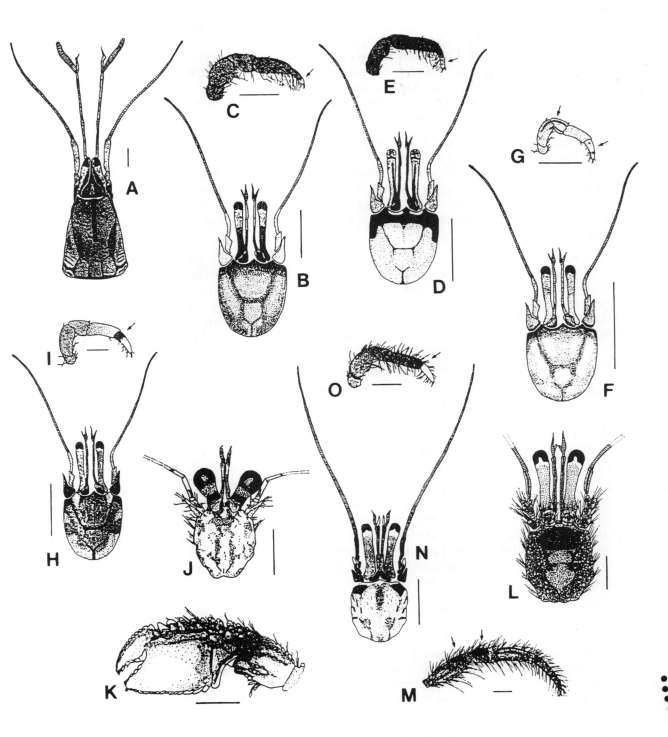

Fig. 41. **A,** *Coenobita perlatus,* dorsal view of head. **B, C,** *Calcinus gaimardii* (colour variant 1): **B,** dorsal view of head; **C,** lateral view of 2nd walking leg. **D, E,** *Calcinus gaimardii* (colour variant 2): **D,** dorsal view of head; **E,** lateral view of 2nd walking leg. **F, G,** *Calcinus laevimanus:* **F,** dorsal view of head; **G,** lateral view of 2nd walking leg. **H, I,** *Calcinus latens:* **H,** dorsal view of head; **I,** lateral view of 2nd walking leg. **J, K,** *Dardanus deformis:* **J,** dorsal view of head; **K,** external, lateral view of left cheliped. **L, M,** *Dardanus lagopodes:* **L,** dorsal view of head; **M,** lateral view of 2nd walking leg. **N, O,** *Clibanarius virescens:* **N,** dorsal view of head; **O,** lateral view of 2nd walking leg. (Scale bars 5 mm).

Calcinus gaimardii, small species. Two colour forms present on the reef. In both carapace greenish-white with shadings of brown, both antennae orange and chelipeds uniform rusty brown with tips of chelae white. Walking legs uniform rusty brown with a narrow white band next to the dark claw. In one form eyestalks dark brown proximally, with dark blue distally and corneas black with white spots. The second form has eyestalks orange laterally and ventrally but with longitudinal brown stripe on dorsal surface. Two narrow bands of light and dark blue immediately below corneas (white on black). Walking legs rusty brown proximally but orange distally with narrow white band present next to the dark claw. Recorded from *Conus, Turbo, Strombus, Trochus, Drupa* and *Cypraea* shells. Like *C. latens,* common from beachrock to reef crest.

Calcinus laevimanus similar to *C. gaimardii.* Carapace is greenish white or grey-green, eyestalks with basal half blue, distal half orange and cornea black or blue. Both antennae with orange flagella. Chelipeds dark brown with fingers showing varying amounts of white. Walking legs light brown proximally, with two dark brown longitudinal stripes on the merus and carpus. Dactyli white, with brown subdistal ring and subproximal spot. Recorded from a variety of shells, including *Nerita, Trochus, Drupa, Turbo, Littoraria, Epitonium* and *Cerithium,* on the reef flat.

Calcinus latens often in association with *C. laevimanus.* Carapace is greenish anteriorly, shading off to mottled green and white posteriorly. Eyestalks uniform greenish pink, corneas black and white spots. Smaller antennae blue with larger ones uniform orange. Chelipeds dark green with a few scattered white tubercles, gradually fading to white fingers. Walking legs dark green with white tubercles proximally, fading to a lighter grey-green and white distally. White dactyli with a deep brownish purple band proximally and dark tips. Recorded from a variety of shells including *Cerithium, Drupa, Trochus, Natica, Cypraea, Strombus* and *Rhinoclavis.* One of the most common species on the reef, from beach rock to rubble crest.

Calcinus minutus basically white with black mouthparts. The carapace is creamy-white, the eyestalks are uniform pale orange with a distal white ring next to the corneas (black with white spots). Small antennae black and large ones orange. Chelipeds and walking legs uniform white with scattered, small orange pits. Last two segments of walking legs tinged orange, dactylus brighter orange with black tips. Recorded from a variety of shells including *Drupella* and *Morula.* Uncommon, sometimes on branching corals (*Acropora* and *Pocillopora*).

Clibanarius corallinus, carapace reddish brown with three prominent, longitudinal stripes of lighter shading. Eyestalks reddish brown dorsally, orange laterally and mesially with blue corneas. Both antennae a uniform orange. Chelipeds reddish brown with white to yellow tubercles, thickly hirsute; chelae black-tipped. Walking legs coarsely hirsute, uniform reddish brown with yellowish tubercles. Common on the beachrock, especially under rocks at low tide with *Clibanarius virescens.* Recorded from *Morula, Peristernia, Cerithium, Littoraria* shells.

Clibanarius taeniatus, carapace, eyestalks, chelipeds and walking legs all conspicuously striped green-brown and creamy-yellow. Corneas whitish. Flagella of both small and large antennae orange to pale transparent yellow. Chelipeds hirsute and tuberculous, chelae black-tipped. Found on border of sand beach and algal zone in shells of *Rhinoclavis, Peristernia, Morula* and *Natica.* Common on the continental shores of eastern Australia but records from Heron Island and neighbouring Masthead Island are the only ones for the reef. The Capricorn-Bunker Group of reefs could be its most northerly limit.

Clibanarius virescens, the background colour varies from yellow, olive-green, green-blue, blue or brown. Dactylar annulus on the walking legs present, absent or incomplete. Carapace olive with shades of dark and light brown. Eyestalks olive or dark brown, except for narrow white ring, proximal to corneas (black with white spots). Smaller antennae olive in colour fading to orange distally, larger ones uniform blue with orange tip. Chelipeds olive or brown with white tubercles and white fingers with black-tips. Walking legs olive or dark brown with darker coloured band at distal end of propodus. Dactyli white with black claws. Recorded from a wide variety of shells including *Cerithium, Cypraea, Nerita, Morula, Rhinoclavis, Strombus, Turbo, Terebra* and *Conus*, commonly at low tide under beachrocks with *C. corallinus*. Common in the Indo-West Pacific and locally abundant on all east coast Australian shores.

Dardanus deformis with large left cheliped used as an operculum to close its shell and with anemones on the shell. Carapace mottled browny-green with a branching pattern on branchial region. Eyestalks short, white with dark brown transverse band subproximally and lighter brown band distally. Corneas vivid light green. Both antennae and their flagella uniformly grey-green. The chelipeds tuberculous, creamy-white with faint orange on dorsal and inner surface. Small irregular orange spots over chelipeds, chelae black-tipped. Left cheliped larger than right, with two to three distinct dorsal rows of tubercles or spines, and ventral edge distinct, with a single row of tubercles. Walking legs coloured as for chelipeds, with distinctively sharp dorsal and ventral edges. Recorded from *Tonna, Turbo* and *Terebra* shells, commonly with two species of anemone attached to the outside of its shell — a larger brown and white striped *Calliactis polypus* on the back of the shell and a smaller species, *Sagartiomorphe paguri*, often attached inside the mouth.

Dardanus guttatus, carapace reddish purple with numerous tan and whitish spots, and large, dark green-blue marking anteriorly. Eyestalks purplish pink with narrow white ring adjacent to black corneas. Both antennae uniform purplish pink with transparent light brown flagella. Walking legs and chelipeds reddish purple with white spots (elongated on second walking leg), dorsal surface of carpus with large, dark green-blue spot covering most of segment. Body including legs and chelipeds, covered with reddish purple setae with white tips. Uncommon, previously recorded from cone shells.

Dardanus lagopodes, two colour forms, a "black" and a "red", often found together. The carapace is mottled red and white with a purplish red (or black) patch anteriorly. The eyestalks pinky-grey with a yellow band distally near black corneas. Both antennae with yellow-orange or pale green flagella. Chelipeds hirsute, tuberculous and mottled red, brown, orange and white with large purplish red or black patch dorsally on carpus (similar to carapace patch). Chelae black-tipped. Walking legs mottled red-brown with flecks of pale violet, carpus with similar patch to that on the chelipeds. Setae on body, chelipeds and legs red with cream tips. Commonly live in broad-mouthed shells such as *Syrinx, Tectus, Latirus, Angaria* and *Lambis* but also in some narrow-mouthed shells such as *Conus* and *Strombus*. On the outer reef flat and crest, the majority of specimens occupy *Tectus* shells.

Dardanus megistos is one of the largest species in this family, sometimes up to 30 cm long. Larger individuals often in deep water, smaller ones on the reef flat and crest. Carapace, antennae, chelipeds, walking legs bright orange-red with white spots ringed with black. Red setal tufts from most of the spots sometimes with white tips on carapace. Eyestalks similar, bright orange-red, corneas black. Tips of chelae black. Dactyli with dark tips. Recorded from a variety of shells including *Turbo* and *Strombus* with larger individuals commonly in *Charonia tritonis* shells.

Dardanus scutellatus, carapace mottled brown, fawn and green with white spots, a darker red-brown patch anteriorly. Eyestalks white with thin orange band adjacent to dark corneas (appearing bright blue dorsally). Basal segments of both antennae white with longitudinal dark dorsal stripes, with orange transparent flagella. Chelipeds and walking legs covered with reddish setae, coloured as for carapace, merus and carpus with similar red-brown patches. Dactyli of legs with black tips. Small brown tips on chelae. Left cheliped is slightly compressed with upper margin spinose and the outer surface granulous. Common on inner reef flat in sand and algal zone, all individuals occupying shells of *Strombus luhuanus*.

Trizopagurus strigatus, rarely seen but vivid coloration allows easy identification. Carapace is pure white, conspicuous, flat, broad and not hirsute. Eyestalks solid dark orange. Both antennae dark orange with transparent flagella. Chelipeds distinctly annulated, though smooth, with alternating bright red and orange bands, fingers solid orange and tips of chelae black. Walking legs as for chelipeds except solid orange dactyli with a black tip. Inner surface of chelae with stridulating apparatus. Young specimens recorded in *helmet, mitre* and *murex* shells. Adults usually in *Conus* shells in deep waters.

119

Paguridae

Paguritta harmsi, small, rarely encountered, inhabits vacated serpulid tubes *(Spirobranchus giganteus)* in massive corals. Carapace yellow-orange, posterior half with four longitudinal red-brown lines. Eyestalks yellow-white with red-brown dorsal and lateral longitudinal stripes. Corneas black with white spots. Both antennae yellow-orange with lateral red-brown stripes, but the larger of the two with red-brown flagella with two rows of yellow, plumose setae. Walking legs compressed and setose with yellow tips. Chelipeds yellow unequal, right slight larger than left, upper surface of right chela flat and thickly covered with spines, setae and downy hairs. Abdomen is soft and straight. They have been recorded from *Astreopora myriophthalma, Millepora platyphyllia, Montipora verrucosa, Cyphastrea* sp., *Goniastrea* sp., and *Porites* corals. This species filter feeds on plankton using its feathered second antennae.

Pagurus hirtimanus, carapace setose, mottled tan and white. Eyestalks short and white with median transverse dark, browny-green band and black corneas. Both antennae blue proximally, smaller pair with yellow-orange flagellae. Chelipeds heavily setose, mottled brown and white (as for carapace). Chelae more uniform brown. Right chela larger than left and used as an operculum when individual withdraws into shell. Proximal segments of heavily setose, walking legs mottled browny-orange with large whitish areas, carpus and propodus whitish with a median brown band. Dactyli whitish with black tips. *P. hirtimanus* sometimes confused with *Dardanus deformis* because of the similarity in eyestalk colour and the large operculum-like chela. *P. hirtimanus* has an unusual habit of withdrawing noisily and rapidly into its shell when handled. This species was collected on the reef flat and was recorded from shells of *Turbo* species.

Key to the Families and Genera of Common Hermit Crabs of the Great Barrier Reef

1. Terrestrial or semi-terrestrial; strongly compressed eyestalks with corneas terminal and lateral .... **Coenobitidae**
   Marine; eyestalks variously separated; corneas terminal only 2

2. Chelipeds equal or subequal, or left distinctly larger than right .... **Diogenidae** — 3
   Left cheliped never larger than right, right usually much larger than left .... **Paguridae** — 7

3. Chelae opening and closing horizontally; chelipeds equal or subequal .... **Clibanarius**
   Chelae opening and closing obliquely or near vertically 4

4. Tips of chelae calcareous .... **Calcinus**
   Tips of chelae corneous and blackened 5

5. Tips of chelae crescent-shaped; left cheliped usually larger than right, the two occasionally subequal .... **Dardanus**
   Tips of chelae hoof-shaped; chelipeds equal or subequal; chelipeds, 2nd and 3rd pereopods transversely ringed 6

6. Posterior carapace with transverse groove; chelipeds and legs with regular transverse scutes or grooves; chelae without stridulating apparatus on inner surface .... **Aniculus**
   Posterior carapace without transverse groove; chelae with stridulating apparatus on inner surface .... **Trizopagurus**

7. Abdomen straight; antennal flagella with two rows of long plumose setae; usually inhabit serpulid polychaete tubes in massive corals .... **Paguritta**
   Abdomen recurved to one side; peropods 1–3 heavily setose; inhabiting gastropod shells .... **Pagurus**

Phylum Mollusca

Molluscs have calcareous shells, a large muscular foot and a rasping tongue (radula). These three characteristics have enabled them to adapt to a wide range of habitats in the sea, rivers, lakes and estuaries, and on land. Their calcareous shells protect their otherwise soft bodies from mechanical damage and desiccation. Some, such as the marine species which survive exposure in intertidal regions, and even above the high tide mark, can accommodate variations in their environment either by closing the shell with an operculum, or by sealing it tightly to rocky substrates (periwinkles and limpets).

Shell form is highly variable and suited to the lifestyle of a particular species. Hence species that live on the seafloor, such as helmets and muricids, tend to have heavy, ornamented shells; those with a foot modified for swimming have light, delicate and often reduced shells. Some, such as nudibranchs, lack shells, but their brightly coloured bodies may protect them from predators instead. Some of the smallest species, such as eulimids, live parasitically on other organisms, and others live interstitially among the fine sand grains of the intertidal zone.

The large muscular foot characteristic of molluscs enhances their capacity to use their environment to the full. With it they can creep or crawl, or they can use it as a wide vane or fin for swimming, or it can be used as a float.

There also is a wide range in the types of food preferred by different molluscs. Their main feeding organ, the tooth-bearing, tongue-like organ called the radula, tears or scrapes and pulls food particles into the mouth. Herbivores use their radula to rasp micro-algae off hard or soft substrates. In some carnivorous species, prey are immobilized by a toxin secreted by a poison gland, and administered by a radula tooth that flicks out on the end of a long proboscis. Other species (especially bivalves) are filter-feeders, straining micro-organisms from the water that flows over their gill filaments.

Molluscs are divided into five main classes: Polyplacophora, Gastropoda, Bivalvia, Cephalopoda, Scaphopoda. There is not, at present, a full list of species from any part of the Great Barrier Reef. It is certain, however, that when such a list is eventually compiled it will be formidable. Commonly occurring species are indicated in the notes that are set out below, and illustrations of some of these are presented as a guide to the major groups. For more detailed descriptions of particular species the works cited in the reference list should be consulted.

Class Polyplacophora — Chitons

Chitons are an ancient group of molluscs, found only in the sea — from the intertidal zone to abyssal depths, and from tropical to polar regions. They are bilaterally symmetrical, usually dorsoventrally flattened, with eight valves (usually articulating) surrounded by a muscular naked, scaly, spiny or spiculose girdle (Fig. 44:1).

The representatives of most families and subfamilies on the Great Barrier Reef are found in intertidal pools and shallow subtidal locations on or under rocks, dead coral, pebbles and shell fragments in sediments. Usually clean sediments are favoured, but Schizochitonidae are in muddy rather than clean sand. Acanthochitonidae occasionally bore into dead coral and limestones. A few species live on seagrasses or mangrove pneumatophores. Acanthopleurinae and Mopaliidae are often exposed by the tide, the former returning to intertidal homesites on rocks and dead coral after feeding, and the latter living in exposed high energy locations. Callochitoninae are found on rocks in deeper water.

Chitons are usually grazers, many feeding on algae from the substrate surface, but some on encrusting animals such as sponges, ascidians and bryozoans.

Lepidopleuridae

Mainly small (<15 mm), colourless; valves lack insertion plates; valve sculpture granulose, e.g., *Leptochiton (L.) liratellus.*

Chitonidae

Small to large (to 130 mm long). Three subfamilies, all represented on the Great Barrier Reef.

Chitoninae, on the Great Barrier Reef, small to medium (to about 40 mm); valve sculpture microgranulose to strongly grooved; girdle with closely packed, smooth or striate scales, e.g., *Tegulaplax hululensis, Rhyssoplax venusta.*

Acanthopleurinae, large to very large (to 130 mm); valves thick, heavy, sculpture coarsely granular to wrinkled, but usually eroded; girdle with dense arrangement of spikes, spines and scales, e.g., *Acanthopleura gaimardi, A. gemmata, A. spinosa.*

Toniciinae, small to large (to 70 mm); valves sculptured with nodules, pits and grooves, usually with striking colour patterns; extrapigmentary ocelli usually numerous on all valves; girdle with microscopic scales and spicules, e.g., *Onithochiton quercinus, Tonicia (Lucilina) fortilirata, T. (L.) lamellosa.*

Ischnochitonidae

Small to large. Six subfamilies, three represented on the Great Barrier Reef:

Ischnochitoninae, small to medium (to 30 mm) on the Great Barrier Reef; valves smooth to sculptured; girdle with scales, e.g., *Ischnochiton (I.) luticolens, I. (Haploplax) adelaidensis, I. (H.) arbutum.*

Callochitoninae, small to medium (to 20 mm); valve sculpture finely granulose; girdle with fine, imbricating spicules, e.g., *Callochiton rufus.*

Callistoplacinae, small to medium (to 20 mm); valves sculptured, usually with elevated ribs; girdle with scales, e.g., *Callistochiton periousius, C. generos, C. granifer.*

Mopaliidae

On the Great Barrier Reef, small (to 10 mm); valves sculptured with pustules and wrinkles; girdle with various hairs, bristles and spines, never scales, e.g. *Plaxiphora (P.) parva.*

Schizochitonidae

Medium to large (to 50 mm); valves with conspicuous ocelli; sculptured with grooves and ridges, girdle scaly with spiculose tufts or hairs, and posteriorly slit, e.g., *Schizochiton incisus.*

Acanthochitonidae

Small to large (to 150 mm); valves usually reduced, sometimes not articulating in adult *Cryptoplax*, insertion plates usually large; girdle fleshy, large, spiculose with sutural tufts; often elongate, even vermiform, and usually flexible, e.g., *Acanthochitona shirleyi, A. complanata, Craspedochiton laqueatus, Cryptoplax larvaeformis*.

Class Gastropoda

Snails

The most diverse group of molluscs with a corresponding diversity in shell, colour, shape and ornamentation, gastropods usually have a single shell coiled into a spiral (Fig. 42) or modified into a cap-like structure (as in limpets). Sometimes, as in nudibranchs, the shell is absent altogether.

Subclass Prosobranchia

Prosobranchs occur principally in the sea, but also are found in fresh water and some are terrestrial. They include most of the single-shelled molluscs prized by collectors (Fig. 43). The muscular foot is used for crawling and only rarely is adapted for swimming or floating. The divisions (orders), based on characteristics of the tooth-bearing radula, are not discussed here. The major families are set out below:

Fissurellidae (False, Slit, or Keyhole Limpets). Shell conical, with a wide aperture and usually perforated either by an apical hole or a slit or notch at the anterior edge of the outer lip. Usually herbivores, grazing over rock surfaces. *Scutus antipodes, Diodora jukesi.*

Haliotidae (Abalone). Shells flat with an enormously expanded and depressed body whorl and a wide open aperture, an iridescent lining and a row of perforations around the outer edge. Live under stones or in crevices. *H. asinina*, with the dull green folds of the body almost covering the shell, is conspicuous in pools and under boulders toward the outer edge of reefs at low tide. Herbivores. *Haliotis asinina, H. varia, H. ovina.*

Trochidae (Top Shells, Wide-mouthed Shells). Shell conical usually with a flattened base. In some species the whorls are depressed and the shell is a wide, shallow cone, often very ornamented. Operculum spiral, circular, horny. Found on rocky substrates and amongst weed. Herbivores. *Trochus maculatus, T. histrio, T. niloticus, Tectus pyramis, Clanculus atropurpureus, Chrysostoma paradoxum, Thalotia marginata, Pseudostomatella maculata, Stomatia phymotis.*

Liotiidae (Wheel Shells). Shell small with rounded and depressed whorls. The operculum partly calcareous. Herbivores. *Liotina peronii.*

Turbinidae (Turbans, Tent or Star Shells). Shell whorls usually rounded and the body whorl expanded. Shells often difficult to distinguish from trochids because the aperture is circular, there is a pearly lining and the whorls are sometimes flattened. Operculum (cats eye) characteristically hard, calcareous. Found in shallow waters. Herbivores. *Turbo argyrostomus.*

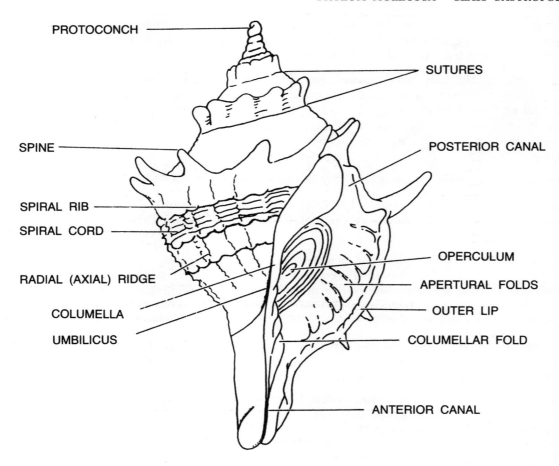

PROTOCONCH

SUTURES

SPINE

POSTERIOR CANAL

SPIRAL RIB

SPIRAL CORD

OPERCULUM

RADIAL (AXIAL) RIDGE

APERTURAL FOLDS

OUTER LIP

COLUMELLA

UMBILICUS

COLUMELLAR FOLD

ANTERIOR CANAL

Fig. 42. Generalized gastropod shell showing main external feature.

Neritidae (Nerites). The basal (or body) whorl of the shell is swollen and there are only few apical whorls. A shelf extends from the inside border of the opening and partially occludes it. The animal is well protected within the shell when the calcareous, pegged operculum is tightly locked against this shelf. They are therefore well suited to intertidal locations. Herbivores. *Nerita albicilla, N. costata, N. plicata, N. polita.*

Patellidae (True Limpets). Shell conical, not coiled. These limpets are able to cling tightly to rocks, and thus avoid desiccation and damage by strong surf and breaking waves. Herbivores. *Patella flexuosa.*

Littorinidae (Periwinkles). Shell generally small, regularly coiled and conical. Live in the intertidal area, usually in clusters. Herbivores. *Nodilittorina pyramidalis, N. millegrana, Littoraria undulata.*

Planaxidae (Cluster Winks). Shells solid, pointed with a long body whorl. Aperture slightly elliptical in contrast to the usually circular littorinid opening. Herbivores. *Planaxis sulcatus* is a common species on beachrock.

Rissoidae. A large group with varied and mostly very minute shells. Often herbivores. Sometimes found on algae.

Calyptraeidae (Slipper Limpets). Shell wide open, delicate and conical with the apex only slightly coiled. An internal shelf creates a shallow cavity in the apex of the shell. Filter-feeders. *Crepidula aculeata.*

Xenophoridae (Carrier Shells). Shell usually with pebble debris and other shells attached to a rather depressed spiral shell. Live on the sea floor. Deposit feeders. *Xenophora solarioides.*

125

Hipponicidae (Horse's Hoof Limpets). Shell small, depressed, limpet-like, often without an apical spiral; thin and wrinkled or with fine radiating ribs. Live permanently attached to rocks or other shells. Deposit feeders. *Hipponix conicus.*

Cerithiidae (Creepers). Shell tapered and elongate often with strong spiral sculpture. Body whorl not usually expanded. Siphonal canal recurved. Operculum with few spirals. Closely related to Potamididae (Mud Whelks usually are found associated with mangroves). Most live in shallow sandy lagoons or offshore waters. Detrital feeders. *Clypeomorus moniliferus* (common on the beachrock), *Rhinoclavis aspera, R. fasciata, R. sinensis, R. brettinghami, R. vertagus.*

Triphoridae. Like small Cerithiidae, but the shell usually is coiled to the left. Sponge feeders.

Siliquariidae (Slit-worm Shells). Shell long, irregularly coiled and often attached to coral or other shells. A long slit, or a series of holes, runs along the shell. Filter feeders. *Siliquaria ponderosa.*

Strombidae (Strombs, Spider or Scorpion Shells). Shell solid, porcellaneous and often brightly coloured with outer lip flared and sometimes extended into pointed projections. Body whorl long, the aperture narrow and elongate. A distinctive notch is on the anterior part of the outer lip. Herbivores and detrital feeders. *Strombus luhuanus, S. mutabilis, S. gibberulus, Lambis lambis.*

Architectonicidae (Sundial Shells). Shell discoidal with a depressed spire and flattened base. Aperture rounded and the umbilicus large and deep. Found on the sea floor in relatively shallow water. Carnivores on cnidarians. *Heliacus variegatus.*

Ranellidae (Tritons, Trumpet Shells, Kookaburra Shells). Whorls rounded and interrupted by varices. Body whorl expanded and extended anteriorly to enclose a narrow canal. Aperture rounded or elliptical. The large Trumpet Shell *(Charonia tritonis),* renowned as a predator of the Crown of Thorns starfish, is protected by law. *Cymatium rubeculum, Gyrineum pulchellum.*

Bursidae (Frog Shells). Very like ranellids but with a more knobbly shell and a posterior canal on the outer lip. Carnivores on polychaete and sipunculid worms. *Bursa granularis.*

Cassidae (Helmet Shells). Shell with spire depressed and body whorl inflated. Aperture large and often with a thickened, toothed outer lip. Often found in shallow waters. Carnivores on echinoderms. *Cassis cornuta, Casmaria erinaceus.*

Tonnidae (Tun Shells). Shell thin, almost spherical with strong spiral cords. Spire depressed and body whorl inflated. Carnivores on echinoderms, bivalves and crustaceans. *Tonna perdix.*

Ficidae (Fig Shells). Shell delicate and fig-shaped. Body whorl expanded, but narrows anteriorly. Carnivores on echinoderms. *Ficus subintermedia.*

Cypraeidae (Cowries). Shell solid, and polished with body whorl extended to envelop and hide the spire. The outer lip turns in and teeth develop along both sides of the elongate aperture. Mostly herbivores. *Cypraea tigris, C. vitellus, C. caputserpentis, C. arabica, C. errones, C. caurica, C. erosa, C. moneta, C. asellus, C. lynx, C. staphylaea, C. talpa.* The small, yellow "ring cowrie" *(Cypraea annulus)* is especially common, under boulders, toward the edge of reefs.

Ovulidae (Egg and Spindle Cowries). Shell similar to that of cowries but sometimes with greatly extended posterior and anterior canals. Carnivores on cnidarians. *Ovula ovum.*

Triviidae (Bean Cowries). Shell small and cowry-shaped, usually with fine cross-ribbing extending from the apertual teeth across the dorsum. Carnivores on ascidians. *Trivirostra oryza.*

Vanikoridae. Shell similar in shape to that of naticids but the surface with conspicuous cancellate sculpture. Detritivores. *Vanikoro cancellata.*

Naticidae (Sand Snails, Moon Shells). Shell solid, porcellaneous, smooth and almost spherical with an inflated body whorl and depressed spire. Umbilicus in the centre of the basal whorl is sometimes conspicuous, only partially occluded or closed by a callus (plug-like thickening of the shell). Common just under the surface on sandy beaches where their trails can be seen as long raised ridges of sand. Carnivores on bivalves and other molluscs. *Natica gualteriana, N. onca, Polinices tumidus.*

Muricidae (Murex Shells, Purples, Mulberry Whelks). Shell ornamentation interrupted by rib-like varices. Body whorl expanded and produced anteriorly to enclose a narrow canal. Aperture circular to elliptical. Like ranellids, but shells usually more ornamented and varices usually more numerous. Carnivores. *Chicoreus brunneus, Drupa morum, Morula spinosa, M. margariticola, M. marginalba, Thais kieneri, Thais tuberosa.*

Columbellidae (Dove Shells). Shell small, solid, and often brightly coloured. Body whorl long and narrows anteriorly. Aperture elongate, often with teeth on the outer lip. Carnivores mainly on crustaceans. *Pyrene testudinaria, Mitrella ligula.*

Nassariidae (Dog Whelks). Shell often strongly nodulose or ribbed with a tapered spire and more or less rounded aperture. A deeply excised notch for the anterior canal and sometimes a conspicuous notch for the posterior canal. Inner lip of the aperture is usually reflected and sometimes denticles are on the outer lip. Scavengers and carnivores. *Nassarius albescens, N. coronatus.*

Fasciolariidae (Tulip Shells, Spindle Shells). Shell large, solid, high-spired with fine spiral ridges and longitudinal ribs. Body whorl extended to enclose a narrow canal. Often plaits are on the inner lip of the aperture. Carnivores on worms and bivalves. *Latirus nodatus, Peristernia australiensis.*

Buccinidae (True Whelks). Shell small to large and solid. Body whorl expanded with a short to long siphonal canal, ribs and/or spiral ridges, and a deep notch for the anterior canal. Carnivores and scavengers. *Cantharus undosus, Engina alveolata.*

Harpidae (Harp Shells). Shell brightly coloured with regular longitudinal ribs, an inflated body whorl and wide aperture. Carnivores on crabs and shrimps. *Harpa amouretta.*

Volutidae (Volutes, Baler Shells). Shell large and highly polished usually with a short spire. Aperture narrow to expanded and with characteristic plaits across the inner lip. Species found at all depths, from shallow to deep waters, on the continental shelf and in lagoons. Carnivores on bivalves, gastropods and hermit crabs. *Cymbiolacca pulchra, Amoria maculata, Melo amphora.*

Olividae (Olive Shells). Shell solid, brightly coloured and polished with a short spire, long oval body whorl, long narrow aperture, numerous plaits across the inner lip and a conspicuous notch for the posterior canal. Carnivores mainly on small bivalves and crustaceans. *Oliva annulata.*

Cancellariidae (Nutmeg Shells). Shell small and spire elevated, often with strong ribs and some concentric sculpture. Body whorl expanded, aperture rounded, and plaits on inner lip. Outer lip thickened and crenulated. *Trigonostoma scalarina.*

Mitridae (Mitre Shells). Shell elongate and high-spired with a long and narrow body whorl. Plaits on the inner lip become more pronounced toward posterior end of the narrow aperture. Carnivores on peanut worms. *Mitra cucumerina, M. mitra.*

Costellariidae (Ribbed Mitres). Shell features generally similar to the Mitridae except for the presence of strong axial sculpture. Carnivores on small invertebrates. *Vexillum plicarium.*

Turbinellidae (Vase Shells). Shell solid with shouldered whorls which have spines or tubercles. The body whorl narrows anteriorly and there are plaits on the internal lip of the aperture. Carnivores. *Vasum ceramicum, V. turbinellus.*

Turridae (Notch Shells). Shells elongate and tapered, whorls rounded or shouldered, usually with both spiral cords and radial ribs. Body whorl narrows anteriorly. A deep notch

127

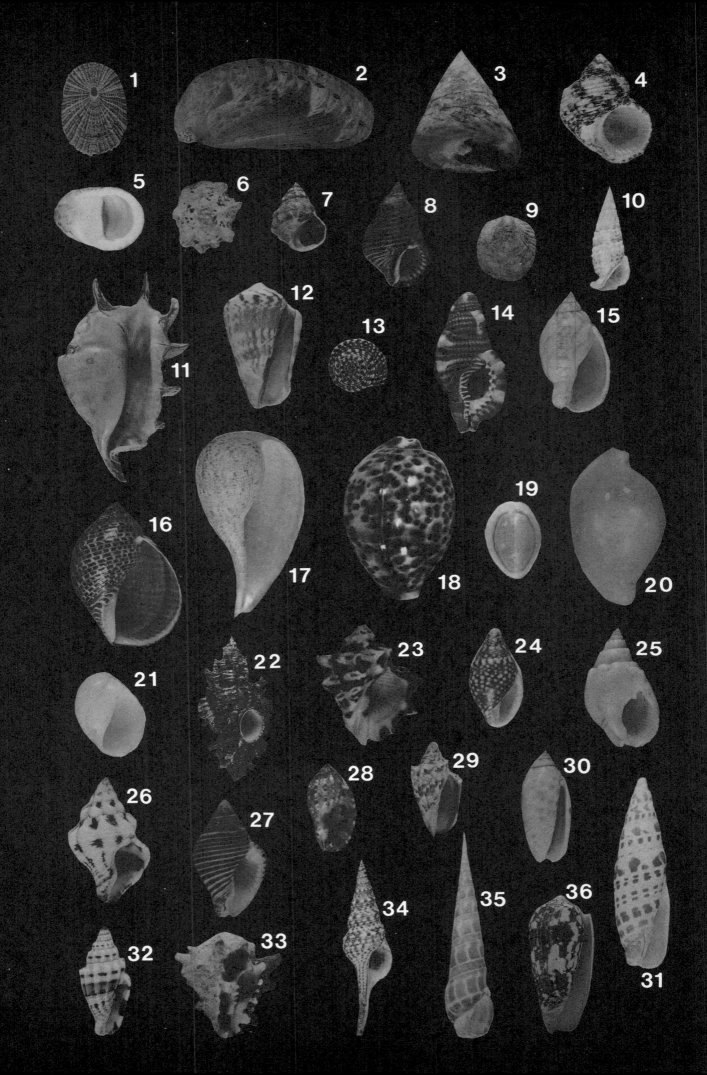

is at the posterior end of the outer lip. An anterior canal is present. Carnivores, with a poison gland associated with their usually needle-like teeth. *Lophiotoma indica, Lienardia rubida.*

Terebridae (Auger Shells). Shell brightly coloured, long and tapered with regular flattened whorls, sometimes sculptured. Body whorl not lengthened, aperture small and outer lip thin. These shells can be confused with those of Pyramidellidae (a family of the opisthobranch molluscs), which generally can be distinguished by the conspicuous pleats on the inner lip of the aperture. Carnivores with poison apparatus. *Terebra dimidiata, T. areolata.*

Conidae (Cone Shells). Shell conical with depressed spire and elongate aperture. Colour pattern variable. These carnivores contain dart-like teeth in the proboscis associated with a poison apparatus. The poison, which immobilizes invertebrate and often vertebrate (fish) prey, is sometimes dangerous to humans. Some species have been implicated in fatalities but care should be taken with all *Conus* because reaction to the poison may depend on individual tolerance. *Conus arenatus, C. capitaneus, C. geographus, C. coronatus, C. generalis, C. lividus, C. miles, C. miliaris, C. rattus, C. virgo, C. ebraeus, C. eburneus, C. flavidus, C. planorbis, C. textile, C. striatus, C. vexillum, C. chaldaeus.*

Fig. 43. Common gastropods of the Great Barrier Reef: 1, *Diodora jukesi.* 2, *Haliotis asinina.* 3, *Tectus pyramis.* 4, *Turbo argyrostomus.* 5, *Nerita polita.* 6, *Patella flexuosa.* 7, *Nodilittorina pyramidalis.* 8, *Planaxis sulcatus.* 9, *Hipponix conicus.* 10, *Rhinoclavis aspera.* 11, *Lambis lambis.* 12, *Strombus luhuanus.* 13, *Heliacus variegatus.* 14, *Cymatium rubeculum.* 15, *Casmaria erinaceus.* 16, *Tonna perdix.* 17, *Ficus subintermedia.* 18, *Cypraea tigris.* 19, *Cypraea annulus.* 20, *Ovula ovum.* 21, *Polinices tumidus.* 22, *Chicoreus brunneus.* 23, *Thais tuberosa.* 24, *Pyrene testudinaria.* 25, *Nassarius coronatus.* 26, *Peristernia australiensis.* 27, *Cantharus undosus.* 28, *Harpa amouretta.* 29, *Cymbiolacca pulchra.* 30, *Oliva annulata.* 31, *Mitra mitra.* 32, *Vexillum plicarium.* 33, *Vasum turbinellus.* 34, *Lophiotoma indica.* 35, *Terebra dimidiata.* 36, *Conus striatus.*

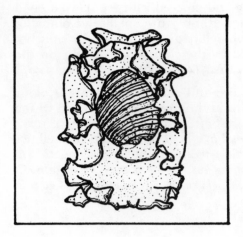

Subclass Opisthobranchia

(Class Gastropoda)

Many people think of opisthobranchs as the spectacularly shaped and coloured nudibranchs and the soft-bodied sea-slugs, which lack a protective shell. However, there are many other orders (some included in the summary below) which have evolved a nudibranch-like form. Within the subclass there are many evolutionary lines showing the progression from "snail" with a large protective shell, to "slug" in which the shell is completely lost (Fig. 44:2–12).

While most are benthic, burrowing through soft sediments or crawling over the bottom, there are some spectacular examples such as the pteropods, which are planktonic.

Opisthobranchs are found throughout the world, and even the brightly coloured nudibranchs are found not only in tropical seas, but also in cool waters, such as the seas around Tasmania, New Zealand and Europe.

Some of the more conspicuous external characters of the major orders are listed below. A more detailed treatment will be found in Thompson (1976).

Order Cephalaspidea (Bullomorpha)

This order contains the Bubble Shells, Tailed Slugs, etc. — a whole range of species from primitive acteonids with large external shells to vividly coloured gastropterids and aglajids with greatly reduced internal shell remnant. Mostly carnivores, some on worms while others, with hard gizzard plates, ingest and crush whole bivalves. Some feed on other bullomorphs. Two families (Bullidae, Haminoeidae) are herbivorous.

Hydatinidae: Thin external shell, with foot developed into large thin folded lobes which partly enclose shell. Specialized vermivores. *Hydatina physis, H. amplustre.*

Acteonidae: Usually infaunal burrowers, with relatively large, heavily calcified external shell. Operculum usually retained. Specialized vermivores. *Pupa nitidula.*

Aglajidae: Greatly reduced flattened internal shell. Foot on each side developed into a large parapodial lobe which folds up to partially enclose body. Often brightly coloured. The genus *Philinopsis* includes infaunal burrowers feeding on bubble shells, while in *Chelidonura*, two long tapering "tails" project from the posterior end of the body, leading to the common name "tailed slugs".

Gastropteridae: Small internal shell. Body with very enlarged parapodial lobes which are used for swimming when animal disturbed. *Sagaminopteron ornatum.*

130

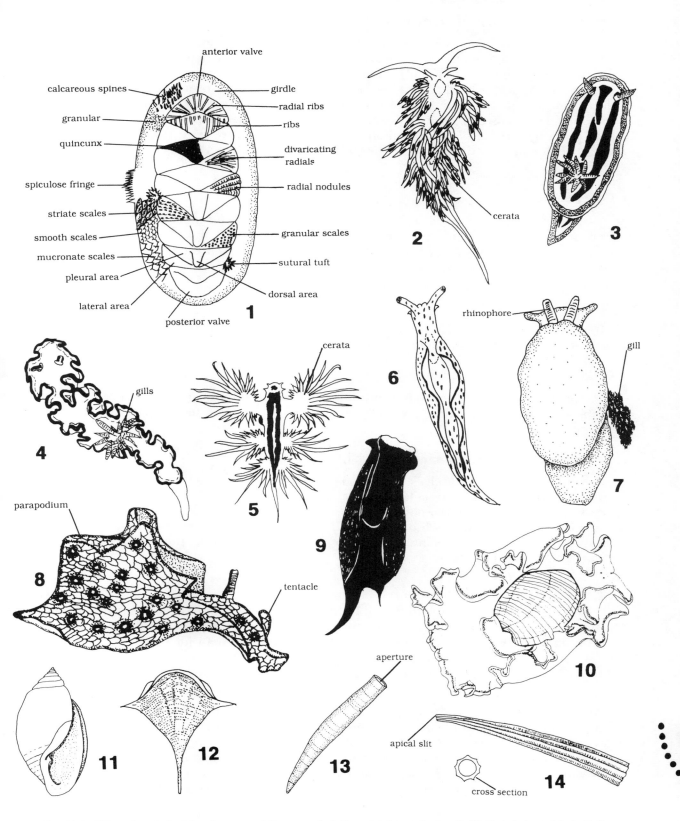

Fig. 44. 1, **Chiton** dorsal view showing general features of girdle and valve sculpture. 2–12, **Opisthobranchia** 2, *Godiva rachelae*; 3, *Chromodoris magnifica*; 4, *Glossodoris atromarginata*; 5, *Glaucus atlanticus*; 6, *Elysia ornata*; 7, *Berthellina citrina*; 8, *Aplysia dactylomela*; 9, *Chelidonura inornata*; 10, *Hydatina physis*; 11, *Pupa nitidula*; 12, *Diacria trispinosa*, a pteropod. 13–14, **Scaphopoda** 13, *Dentalium* sp.; 14, *Cadulus* sp. (Scale Lines = 1 cm).

131

Order Anaspidea (Aplysiomorpha)

Commonly known as "Sea Hares" from classical times, because of the resemblance of a Mediterranean species to the European Hare, when sitting. They have a reduced flattened internal shell. The foot is usually large and muscular and there is usually a large lateral parapodial flap on each side enclosing the mantle. Many species produce a purple ink when disturbed. Their colour is usually a nondescript patterning of browns and greens, camouflaging them well amongst their algal food. Often their presence is only detected in tidal pools by a cloud of purple ink appearing after they have been stood on or partially squashed by an overturned rock. The most familiar family is Aplysiidae, containing the genus *Aplysia*.

Order Sacoglossa

The saccoglossans are so named because of a special sac in their mouth to hold used radular teeth. Their teeth are knife-like blades used to pierce algal cells so that they can suck out the cell sap on which they feed. There are forms representing all stages in the evolution from a shelled snail to a shell-less "nudibranch".

Polybranchidae. Without shell. Body covered with leaf-like cerata, which can produce a sticky white secretion when disturbed. *Cyerce nigricans*.

Elysiidae. Without shell. Body dominated by pair of large flattened parapodial lobes which usually lie folded over each other. *Elysia ornata*.

Orders Thecosomata, Gymnosomata

Shelled and naked pteropods, morphologically adapted for planktonic existence. Shelled forms are phytoplankton feeders while gymnosomes apparently feed exclusively on other pteropods.

Order Notaspidea (Pleurobranchomorpha)

Side-gilled slugs, Umbrella shells, mostly with reduced, flattened internal shell, although the primitive *Umbraculum* has a large limpet-like external shell. They have a large flattened oral veil, and as the common name suggests the large gill is found on the right side of the body. Common genera are *Pleurobranchus*, *Berthellina*. They are carnivores: most specialize on sponges, ascidians or coelenterates, but others seem to feed on a range of dead or dying carcases. *Berthellina citrina*.

Order Nudibranchia

Sea-Slugs, without a shell in the adult. Body bilaterally symmetrical (apart from renal, genital openings and anus). Body often brightly coloured, and often defensive glands are incorporated in the skin. All are carnivores. They have evolved a wide variety of shapes but most have evolved a pair of antero-dorsal chemosensory tentacles, known as "rhinophores". The higher classification of the group is not clearly resolved. Three major suborders are listed below.

Suborder Doridoidea — Most dorids are characterized by a circlet of gills arranged around a poster-dorsal anus. The phanerobranch (Anadoridoidea) dorids usually have a high elongate body and feed on a wide variety of fouling organisms including bryozoans (*Polycera*, *Corambe*), ascidians (*Goniodoris*, *Nembrotha*), sponges (*Notodoris*), and other nudibranchs (*Robastra*, *Gymnodoris*). On the other hand, the cryptobranch (Eudoridoidea) dorids have a flattened ovate body, and are usually sponge-feeding (*Asteronotus*, *Discodoris*, *Platydoris*, *Halgerda*, *Rostanga*).

The family **Chromodorididae** is represented here by *Glossodoris atromarginata*. Characterized by brilliantly coloured species, the colour patterns are considered, in some cases, to be warning coloration, advertising the presence of distasteful chemicals, which the slugs remove from the sponges they feed on and store in characteristic glands around the mantle edge. Other genera include *Chromodoris, Hypselodoris* and *Ceratosoma.*

The family **Hexabranchidae** is characterized by gills which do not have a common pocket in which to retract. Probably only one species, *Hexabranchus sanguineus,* in which the mantle edge is greatly enlarged into a pair of flaps, which usually lie folded over the body. When disturbed, *Hexabranchus* is able to swim vigorously, with the aid of these flaps. The common name, "Spanish Dancer" is based on the resemblance of the beautiful colour pattern, so brilliantly displayed when the animal is swimming, to the dress and movements of a traditional flamenco dancer.

Suborder Aeolidoidea — Body elongate with many tubular papillae or "cerata" on the back. Each ceras contains a branch of the digestive gland, and the shape and arrangement of the cerata into patterns and groups, are considered important characters for classifying these animals. Almost all feed on cnidarians and many store undischarged nematocysts from their food in special cnidosacs at the tip of each ceras. Some major families illustrating the diversity of the suborder are:

Aeolidiidae. Anemone feeders in which the cerata are arranged in many crowded transverse rows. *Cerberilla, Aeolidiella, Aeolidiopsis, Spurilla.*

Glaucidae is a large diverse family. Most are hydroid feeders. Exceptions are *Phyllodesmium,* specialized soft-coral feeders often with symbiotic zooxanthellae in their tissues; *Favorinus* which feed almost exclusively on the eggs of other gastropods (usually opisthobranchs); and *Glaucus,* a wholly pelagic species which floats upside down on the water surface and feeds on *Physalia* and *Velella.*

Tergipedidae are usually small, hydroid feeding species *(Cuthona)* but in tropical waters species of *Phestilla* have evolved to feed on corals such as *Porites, Goniopora* and *Tubastrea.*

Suborder Dendronotacea — Includes a wide range of forms usually with a row of cerata or gills down each side of the body. All have rhinophores enclosed by a characteristic sheath. The most speciose family, Tritoniidae, have a series of gills down each side of the body and feed exclusively on soft corals. Another family reminiscent of the aeolids, and well represented in the tropics, Bornellidae, has a set of cerata down each side of the body, and feeds on hydroids.

Subclass Pulmonata
(Class Gastropoda)

These are mainly land snails. They lack external gills. Respiration takes place through the wall of the mantle cavity, modified to form an almost totally enclosed pulmonary sac or lung.

Aquatic pulmonates do exist, and although the majority of these are in fresh water, a small number occur in marine environments usually in fringe zones such as estuaries, intertidal sands and rocky shores. At least two families occur on Heron Island and probably will be found on other coral cays.

Siphonariidae (Siphon Limpets). The shell flattened and limpet-like. Usually they live on beachrock or large boulders at upper levels of the intertidal zone. Herbivores. *Siphonaria laciniosa.*

Onchidiidae. Medium to large-sized, air-breathing slugs without a mantle cavity. Leathery, often papillate or tuberculate dorsal surface. They live in the littoral zone in sheltered situations. Detrital feeders. *Onchidium damelii.*

Class Cephalopoda

(Phylum Mollusca)

The class was more diverse in the Mesozoic than it is today. The extant Cephalopoda are in two subclasses, Nautiloidea (order Nautilida — chambered nautili), and Coleoidea (Orders Sepioidea — cuttlefishes, Teuthoidea — squids, Octopoda — octopods, and Vampyromorpha). All except Vampyromorpha are represented in the waters of coral reefs.

Nautilus, the last surviving genus of the subclass Nautilida occurs only in the tropical waters of the Indo-Pacific region. Five species are recognized: *N. macromphalus* (New Caledonia), *N. scrobiculatus* (Papua New Guinea), *N. belauensis* (Palau), *N. stenomphalus* (Great Barrier Reef) and *N. pompilius* (widespread throughout the region). The animals normally live in waters of 200–300 m, but shells of *N. pompilius* (Fig. 45:16) and *N. stenomphalus* occasionally are found on the beaches of the Great Barrier Reef region. The surface of the chambered shells are white or cream with pale brown or orange coloured markings. In life, the chambers contain buoyant gases and the soft parts of the animal occupy the last chamber.

Cuttlefishes are represented by many species in the waters of the Great Barrier Reef (Fig. 45:1–14). They range from the small, *Metasepia pfefferi*, about 6 cm in mantle length, to the giant *Sepia latimanus* with a mantle length up to 50 cm. On the beaches of Heron Island, cuttlebones of *Sepia plangon* and *S. papuensis* abound. Other species such as *S. rozella, S. pharaonis* and *S. opipara* are also frequently found. Further north, on the beaches of Lizard Island one finds the cuttlebones of *Sepia latimanus, S. pharaonis, S. elliptica, S. whitleyana* as well as the abundant *S. papuensis*. The shells of *Spirula spirula*, a distant relative of true cuttlefish, coiled and chambered and resembling ram's horns in appearance, are frequently found washed up on tropical beaches (Fig. 45:15), but the animal lives in the open ocean. On the sandy, gravelly and shelly bottom of the lagoon of Lizard Island, the small *Sepiadarium kochi*, another distant relative of cuttlefish, often buries itself in sand with only the eyes exposed, waiting for unsuspecting prey, such as prawns, to pass by. Several species of *Euprymna*, commonly known as bottle squid, are also common in the lagoons. Although related to cuttlefish, they have no shells.

The reef squid, *Sepioteuthis lessoniana*, often seen schooling in the waters of coral reefs, reaches a maximum size of about 35 cm. Fragments of its chitinous internal shell (gladius) are occasionally found on the beaches. Other squids such as *Loligo chinensis* and many species of open ocean squid are also found in the region but rarely encountered on coral reefs.

Many species of octopods live in the crevasses in the reef. They range from small species with a mantle length of 1 or 2 cm to the large *Octopus cyanea* with a mantle length of up to 16 cm and weighing up to 4 kg. Octopods are shy animals, most being active at night or

134

Fig. 45. Cephalopod remains frequently found on the island beaches of the Great Barrier Reef: **1–2,** *Sepia elliptica.* **3–4,** *Sepia opipara.* **5–6,** *Sepia papuensis.* **7–8,** *Sepia plangon.* **9–10,** *Sepia pharaonis.* **11–12,** *Sepia smithi.* **13–14,** *Sepia whiteleyana.* **15,** *Spirula spirula.* **16,** *Nautilus pompilius.*

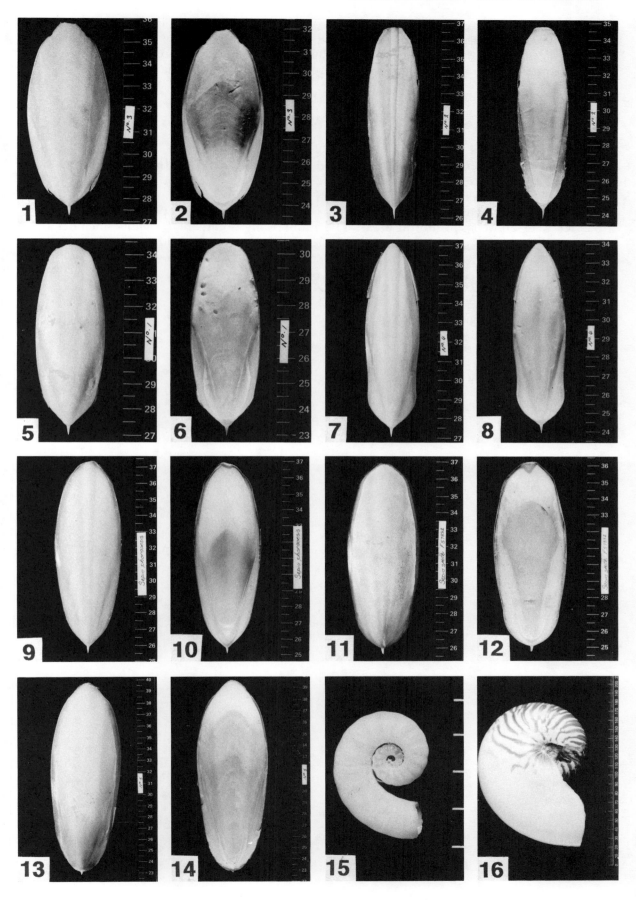

dusk and dawn only. *Octopus cyanea* hunts in the daytime on reef flats and is the most commonly sighted large octopus. At least one species of the venomous blue-ringed octopus *Hapalochlaena* is known to occur in the shallow tropical waters close to coral reefs on sandy silt substrates — specimens have been captured in waters around Lizard Island.

Class Scaphopoda
(Phylum Mollusca)

Scaphopoda (Tusk Shells) have a long, curved and tapered shell. The broad end, containing head and foot is buried in the substrate. The apex or pointed end projects into the water. Both ends of the shell are open (Fig. 44:13,14). Buried in sand or mud, scaphopods feed on microscopic animals such as foraminifers or detritus. Two genera occur along the Great Barrier Reef and coastal littoral areas. The numerically dominant *Dentalium* includes the larger species. *Cadulus*, with relatively few representatives, has shells with a central swelling.

PLATE 5

Centropages furcatus (Copepoda, Calanoida).

Stenopus hispidus (Decapoda, Stenopodidea), the Banded Coral Shrimp.

Allogalathea elegans, (Decapoda, Anomura), a symbiont of crinoids, it is seen amongst the arms of its host. (Photo courtesy of Roger Steene.)

Eriphia sebana (Decapoda, Brachyura), the Red-eyed Crab. (Photo courtesy of P. Davie.)

Cypraea tigris (Gastropoda, Prosobranchia).

Conus textile (Gastropoda, Prosobranchia), a carnivore dangerous to man.

Haminoea cymbalum (Gastropoda, Opisthobranchia).

Tridacna sp. (Bivalvia), a giant clam.

PLATE 6

Comanthus sp. (Crinoidea).

Culcita novaeguineae (Asteroidea), two colour varieties.
(Photo courtesy of I. Bennett).

Acanthaster planci (Asteroidea), Crown-of-Thorns Starfish.

Heterocentrotus mammillatus (Echinoidea), Slate Pencil Urchin.
(juvenile)

Ophiarachna incrassata (Ophiuroidea).

Holothuria atra (Holothuroidea) (with black spots), *H. leucospilata*
and *Stichopus variegatus* (brown).

Phallusia julinea (Phlebobranchia, Ascidiidae), anterior part of the body
showing its yellow chromatophores. (Photo courtesy of E. Lovell.)

Pycnoclavella diminuta (Aplousobranchia, Pycnoclavellidae).
(Photo courtesy of N. Coleman.)

Class Bivalvia

(Phylum Mollusca)

Second only to prosobranch gastropods in diversity, these highly modified molluscs are laterally flattened between two shells (*valves*; Fig. 46). Some are fixed (by the shells, or by threads secreted from the foot — *byssus*). Some burrow into sand, rock or wood by means of the laterally compressed foot. Some, free-living, are propelled by a jet of water expelled as the valves close (e.g., Pectinidae and Limidae). The two shells are held together by a ligament and have a hinge consisting of teeth that fit into sockets on the opposing valve. The most primitive have numerous simple teeth along the hinge line. More complicated hinges evolve as more effective mechanisms are selected. Sometimes the valves, when closed by the muscles of the living animal, form an impregnable refuge from all except predators that crunch up the whole shell or bore through it. In other species adapted for life in the sand, or for boring into calcareous rocks and other debris, the shells often gape or are some other special shape. Most bivalves are filter feeders with ciliated cells on the gill filaments that draw water over them. Here the food (organic particles) is trapped in mucus, and is moved into the mouth by other cilia. The major families (Fig. 47) are:

Nuculidae (Nut Shells). Solid valves with a hairy outer layer (periostracum) and numerous teeth along the obtusely angled hinge line. Internally the valves are pearly. *Ennucula superba.*

Glycymerididae (Dog Cockles). Heavy, compressed and oval valves with a straight hinge line and an arc of simple teeth. *Tucetona pectunculus.*

Arcidae (Arks). Valves elongate (antero-posteriorly), often with prominent radial ridges and a long straight hinge-line with numerous teeth and horny black ligament. *Anadara antiquata.*

Pteriidae (Pearl Shells, and Winged Oysters). Irregular, scaly asymmetrical valves with a pearly interior and a long smooth straight hinge line with or without teeth. The Black-Lip and the Golden Lip Pearl Shells are the basis of the Australian pearl shell industry. *Pteria penguin, Pinctada margaritifera.*

Malleidae (Sponge Fingers, Hammer Oysters). Valves long with a simple hinge held together by an oblique ligament seated in a deep pit. *Vulsella vulsella.*

Isognomonidae (Tree Oysters). Valves scaly, long, with a series of ligament pits separated by long flattened teeth. *Isognomon isognomon.*

Pectinidae (Fan Scallops). Valves usually with radial ribs. Apex (umbo) of the shell more or less in the centre of a fairly long hinge line held together by a round ligament. One valve usually more convex than the other. *Gloripallium pallium.*

Propeamussiidae (Saucer Scallops). Valves equally convex without prominent ribs and sculptured with concentric incised lines. These are the basis of an important commercial scallop industry in Queensland. *Amusium balloti.*

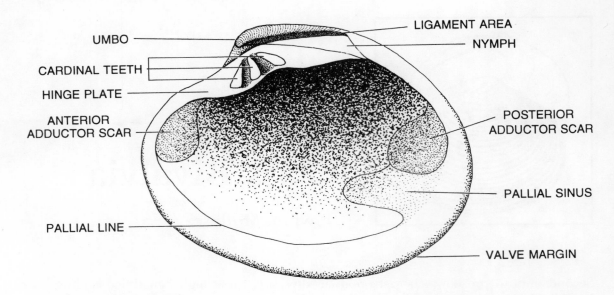

Fig. 46. Interior of right valve of a veneroid bivalve.

Limidae (File Shells). Valves elongate, usually white with radial ribs and a short hinge line with a strong ligament. *Limaria fragilis, Lima lima.*

Spondylidae (Thorny Oysters). Valves unequal, the uppermost sculptured with numerous spines, the lower usually fixed to the substrate. Hinge with prominent teeth on each side of a central round ligament. *Spondylus squamosus.*

Ostreidae (Oysters). Irregularly shaped valves, one attached to the substrate. Closely related to the commercially cultured oyster of New South Wales, the tropical rock oyster, *Saccostrea amasa,* occurs as a distinct band at mid-tidal level on rocky shores along the Queensland coast and offshore islands. The giant Cockscomb Oyster, *Lopha cristagalli,* the largest of the edible oysters, has deeply serrated, thick valves, one attached to coral boulders. It is found at low tide down to several metres depth.

Anomiidae (Jingle Shells). Valves delicate, thin and translucent. Certain species adhere to rocks by a ligament that passes through a hole in the lower valve. *Patro australis.*

Mytilidae (Mussels). Valves darkly coloured with a weak hinge and few small teeth. The apex (beak or umbo) of the shell is at one end of the long hinge line held together by a long ligament. They are usually attached by a byssus (a bundle of hair-like threads associated with the foot). Some are coral borers. *Modiolus agripeta, Septifer bilocularis.*

Chamidae (Jewel Boxes). Valves irregular and solid, the lower one sometimes fixed to the substrate, the upper valve fitting it like a lid. With irregular teeth on the hinge. *Chama pacifica.*

Crassatellidae. Valves large, elongate. Solid triangular hinge with a plate. *Eucrassatella cumingii.*

Carditidae (False Cockles). Shell with solid radiating often scaly, striated, or nodulose ribs and crenulate margin. The beak is turned toward the anterior end of the shell. *Cardita variegata, C. incrassata.*

Fig. 47. Common bivalves of the Great Barrier Reef: 1, *Ennucula superba.* 2, *Tucetona pectunculus.* 3, *Anadara antiquata.* 4, *Pteria penguin.* 5, *Pinctada margaritifera.* 6, *Vulsella vulsella.* 7, *Isognomon isognomon.* 8, *Gloripallium pallium.* 9, *Lima lima* (sub sp. *vulgaris*). 10, *Spondylus squamosus.* 11, *Patro australis.* 12, *Septifer bilocularis.* 13, *Chama pacifica.* 14, *Cardita variegata.* 15, *Codakia tigerina.* 16, *Fragum fragum.* 17, *Tridacna maxima.* 18, *Antigona puerpera.* 19, *Globivenus toreuma.* 20, *Tellina staurella.* 21, *Gari maculosa.* 22, *Mactra maculata.* 23, *Paphies striata*

Lucinidae (Saucer Clams). Valves regular, symmetrical and flattened, with fine radial and concentric sculpture. Hinge with a long ligament in a deep groove. *Codakia paytenorum, C. tigerina.*

Cardiidae (Cockles). Valve with conspicuous radial ribs and crenulated edges, often swollen and heart-shaped. Hinge with well developed teeth. *Fragum fragum.*

Tridacnidae (Giant·Clams). Valves with radial folds or plaits, continued out to the uneven margin, and scales on the external surface. Hinge plate large and massive. Included are the giant and the horse-shoe clams of northern Great Barrier Reef waters. Smaller species are commonly seen on the reef flat, the lips of the mantle protruding from the shell are brilliantly coloured by the enclosed zooxanthellae. *Tridacna maxima, T. crocea.*

Veneridae (Venus and Tapestry Shells). Valves with concentric sculpture and occasional radial ridges, usually rounded but sometimes lengthened anteroposteriorly and sometimes swollen. Three cardinal teeth in each valve. Umbo deep and prominent. *Antigona puerpera, Globivenus toreuma.*

Tellinidae (Tellins). Valves delicate, compressed, slightly asymmetrical with two small teeth in each and a conspicuous rounded external ligament. Species live in shallow seas and are active burrowers. *Tellina staurella.*

Psammobiidae (Sunset Clams). Valves compressed, rather thin elongately oval and with radiating markings. Hinge with small teeth and a short prominent external ligament. Valves resemble tellins. They inhabit the sea floor at shallow depths and are deposit feeders. *Gari maculosa. G. squamosa.*

Donacidae (Wedge Shells). Valves are wedge-shaped, distinguished from all others in having the anterior end (without the ligament) longer than the posterior end. The ocean beach pipi is used extensively as bait and is also used as a base for clam soup in Australia. *Donax faba.*

Mactridae (Trough Shells or Surf Clams). Valves have more or less symmetrical shells with a well developed hinge-line containing a deep pit for a rounded internal ligament and well developed teeth on each side. *Mactro maculata.*

Mesodesmatidae. Related to the Mactridae but with more solid, heavier valves and thicker hinge teeth. The species common in the islands of the Capricorn and Bunker Group is *Paphies striata* and it is known as the Beach Ugarie, burrowing into the intertidal sand.

Teredinidae (Shipworms). A long worm-like body with a pair of small valves at one end and a pair of posterior "pallets" used to drill out the tunnel in the wood, or sometime sand, in which they live. *Bankia australis* has been recorded from wooden piles in Gladstone Harbour. This and other species also may occur in drifting timber and in mangroves.

Phylum Bryozoa

Lace Corals and other Moss Animals

Bryozoans are fixed, colonial, coelomate, filter feeding invertebrates of uncertain affinities. Their common name, moss animals, relates to their moss-like habit, encrusting or otherwise attached to sand, rocks, weed and other substrates. The majority live in the sea, a few in fresh and brackish water. The colonies are made up of replicated individuals (zooids) with horny or calcified skeleton. Zooids are polymorphic, some for feeding (autozooids) and others (heterozooids) for special functions. Each autozooid has a U-shaped digestive tract, the anus opening at the top outside the circle of tentacles *(lophophore)* that surrounds the mouth. The tentacles of the lophophore have cilia moving food particles down into the mouth. The orifice of the zooid is surrounded by the rim of the horny or calcified body wall, inside which the whole zooid can be withdrawn. Sometimes an operculum (which in many calcified species pivots on hinge teeth — *condyles*) is present to close the orifice. Heterozooids include *avicularia,* in which the operculum is modified into a large jaw; and *vibracula,* in which it has lengthened into a bristle *(seta).* If the cuticular wall of the zooid is calcified, the upper surface (front) often remains membraneous to sustain changes in intra-zooid pressure which cause introversion or extroversion of the lophophore ring. The frontal membrane is often protected by calcified spines, or it becomes a calcified frontal wall with changes in internal pressure being effected through a hydrostatic sac *(ascus)* which opens to the exterior.

Bryozoa are abundant in the Great Barrier Reef province, as in Australian coastal waters elsewhere, but the fauna is known mainly from undescribed collections and a few short papers. On inner reef flats conditions are unsuitable for bryozoans but coral boulders on outer intertidal flats support a diverse fauna of up to at least 80 species. The concave under surface of *Acropora hyacinthus* boulders, for example, shelters erect, branching forms such as *Margaretta triplex* (Fig. 49:8) and the lace-coral *Reteporella graeffei* (Fig. 49:11) as well as encrusting species including *Hippopodina feegeensis* (Fig. 53:53) and *Stylopoma duboisii* (Fig. 53:54,55). Subtidally bryozoans are even more common, found under heads of *Acropora* and plate-like growths of *Montipora.* Although they occupy less space than sponges, such species as the violet and white lace-corals (*Iodictyum, Triphyllozoon*), branching cyclostomes (*Mesonea, Nevianopora*) and pendent tufts or fronds of *Bugula, Euthyrisella* and *Nellia* are often conspicuous.

Most of the common species referred to below have a wide range in the Indo-West Pacific, or at least the western Pacific sometimes from Hawaii to Mauritius, and New Zealand to Japan, to about 200 m depth. A few have a pan-tropical range. The few species known only from the Great Barrier Reef and Torres Strait may eventually be found to have a wider geographic range.

Labelled figures (Fig. 48:1–6) here explain many of the morphological terms (see also Ryland 1970) given to the four major bryozoan taxa and to the genera of lace-corals.

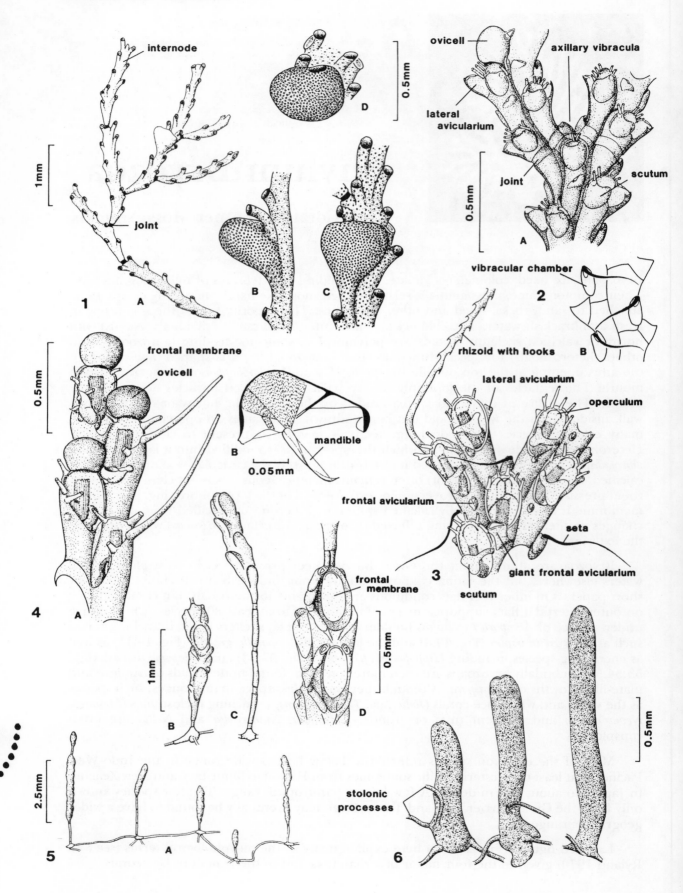

Key to the Higher Taxa of Marine Bryozoa

1. Non-calcified bryozoans. Colonies form gelatinous incrustations, stoloniferous networks of erect cylindrical zooids (generally 0.5–3 mm high) or dense soft tufts. Zooids semi-transparent or (Fig. 48:6) rendered opaque by a fine cover of sand; orifice without operculum, terminal in cylindrical species, frontal in crustose forms .... Order **CTENOSTOMATA**

   Calcified bryozoans (not always densely). Colonies pendent, erect, creeping or encrusting. Zooids with at least vertical walls calcified, frontal (i.e., upper) surface transparent or opaque; often a rigid, calcareous formation in which the position of each zooid is indicated only by the orifice 2

2. Colonies erect and branched (rigid or jointed), or forming discoid, hemispherical or irregular incrustations. Zooid walls completely calcified, orifice terminal and circular (Figs 48:1; 50:16,18). Brood chambers (gonozooids) form stippled, swollen regions (Figs 48:1; 50:18). No avicularia, vibracula or ovicells (cf. Fig. 48:2,4) .... Order **CYCLOSTOMATA**

   Colony pendent, erect, creeping or encrusting. Orifice subterminal or frontal, almost invariably closed by a hinged operculum (Fig. 48:3,5D; 50:19,21). Frontal surface often partly membranous. Slender spines often present around the margin of the zooid or its orifice (Fig. 48:3–5). Avicularia, vibracula and/or ovicells (Fig. 48:2,4) sometimes present (Order **CHEILOSTOMATA**) 3

3. Colonies encrusting or erect, frequently jointed. Zooids with at least part of frontal surface membranous, so that internal structures sometimes are visible (Fig. 48:3,4). The membrane, in which the operculum is set, comprises a greater or lesser part of the frontal surface; it may be underlain by a concave, calcareous shield (cryptocyst) or overarched by ribs, but is always present .... Suborder **ANASCA**

   Colonies encrusting or erect. Zooids with the frontal wall (apart from the operculum) calcified; smooth, rugose, sculptured or variously porous (Fig. 51:22–36). Secondary calcification sometimes adds strength and obscures zooid boundaries .... Suborder **ASCOPHORA**

Order Cyclostomata

Crisia — colonies small, erect, forming tufts of branching, jointed stems; three to many, biserially arranged zooids in each internode; gonozooids pyriform.

   C. elongata (Fig. 48:1), common, to about 15 mm high, with long internodes with black joints, and opening of gonozooid a sessile, transverse slit (Fig. 48.1D).

Mesonea radians (Figs 49:13; 50:16–17) — colony of slender, bifurcating stems, spreading to a saucer shape, to 25+ mm diameter. Branches triangular in section. Zooids in short, alternating rows of two to three, highest medially, sessile laterally (Fig. 50:16); gonozooids at bifurcations, occupying the space between several zooid rows; basal surface with about three series of conspicuous pores (Fig. 50:17).

Nevianopora pulcherrima (Figs 49:12; 50:18) — colony of slender, irregularly branching and anastomosing stems, rooting at intervals, to at least 45 mm across. Frontal surface of branches without median ridge. Zooids separated, in rows of two to three (rarely four), highest laterally; gonozooid spreading between the zooids at a bifurcation, its opening on a short, flaring tube (Fig. 50:18).

Lichenopora novaezelandiae (Fig. 52:37,38) — colony encrusting, domed, often with an elongate oval outline; to 10 mm long but usually smaller. Autozooids in single connate rows, radiating from centre of colony, longest centrally, shortest at the edge. Areas between autozooid rows divided by calcified struts into tubular alveoli, with pinhead-shaped processes projecting into their lumina. Brood chambers indicated by calcified areas occluding the alveoli; opening (essential for certain identification) a simple tube just protruding above level of alveoli. Often common in cryptic reef habitats.

Fig. 48. Bryozoans: 1, *Crisia elongata*: A, part of colony; B, C, D, gonozooid from side, front and above. Suva, Fiji. 2, *Scrupocellaria maderensis*: A, bifurcation in frontal view; B. vibracula in basal view. Pacific Harbour, Fiji. 3, *Scrupocellaria diadema*: bifurcation in frontal view; Suva, Fiji. 4, *Bugula dentata*: A, zooids in frontal view; B. avicularium. Heron I. 5, *Nellia tenuis*: A; part of colony; B, C, enlargements of erect branches to show stems; D, zooids. Suva, Fiji. 6, *Nolella papuensis*: three zooids. Suva, Fiji.

Order Ctenostomata

Nolella papuensis (Fig. 48:6) — colony of erect cylindrical zooids, 1.5–3.0 mm high, about 0.2 mm diameter, sparse to crowded, on hydroids, algae, coral rock, etc. Zooid surfaces opaque, containing fine earthy particles; basally with four or more slender, adnate stolonic outgrowths, which sometimes divide before producing a new zooid. About 18 tentacles; embryos (several at a time) brooded distally in the zooids.

Order Cheilostomata

Suborder Anasca

Retiflustra cornea (Fig. 52:40) — colony erect, saucer-shaped, convex face uppermost, with regularly fenestrate flexible branches spiralled around the vertical axis; attached by rootlets. Autozooids on one surface of branch only; frontal wall entirely membranous, with a narrow, cryptocystal border. Ovicell small, spherical, imperforate. No spines or avicularia.

Bugula — zooids unidirectional, fronts about two-thirds membranous; operculum absent; transverse walls forked when seen basally. Pedunculate, "bird's head" avicularia usually present.

The distinctive, bottle-green *B. dentata* (Figs 48:4; 49:10C) forms loose, pendent tufts about 6 cm high, with repeatedly bifurcating branches around indefinite axes. Zooids biserial, with three spines (one or more large) on outer angle, one on inner; ovicells subglobular, orthogonal or oblique to branch axis, with cuticularized closing membrane; bird's head avicularia about 0.2 mm long (Fig. 48:4B), occasionally giant, attached midway or in lower half of the bearing zooid. Widely distributed in tropics and subtropics. Well known from Heron Island.

Scrupocellaria — colonies free and branched but usually straggling (anchored by rootlets) rather than bushy (Fig. 49:7). Zooids unidirectional, rhombic, with oval frontal membrane, arranged biserially in branches jointed at bifurcations (Fig. 48:2). Sessile avicularia sometimes laterally and frontally. Vibracular chambers with long setae, usually laterobasally, sometimes giving rise to anchoring rootlets. Spines around frontal membrane, one often modified as a shield (scutum). Significant characters include number of vibracula (0–2) in branch axils, presence/absence and form of scutum, frontal and lateral avicularia, and rootlets.

S. maderensis (Fig. 48:2) with large scutum, fitting caplike over frontal membrane; lateral avicularia prominent and frontal ones small (or absent) and displaced when ovicells are present (Fig. 48:2, top left); two axillary vibracula, and the vibracular setae lying across basal surface (Fig. 48:2B).

S. diadema (Fig. 48:3) with scutum variable (sometimes absent); lateral avicularia small, the frontal ones occasionally giant; a single axillary vibraculum.

S. spatulata (Fig. 42:39) with narrowly oval scutum covering only central area of frontal membrane. Lateral avicularium dimorphic, usually tiny, but often giant with a slender, digitate rostrum parallel to long axis of branch; single axillary vibraculum.

Caberea — related to *Scrupocellaria* but forming coarse, tufted colonies; branches not jointed. Zooids in two to several series. Vibracula large, with long, usually serrate, setae. Scutum present or absent.

145

Fig. 49. Bryozoans (continued; scales indicated) 7, *Scrupocellaria diadema* with didemnids, underside of boulder. Suva, Fiji. 8, *Margaretta triplex* with *Reteporella graeffei*, underside of boulder Heron I. (15 cm). 9, *Caberea lata* Tomberua Passage, Fiji (10 mm). 10, A. *Euthyrisella clathrata*; B. *Nellia simplex*; C. *Bugula dentata* Heron I. (28 mm). 11, *Reteporella graeffei* (37 mm) and *Margaretta triplex*, as 8. 12, *Nevianopora pulcherrima* Great Astrolabe Reef, Fiji (colony width 30 mm). 13, *Mesonea radians* Great Astrolabe Reef, Fiji (colony diameter 12.5 mm). 14, *Cigclisula occlusa* Heron I. (bottom L to top R 72 mm). 15, *Reteporellina denticulata* Yanuttha, Fiji (height 30 mm).

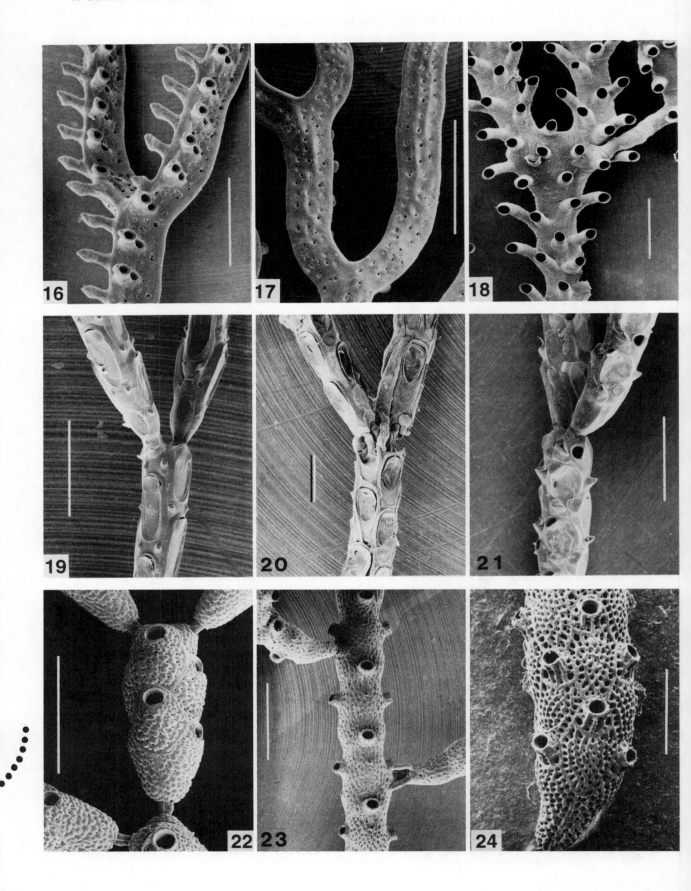

C. lata (Fig. 49:9), tufts to about 70 mm high usually with 4-serial branches, no scuta, and small frontal avicularia (usually in pairs).

Nellia — colonies erect; branches 4-serial, jointed at bifurcations. Zooids in alternating pairs; frontal membrane oval; no spines; avicularia small (disposed in pairs) or absent; ovicells often inconspicuous.

N. tenuis (Fig. 48:5), diminutive with slender stems projecting on wire-like stalks from thin stolons form a turf, with other erect species, under boulders. Common.

N. simplex (Figs 49:10B; 50:20), diffuse but firm yellow-brown tufts about 30 mm high; internodes to about 10 mm long, 0.5 mm in width. Frontal membrane oval; paired avicularia absent; ovicells subglobular. From Torres Strait to Heron Island.

N. oculata (Fig. 50:19), fine, densely branched, white colonies to about 25 mm high; internodes 1.5 mm long, 0.2 mm wide. (The form with squared-off internodes is var. *quadrilatera*). Frontal membrane elongate-oval; paired avicularia present; ovicells vestigial.

Poricellaria ratoniensis (Fig. 50:21) — erect colony, jointed branches about 0.3 mm wide, attached by rootlets (similar to *Nellia oculata*). Zooids 4-serial, in alternating pairs, asymmetrical; membranous frontal area roughly oval, underlain by a calcified lamina (cryptocyst) perforated by a single, off-centre, elongate opening (opesiule); orifice clearly defined, D-shaped, oblique to branch axis; one avicularium proximally on each zooid, positioned transversely.

Steginoporella — flat, encrusting sheets, sometimes with erect, frondose or narrowly branched growths. Autozooids dimorphic; A zooids with a conspicuous brown operculum, as wide as the zooid and half as long; B zooids with a proportionately larger operculum with a series of large teeth around its edge. Both types of autozooid have feeding polypides.

S. magnilabris (Fig. 42:41) colonies are deep reddish brown or horn coloured sheets, or occasionally partly erect uni or bilaminar plates. Membranous frontal wall of autozooid underlain for half its length by a thickened, concave cryptocyst with its distal edge complexly lobed descending to floor of zooid chamber, subdividing it. The polypide in the proximal half is extruded through a tubular foramen, the "polypide tube".

Thalamoporella — colonies develop as encrusting sheets or erect, bilaminar fronds. Membranous frontal surface of autozooid underlain by a complete cryptocyst, with only two large foramina (opesiules) for depressor muscles of the membrane. Orifice uncalcified. Vicarious avicularia frequent, often characteristic for the species. Embryos brooded in conspicuous, bivalved brood chambers. Small calcarous spicules (compasses and calipers), of unknown function but characteristic form in body cavity of autozooid. The two species, below, common at Heron Island, form broad, brownish sheets.

T. granulata (Fig. 52:43,44), presently known only from the Torres Strait and the Great Barrier Reef, has characteristic avicularium narrowly spatulate and curved to one side. The autozooid adjoining the concave side of an avicularium always asymmetric.

T. stapifera (Fig. 52:42), with smaller avicularium and elongate, symmetrically oval rostrum, distinguished from similar species by widely open compass spicules, and large, wishbone-shaped calipers.

Suborder Ascophora

A. Branches flat and flexible

Euthyrisella clathrata (Fig. 49:10A) — colonies brick-red; branches, flat, horny, bifurcating, parallel-sided with truncated ends, attached basally where fronds are narrowest; without

147

Fig. 50. Bryozoans (continued; scales indicated): **16,** *Mesonea radians* (as 13), oblique frontal view (1 mm). **17,** *M. radians* (as 13), basal view (1 mm). **18,** *Nevianopora pulcherrima* (as 12), frontal view of bifurcation with gonozooid (1 mm). **19,** *Nellia oculata* Townsville (0.5 mm). **20,** *Nellia simplex* (as 10B); (0.5 mm). **21,** *Poricellaria ratoniensis* Townsville (0.5 mm). **22,** *Tetraplaria ventricosa* Etty Bay, Queensland (1 mm). **23,** *Margaretta gracilior* Great Astrolabe Reef, Fiji (1 mm). **24,** *Margaretta triplex* (as 8) (1 mm).

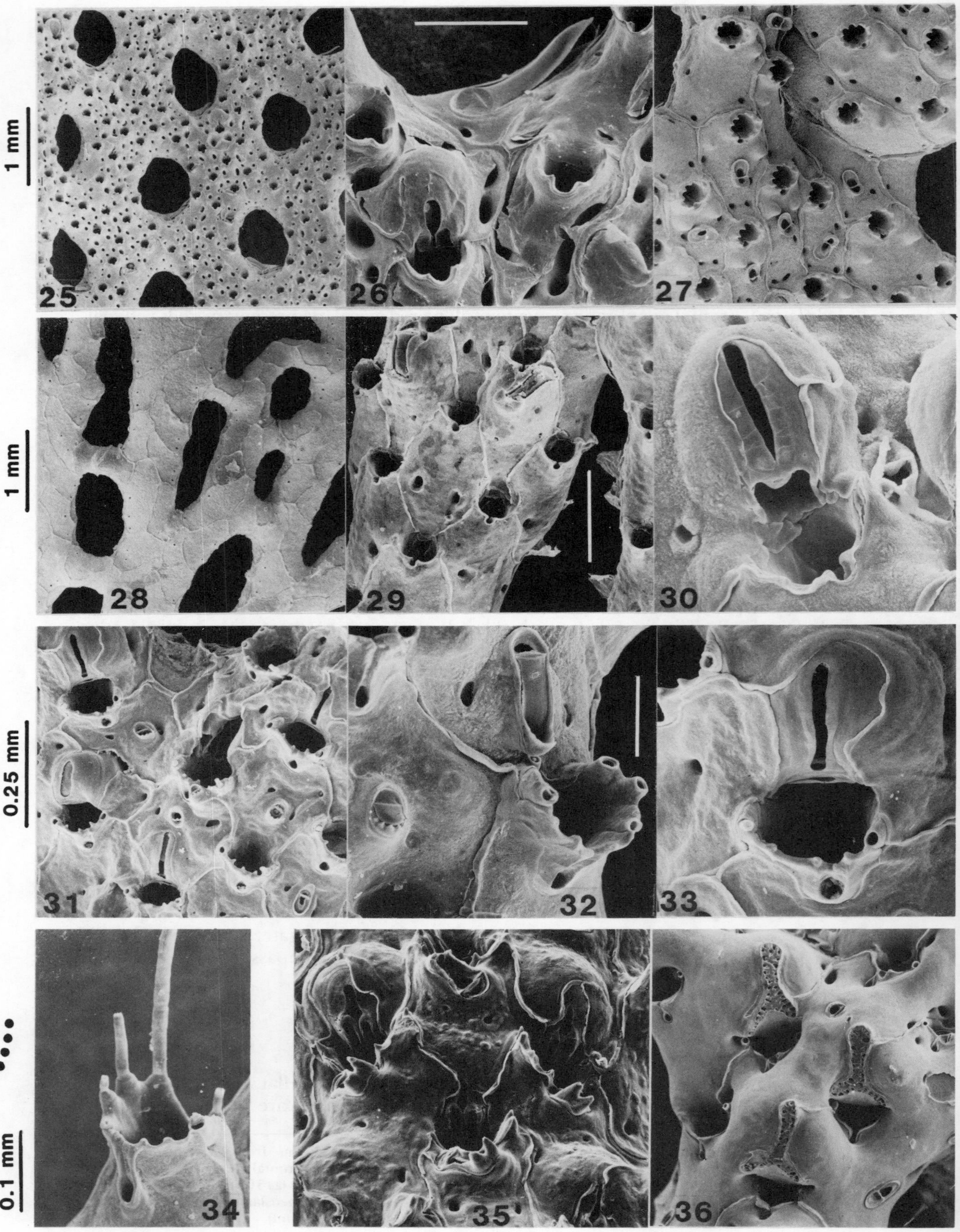
1 mm
25
26
27
1 mm
28
29
30
0.25 mm
31
32
33
0.1 mm
34
35
36

rootlets; 10–11 cm high, sometimes to 19 cm, branches 3–6 mm wide. Unilaminar, zooids all opening on same side. Opercula immediately noticeable, large, almost rhomboid, in diagonal rows; dimorphic (about one-quarter being wider at hingeline); each with a conspicuous T-shaped sclerite. Network of calcified bars visible through cuticle, apparently radiate from the midproximal point of operculum. Known from New South Wales and Queensland. Found washed up on the shore. Often supports rich epizoic fauna of other bryozoans and hydroids.

B. Branches flat and rigid

Cigclisula — colonies branch in three dimensions, with flat, hard fronds. Bilaminar, zooids opening on both sides of branches. Frontal wall of zooid at first with marginal pores (areolae) and a few central ones, but calcification rapidly becomes thick and nodular. Orifice at first ovate-oblong, with a sinus, becoming deeply immersed at the bottom of a tube (peristome) as calcification progresses; a small avicularium situated in proximal wall of peristome. Ovicells porous frontally, opening into peristome. At least two species occur: *C. occlusa* (Fig. 49:14) and *C. cautium*, distinguished principally by opercula and avicularia (see Hastings 1932).

C. Branches cylindrical and jointed

Margaretta — colony erect, branched, consisting of nearly cylindrical elongate internodes separated by chitinous joints. Zooids in alternating whorls of two to six. Frontal wall porous. Calcification around orifice elevated as a cylindrical peristome, containing the ascopore proximally. Ovicells opening into the peristome. *M. gracilior* (Fig. 50:23) a slender species with two zooids per whorl. *M. triplex* (Figs 49:8; 50:24) thicker, with four zooids per whorl; internodes reach to 30 mm in length and 2 mm in width. Known from Torres Strait to Heron Island, where it is common. Other species with more than two zooids per whorl may occur.

Tetraplaria — colony erect, jointed, repeatedly bifurcating, 4-serial; internodes connected by chitinous tubes, the longest distally. Zooids in alternating pairs, porous, cuticle distinct in life; orifice with a sinus; no avicularia. Two species recorded from the Great Barrier Reef: *T. ventricosa* (Fig. 50:22), with porous ovicells and individually convex zooids separated by distinct sutures, an Indo-Pacific species; and *T. immersa* with scarcely convex zooids separated by indistinct valleys, fertile zooids inflated, and without ovicells known only from Queensland.

D. Colonies fenestrate

Fenestrate bryozoan colonies, which fit the common designation "lace coral" branch repeatedly and regularly, and anastomose forming a web of branches (trabeculae) and windows (fenestrae). Zooids are confined to one surface. They occur in Cyclostomata (*Mesonea, Nevianopora*) and the anascan genus *Retiflustra,* Fig. 52:40). Two fenestrate families are in the Ascophora, viz. Petraliidae (single genus *Petralia*) and Phidoloporidae (formerly Sertellidae). *Petralia,* a well-known Australian genus attached by rhizoids sometimes forming a stem, and with flat fronds, is not associated with coral reefs.

Phidoloporids are common components of coral reef ecosystems and comprise the majority of taxa referred to as "lace corals". They form saucer-like or cup-like colonies, or are scrolled like brandy-snaps. Zooids normally face inwards. The basal surface is reinforced

Fig. 51. Bryozoans (continued; scales indicated): **25,** *Iodictyum* (sect. A) spp., part of colony. Heron Island. **26.** *Iodcytum* as 25, ovicell and infrafenestral avicularium (0.25 mm). **27.** *Iodictyum* (sect. B) sp. Heron Island. **28,** *Reteporellina denticulata,* basal surface. Heron Island. **29,** *R. denticulata* as 28, frontal surface showing avicularia (0.25 mm). **29,** *R. denticulata* as 28, frontal surface showing avicularia (0.25 mm). **30,** *R. denticulata* as 28, ovicell. **31,** *Reteporella graeffei* Amirante Island. **32,** *R. graeffei* orifice and frontal avicularia (0.25 mm). Heron Island. **33,** *R. graeffei* as 32, ovicell. **34,** *R. graeffei* as 31, spines and labial pore. **35,** Unidentified Port Jackson, New South Wales. **36,** *Triphyllozoon mucronatum* ovicells Heron Island.

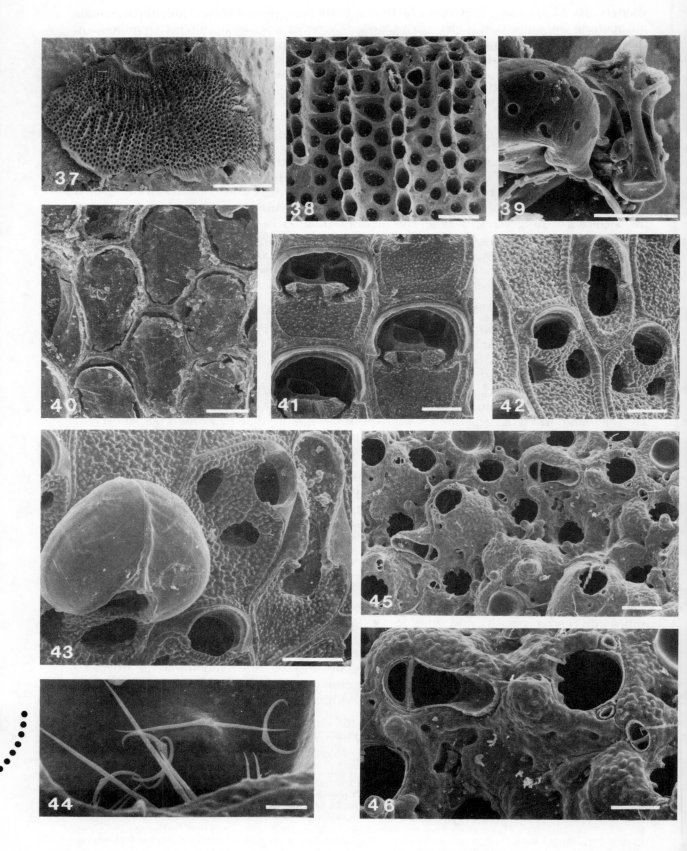

by flat, non-feeding zooids (kenozooids), devoid of external structures, and separated by distinct septal lines (vibices). Origin of colony cemented to substratum. Orifice primitively sinuate, often seen in this condition in young zooids near the edge of the colony; in some species, however, the sinus is separated off as a labial pore. There is frequently a raised margin or peristome.

Ovicells are important in defining phidoloporid genera (Harmer 1934); a lip, usually cleft, that descends into the peristome is the *labellum* (Fig. 51:26,35), while an uncalcified window is the *fissure*. Avicularia are varied, large ones sometimes occur in an angle of the fenestrae (Fig. 51:26); zooids have small or larger frontal avicularia (including some basal kenozooids) and sometimes one associated with the peristome *(labial avicularium)*. The group is difficult to classify and identify, except with the aid of a scanning electron microscope.

Key to Australian Phidoloporidae
(* not recorded from Great Barrier Reef)

1. Colony ramose, with or without anastomoses and slender cross-connections; fenestrae long and slender (Fig. 49:11,15) 2
   Colony truly fenestrate, the fenestrae round-ovate, separated by trabeculae of even width (Fig. 51:25)   4
2. Orifice surrounded by spines joined by webs (see young zooids); labial pore present (Fig. 51:34); avicularia various but not terminally bidentate .... *Reteporella (graeffei)*
   Orifice with cylindrical peristome, with or without pore; with teeth but no spines. Usually some avicularia bidentate (Fig. 51:35) 3
3. Ovicells subglobular, with median fissure but virtually no labellum (Fig. 51:30); peristome with labial sinus .... *Reteporellina (denticulata)*
   Ovicells with median fissure and well-developed cleft labellum (Fig. 51:35); peristome with labial pore .... new genus (unidentified species)
4. Colony carmine, pink or violet; zooids with four to seven large frontal pores (Fig. 51:26) ....
   .... *Iodictyum* section A
   Colony white (rarely pale pink); frontal pores small or absent 5
5. Ovicell not frontally emarginate but with linear or Y-shaped fissure (Fig. 51:33,36) 6
   Ovicell frontally emarginate or not, but without frontal fissure 7
6. Ovicell with linear fissure; basal vibices numerous .... *Sertella**
   Ovicell with Y-shaped fissure (Fig. 51:36); basal vibices few .... *Triphyllozoon mucronatum*
7. Margin of ovicell projecting as obtuse median point .... *Phidolopora**
   Margin of ovicell emarginate or widely cleft 8
8. Labellum interior, downward-projecting underlying cleft in ovicell ..... *Iodictyum* Section B (Fig. 51:27)
   Labellum absent; ovicell with front wide open 9
9. Orifice of young zooids with wide sinus .... *Schizoretepora**
   Orifice of young zooids with narrow sinus delimited by projections .... *Hippellozoon**

Reteporella (*R. graeffei*, Figs 49:11; 51:31–34) — colony spreading, branches anastomosing (zooids 4–6 serial), enclosing long slender fenestrae (in Heron Island material); no transverse trabeculae. Generally two series of basal kenozooids, with scattered pores and minute avicularia. Frontal surface of zooids flat, usually with two pores. Peristome a ring of slender, basally flaring spines (appearing webbed), with separate pore (Fig. 51:34). No labial avicularia in Heron Island material; frontal avicularia oval or elongate, with or without a series of small teeth terminally; occasionally giant, beaked avicularia present (Fig. 51:32). Ovicells developing from saucers to ovoids, leaving a long slender frontal fissure; no labellum (Fig. 51:33).

Reteporellina (*R. denticulata*, Figs 49:14; 51:28–30) — colony delicate, branches anastomosing (zooids 3–5 serial) enclosing long, slender fenestrae, and a few short transverse trabeculae

151

Fig. 52. Bryozons (continued; scales indicated): **37**, *Lichenopora novaezelandiae* entire colony (2 mm). **38**, *L. novaezelandiae* zooid rows, with an ooeciostome (top, right of centre) (0.25 mm). **39**, *Scrupocellaria spatulata*, the characteristic avicularium, adjacent to an ovicell (0.10 mm). **40**, *Retiflustra cornea*, group of autozooids (0.2 mm). **41**, *Steginoporella magnilabris* (0.25 mm). **42**, *Thalamoporella stapifera* autozooids and an avicularium (0.2 mm). **43**, *T. granulata* autozooids, an avicularium and an ovicell (0.2 mm). **44**, *T. granulata* compasses and calipers (0.025 mm). **45**. *Celleporaria tridenticulata* autozooids and avicularia (0.2 mm). **46**, *C. tridenticulata*, detail note primary orifice and thickened spine bases (0.10 mm).

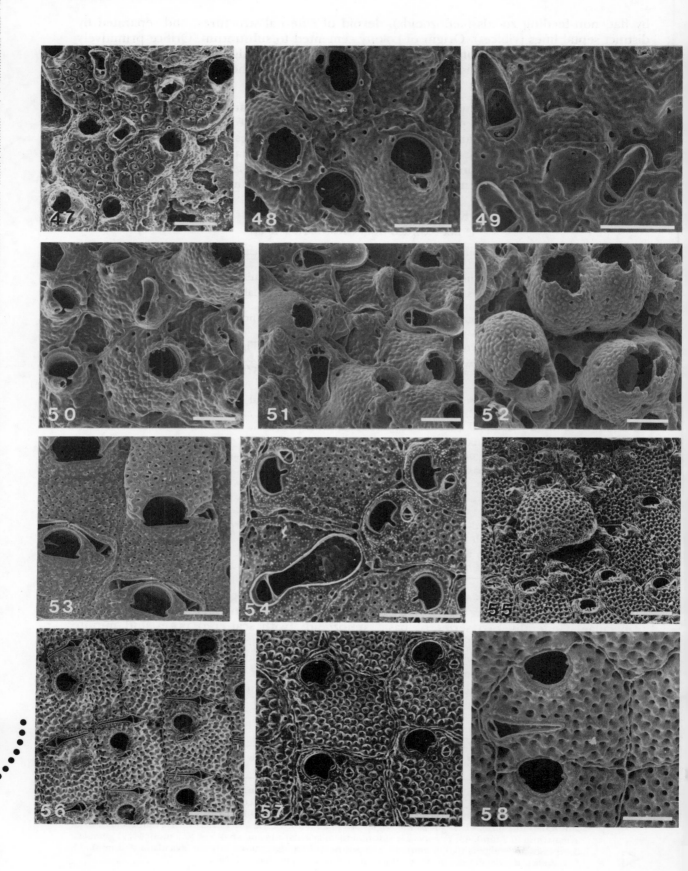

(Fig. 51:28). Mainly two series of basal kenozooids, with a few marginal pores, separated by vibices. Frontal surface of zooids flat, usually with two pores. Peristome of blunt teeth, with proximal sinus. Labial avicularia absent, present or modified (usually greatly enlarged and sometimes terminally bidentate). Ovicells developing from saucers to spheres, leaving frontal fissure, with short labellum.

New genus (unidentified species; Fig. 51:35). An unrelated species, assigned, erroneously, to *Reteporellina denticulata* (see Harmer 1934) in the literature, is distributed from New South Wales, through Torres Strait to the Indian Ocean. It has non-fenestrate colonies; zooids with about three pores; tall flaring, toothed peristomes and well-developed labial pore. Labial avicularia are absent, or present unmodified or enlarged and terminally bidentate. Ovicells have a well-developed, cleft labellum distinguishing the species from *R. denticulata*.

E. Colonies encrusting

Tremogasterina spathulata (Fig. 53:47) — colonies usually small, less than 5 mm diameter, and inconspicuous. With 2–20 thick-rimmed foramina on frontal wall of the autozooid, and shoe-shaped avicularia. Common in shallow reef habitats and one of the few bryozoans sometimes abundant on the inner reef flat.

Celleporaria — colonies usually encrusting, multilaminar, often nodular or mamillate, sometimes deeply pigmented, and usually conspicuous, to 100 cm². Orifice of autozooid semicircular to oval, a few species with two or three delicate denticles on its proximal edge. A peristome proximal to the orifice, usually incorporating an avicularium, sometimes with a characteristic notch. Oral spines present in some species. Ovicell small without pores. Vicarious avicularia, usually species characteristic, are often infrequent. Common in all shallow reef habitats. At least eight species on Heron Island reef flats, but only three are well characterized. *C. aperta* (Fig. 53:48,49) has a shallow sinus in the proximal border of the orifice, and a widely spaced pair of oral spines, often particularly long and prominent in newly budded autozooids. Oral avicularium short, with finely dentate rostral rim; vicarious avicularia rounded and often slightly tapered distally, also dentate. In *C. tridenticulata* (Fig. 52:45,46) the orifice has three denticles on its proximal edge, the middle one often broad, and sometimes bifid. The two to four distal oral spines have thickened bases, visible even in old autozooids. Suboral avicularium small and peristome only poorly developed, without median notch. Vicarious avicularium slender, spatulate, with toothed rostrum; the rather stout crossbar lacks a columella. In *C. vagans* (Fig. 53:51,52) the orifice lacks oral spines but has three denticles, thin, pointed, and never bifid. The suboral avicularium, scarcely larger than in *C. tridenticulata*, is in a well-developed peristome which has a deep, rounded notch adjacent to the avicularium. Ovicell almost spherical with few pores; aperture rim tends to uneveness and often has a small avicularum. Vicarious avicularium, spatulate distally, has a smooth edge to the rostrum, and the slender crossbar bears a small columella.

Hippopodina feegeensis (Fig. 53:53) — colonies thin, unilaminar, light-yellowish brown sheets. Frontal membrane glistening in dried specimens. Autozooids long (to 1 mm), lightly calcified, with regular tiny pores in the nodular frontal wall. Orifice bell-shaped, in many autozooids bordered distally by the slender rostra of a pair of lateral oral avicularia. Ovicell large, conspicuous, with calcification and perforations like autozooid frontal wall. Common in all reef habitats.

Calyptotheca — colonies often multilaminar and extensive. Autozooids with densely perforated frontal walls, characteristically bounded by raised sutures. Orifice shallowly

153

Fig. 53. Bryozoans (continued; scales indicated): **47,** *Tremogasterina spathulata* (0.25 mm). **48,** *Celleporaria aperta*, group of autozooids, note primary orifice and spine bases (0.2 mm). **49,** *C. aperta* vicarious avicularia (0.2 mm). **50,** *C. vagans*, group of autozooids, note primary orifice, lacking spines (0.25 mm). **51,** *C. vagans*, autozooids and vicarious avicularia (0.25 mm). **52,** *C. vagans*, ovicelled autozooids (0.25 mm). **53,** *Hippopodina feegeensis* (0.25 mm). **54,** *Stylopoma duboisii*, autozooids and a vicarious avicularium (0.25 mm). **55,** *S. duboisii*, autozooids and an ovicell (0.25 mm). **56,** *S. viride* (0.5 mm). **57,** *S. thornelyae* (0.25 mm). **58,** *Calyptotheca tenuata* (0.2 mm).

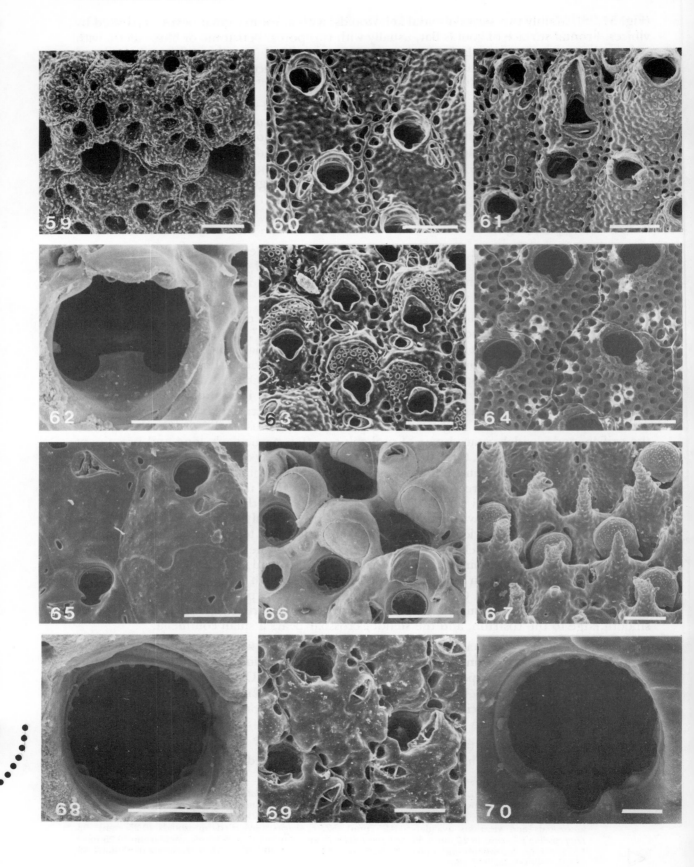

sinuate, with distinct proximolateral condyles; dimorphic, usually being larger and broader in brooding zooids. Ovicell large and conspicuous, with crowded pores in nodular surface. Adventitious avicularia sparse. Several species occur at Heron Island but they are confused. *C. tenuata* (Fig. 53:58) has transversely oval orifice, with shallow U-shaped sinus, and lateral avicularium with a slender rostrum medially directed, passing proximal to the orifice.

Stylopoma — colonies multilaminar, extensive, massive or nodular. Autozooids thickly calcified; the frontal wall densely punctured and sometimes coarsely nodular in later ontogeny. Primary orifice with distinct U or V-shaped sinus, lacks oral spines. Vicarious avicularia sporadic typically with spatulate mandibles; usually a single adventitious avicularium on each autozooid, close to the orifice. Huge spherical ovicell completely enclosing orifice of maternal autozooid, obscuring the distally succeeding autozooid. A pantropical genus, most of the species occurring in reef habitats. Three species at Heron Island, each readily distinguished by orifice shape and type of avicularia: *S. duboisii* (Fig. 53:54,55) with a semi-circular orifice and a slit-like sinus, and adventitious avicularium with short, triangular mandible situated proximo-lateral to the orifice; *S. thornelyae* (Fig. 53:57) with a deep V-shaped sinus and adventitious avicularia smaller than in *S. duboisii* and directed more distally; *S. viride* (Fig. 53:56) with longer than wide orifice, a U-shaped sinus, adventitious avicularia dimorphic, consistently with an elongate, slender type distal to the orifice, and some autozooids with a shortly triangular type proximo-lateral to the sinus. In some populations the colony is a bright, vivid, permanent green.

Cigclisula areolata (Fig. 54:59) — colony a thick, multilaminar crust. Autozooids with a granular frontal wall bordered by few, very large pores. Primary orifice bell-shaped, with inconspicuous condyles, partly hidden by a thickened peristome, notched on its proximal edge; a tiny, vertically orientated avicularium on one side of the notch. Ovicell grossly inflated, often crossed by sutures, has four to eight large foramina frontally. Large vicarious avicularia sporadic. Known only from the Torres Strait and the Great Barrier Reef; common around Heron Island, but can be confused with others.

Pleurocodonellina signata (Fig. 54:60) — colonies extensive, pinkish brown, unilaminar sheets; found in most reef habitats. Autozooid with a nodular frontal wall bordered by a single series of large pores. Orifice sinuate and completely surrounded by a thin, raised peristome. A single adventitious avicularium on each autozooid, proximo-lateral to the orifice, proximally directed; rostrum elongate triangular, slender. Ovicell thinly calcified and flattened frontally, with a few small distal pores.

Parasmittina — characterized by the primary orifice of the autozooid, having a medioproximal tooth *(lyrula)* and, usually, distinct lateral condyles. Oral spines sometimes present and peristome variably developed. Frontal wall of autozooid with marginal pores. Avicularia adventitious, polymorphic and located off the midline of the autozooid, with varying orientation. Ovicell perforated frontally. A cosmopolitan genus with many species in reef habitats but all in need of taxonomic revision. As many as six species occur on Heron Island reef flats, but only one common, viz. *P. hastingsae* (Fig. 54:61–63), with two (rarely three) distal oral spines; lyrula occupying about half the proximal width of the orifice and the curved edge with pointed corners. Peristome with pronounced median notch, on each side of which calcification is distinctly thickened. Several types of avicularia occur: lateral oral type with oval rostrum; or occasionally an enlarged type with slender, tapered, serrate rostrum; and, typically, a frontally positioned type with elongate oval or tapered rostrum directed distally.

Fig. 54. Bryozoans (continued; scales indicated): **59**, *Cigclisula areolata* two ovicelled autozooids (0.2 mm). **60**, *Pleurocodonellina signata* (0.2 mm). **61**, *Parasmittina hastingsae* autozooids and an enlarged avicularium (0.2 mm). **62**, *P. hastingsae* primary orifice (0.1 mm). **63**, *P. hastingsae* ovicelled autozooids (0.2 mm). **64**, *Sinupetraliella litoralis* (0.25 mm). **65**, *Schedocleidochasma porcellanum* (0.2 mm). **66**, *Rhynchozoon compactum* (0.2 mm). **67**, *R. tubulosum*, (0.25 mm). **68**, *R. tubulosum* primary orifice (0.10 mm). **69**, *R. rostratum*, (0.2 mm). **70**, *R. rostratum* primary orifice (0.025 mm).

Sinupetraliella litoralis (Fig. 54:64) — colony deep brown, loosely encrusting, unilaminar sheet. Autozooids large, with rugose frontal wall densely punctured by large round pores. Primary orifice asymmetrically sinuate, partly hidden by thickened peristome with a tiny, vertically orientated avicularium in its proximal lip. Similar, small frontal avicularium occasionally present. Ovicell thinly calcified, prominent, its frontal surface speckled with tiny pores.

Schedocleidochasma porcellanum (Fig. 54:65) — colony a unilaminar sheet, brilliantly white, appearing porcellanous. Frontal wall smooth, with few marginal pores, and the orifice distinctly keyhole-shaped. Single lateral suboral avicularium on every autozooid, with slender rostrum laterally directed. A pantropical-subtropical species often abundant in coral reefs.

Rhynchozoon — colonies small to massive, nodular or mamillate, and multilaminar. Characters include a usually sinuate denticulate primary orifice; suboral avicularium, sometimes with a tooth-like uncinate process projecting above the orifice, and a proliferation of polymorphic frontal avicularia. The genus occurs throughout the marine realm, except in polar seas, and includes numerous reef-associated species. At least nine species occur around Heron Island but only three are well characterized. *R. compactum* (Fig. 54:66) colony small, of thickly calcified, steeply convex autozooids; frontal wall smooth, with few distinct marginal pores; orifice with small, U-shaped sinus and low peristome, not obscuring the orifice; elongate suboral avicularium laterally directed, lacking a projecting uncinate process; frontal avicularia sparse, small, and elongate oval in outline. *R. tubulosum* (Fig. 54:67,68) with broadly sinuate orifice hidden by massive, spiked development of the peristome, which may be knobbed or branched apically, with tiny, rounded avicularia; large suboral avicularium transversely oriented on distal side of this spike, towards its base; frontal avicularia sometimes proliferate in older parts of colony, and are proximally directed, with elongate rostra extending the whole length of the autozooid bearing them. *R. splendens* (Fig. 54:69,70) has a massive lateral suboral avicularium, hooked distally, with a stout proximal uncinate process projecting over the primary orifice, and small U-shaped sinus; frontal avicularia small, diamond-shaped, and numerous, with varying orientation.

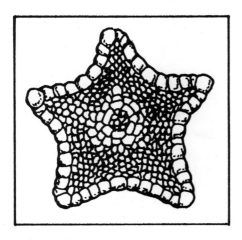

Phylum Echinodermata

Sea Stars and their Relatives

Echinoderms are colourful and conspicuous reef invertebrates. Their name, derived from Greek words meaning "spiny skin", because their skin is filled with large or small calcareous plates or spines. So crowded can these be that even in death the animal's shape is preserved.

The best known are "starfish" (Asteroidea), so-called because they have a five-rayed (pentameral) symmetry. Lacking a front and a back or a left and a right, echinoderms generally are thought of as having an oral (usually the under) surface and an aboral one (usually the upper).

They move on hundreds of hollow papillae (tube feet), radially arranged and operated by a unique hydraulic system — the water vascular system. In starfish, these tube feet are in grooves *(ambulacra)* along the underside of the radial arms.

Most echinoderms are harmless, yet severe puncture wounds can be inflicted by the long, sharp spines of some urchins and, worse, the spines of the notorious coral predator the Crown-of-Thorns, *Acanthaster planci*, which are covered with toxin filled tissues.

Some echinoderms feed by filtering plankton from the water, others by digesting micro-organisms from the sediments, or by grazing algae from rocks. Othere are aggressive predators. Their often large and complex bodies offer homes to a great complex of symbionts — molluscs, crustaceans, worms and protozoans.

Sexes are separate and fertilization is external. The animals congregate, often in large numbers, and after a slow communal dance they pour their gametes into the sea. This synchronous release ensures maximal concentrations of gametes, providing ample opportunities for fertilization to take place so that eggs and sperm are not wasted. Delicate larvae live briefly in the plankton before dramatic metamorphosis and settlement.

On the Great Barrier Reef five major groups, classes, of echinoderms are commonly found. The crinoids or "feather stars" have mouth and anus directed up. The asteroids, "sea stars", have mouth down and anus up as do the ophiuroids ("brittlestars") and most echinoids ("sea urchins"). The holothurians — the "sea cucumbers", "trepang" or "bêche de mer" — lie on their "side" with mouth and tentacles at one end and anus at the other.

Picture keys to the families are presented as a guide to identification (Figs 55–59). For more comprehensive treatments reference should be made to Clark (1946) and Clark and Rowe (1971). Endean (1953, 1956, 1961) reported on the Queensland fauna. For recent literature consult Arnold and Birtles (1989).

CRINOIDEA

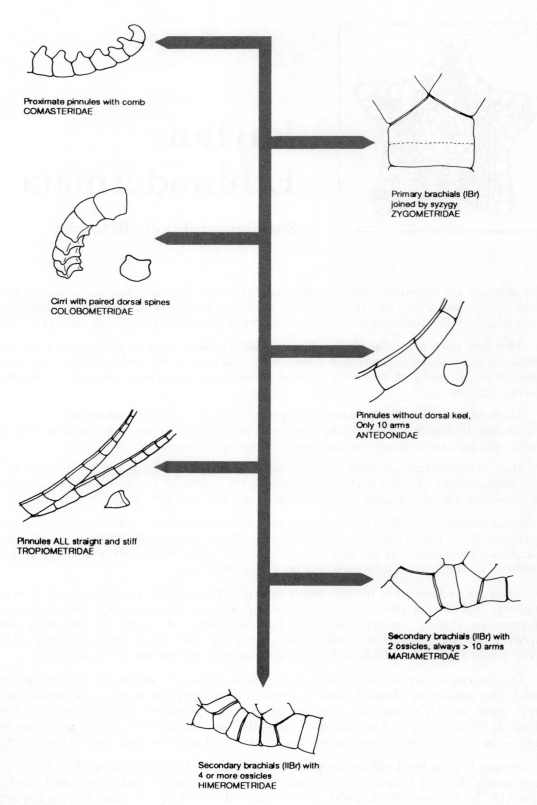

Proximate pinnules with comb
COMASTERIDAE

Primary brachials (IBr)
joined by syzygy
ZYGOMETRIDAE

Cirri with paired dorsal spines
COLOBOMETRIDAE

Pinnules without dorsal keel,
Only 10 arms
ANTEDONIDAE

Pinnules ALL straight and stiff
TROPIOMETRIDAE

Secondary brachials (IIBr) with
2 ossicles, always > 10 arms
MARIAMETRIDAE

Secondary brachials (IIBr) with
4 or more ossicles
HIMEROMETRIDAE

Fig. 55. Crinoidea.

Class Crinoidea — Feather Stars

These colourful animals have a thin veneer of tissue over their calcareous plates. They are thought to be the most ancient of echinoderms. Five arms, often branched and pinnate, rise from a small cup (theca). Both mouth and anus open on the membranous cover of the ·theca and a cluster of cirri project below it to grip the substrate. Crinoids use their tentacles or pinnules to gather plankton which is then moved down the arms to the mouth. Clark (1975) reported on the crinoids of the Swain Reefs.

Crinoids are delicate animals and often difficult to identify (Fig. 55). They tend to hide under ledges at 5–20 m. Two common species, in the Comasteridae, are *Comanthus parvicirrus* which is green with yellow tipped pinnules and *C. samoanus* also green but its pinnules have red tips. A dark red species with grey pinnules often found on coral heads at 5–15 m is *Himerometra robustipinna* (Himerometridae). Two species often found with gorgonians or other corals are the speckled *Stephanometra oxyacantha* (Mariametridae) at 5–12 and, slightly deeper at 10–20 m, the multicoloured *Oligometra serripina* (Colobometridae).

Class Asteroidea — Sea Stars, Pin-cushion Stars

These are starfish (or seastars). Typically they have five arms in continuation with the central disc. Sometimes the arms are long relative to the disc and sometimes short, so short in *Culcita novaeguineae* (Oreasteridae) as to be almost non-existent. Below the arms are the distinctive ambulacral grooves with the tube feet. The ambulacral grooves converge on the mouth in the centre of the lower surface. The anus and one or more madreporites (through which water is drawn in to fill and control the water vascular system) are in the centre of the upper disc surface. Asteroids are detritus feeders, omnivores or predators. Both *Culcita* and *Acanthaster planci* (Acanthasteridae) are predators of hard corals. Controversy about the nature of the impact of *A. planci* on the Great Barrier Reef has raged for nearly 25 years. For the most recent overview consult Wilkinson (1990). The major taxa are set out in Figure 56.

One of the most characteristic species and most noticeable on the reef flats is the brilliant blue *Linckia laevigata* (Ophidiasteridae). A common but duller relative with thinner arms is *L. guildingi*. The mud-coloured *Archaster laevis*, with prominent projections along the arms is common on the northern sand flats. Other common ophidiasterids on the reef flats are the mustard yellow *Nardoa novaecaledoniae* (with bosses becoming smaller toward the end of the arms) and *N. pauciforis* (with bosses of even size along the arms). The small, deep red *Fromia elegans* is found on the slopes. Also on the flats are the almost black/red *Echinaster luzonicus* (Echinasteridae) with thin arms and a slightly prickly skin.

The crimson *Tosia queenslandia* (Goniasteridae), with quite short arms and distinct marginal plates, is found in rubble areas together with two smaller members of the Asterinidae — *Asterina burtoni* (rough and usually orange) and *Diasterina leptalacantha* (smooth and cream or green). On sand flats, often partially buried, is *Astropecten polyacanthus* (Astropectinidae) with characteristic large cream spines along the edges of the arms.

Large spectacular, heavy-bodied sea stars, *Protoreaster nodusus* (with very dominant nodules on the aboral surface) and *Pentaceraster regulus* (with less prominent nodules) are found in deeper waters on sandy bottoms.

Class Ophiuroidea — Brittlestars, Basketstars

Brittlestars characteristically have five long, slender arms each well set off from the central disc, and easily broken off it. The central disc usually is leathery. These animals can move with surprising speed. Most are detritus feeders or use mucous webs to catch small prey; some are carnivores and catch small organisms. The major taxa are set out in Figure 57.

The basketstars such as *Euryale aspera* (Euryalidae), unlike other brittlestars, have branching arms. These remarkable animals are usually found entwined among gorgonians at some depth.

159

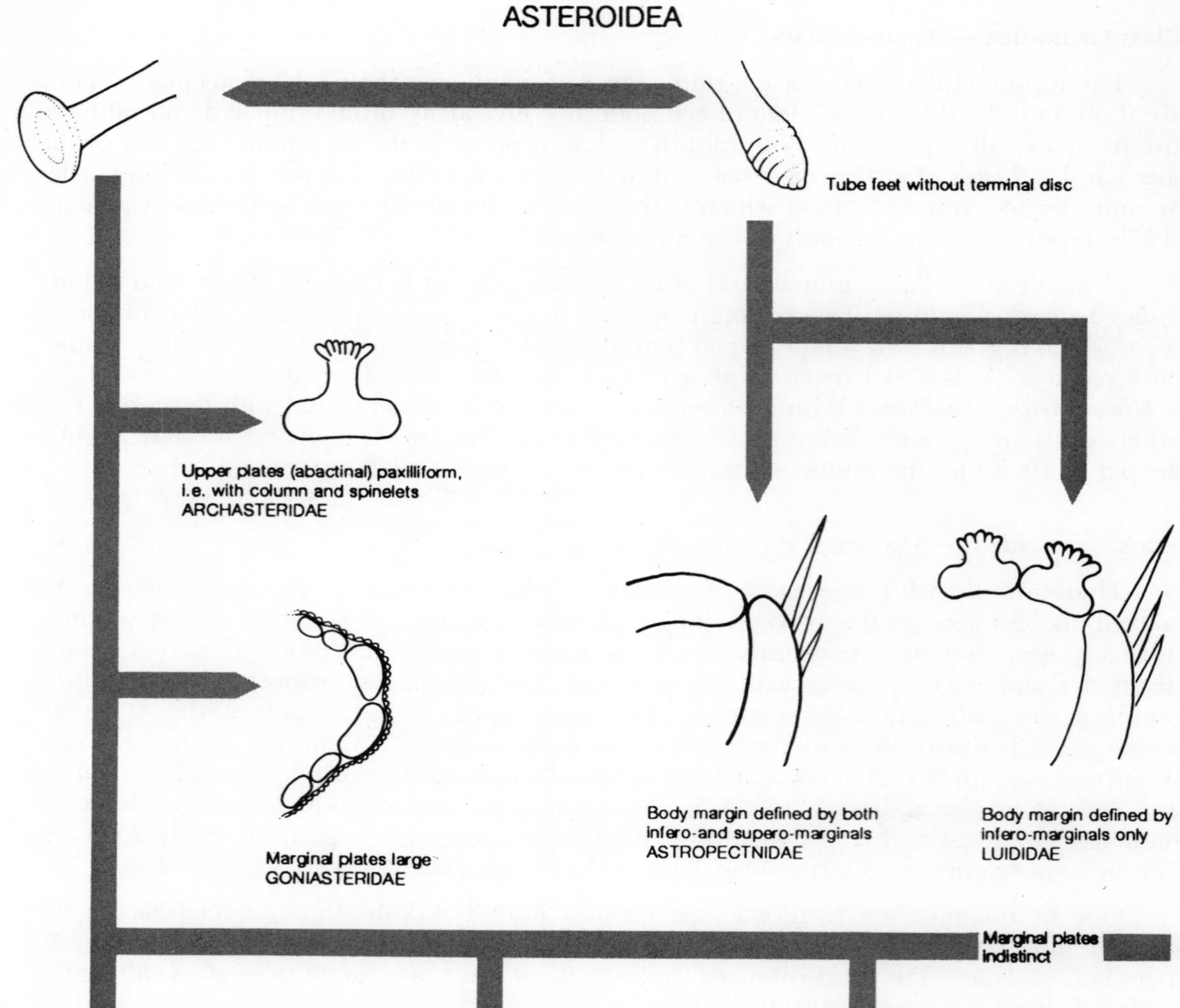

ASTEROIDEA

Tube feet without terminal disc

Upper plates (abactinal) paxilliform,
i.e. with column and spinelets
ARCHASTERIDAE

Body margin defined by both
infero-and supero-marginals
ASTROPECTNIDAE

Body margin defined by
infero-marginals only
LUIDIDAE

Marginal plates large
GONIASTERIDAE

Marginal plates
indistinct **A**

Arms long and cylindrical, marginal
plates distinct, skeleton solid

Upper (aboral) skeleton
reticulate, usually
massive, R>100mm
OREASTERIDAE

Body flat below, upper plates
overlap inwards, arms variable
ASTERINIDAE
(*Asteropsis* with obscuring skin)

B

Fig. 56a. Asteroidea.

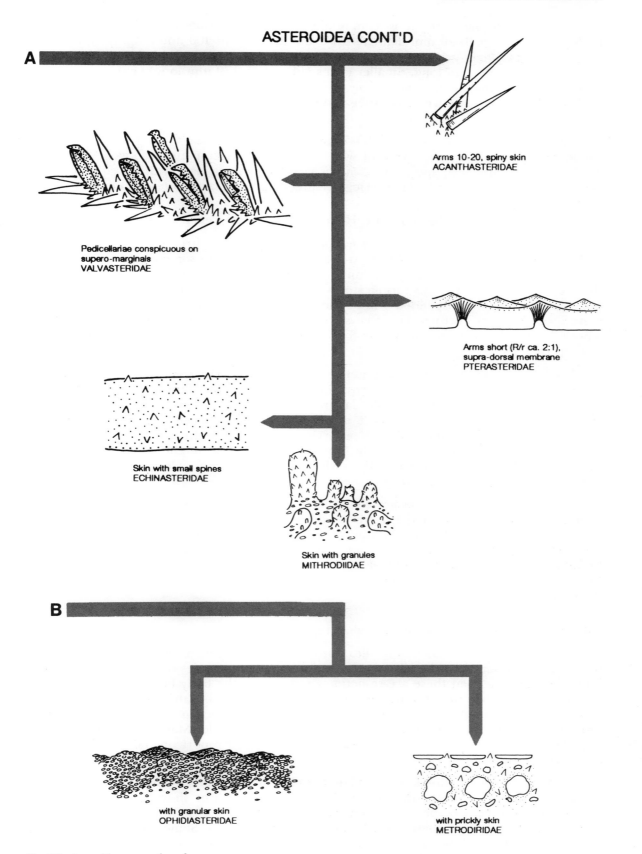

ASTEROIDEA CONT'D

A

Arms 10-20, spiny skin
ACANTHASTERIDAE

Pedicellariae conspicuous on
supero-marginals
VALVASTERIDAE

Arms short (R/r ca. 2:1),
supra-dorsal membrane
PTERASTERIDAE

Skin with small spines
ECHINASTERIDAE

Skin with granules
MITHRODIIDAE

B

with granular skin
OPHIDIASTERIDAE

with prickly skin
METRODIRIDAE

Fig. 56b. Asteroidea — continued.

161

On reef flats one of the most common brittlestars is *Macrophiothrix longepeda* (Ophiotrichidae) with a small 20 mm diameter disc, but arms up to 400 mm long. Another large species with a brilliant green 50 mm disc is *Ophiarachna incrassata* (Ophiodermatidae) which has arms up to 200 mm long. Smaller (arms about 100–150 mm long) yet quite common species in the Ophiocomidae are *Ophiocoma erinaceus* with both upper and lower surfaces dark and *O. scolopendrina* which is variegated grey/brown above and white below around the mouth.

Smaller still with arms only about 50–70 mm long and living near the reef crest is *Ophioplocus imbricatus* which is grey or olive and with a dark, rectilinear pattern above. Among the smallest, yet commonest, species is *Ophiactis savignyi* (Ophiactidae) with a disc only 5 mm across and arms 25 mm long. It is a variegated green and white, and often found in sponges.

Class Echinoidea — Sea Urchins, Heart Urchins, Slate Pencil Urchins

Sea urchins lack arms and the dermal plates fuse to form a firm test covered externally with spines. They usually are globose (regular urchins) though some of the sand dwelling ones are flattened discs (irregular urchins). Tube feet are arranged in five zones *(ambulacra)* that in some irregular urchins form a stellate or petaloid pattern on the upper surface (Fig. 58). The viscera are suspended within the firm test. Urchins are browsers and detrital scavengers. Their powerful scraping jaws are mounted in a skeletal frame *(Aristotle's lantern)*. Those living below the sand may pass food to the mouth by currents set up by the waving of their tube feet.

Spectacular urchins often encountered on reef flats are *Diadema savignyi* and *D. setosum* (Diadematidae) about 80–100 mm across the test, but with very long (about 200 mm) fine needles. The former is all black, the latter has some white about the mouth. Also with spectacular, but large and flattened spines, is the slate pencil urchin *Heterocentrotus mammillatus* (Echinometridae). A much more common species in the same family, with strong simple spines with white tips, usually found in holes bored in the coral, is *Echinometra mathaei*. Another urchin of the reef flat with bright orange spines alongside the ambulacra is *Tripneustes gratilla* (Toxopneustidae).

In the sand off the slope are the pale green "regular" urchins *Salmacis sphaeroides* (Temnopleuridae), while in the sands of the lagoons live flattened, "irregular" urchins *Clypeaster telurus* (Clypeasteridae) of up to 120 mm across and the smaller (50 mm) *Laganum depressum* (Laganidae). Also found in sandy areas are the more robust "irregular" urchins *Lovenia elongata* (Lovenidae) and *Brissus latecarinatus* (Brissidae). *Maretia planulata* (Spatangidae) occurs in large numbers on the sea-floor between Heron and Sykes Reefs in the Capricorn Group.

Class Holothuroidea — Sea Cucumbers, Trepang

The sea cucumbers have their calcareous skeleton very much reduced. There is a ring of internal plates around the oesophagus and microscopic spicules of great diversity in the body wall, though even these are sometimes reduced so the body becomes quite soft and flaccid. The mouth is ringed with tentacles and lies at one end of the sausage shaped body. The gut loops through the body to discharge through the anus at the other end. In some groups tube feet are concentrated in rows on the lower side. Major taxa are shown in Fig. 59. Consult Cannon and Silver (1987) for a detailed report on the holothurians of northern Australia.

Reef regions are dominated by the families Holothuriidae and Stichopodidae, both with peltate tentacles, i.e., short with a plate-like end. These feed by shovelling sediments into the mouth and digesting the microfauna within. Off the reefs or in sandy regions are those with dendritic tentacles; these are spread to collect plankton. Some lack tube feet: most conspicuous among these are the long synaptids which because of their peculiar anchor-shaped spicules feel sticky when handled.

OPHIUROIDEA

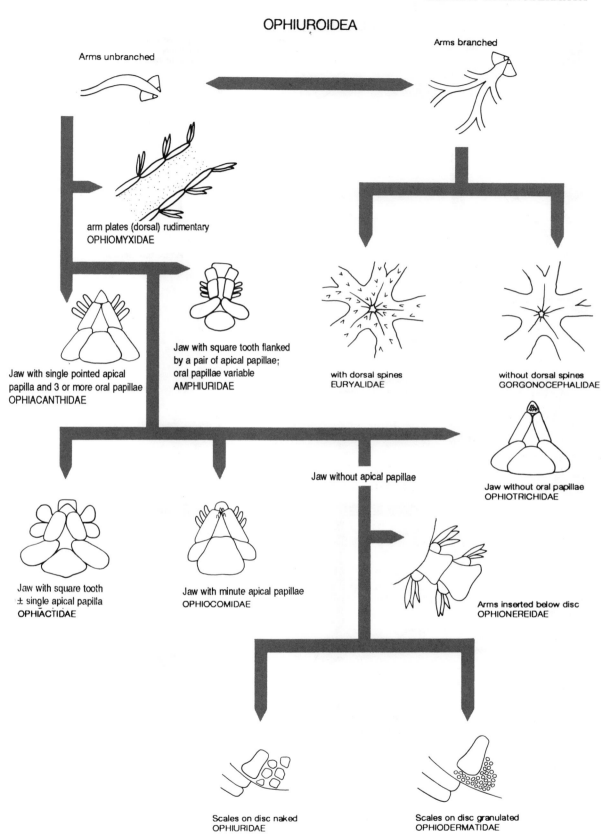

Arms unbranched

Arms branched

arm plates (dorsal) rudimentary
OPHIOMYXIDAE

Jaw with square tooth flanked
by a pair of apical papillae;
oral papillae variable
AMPHIURIDAE

with dorsal spines
EURYALIDAE

without dorsal spines
GORGONOCEPHALIDAE

Jaw with single pointed apical
papilla and 3 or more oral papillae
OPHIACANTHIDAE

Jaw without apical papillae

Jaw without oral papillae
OPHIOTRICHIDAE

Jaw with square tooth
± single apical papilla
OPHIACTIDAE

Jaw with minute apical papillae
OPHIOCOMIDAE

Arms inserted below disc
OPHIONEREIDAE

Scales on disc naked
OPHIURIDAE

Scales on disc granulated
OPHIODERMATIDAE

Fig. 57. Ophiuroidea.

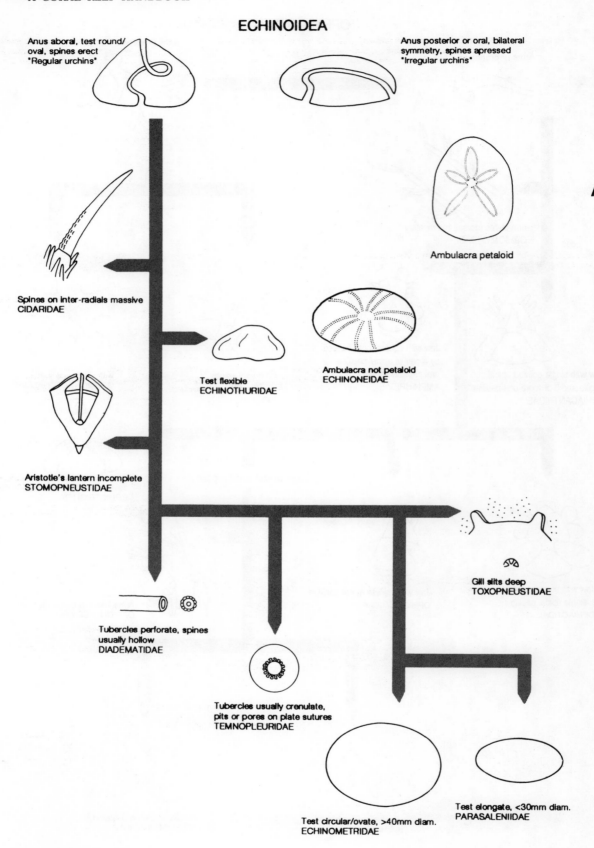

ECHINOIDEA

Anus aboral, test round/oval, spines erect "Regular urchins"

Anus posterior or oral, bilateral symmetry, spines apressed "Irregular urchins"

A

Ambulacra petaloid

Spines on inter-radials massive
CIDARIDAE

Test flexible
ECHINOTHURIDAE

Ambulacra not petaloid
ECHINONEIDAE

Aristotle's lantern incomplete
STOMOPNEUSTIDAE

Gill slits deep
TOXOPNEUSTIDAE

Tubercles perforate, spines usually hollow
DIADEMATIDAE

Tubercles usually crenulate, pits or pores on plate sutures
TEMNOPLEURIDAE

Test circular/ovate, >40mm diam.
ECHINOMETRIDAE

Test elongate, <30mm diam.
PARASALENIIDAE

Fig. 58a. Echinoidea.

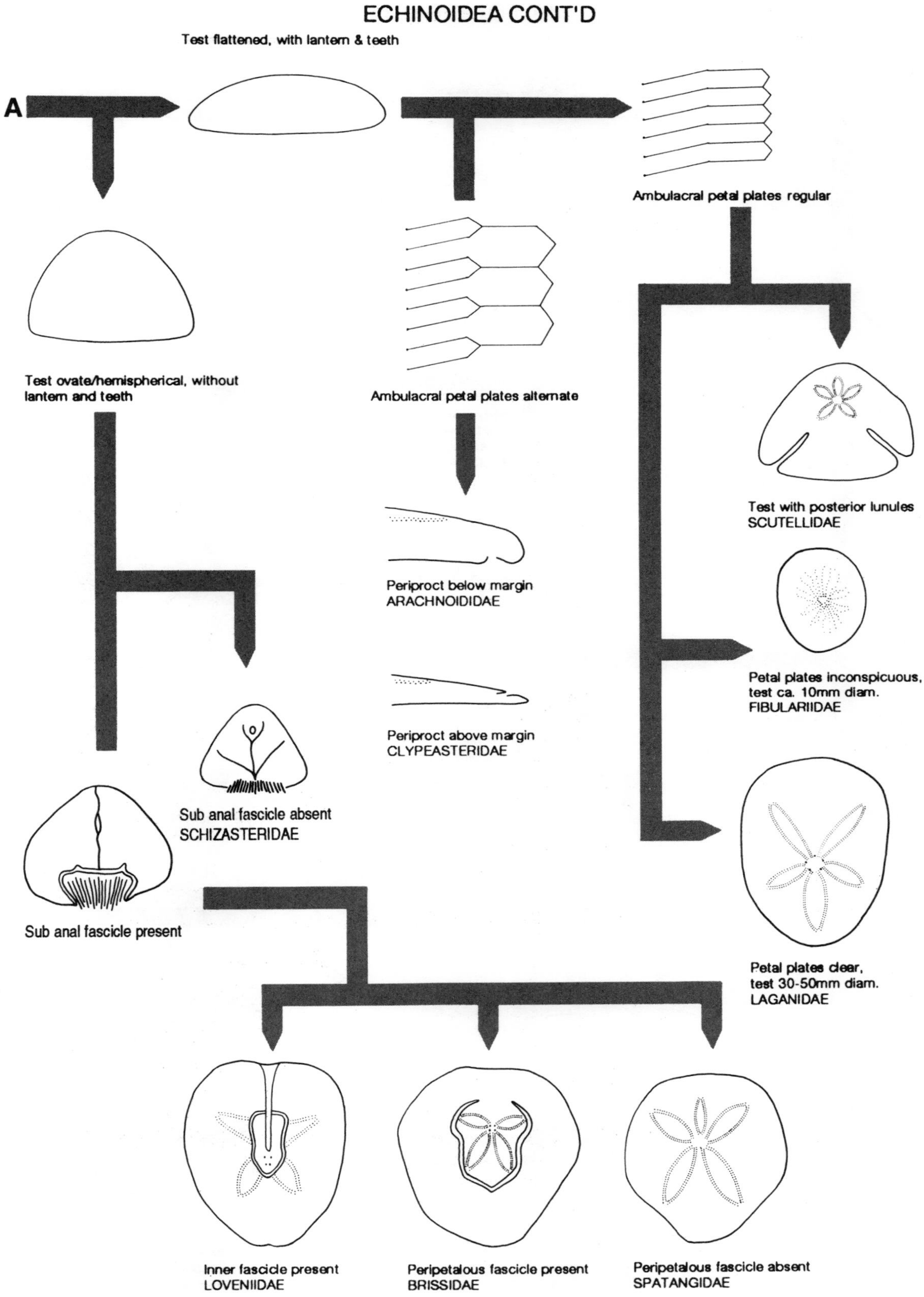

ECHINOIDEA CONT'D

Test flattened, with lantern & teeth

A

Ambulacral petal plates regular

Test ovate/hemispherical, without lantern and teeth

Ambulacral petal plates alternate

Periproct below margin
ARACHNOIDIDAE

Periproct above margin
CLYPEASTERIDAE

Test with posterior lunules
SCUTELLIDAE

Petal plates inconspicuous,
test ca. 10mm diam.
FIBULARIIDAE

Sub anal fascicle absent
SCHIZASTERIDAE

Sub anal fascicle present

Petal plates clear,
test 30-50mm diam.
LAGANIDAE

Inner fascicle present
LOVENIIDAE

Peripetalous fascicle present
BRISSIDAE

Peripetalous fascicle absent
SPATANGIDAE

Fig. 58b. Echinoidea — continued.

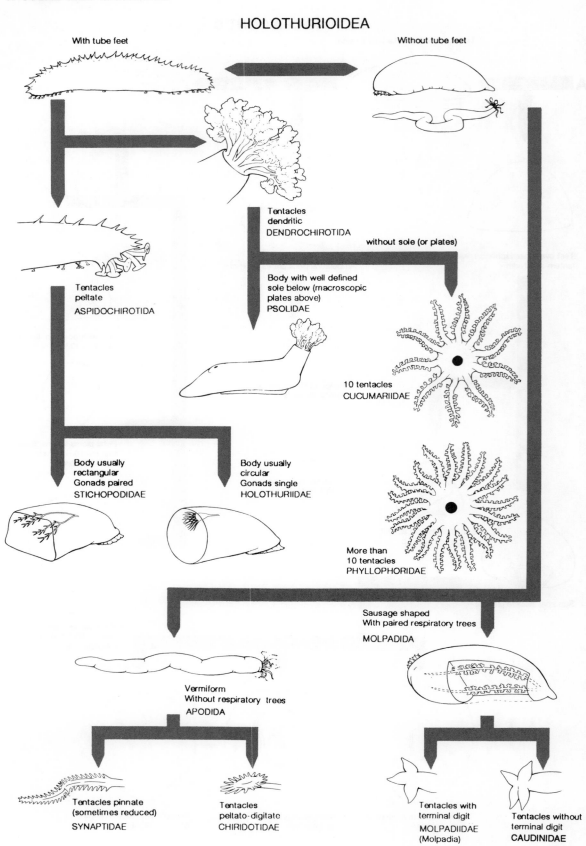

HOLOTHURIOIDEA

With tube feet

Without tube feet

Tentacles
dendritic
DENDROCHIROTIDA

without sole (or plates)

Tentacles
peltate
ASPIDOCHIROTIDA

Body with well defined
sole below (macroscopic
plates above)
PSOLIDAE

10 tentacles
CUCUMARIIDAE

Body usually
rectangular
Gonads paired
STICHOPODIDAE

Body usually
circular
Gonads single
HOLOTHURIIDAE

More than
10 tentacles
PHYLLOPHORIDAE

Sausage shaped
With paired respiratory trees
MOLPADIDA

Vermiform
Without respiratory trees
APODIDA

Tentacles pinnate
(sometimes reduced)
SYNAPTIDAE

Tentacles
peltato-digitate
CHIRIDOTIDAE

Tentacles with
terminal digit
MOLPADIIDAE
(Molpadia)

Tentacles without
terminal digit
CAUDINIDAE

Fig. 59. Holothuroidea.

Of particular interest among the sea cucumbers are those which are prized as delicacies throughout south-east Asia and some parts of the Pacific. Those of the genus *Actinopyga* with five hard anal "teeth" are especially sought, though other genera are taken. There are colloquial names for some of the species. Generally the animal is dried and the tough body wall is used in soups and stews. The trepang or bêche de mer fishery was one of Queensland's biggest 100 years ago and interest is being revived.

The reef flats can be covered with holothurians especially the red/black *Holothuria atra* or the brown/black *H. leucospilota* which readily ejects sticky white cuvierian tubules. Often found under coral clumps are red *H. edulis*, the soft brown *H. hilla* with white papillae and the rough pink/grey/brown papillate *H. impatiens,* all Holothuriidae. Also in the same family are the beautifully patterned *Bohadschia argus* or Tiger-fish and the heavy bodied *Actinopyga* spp. found on the reef slopes.

Generally favouring regions of rubble or coral are members of the Stichopodidae, most commonly the dark green *Stichopus chloronotus* or the large (to nearly 1m) red/purple *Thelenota ananas. Synapta maculata* (Synaptidae) also is found in coral or rubble areas. It is a mottled green/brown and white and can reach 1 m or more.

Under rocks even close to the beach are small red *Chirodota rigida* (Chirodotidae) which like the synaptids lack tube feet. Another inhabitant of rocky areas of the reef flat is the small purple *Afrocucumis africana* (Phyllophoridae), one of the dendrochirotes or branched tentacled holothurians. This group is much better represented in deeper water between the reefs where a dominant genus is *Pentacta* (Cucumariidae).

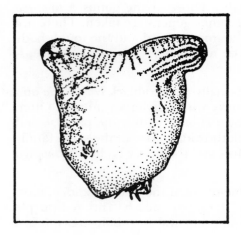

Subphylum Tunicata

Sea Squirts, Salps and Larvaceans

Sea squirts (Ascidiacea), are fixed invertebrates, one of the three classes of filter feeding animals in the subphylum Tunicata of the Chordata. The other classes are the planktonic salps (Thaliacea) and appendicularious (Larvacea).

The tunicate relationship with chordates is based on their perforated pharynx, notochord-like cells in the larval tail, and, also present only in the larvae, a hollow dorsal nerve cord and cerebral vesicle. A mucus-secreting groove in the mid-ventral line of the pharnyx with an iodine-binding capacity like the vertebrate thyroid gland provides even more compelling evidence of chordate affinity. The relationship between tunicates and other invertebrates, however, is obscure.

The name Tunicata, is from the tunic or test secreted by the ectoderm of salps and ascidians. It is composed of fibres of a cellulose-like material (tunicin) in a protein matrix and is traversed by ectodermal vessels from the body wall of the animal. Ascidians and salps also resemble one another in having a peribranchial or atrial cavity invaginated from the dorsal surface to surround the large perforated pharynx (Fig. 60).

In the class Larvacea there is a mucus "house" surrounding the animal but no tunicin test. Larvaceans are distinguished from the other two classes in that development is direct and the tail (lost on metamorphosis in salps and ascidians) is retained throughout their life. Further, there is no peribranchial cavity and the pharyngeal perforations open directly to the exterior.

Tunicates are an important part of the food chain, filtering prodigious quantities of water from which minute plant cells and particulate organic matter are strained. In both ascidians and salps water is drawn into the pharynx and out through its perforated wall by the synchronous beating of cilia that line the perforations (stigmata). Food is caught on a sheet of mucus that moves from the endostyle, up over the pharyngeal wall, back along the mid-dorsal line and into the oesophagus. Larvaceans strain their food through filters in the mucous house from a current of water created by the beating tail (Alldredge 1978).

Both salps and larvaceans in Australian waters are documented by Thompson (1948). Larvaceans are all small (less than 1 cm). Salps make up a large part of the gelatinous plankton that is sometimes very common in oceans of all parts of the world. They usually are in the vicinity of 1–3 cm. However, *Pyrosoma atlanticum*, a cosmopolitan colonial species, sometimes grows so large that divers can swim into the central cloacal cavity that is surrounded by a cylinder of minute zooids embedded in the common test.

Class Ascidiacea

There are about 200, mostly brilliantly coloured, species in the Great Barrier Reef and most occur along its whole length from north to south. SCUBA divers will see the largest specimens on the reef slope, growing around the base of coral colonies, on rocks, around the sides and lining the roof of caves. Most species can also be seen on the under surface of rocks and rubble behind the reef crest, lining tidal pools, and binding together coarse sediments where they gather in hollows near the edge of the reef. Individuals in the intertidal zone behind the reef edge do not usually grow very large. They appear to be grazed by predators, especially *Turbo argyrostomus*, and probably are mechanically removed from rubble and rock substrates as waves move them about on the reef flat.

Amongst the most conspicuous ascidians in coral reefs are the green colonies that gain their colour from single-celled green prokaryotic (without a nucleus) algal symbionts. The most interesting of these algal cells is *Prochloron,* a group that was not known before 1973 and that has not been found anywhere else except in association with ascidians. Blue-Green algae (Cyanophyta) are also found in similar associations with ascidian species. In some species of the family Didemnidae the relationship is one in which the host and symbiont are mutually dependent. The larval ascidians even have special devices to carry the green algal cells with them to multiply in the cloacal cavity or test of the new colonies they form. In other cases the plant cells are only present sometimes, usually on some part of the surface of the colony, and can be wiped off very readily. These plant-ascidian symbioses often are found forming carpets on the sandy surface of the reef flat. Ascidian colonies are able to shade the plant cells from sunlight by arranging carotenoid pigments and calcareous spicules in their upper surface. When in cryptic shaded habitats both pigments and spicules are lost from the upper surface and colonies are green.

Of the three suborders of the Ascidiacea, one (Aplousobranchia; Fig. 61A,B) is almost exclusively colonial, forming colonies by replication of the zooids. The other two (Phlebobranchia and Stolidobranchia; Fig. 61C,D) contain both solitary and colonial forms. In colonial forms the zooids are sometimes joined to one another by fine strands of test (stolons; Fig. 62A,a), but in others, they are embedded in the common test (Fig. 62B–D, b–c). All suborders are represented in the waters of the Great Barrier Reef, but colonial species are especially numerous.

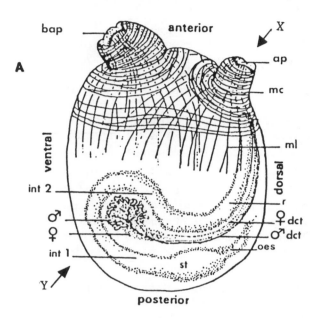

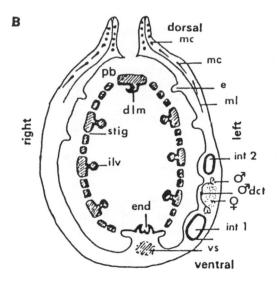

Fig. 60. Terms used to describe ascidian morphology: A, imaginery solitary ascidian removed from the test; **B**, oblique section through A, X–Y (antero-dorsal–postero-ventral). For key to symbols used see caption to Figure 61.

In the field, the two apertures (branchial or incurrent and atrial or excurrent) of the larger solitary ascidians are readily seen (Fig. 60-bap,ap). They are less conspicuous in some of the smaller zooids of colonial species, and when zooids are completely embedded in the test the apertures are often very difficult to see. Sometimes, both branchial and atrial apertures open onto the surface of the test (Fig. 62B,b), but in others the zooids are organized into colonial systems in which the atrial apertures open into spaces inside the test (common cloacal cavities) and the surface of the test is interrupted by minute star-shaped branchial openings and large common cloacal apertures (Fig. 62C–D, c).

As colonies evolve (from Diazonidae to Didemnidae), zooids replicate themselves at a greater rate and there is a progressive reduction in zooid size (Fig. 62A–D). Colony organization is also associated with the evolution of viviparous larvae. In the better organized colonies fertilization is internal, fewer eggs are produced, embryos are incubated in the colony, and are released at an advanced stage, with well developed tail and sense organs.

In order to investigate the morphology of ascidians it is usually necessary to remove the body from the test. For solitary species (Fig. 61 C,D), this is done by cutting the test around the ventral mid-line from one aperture to the other (the long way around). If the cut has not been too deep, the body will be entire and can be removed by gently detaching each aperture where it overlaps the test. The body itself should then be opened around the mid-line (the endostyle) and pinned open. The branchial sac (pharynx) can then be carefully removed (to expose the atrial cavity) by cutting through the connectives. The body organs (gut and gonads) can then be seen embedded in the outer body wall and the genus can be readily identified.

Colonial species (Figs 61B, 62) in which zooids are embedded are best examined by cutting a thin vertical wedge out of the colony. Zooids can be removed or they can be examined *in situ* with stereo-microscope. Usually it is not necessary to dissect the fragile transparent zooids of colonial species. The star-shaped calcareous spicules of the family Didemnidae can be examined by holding a very small piece of test in a flame (a match will do) in order to burn the test. This will free the spicules so that they disperse into a drop of glycerine on a microscope slide.

Characters that will aid recognition of family and higher level taxa are set out in the graphic key to the Class Ascidiacea and are illustrated in Figures 60–62. The more common and readily identified species occurring in the area are referred to below. It should be noted that colours are always lost in preservative. More detailed keys to genera and families are available in Kott (1985, 1990, 1992).

Diazonidae is represented by the large (up to 6 or 7 cm long) solitary zooids of *Rhopalaea crassa*. It is opaque yellow or blue, or colourless with fine black markings along the blood vessels and longitudinal body muscles, and with yellow around the rims of the apertures. The firm, cylindrical to irregular stalk is firmly embedded in rubble and is hard to extricate. These zooids appear to regenerate thoraces from persisting stalks. They are found at shallow (2 or 3 m) to greater depth down the reef slope.

Clavelinidae zooids are smaller than diazonids, and usually at least partially embedded or joined by basal stolons. They are gelatinous, translucent and often blue. The common *Clavelina moluccensis* has three blue pigment patches in a line between the apertures; *C. fecunda* has smaller (less than 1 cm) blue zooids with some yellow patches anteriorly; *C. oliva* is small, solitary and reddish brown, most common in the north. *Nephtheis fascicularis*, common around northern Australia and in the Western Pacific, has blue embedded zooids around a conical head, on a short, thick cylindrical stalk. A cylindrical mesh of blood vessels beneath the surface test of the stalk distinguishes the genus.

Pycnoclavellidae are usually small pea-shaped to oval naked thoraces on long thin stalks often tangled with sand and epiphytes basally. The common *Pycnoclavella diminuta*, with oily brown vesicles in the stalk, has blue, white or brownish pea-shaped thoraces with four rows of stigmata, while *P. detorta* has glowing green-blue flourescent thoraces turned through 90° at the top of the stalk so that atrial apertures are terminal and branchial apertures are at the side.

												Subfamily	Family	Order
gut loop behind pharynx	colonial, and/or gut loop vertical	no internal longitudinal vessels or forked vestiges	branchial apertures 6-lobed	replicates generated by division of zooids	replicates not by oesophageal budding	gonads in posterior abdomen	stigmata in more than 3 rows	stomach halfway down short abdomen	heart in posterior abdomen	cloacal systems absent	posterior abdomen not constricted		RITTERELLIDAE n. fam.	APLOUSOBRANCHIA
											posterior abdomen constricted		PROTOPOLYCLINIDAE n. fam.	
										cloacal systems present			POLYCLINIDAE emend.	
									heart in abdomen				PLACENTELIDAE n. fam.	
								stomach at posterior end of long abdomen					EUHERDMANIIDAE	
							stigmata in 3 rows						PSEUDODISTOMIDAE n. fam.	
						gonads in abdomen							POLYCITORIDAE	
				replicates by oesophageal budding									DIDEMNIDAE	
				replicates generated in vegetative stolons	lobes of apertures smooth								HOLOZOIDAE	
					lobes of apertures denticulate								STOMOZOIDAE	
			branchial apertures not lobed	abdomen more than twice length of thorax; embryos fertilised at base of oviduct; larval adhesive organs inverted tubes									PYCNOCLAVELLIDAE	
				abdomen not more than twice length of thorax; embryos fertilised at top of oviduct; larval adhesive organs with axial cone									CLAVELINIDAE	
		internal longitudinal branchial vessels or forked vestiges											DIAZONIDAE	
	solitary, and gut loop horizontal												CIONIDAE	
gut loop at side of pharynx	gut on right side of pharynx						stigmata straight					RHODOSOMATINAE	CORELLIDAE	PHLEBOBRANCHIA
							stigmata coiled					CORELLINAE		
	gut on left side of pharynx	internal longitudinal branchial vessels represented by papillae											AGNESIIDAE	
		internal longitudinal branchial vessels entire	pharynx flat; gonads on left side only	gonads not embedded in the test	solitary								ASCIDIIDAE	
					colonial								PEROPHORIDAE	
				gonads embedded in the test									PLURELLIDAE	
			pharynx folded; gonads on both sides	simple branchial tentacles	solitary							STYELINAE	STYELIDAE	STOLIDOBRANCHIA
					colonial	cloacal systems absent						POLYZOINAE		
						cloacal systems present						BOTRYLLINAE		
				branched branchial tentacles	rectangular stigmata; no renal vesicle								PYURIDAE	
					stigmata not rectangular; renal vesicle present	pharynx whole body length, perforated by spiral or irregular stigmata							MOLGULIDAE	
						pharynx short anterior band, perforated by circular stigmata							HEXACROBYLIDAE	

Holozoidae are represented by the opaque blue rope-like *Sigillina cyanea* with separately opening zooids around a central test core through which the long posterior vascular stolons extend into the basal stalk. *Sigillina signifera,* most common in the north, forms navy blue to bottle green translucent carpets of separately opening upright zooids. *Hypodistoma deerratum* has large flask-shaped colonies with terminal cloacal apertures and minute zooids with long atrial siphons opening into posterior abdominal cloacal cavities. Also, there are several soft violet-pink-blue, mushroom shaped *Distaplia* spp. in reef waters.

Polycitoridae with its gelatinous, sometimes sandy colonies of completely embedded but separately opening zooids, is one of the best represented families in the Reef. *Polycitor*, with four or more rows of stigmata is less diverse than *Eudistoma* (with only three rows of stigmata). *Cystodytes* (four rows of stigmata) and *Polycitorella* (more than four rows of stigmata) have calcareous spicules in the test, but long abdominal gut loops to distinguish them from Didemnidae. Common in the rubble zone are smooth, shiny-surfaced cushions of *E. purpureum* (purple), *E. glaucus* (green), *E. muscosa* (yellow-brown), and large investing colonies of *E. amplus* with its zooids in rudimentary cloacal systems, red or green, symbiotic cells in the test and green prochloron on the surface. Sandy colonies of *E. ovatum* (with yellow zooids) and *E. angolanum* (red test and zooids) are tucked into crevices. Purple *E. reginum* also has some embedded sand and large red symbionts in the test between the zooids. Common species of *Polycitor* are *P. annulus* with colourless test and black rims around the apertures, the small *P. translucidus* with parallel vertical zooids, and the massive, white, fleshy, *P. circes* and *P. giganteus*.

Euherdmaniidae are represented by the firm, gelatinous colonies of separately opening *Euherdmania dentatosiphonis* (with dentate lobes around the apertures) and the solitary, yellow zooids of *E. digitata*.

Protopolyclinidae has only a single species, *Condominium areolatum*, reported from reefal waters. It has a single layer of zooids embedded, parallel to one another, in a flat sandy lamella which has its upper rim projecting above the sand in which it stands vertically.

Pseudodistomidae are not diverse in reefal waters, although the massive *Pseudodistoma gracilum* (with mucus-like soft test), and golden translucent plates of *P. aureum* often occur.

Ritterellidae are more often encountered in temperate than tropical waters. However, pinkish-blue slightly iridescent plates of *Ritterella dispar*, which separate out into clumps of flat-topped lobes when collected, are common high in the intertidal.

Polyclinidae is, after the Didemnidae, the most diverse family in reefal waters. All taxa have narrow, thread-like zooids arranged in circular to complex branching common cloacal systems. Common genera are *Polyclinum* (with sac-like posterior abdomen, twisted gut-loop and usually branchial papillae), *Synoicum* (with smooth or mulberry-like stomach), and *Aplidium* (with longitudinal stomach folds).

The yellowish-black, thick, almost rubbery sheets of *Polyclinum vasculosum* are common in the rubble zone; and sometimes colonies of *P. glabrum* with opaque yellow zooids showing through the clear-yellow test are found under rocks. A firm sandy outer layer of test protects the zooids embedded in the soft internal test of *P. saturnium* (purple or red internally with yellow zooids), *P. solum* (with a long, narrow posterior abdomen and lacking branchial papillae) and *P. tsutsuii* (with a brood pouch projecting from the thorax).

Fig. 61. Ascidian morphology: **A**, solitary aplousobranch with internal longitudinal branchial vessels and gonads in the gut loop (*Rhopalaea*, Diazonidae); **B**, colonial aplousobranch, without internal longitudinal vessels and gonads in the posterior abdomen (*Aplidium*, Polyclinidae); **C**, solitary phlebobranch (*Ascidia*, Ascidiidae); **D**, composite stolidobranch with branched branchial tentacles (Pyuridae, Molgulidae), dorsal languets (*Pyura*, Pyuridae), liver diverticulum (*Pyura*, Pyuridae), kidney (Molgulidae), large endocarps enclosed in gut loop (Styelidae), gonads outside the gut loop, long and branched ovarian tubes with testis follicles applied closely along the sides (*Cnemidocarpa*, Styelinae) and siphonal armature (Pyuridae).

In C and D the body has been cut around the mid-ventral line and opened out; and, except for a small fragment anteriorly and posteriorly, the branchial sac has been removed. Key to symbols — ab, abdomen; ap, atrial (excurrent) aperture; an, anus; b, branchial tentacles (b1, simple; b2, branched); bap, branchial (incurrent) aperture; bf, branchial fold; bs, branchial sac; bw, body wall; cap, common cloacal aperture; ccc, common cloacal cavity; dct, gonoduct; dlm, dorsal lamina; dln, dorsal languets; dt, dorsal tubercle; e, endocarp (e1, on gut; e2, in gut loop); end, endostyle; g, gonad (o follicle, o ovarian tube); h, heart; ilv, internal longitudinal branchial vessel; int, gut loop (int1, ascending limb; int2, descending limb); l, liver diverticulum; oc, ocellus; oes, oesophagus; pab, posterior-abdomen; pb, peribranchial (atrial) cavity; pg, prebranchial (prepharyngeal) groove; r, rectum; s, siphonal spines; sl, siphonal lining; st, stomach; stig, stigmata (pharyngeal perforations); t, test; th, thorax; tv, test vessel; vs, ventral sinus.

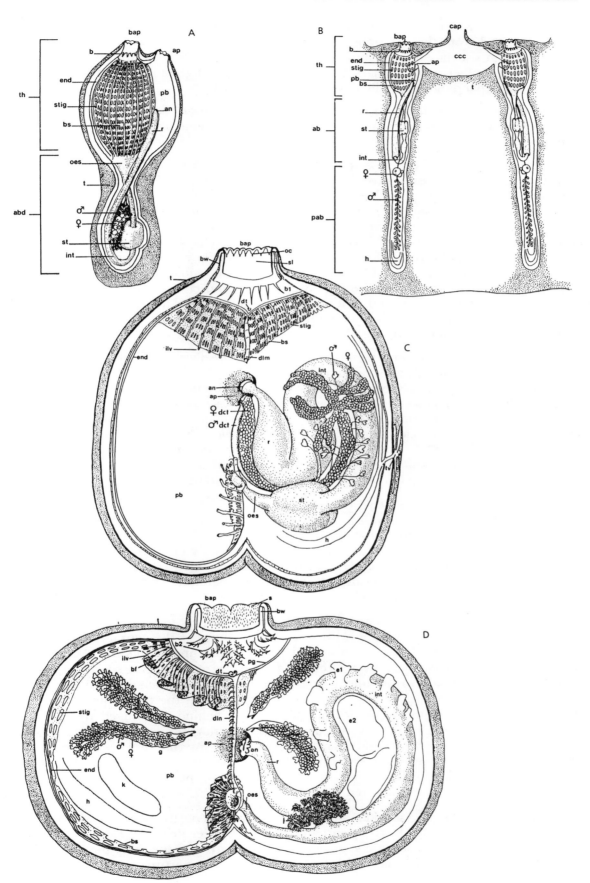

173

Tightly packed reddish-black lobes of *Synoicum suarenum*, looking like a pigs kidney when removed from the substrate, are found attached to rocks near the intertidal zone; *S. intercedens,* its surface divided into naked, brown to bright red lobes with sand around the margins, has mulberry-like stomachs; and *S. buccinum* has tough sandy cylindrical branching stalks, each expanding terminally into naked yellow heads.

In deeper waters there are massive, gelatinous colonies of *S. castellatum* and *Aplidium crateriferum* with zooid systems opening into surface depressions, around protuberant cloacal siphons.

Aplidium is one of the most diverse genera of the Ascidiacea, and only the most conspicuous of its representatives in tropical waters are referred to here: *Aplidium multiplicatum* has soft, orange-pink sheet-like colonies, double rows of zooids, and each aperture is outlined in white opaque cells. Sometimes it has green *Prochloron* on the surface, and in common cloacal canals. *Aplidium protectans* has large, firm, spherical, rosy colonies with zooids arranged in circles. Sheet-like colonies of the spectacular, orange *A. tabascum* have test areas between the rows of zooids outlined in a single row of sand-particles like the contours of a map, and the zooids of *A. lenticulum* are in double rows surrounding circular areas of zooid-free test. There also are species, with sand crowded in the test, such as *A. caelestis, A. clivosum, A. ritteri* and *A. triggsense* (with many larval adhesive organs). *Aplidium uteute* has small, cushion-like colonies through which the orange or scarlet zooids with maroon-coloured embryos are clearly seen.

Didemnidae is the most diverse family occurring in coral-reef waters. It contains a bewildering number of species not always readily distinguished from one another. The zooids of all genera are small and simplified, and the taxonomy of the family is difficult. Most contain stellate calcareous spicules in the test which obscure the zooids and the cloacal systems. Many (about 25) of the tropical species have obligate symbioses with the minute prokaryotic *Prochloron* in the test or cloacal cavities. The *Prochloron*-containing didemnids have been revised (Kott 1980, 1982), and *Didemnum molle, Lissoclinum patella, L. bistratum, Diplosoma virens, D. similis, Trididemnum cyclops* and *T. paracyclops* are all conspicuous in shallow areas from north to south. Only *L. voeltzkowi* does not appear to be present in the south.

The family contains the genera *Didemnum* and *Trididemnum* (with four and three rows of stigmata respectively, and with a coiled vas deferens); *Diplosoma* (without spicules and with a straight vas deferens); *Lissoclinum* (with a straight vas deferens); *Leptoclinides* (with numerous testis follicles, coiled vas deferens and posteriorly oriented atrial siphon); *Polysyncraton* (with numerous male follicles, coiled vas deferens, but no posteriorly oriented atrial siphon); *Atriolum* (with a single testis follicle, coiled vas deferens, posteriorly oriented atrial siphon, and a thoracic brood pouch).

Ascidiidae, a family of large, generally naked, firm gelatinous forms, brightly coloured in life, contains two genera, *Phallusia* (with accessory openings of the neural duct behind the dorsal lamina) and *Ascidia.* Cream to brown with bright yellow chromatophores, *Phallusia julinea* is commonly seen projecting from crevices. *Ascidia* spp. are more diverse, species often being attached by the left side to the under surface of rubble. They include *A. archaia,* with a smooth, glassy test that magnifies commensal crustaceans in the peribranchial cavity; *A. liberata* with blackish pigment anteriorly, a deep groove behind the fringed apertures, and pointed papillae along the siphons; *A. glabra,* a translucent green coloured test; *A. capillata* with pink pigment anteriorly, and membranes from the internal test projecting into the body wall around the gut; *A. sydneiensis,* with fringed apertures, a mud-filled gut and short parallel muscle bands around the margin of the left side of the body; *A. kreagra* has a long body with canary yellow test and red siphons.

Corellidae are similar to Ascidiidae but have the gut loop on the right. *Corella* has spiral stigmata and is represented by *C. japonica* in the Great Barrier Reef. *Rhodosoma turcicum,* the genus characterized by its straight stigmata, has a deep groove converting the anterior part of the right side of body to a lid which folds down over the apertures.

Plurellidae a small family of one colonial genus *(Plurella)* and one solitary one *(Microgastra)* is more often reported near the mainland. Both genera have been recorded from the Western Pacific. Both have a brittle, sand encrusted test, in which the heart, gonads and neural complex are embedded. *Microgastra granosa* is known from Low Island in the Great Barrier Reef. A species of *Plurella* is known to occur in the Philippines, and very likely the genus will be found in the Great Barrier Reef.

Perophoridae contains two genera *(Perophora* and *Ecteinascidia),* both forming similar colonies of short-stalked zooids joined by basal or axial stolons. Generally, *Perophora* species are small, with no more than eight rows of stigmata, and club-shaped or undivided male follicles. *Ecteinascidia* zooids are larger, with more than eight rows of stigmata, and short, pear-shaped male follicles. A number of species commonly occur in the Great Barrier Reef. Small colourless zooids of *P. multiclathrata* have a single male follicle and only five rows of stigmata; *P. modificata* (recorded only from the north) has opaque yellow zooids and a complex vascular network in the stalk. *P. namei* has upright horny, rigid stalks and four rows of stigmata. Transparent *E. diaphanis* (with orange-red bands or spots around the apertures), and cloudy yellowish-green or blue *E. nexa* (with a complex network of basal stolons making it difficult to remove) form extensive mats on undersurfaces.

Styelidae (Styelinae): *Polycarpa,* one of the most diverse genera of solitary species in tropical waters, has distinctive short gonads (polycarps) scattered over the body wall. *Styela* and *Cnemidocarpa,* the other two genera that occur here, with long gonads stretching from the ventral line to the atrial aperture, are less diverse. *Styella* (represented only by *S. canopus)* has male follicles on the body wall rather than clustered around the gonad to form a compact rod as in *Cnemidocarpa. Cnemidocarpa areolata* is a common species fixed by the ventral surface, with smooth, naked purplish test, and short siphons with red-striped linings which turn black in preservative. The related *C. stolonifera* is stalked, often partially embedded in the interreefal sediments, its long, grooved parallel siphons close together and project vertically upwards.

Over most of the length of the Great Barrier Reef except in the south, the most conspicuous species of the diverse genus *Polycarpa* is the boat-shaped, golden-whitish-purple tough, leathery, naked *P. aurata,* with gold-lined siphons well separated from one another. Also naked, the orange, thick-stalked, fleshy *P. clavata,* with siphons on the side of the vertically lengthened head directed away from one another, has a similar geographic range. Found along the reef slopes, *P. pigmentata* is also a common species, and is readily distinguished by its wrinkled leathery test with some epibonts, and its blue siphonal linings. Superficially similar, *P. obscura* has orange siphon linings, and probably is the largest ascidian known from reefal waters, growing to 20 cm or more. In interreefal areas, the common *Polycarpa* is *P. papillata,* often tapering anteriorly to a terminal branchial aperture, and with longitudinal red stripes on the otherwise whitish, naked test. As individuals of this species age, the test becomes rough and wrinkled, and the orientation of the body changes from being upright to recumbent (lying on its ventral surface). The species is readily distinguished by its oval, upright gonads, attached to the body wall by a narrow ligament, and by its habit of eviscerating the whole gut through the branchial aperture when it is collected. The smaller, cryptic species of *Polycarpa* present in reefal waters include two with sandy brittle test and an open curved, rather than looped, gut, viz. the sandy crescent-shaped *P. chinensis,* half embedded in sandy substrates and the upright, oval *P. procera.* Both are usually found in large aggregates.

Other upright sandy species with brittle tests, but with the more normal looped gut, are *P. reniformis* (with a cushion-like projection of the body wall — endocarp — enclosed in the gut loop), *P. lucilla* (without any endocarps), and *P. papyra* (with small scattered endocarps). *Polycarpa aurita* (named for the large opening of the neural duct that looks ear-like) is either naked or covered with sand, attached to test hairs. It has very numerous embedded gonads that appear to coalesce with one another between fleshy papilla-like

175

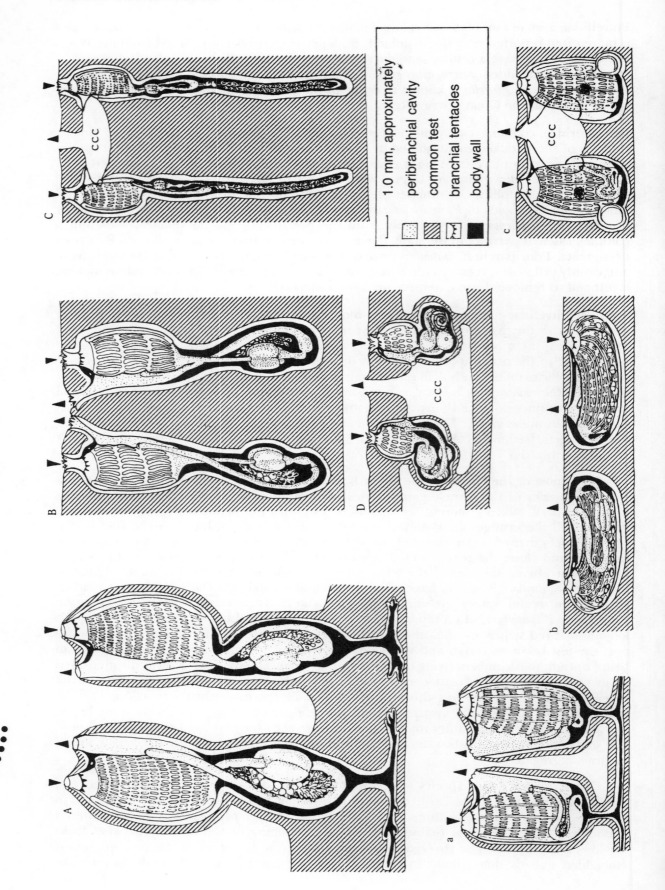

endocarps. An externally irregular species, *P. biforis,* also has a large opening of the neural gland, but its gonads are upright and clustered around the base of the connectives joining the body wall to the pharynx, and it has no endocarps.

The only species of *Polycarpa* with external spines around the apertures is *P. olitoria.* Externally and internally it resembles *P. papillata,* with numerous endocarps and gonads in a row on each side, however, its gonads are recumbent rather than upright and its gut does not eviscerate.

Styelidae (Polyzoinae, Botryllinae): These are colonial styelids with apertures opening separately to the exterior. They usually are small, the evolution of replication being associated with reduction and simplification of individual zooids.

Polyandrocarpa are least simplified having the characters of *Polycarpa,* albeit usually only single rows of gonads *(polycarps)* along each side of the ventral line, but retaining four branchial folds on each side. *Eusynstyela latericius,* common on the undersides of boulders, forms flat, red mats of dorso-ventrally flattened zooids, embedded in common test. Similar colonies but more delicate and thinner, with smaller zooids, *Symplegma* spp. are pink or yellowish with only four internal longitudinal vessels, and single gonads in the middle of each side of the body wall.

In contrast with Polyzoinae, in which each zooid in the colony has separate atrial and branchial openings to the exterior, the Botryllinae have zooids lining long canals and circular cloacal cavities like Aplousobranchia. There are several abundant species of this family in coral reef waters. They usually have regular patterns of at least two colours (not always the same). The relationships of the various populations and colour variants in the seemingly cosmopolitan taxa of *Botrylloides magnicoecus, B. leachi,* and *Botryllus schlosseri* are not resolved. Botryllidae contains some of the most brilliant and conspicuous members of the Ascidiacea in coral reef waters.

Pyuridae: Like Styelidae, the Pyuridae are solitary often large, ascidians, with tough, often rough, wrinkled, leathery tests. They are seldom brightly coloured and often have scale-like hardenings of the outer cuticle or they have adhering sand and calcareous particles, and epibionts. The apertures usually are protected by minute scales or spines (seldom more than 0.1 mm long) which line the siphons and sometimes continue, out on the outer surface of the test around the siphons. Of the most commonly occurring genera, *Halocynthia, Herdmania* and *Pyura* have small, pointed tentacle-like languets along the dorsal mid-line in the pharynx, while *Microcosmus* has a plain-edged dorsal lamina in this position. *Pyura elognata* is a sessile leathery flattened species fixed along the ventral surface with apertures at opposite ends of the upper surface, polygonal thickenings in the test, and minute cusp-like scales lining the siphons. More conspicuous, pointed iridescent scales line the siphons of the oval to spherical sandy *P. arenosa,* naked *P. curvigona,* large tuberculated *P. sacciformis,* and the upright *P. obesa* with black and white stripes converging to the apertures. Peach-coloured, translucent, *Herdmania momus,* with its inflated spherical body, and diverging cylindrical siphons, is often found under rubble on the reef flat. Care should be taken when handling it because of its armed spindle-shaped spicules in the body wall.

Microcosmus is represented by the ubiquitous *M. pupa* and *M. exasperatus,* both with pointed siphonal spines; *M. squamiger* with cusp-like scales; *M. helleri* with cartilaginous projections in the base of the siphon; and *M. tuberculatus* with broadly based curved spines.

Molgulidae: Always solitary, with a large kidney-shaped vesicle on the right body wall, and stigmata curved around infundibulae in the branchial wall. The family is not well represented in the reefal fauna, and the species occurring here are small and inconspicuous, never

Fig. 62. Convergent evolutions of colonial systems in the Ascidiacea (diagrammatic): **A–D,** Aplousobranchia; a–c, Phlebobranchia and Stolidobranchia. **A,** (*Podoclavella,* Clavelinidae) and a (*Ecteinascidia,* Perophoridae), zooids largely independent, joined basally by common test or stolons; **B,** (*Eudistoma,* Polycitoridae) and b (*Eusynstyela,* Polyzoinae) zooids completely embedded in common test but opening independently to the exterior, **C,** (*Aplidium,* Polyclinidae) and c (*Botrylloides,* Botryllinae) atrial aperture of each zooid opens into common cloacal cavity; **D,** (*Leptoclinides,* Didemnidae) an extensive common cloaca between and behind the zooids.

brightly coloured and often with sand-encrusted and very brittle test. Both *Molgula ficus* and *M. mollis* has been recorded from Heron Island, but not often. The former is tough and spherical, with apertures on siphons directed away from one another; the latter has brittle thin test, and the sessile apertures are withdrawn into a narrow, long depression around the anterior edge of the body that is caused by contraction of body muscles. Other species, known from the Western Pacific and Indian Ocean may eventually be found to occur in the Great Barrier Reef.

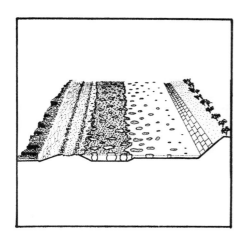

Reef Zonation

The Great Barrier Reef consists of two to three thousand reefs and islands, each one different. Each reef has a different history and a different shape; and each reef, and each part of a reef is subjected to different physical influences — such as sun, wind and currents — that affect the distribution of organisms on it.

Coral reef organisms usually are distributed in zones that result from the requirements of the organisms themselves. Zonation is particularly conspicuous on all reefs which have some parts completely exposed at low water, and others covered only by shallow water; or when, as on some reefs, there is a lagoon. Some lagoons are small, others are extensive, some are shallow with a very sandy bottom, and others are deep with coral outcrops and dense coral growth along the margins. These lakes in the reef, insulated from the oceanic waters surrounding the reef for at least part of the day (at low tide) greatly affect the zonation of fauna on the reef itself.

Brilliantly coloured living corals are to be found where they are kept free of sand and silt, especially where highly oxygenated, nutrient rich waters provide ideal conditions for them along the far seaward edges of the reef or along the outer margins of a deep lagoon within a reef. Cryptic species are found under dead coral boulders, either attached to the undersides, or, in the case of more mobile species, sheltering or burrowing in the substrate below. Burrowing molluscs, such as the volutes and olives, some holothurians and worms will only be found in sandy areas of the reef flat. Numbers of species shelter among algae and coral (both living and dead). Certain shrimps are found only as commensals in anemones and molluscs. One species of small crabs lives only in clumps of Turtle weed, the green algae *Chlorodesmis*, another in *Halimeda*, so perfectly adapted to the shape of the algal fronds that it is difficult to find. Other crabs live in or among living coral colonies.

Latitude and longitude must also be taken into consideration. Some species e.g., the Giant and Horse's Foot clams, will only be found in the northern region. Reefs in close proximity to the mainland will differ from those on the far outer edges of the continental shelf. Reefs such as Cairns and Pickersgill in the northern region have large sand flats exposed at low water. In this same region, especially on reefs close to the mainland, mangroves have become established and these in turn have a considerable effect on the nature of the surrounding reef. On Low Isles, for example, there is a dense mangrove area to seaward, east of the sand cay, and connected to it by an extensive sand flat, mostly uncovered by low spring tides.

Reef zonation varies as a result of temporal changes in the reef. For instance, cyclones, natural depredation, crown-of-thorns and human contact play a major role in altering certain reefs.

Long-term changes over decades result from reef growth and the maturation of some of its communities. These are not always easy to detect owing to the lack of base-line studies. One of the few locations where such studies are available is Low Island, off Port Douglas. It was the site of the Great Barrier Reef Expedition of 1928–29 — the first time that a coral reef had been studied continuosly over a year, and from many different aspects (ecology, physiology, chemistry and physics of the sea water, plankton production and growth rate of corals). Later, in 1953, the site was revisited to assess the changes.

As an example of the intertidal zonation of invertebrates, their distribution on the reef flat (from the beach of the cay to the reef rim) Heron Island reef is described.

Sandy Beach

Burrows of the Ghost crabs (*Ocypode* spp.) will be obvious, although normally the crabs emerge only at night.

Where the beachrock is absent, and the sandy beach merges into the Inner Reef Flat, as along the northeastern and eastern margins of the cay, the small burrowing bivalve, *Paphies striata,* is very common just below the surface of the sand. A very small pink holothurian, *Chirodata rigida,* also occurs here, buried in the sand, and the black *Holothuria atra* lies along the low tide line.

Beachrock

The amount of beachrock exposed on each side of the cay varies considerably from year to year, according to weather conditions. Beachrock fauna on the northern shore of the cay is sparse (with only a few mobile species under slabs of rock), presumably due to scouring and recurrent cyclonic activity. Populations are more obvious on the southern shore where the beachrock can usually be seen as three fairly clearly marked bands.

1. An upper, friable band with broken rubble and slabs of small rock. Here, the gastropod, *Planaxis sulcatus,* is the dominant mollusc, usually occupying cracks and crevices during day-light. Two obvious populations of *Planaxis,* the smaller animals (about half the size of the larger) occur nearer the beach. Clusters of *Clypeomorus monniliferus,* (Moulton 1962), also seem to vary due to weather conditions. Areas of flat rock uncovered one year are not visible another and in 1978 the populations recorded by Moulton were absent, but very large aggregations, not recorded by Moulton, were to be seen at the back of the western end of the northern beachrock.

   Where rubble and small slabs of rock occur along the southern beachrock, the nerites, *Nerita polita* and *N. striata* are found. Among more mobile species are the swift-footed crab, *Grapsus albolineatus* and the Red-eyed Crab, *Eriphia sebana*. The small porcelain crab, *Petrolisthes lamarcki,* small hermit crabs, mostly *Clibanarius virescens,* the anemone, *Actinia tenebrosa,* amphipods and small blennies, shelter among and under the boulders.

2. The second band of beachrock is much harder, and pitted with jagged projections. The large chiton, *Acanthopleura gemmata* occurs here, sometimes in numbers, in depressions and crevices facing south during daylight, but the mollusc is more obvious at night when browsing over the rock. The nerites, *Nerita albicilla* and *N. plicata* are also found here, together with a few *Siphonaria australis*.

3. At its lowest levels, the beachrock is generally smooth and softer, with a dense covering of small algae.

The Reef Flat

(Covered at E.L. W.S. by water of variable depths from a few centimetres to 1–2 m in deeper pools).

Inshore Sandy Zone

The reef flat is a mixture of sandy areas, dead coral rubble, algal-covered coral bounders (part-living and part-dead coral), and occasional micro-atolls of the solid *Porites lutea,* or the branching *P. cylindrica*. The latter is the dominant species at the eastern end of the cay.

Amongst living corals here the large brown, blunt-topped *Acropora palifera,* small colonies of *Pocillopora damicornis,* the branching yellow *Porites cylindrica, Goniopora* (obvious with its polyps extended during daylight with colours of brownish-yellow, blue, green and mauve), sporadic colonies of smaller *Acropora* spp. and a few faviids are most obvious.

If algal-covered boulders are turned over, a number of species will be found sheltering either in the sandy substrate, attached to, or burrowing into the dead coral rock. Conspicuous here are the cosmopolitan polychaete, the bristle-worm, *Eurythoe complanata* (which should not be picked up with bare hands), the tube-building *Reteterebella queenslandia* (whose presence in numbers across the reef flat is usually indicated by its long white thread-like feeding tentacles spread out, through, and over the boulders and on the sand), the swimming Lima, *Limaria fragilis* (easily identified by its bright red mantle processes), and two or three species of *Holothuria* (*H. impatiens* and *H. pardalis*) are also found.

The Outer or Living Coral Zone of the Reef Flat

This is the "moat" area of some authors. To the east of the cay, it is separated from the inshore sandy zone by an obvious large, shallow and sandy lagoon, but below the Research Station and on the northern side of the cay, they merge with another.

Many of the species already mentioned are present, but deeper pools and drainage channels have more and larger colonies of living corals. Species of *Acropora* and encrusting *Montipora* sometimes dominate, but large colonies of other species occur. The delicately branched *Seriatopora hystrix* shelters down at slightly lower levels among large patches of stouter species. Colonies of pink or brown *Pocillopora damicornis* usually grow along the sides of pools attached to either dead corals or other species. Colonies of *Pavona, Pachyseris,* micro-atolls of *Porites lutea* and *P. cylindrica,* solitary fungiids, several species of *Favia* and *Favites,* and the meandrine *Platygyra* and *Leptoria,* the delicately foliose *Echinopora lamellosa, Galaxea, Acrhelia* with their beautifully sculptured corallites, and the large brain corals, *Lobophyllia* and *Symphyllia,* are all to be found here.

Where the outer reef flat merges into a boulder zone, as along part of its northern side, boulders carry a very much richer crypto-fauna than those of more inshore areas. Attached or encrusting forms, especially compound ascidians, bryozoans, sponges, hydroids, and tube worms occur in multi-coloured profusion.

The Reef Rock Rim

The southern margin of the Heron Island reef shows a rather assorted series of habitats along its length from a large dead boulder zone east of the Cay to a more typical cemented "lithothamnion" zone.

Large dead coral boulders (1–2 m in height) provide a substrate not found elsewhere on the outer reef for animals such as the barnacles, *Tetraclita vitiata* and *T. coerulescens,* the rock oyster, *Saccostrea amasa,* the chiton of the beach rock, *Acanthopleura gemmata,* together with the pulmonate, *Siphonaria australis* and the limpet, *Patella flexuosa.*

On the more consolidated outer slope of the reef crest, dominated by coralline and other small algae, are carpets of mustard coloured zoanthids (mainly *Palythoa caesia*), followed by the corals. Coral growths with shoals of brilliantly coloured reef fishes among them, are luxurious in deep pools. Mobile species such as brittlestars, crabs, shrimps, polychaete worms, the tropical abalone, *Haliotis asinina,* cowries, cones, turban shells and trochids also occur.

The Reef Slope

Coral colonies, with plate-like and short *Acropora* spp. dominating the scene, flourish in profusion from the crest and down the slope to where, in deeper water, they are replaced by the larger branching Staghorn *Acropora* spp. and massive rounded colonies of other species.

The hydrocoralline, *Millepora platyphylla,* a short lamellate brown species with flattened yellowish tips on its stunted branches, is common, especially along the northern margin of the reef. Sometimes it occurs among corals, but in some instances large colonies line the sides of the pools along the reef edge.

Otherwise, among the more obvious species which may be found in a short visit to the reef flat, are the following:

Protozoa: Numbers of living foraminifers are attached to the various species of brown algae and species of *Halimeda* growing on the coral boulders. Where it occurs, the large round *Marginopora vertebralis* is easily recognized. A handful of sand from the bottom on one of the deeper pools will possibly show the shells of several species of foraminfers.

Porifera: The most obvious species on the reef flats is the large round, dark brown *Jaspis stellifera* up to 30 cm or so in diameter, attached to algal-covered boulders, especially on the flats off the northeastern end of the cay. The cup sponge, *Carteriospongia foliascens,* and *Dysida herbacea* (the thin, upright lamellae of which, with their sculptured sides resemble *Carteriospongia*) occur sporadically.

Under boulders, species of the spherical *Tethya* (the pinkish *T. robusta* and the pale brown *T. seychellensis*), the spherical grey *Cinachyra australiensis,* encrusting species of *Callyspongia* and *Adocia* may be found together with clusters of a small syconid. Species of *Cliona* bore into corals such as *Acropora* and *Stylophora.*

Cnidaria (excluding corals): Various species of small hydroids are found under boulders, the largest of which will probably be the stout *Solanderia fusca* (which also grows as larger colonies down to considerable depths on the reef slopes). Nassariid shells along the sandy and inner shore often carry a fine "fur" coating of colonies of the hydroid, *Cytaeis niotha.*

Clumps of the large brown fern-like *Aglaophenia cupressina,* several cm in height occur sporadically attached to boulders in pools on the reef. (It should not be handled).

Apart from the corals, there are small colonies of alcyonarians, the most obvious being the Organ-pipe coral, *Tubipora musica* (whose red skeleton may be obvious below the greenish polyps), the blue-grey *Xenia* with its long extended polyps, the large, flat yellowish *Sarcophyton trocheliphorum,* and small colonies of grey or brown *Sinularia* and *Lobophytum.*

Among coral rubble are species of *Radianthus* and a few large anemones — *Heteractis crispa, Stichodactyla gigantea* and *Entacmea quadricolor.* In the latter, what may appear as a single large anemone will generally be found to be a considerable number, each attached to separate branches of dead coral.

The commensal anemone, *Calliactis polypus,* is sometimes seen attached to shells containing hermit crabs.

Platyhelminthes: Several species are usually found under boulders, but sometimes the spectacular black and brown *Pseudoceros bedfordi* is seen swimming in pools among the corals.

Nemertea: Two conspicuous, long, black and white ribbon worms, *Baseodiscus quinquelineatus,* with two black lines, and *B. hemprichii,* with one black line along the white body, are sometimes seen among coral rubble.

Annelida, Polychaeta: Apart from the two polychaetes mentioned above, a number of errant species such as species of *Nereis* and *Eunice,* occur in rubble areas and in the sandy substrate beneath dead coral boulders. There are extremely large populations of small to minute polychaetes living among coral colonies as shown by Grassle (1973), who extracted over 1 400 worms belonging to 103 species from a single head of the coral *Pocillopora damicornis* on the Heron reef.

There are also a number of rather small tube-building species. Of these, the most conspicuous and possibly the best known of the reef worms is the serpulid, *Spirobranchus giganteus,* whose double whorls of branchiae may be found in all colours from black and white, to browns, grey, blue, yellow, orange or brilliant red. They occur commonly down the growing perimeter of micro-atolls of *Porites lutea*. Colonies of the tiny tube worm *Filograna implexa* are common under boulders.

Oligochaeta once unsuspected as members of a coral reef fauna, are represented on the Heron Island reef (in sub-littoral sand of the reef flat) by worms from a few mm to less than 3 cm long in the families Tubificidae and Enchytraeidae.

Bryozoa: Colonies are common among the cryptic fauna of the reef flats, the undersides of boulders often providing shelter for several different species. A rich fauna of encrusting forms is present down the outer reef slopes, as well as the tufted green *Bugula denticulata*. Species such as the lace-coral, *Reteporella graeffei* and the tufted *Margaretta triplex*, together with encrusting forms such as *Hippopodina feegeensis* and *Stylopoma duboisii* are to be found under boulders on the outer flat.

Crustacea, Cirripedia: Apart from species of *Lepas* and *Conchoderma* which are washed on to the reefs attached to floating objects, and the beautifully sculptured *Chelonibia testudinaria* which grows on the carapace of turtles, the only species common on the Heron reef is the small grey *Tetraclita vitiata*, found at its preferred tidal level only where there is suitable substrate, such as large dead boulders on the outer boulder zone or man-made objects such as concrete blocks or stakes driven into the reef flat.

Stomatopoda: Mantis shrimps, *Gonodactylus chiragra*, sometimes common dart among low growing corals and rubble. Other species live in burrows on the sand flat, especially at the eastern end of the cay.

Decapoda: The small mottled green carid shrimp, *Saron marmoratus*, is common among boulders together with free-living alpheids. Commensal shrimps — *Periclimenes* spp. and other pontoniines, alpheids and hippolytids — have been recorded from various hosts such as sponges, coelenterates, molluscs and echinoderms. The red Hunch-back prawn, *Metapenaeopsis lamellata* is common round the various reefs but is rarely seen since it hides within the coral colonies in deeper waters.

The Banded Coral Shrimp, *Stenopus hispidus*, white with bright red bands across body and chelae, lives in crevices, and down the reef slope, where it is known to form cleaning stations.

Two or three closely related species of Painted Spiny Lobsters of the genus *Panulirus* are found on the reef. Whilst normally in deeper waters down the slope, they are seen occasionally in deeper pools on the reef flat, their presence only obvious by the waving of the antennae down among the corals.

The bright red, white-spotted, hermit crab, *Dardanus megistos* is the largest hermit crab to be found on the reef and, usually occupying one of the ton shells, is often seen scuttling among coral and rubble at low tide.

Apart from the species mentioned above as part of the Sandy Beach and Beachrock fauna, crabs commonly seen on the reef flat are the Red-eyed *Eriphia sebana*, the Shawl crab, *Atergatis floridus,* and the Box crab, *Calappa hepatica*, with occasional specimens of the striking red, white spotted *Lophozozymus pictor* with the heavy black claws. Several species of swimming crabs of the family Portunidae also occur on the reefs, the very fast-moving aggressive *Thalamita stimpsoni* and *T. prymna*, brownish with blue and green mottling, being amongst the most numerous, with *Percnon planissimum* under boulders.

At least two or more individuals of the gall-forming crab, *Hapalocarcinus marsupialis* occur in colonies of the slender pink branching coral, *Seriatopora hystrix* and in the corals *Pocillopora* and *Stylophora*. Other crabs living commensally are species such as *Huenia proteus,* found among clumps of the alga *Halimeda*, *Caphyra laevis* among the polyps of *Xenia*, and *C. rotundifrons* among the bright green clumps of the turtle weed *Chlorodesmis*. Several species of small coral crabs of the genus *Trapezia* are usually found sheltering among clumps of *Pocillopora damicornis*.

Mollusca: On inshore sandy areas, various species of Moon snails of the family Naticidae occur, together with the purple-mouthed *Strombus gibberulus* and species of *Nassarius*. Further offshore and in rubble areas, the red-lipped *Strombus luhuanus* is dominant with occasional species of *Conus*.

Apart from the large Tiger Cowry, which browses in the open, several species of cowries, *Cypraea* spp. occur under boulders together with the Ass's Ear shell, *Haliotis asinina*.

The small clam, *Tridacna crocea*, burrows into coral boulders, and the larger *T. maxima*, with its brilliant multi-coloured mantles, is found occasionally among the living corals.

Echinodermata: Fawn coloured sea-stars of the genus *Nardoa* are often seen on the reef flat, with occasional large Pincushion Stars, *Culcita novaeguineae*, in pools. The oval-shaped, white-tipped *Echinometra mathaei*, in varied shades from a mauve to olive green, is the commonest echinoid, burrowing in coral boulders, and occasionally Needle-spined Urchins, *Diadema setosum*, and rarely *Echinothrix calamaris*, occur in deeper pools among corals.

With the exception of the beautiful green *Ophiarachna incrassata* (the largest brittle-star found in the Great Barrier Reef), most ophiuroids live in crevices or sheltering under boulders during daylight. One or two very long arms searching over the rubble probably will be the only indication of *Macrophiothrix longipeda*.

Various species of holothurians occur in sandy pools among corals, especially the black *Holothuria atra*, easily distinguished because it partially covers itself with sand, and *H. leucospilota*. *Holothuria edulis*, *Bohadschia argus*, *Stichopus variegatus*, all conspicuously coloured, are sometimes seen in pools.

On outer rubble areas, the shiny dark green *Stichopus chloronotus* is most obvious, along with the reddish-brown sea-star, *Echinaster luzonicus*, and rarely, the beautiful blue star, *Linckia laevigata*.

Ascidiacea: Ascidians, especially the colonial forms, are among the most numerous species found under boulders, especially towards the outer edge of the reef flat. They also occur in caves and overhangs down the reef slope.

With a bewildering array of colour and form they are among the most beautiful and spectacular of the cryptic fauna of the reef flat. Up to 18 species have been identified on only one upturned rock in the boulder zone. Colonial ascidians of the family Didemnidae are most common, coloured many shades of pink, red, orange and grey. The small yellow bubble-like zooids of *Ecteinascidia nexa* also cover extensive areas, *Botrylloides leachi* in shades of purple to yellow with white and black lace-like markings outlining the apertures are conspicuous where they occur. High up in the intertidal zone mosaic-like blocks of pinkish *Ritterella dispar* abound, and occasionally large translucent peach coloured specimens of *Herdmania momus* are found. This species has needle-like barbed spicules embedded in it and it should not be held in bare hands.

In the crevices and hollows near the edge of the reef large sheets of green/irridescent blue *Diplosoma similis* are found binding the coral rubble together. The green colour is caused by the masses of minute blue-green algal symbionts in the cloacal cavity of the colony.

Fishes

To the layman, the most conspicuous components of coral reef fauna are the fishes. Their abundance and diversity is almost overwhelming: a small area of reef of less than 1 ha may contain as many as 200 species. Many are bizarre and colourful; and they range in size from minute gobies (only 10 mm in length), to the whale shark, *Rhincodon typus,* the largest of all fishes (reaching a size of 18 m and weighing over 15 tonnes).

At the southern end of the Great Barrier Reef, in the Capricorn-Bunker Group alone, some 960 species have now been recorded. More are likely to be added to the list, particularly from the northern part of the Great Barrier Reef and the poorly known inter-reefal areas. If pelagic and demersal fishes are included, it is estimated that the number of fish species in the whole of the Great Barrier Reef region may exceed 2 000. This is comparable with other tropical areas such as the Philippines (2 700+ species) and Indonesia (3 000+ species; and is more than half of the estimated total number from Australian waters (3 600 species).

Why there are so many species and how they co-exist are questions largely unanswered, although some clues are provided by their diversity of form, colour and behaviour. Clearly, many have coevolved a relationship like that between an anemone and anemone fish. Others are specialized for living in certain microhabitats, and others have specific food and feeding habits.

Often the distribution of fishes on coral reefs is restricted, and various reef zones and habitats support markedly different fish assemblages. In a study of One Tree Reef, only about 7% of the species found were cosmopolitan, and about 50% were restricted to just one or other major habitat. In some cases behavioural requirements limit distribution. Thus anemone fishes of the genus *Amphiprion* live with anemones; gobies that inhabit sandy burrows are restricted to sandy patches; and many nocturnally active fishes (e.g., cardinalfishes and squirrelfishes) require caves and overhangs.

Many reef fishes are territorial or home-ranging. Territories may be more or less permanent areas that the occupant defends for feeding purposes, as do some herbivorous damselfishes and surgeonfish that maintain algal ("garden") patches. Many species vigorougly defend territories only during the breeding season to protect their clutches of eggs. In other species, such as wrasses and angelfish *(Centropyge),* the males sometimes maintain tightly controlled harems of breeding females within their territories all year round. Most medium to large species are home-ranging, and frequently have a sleeping site to which they return and aggressively defend at dusk.

Almost all species show strong night and day patterns of behaviour and distribution. The majority including the mass of brightly coloured benthic feeders (parrotfishes, wrasses, surgeonfishes, butterflyfishes and many others), schools of plankton feeders (damselfishes, fusiliers), and small predators (groupers and dottybacks) are active during the day. At night, a much smaller number of nocturnal species is active. Many of these, such as cardinalfishes and squirrelfishes that shelter during the day, move out into midwater to feed at night. Others such as snappers, sweetlips and emperors that occur in largely inactive schools by day, at night disperse over the bottom to feed.

Reproduction in reef fishes is varied and often complex. Most species lay eggs, live-bearing of young being common only among cartilaginous fishes (sharks and rays). Spawning is demersal or pelagic. Demersal spawners generally are in pairs, and eggs are laid in small clutches or nests that are vigorously defended, usually by the male. Pelagic spawning is either by pairs or *en masse,* and often occurs at dusk and on an outgoing tide when conditions are more likely to ensure that the eggs escape the hungry mouths of diurnal plankton feeders. Eggs of both demersal and pelagic fishes are typically small (1–2 mm diameter) and take about five days to hatch. They hatch into larvae that generally have a pelagic dispersal phase ranging from a few days to two months or more. To ensure that local populations are maintained some species migrate to the reef edge to spawn near gyres and local current eddies in which eggs and larvae will develop and eventually return to the natal or nearby reef. A few fishes have evolved ways of caring for their developing young, including mouth brooding of eggs (cardinalfish), pouch brooding of eggs by the male (pipefish), and parental care of both eggs and young (damselfish, *Acanthochromis polyacanthus).*

Most reef fishes undergo sex reversal (sequential hermaphroditism) some beginning their lives as females before changing into males (protogyny), others changing from male to female (protandry). Wrasses and parrotfishes are typical examples of protogynous hermaphrodites, beginning their lives as either males or females, each with a similar, usually rather dull colour pattern. The males of these primary or initial phase individuals are usually incapable of changing sex, but the females can change to brightly coloured secondary or terminal phase males. The change of sex is usually socially controlled, the presence of a number of terminal males stopping other females from changing. If the number of terminal males is reduced, the dominant female will change to male. Terminal males generally pair spawn with numerous females of their own choice, but primary males are less selective, often group-spawning with the females. In other species, such as cleanerfish, *Labroides dimidiatus,* all males are terminal, and usually a single male maintains a harem of females. If the male is removed the dominant female changes sex, thus ensuring continuity in reproduction. In protandrous hermaphrodites, such as anemone fishes, the social hierarchy of the sexes is reversed: in these groups the female is the largest and most dominant, and if removed it is the male that changes sex.

Strategies for avoiding of predators and catching prey have also been selected as species have evolved. Many groups have poisonous defensive spines, and a few also have skin toxins that are lethal to predators, including man. Some species live in close relationships with animals such as spiny sea urchins or stinging anemones to take advantage of their defence mechanisms. Some (such as pipefishes) use their cryptic colouration to hide, and some predators (such as scorpion fish) are camouflaged to hide them from unwary prey. Through evolution of behaviour as well as colour pattern certain reef fishes also mimic other organisms. Thus a harmless or unprotected species (the mimic) will sometimes have come to resemble an unpalatable species (the model). An example of this, known as Batesian mimicry, is in the mimicry of poison-fanged blennies *(Meiacanthus)* and blennies of the genus *Petroscirtes.* Less common is Mullerian mimicry, where two or more unpalatable species resemble one another. A further type is Aggressive mimicry, where the mimic is a predator exploiting its resemblance to another species in order to attack its prey as in the predatory blenny, *Aspidontus taeniatus* and the cleaner wrasse, *Labroides dimidiatus.*

Taxonomic diversity of the fishes of the Great Barrier Reef is reflected in the large number of families recorded. These, together with some of their characteristics, are given below. Although many are associated with particular habitats, most of the families have a geographic range extending over the whole of the region. Ranges that are more restricted are specifically defined in the documentation given. The classification used here is based on Eschmeyer (1990). Families are arranged under their respective orders (the number that precedes the family name, refers in each case to the corresponding outline drawing in Figs 63, 64). For detailed descriptions and illustrations of many of the more common species the reader is referred to Randall *et al.* 1990.

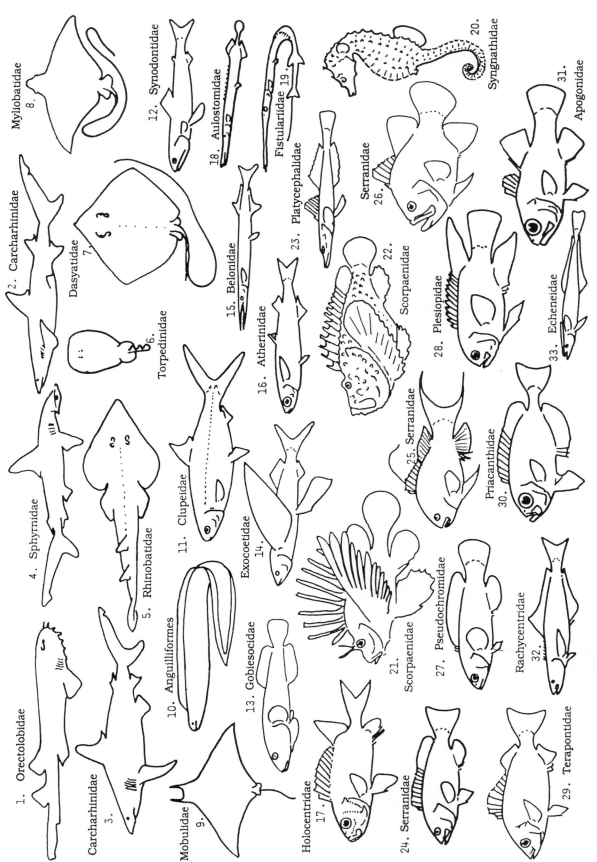

1. Orectolobidae
2. Carcharhinidae
3. Carcharhinidae
4. Sphyrnidae
5. Rhinobatidae
6. Torpedinidae
7. Dasyatidae
8. Myliobatidae
9. Mobulidae
10. Anguilliformes
11. Clupeidae
12. Synodontidae
13. Gobiesocidae
14. Exocoetidae
15. Belonidae
16. Atherinidae
17. Holocentridae
18. Aulostomidae
19. Fistulariidae
20. Syngnathidae
21. Scorpaenidae
22. Scorpaenidae
23. Platycephalidae
24. Serranidae
25. Serranidae
26. Serranidae
27. Pseudochromidae
28. Plesiopidae
29. Terapontidae
30. Priacanthidae
31. Apogonidae
32. Rachycentridae
33. Echeneidae

Fig. 63. Representative fishes of some families occurring on the Great Barrier Reef.

187

Class Elasmobranchii

Order Hexanchiformes

Hexanchidae (Cow Sharks) — large, with six or seven gill slits (most sharks have five), a single relatively small dorsal fin, and blade-like, comb-shaped teeth. Occur mainly in deeper water and rarely encountered.

Order Heterodontiformes

Heterodontidae (Bullhead and Horned Sharks) — small with a squarish head and a stout sharp spine at the front of each dorsal fin. Slow moving, bottom dwellers, generally harmless. A single genus, *Heterodontus*.

Order Orectolobiformes

Rhincodontidae (Whale Sharks) — broad, flat head and terminal mouth with minute teeth, the group contains a single species, *Rhincodon typus*, the world's largest fish. It is a suction filter feeder, and takes a variety of small pelagic organisms. It is considered harmless and may be approached at close range by divers.

Brachaeluridae (Blind Sharks) — small, bottom-living, inhabiting shallow coral areas. Nocturnally active. Harmless.

Orectolobidae (Catsharks, Carpetsharks) — small to medium-size bottom-living, with camouflage colouration, inhabiting coral-covered areas in shallow and deeper parts of the reef. Not considered dangerous unless cornered or handled (Fig. 63:1).

Hemiscyllidae (Bamboo Sharks) — medium-sized, bottom-living in lagoon and reef flat habitats. Not considered dangerous unless cornered or handled.

Stegostomatidae (Leopard Sharks) — moderately large, bottom-living sharks inhabiting coral covered areas. Not considered dangerous unless cornered or handled.

Ginglymostomatidae (Nurse Sharks) — moderately large, bottom-living inhabiting coral covered areas. Not considered dangerous unless cornered or handled.

Order Lamniformes

Odontaspididae (Sand Tiger Sharks) — large and bulky with a pointed snout, long mouth, pair of similar-sized dorsal fins, and sharp dagger-like teeth. Best known member is the Grey Nurse Shark, *Eugomphodus taurus*. Mainly inoffensive and nonaggressive, its notoriety as a maneater is undeserved.

Alopiidae (Thresher Sharks) — have a particularly elongate upper caudal lobe used for herding prey fish or squids. Oceanic, rarely seen over the reef region. A single genus, *Alopias*.

Lamnidae (Mackeral or Mako Sharks) — large, powerful, and rapid swimmers capable of spectacular leaps at the surface when chasing prey. Highly aggressive, and dangerous, responsible for attacks on swimmers and surfers, this group also includes the notorious White Pointer *(Carcharodon carcharius)* a cooler water species that sometimes occurs in the southern portion of the Great Barrier Reef.

Order Carcharhiniformes

Scyliorhinidae (Catsharks) — the largest family of sharks, all generally small and harmless.

Carcharhinidae (Whaler Sharks) — fast-swimming, streamlined, of medium to large-size encountered more frequently along the reef slope by day and often over the reef flat at night. They display plain colouration and obliterative countershading. Mostly piscivorous, but some species will attack man (Fig 63:2,3).

Hemigaleidae (Weasel Sharks) — small, inhabiting open waters near the reef. Not considered dangerous.

Sphyrnidae (Hammerhead Sharks) — with dorso-ventrally flattened heads extending laterally into highly enervated hammer-shaped lobes containing optical and olfactory organs. They are rarely seen over reefs, but frequent the deeper off-reef waters. Large and voracious, known to attack man and common to tropical and subtropical waters (Fig. 63:4).

Order Squaliformes

Squalidae (Dogfish Sharks) — small to medium-sized, mostly in deeper waters between reefs.

Order Torpedinformes

Torpedinidae (Electric Rays) — can produce an electric current across the body. Voltages of over 200 volts have been recorded, while most species produce 70 to 80 volts from their specialized muscle tissue called electroplates. If picked up, they can produce a lethal shock. The electric current may be a defensive mechanism when discharges are large, or a navigational mechanism when microvoltages detect objects in the surrounding water mass. They are seen infrequently, usually on the reef slope (Fig. 63:6).

Order Rajiformes

Rhinobatidae (Guitarfishes and Shovelnose Rays) — wedge-shaped with strong, muscular tails that superficially resemble a shark's. Sluggish, confined almost entirely to the sandy lagoon and reef flat areas where they forage for crustaceans. Small individuals can be seen feeding along the waters edge, and specimens to 2 m long are common in the deeper lagoon (Fig. 63:5).

Rajidae (Skates) — diamond-shaped fishes with the caudal fin reduced or absent; an extremely slender tail; and often with prickles on the back. They occur in deeper water between the reefs.

Order Myliobatiformes

Dasyatididae (Stingrays) — small to large stingrays found over the entire region and in deeper water between reefs. They forage principally for crustaceans and worms on the sandy lagoon floor and between the coral patches of the reef flat and slope. Dangerous only if handled or stepped on. Resting individuals bury themselves in the sandy bottom or hide in crevices under coral formations (Fig. 63:7).

Gymnuridae (Rat-tailed Rays) — with broad discs and short tails. They occur in deeper water between reefs.

Myliobatidae (Eagle Rays) — with a projecting snout capable of digging for and manipulating prey, and a "swept back" appearance of the pectoral flaps. Most common over the sandy lagoon floor where they forage for crustaceans. Not dangerous unless handled (Fig. 63:8).

Mobulidae (Manta Rays) — among the largest of living fishes. Their specialized cephalic lobes allow for a planktivorous diet of small fishes, crustaceans, and ctenophores. They are harmless, measuring over 4 m from wing tip to wing tip. They are commonly seen along the reef edge and near areas used as "cleaning stations" in deeper water along the slope (Fig. 63:9).

Class Holocephali

Order Chimaeriformes

Chimaeridae (Ghost Sharks) — bizarre and shark-like, with blunt, rounded snouts and elongate tapering tails. Inhabit deeper water.

Class Actinopterygii — Bony fishes

Order Albuliformes

Albulidae (Bonefishes) — a small family of primitive teleosts with an elongate, compressed body, a distinctive overlapping snout ventral mouth and a leptocephalus larval stage similar to that of eels. Typically found on shallow sand flats.

Order Anguilliformes (Fig. 63:10)

Moringuidae (Worm Eels) — elongate, thread-like, sand burrowing bodies, with reduced eyes, gill openings low on the body, and the dorsal and anal fins are reduced to low folds confluent with the caudal fin.

Chlopsidae (Reef Eels) — elongate with well-developed dorsal and anal fins confluent with the caudal fin, gill openings are small roundish apertures at the base of the pectoral fin. Little is known of their habits.

Muraenidae (Moray Eels) — medium to large, mostly brightly coloured, ferocious carnivores, sometimes dangerous. Most are aggressive piscivores, feeding nocturnally largely by scent. Owing to their secretive habits, this extremely common group is usually underestimated in terms of numbers of individuals.

Ophichthidae (Snake Eels) — long (up to 0.5 m) with sharply pointed tails used for entering the sandy bottoms in which they live. Probably entirely piscivorous. Most active at night and rarely seen during the day.

Congridae (Conger Eels) — medium-sized fishes, and said to be excellent eating. These eels are not well represented, but when present are usually associated with coral covered areas.

Nettastomatidae (Wire Eels) — elongate, compressed, with long pointed snouts and lacking pectoral fins. They inhabit deeper water between the reefs.

Order Clupeiformes

Clupeidae (Round Herrings, Sprats) — small herring-like, usually in large schools along the reef edge where they feed on plankton. Marked seasonal variations in numbers occur. The school tend to remain in shallow water particularly in the groove and buttress system where they are preyed upon heavily by groupers (Fig. 63:11).

Engraulidae (Anchovies) — small herring-like with the lower jaw typically overhung by the tip of the snout. Large schools usually occur in the lagoon or along the outer reef edge where they feed on plankton.

Order Gonorynchiformes

Chanidae (Milkfish) — superficially herring-like in appearance, up to 1.8 m long. Uncommon, inhabits shallow waters and feeds on algae. Found throughout the tropical Pacific and Indian Oceans, these fish are cultured in ponds for food. A single species, *Chanos chanos*.

Gonorhynchidae (Rat Fishes) — small eel-like with inferior mouths, protractile upper jaw and barbel at the tip of the snout. Occur in deeper inter-reefal waters.

Order Siluriformes

Plotosidae (Eeltail Catfishes) — eel-like body, the tail pointed or bluntly rounded. Usually with four pairs of barbels on the chin. The first dorsal and pectoral fin spines are poisonous and can inflict painful wounds.

Order Aulopiformes

Synodontidae (Lizardfish, Grinners) — small, slender, voracious carnivores live in sand, often partially buried, or on coral over the entire reef. Most commonly observed in the lagoon. They lie in wait for passing prey which they then dart at from their hiding place (Fig. 63:12).

Order Gadiformes

Euclichthyidae (Euclicthyid Cods) — elongate, tapering cod-like bodies. They occur in deeper water between reefs.

Order Ophidiiformes

Ophidiidae (Blindfishes) — medium-sized, but very rare on the reef. They are basically deep-water forms with rudimentary eyes and large mucus glands.

Carapidae (Pearlfishes) — small, elongate with pointed tails. Some live in the internal organs (intestine, branchial chamber) of invertebrates (e.g., holothurians and molluscs).

Bythitidae (Cusk Eels) — small, nocturnally active with only rudimentary eyes. They often are abundant on reefs but are rarely seen.

Order Batrachoidiformes

Batrachoididae (Frogfishes) — small, benthic carnivores, sluggish and seldom seen being well-camouflaged with elaborate extensions of the skin which resemble algal growth.

Order Lophiiformes

Antennariidae (Anglerfishes) — small balloon-shaped with loose skin, and the first dorsal fin modified into a "fishing pole" located in front of the eyes above the mouth. Anglerfishes occur over the entire reef but are cryptic and rarely seen.

Ogcocephalidae (Handfishes) — with greatly depressed bodies, large mouths, tubercule-like scales and arm-like pectoral fins. Benthic, in deeper water between reefs.

Order Gobiesociformes

Gobiesocidae (Clingfishes) — small, benthic, similar to gobies but with a well-developed sucking disc, and only one dorsal fin (Fig. 63:13).

Order Atheriniformes

Atherinidae (Hardyheads) — small, pelagic schooling fishes most common along the reef edge where they prey on zooplankton. They are important in the food web of the reef when they occur in enormous schools over the coral (Fig. 63:16).

Order Beloniformes

Belonidae (Needlefish, Long Toms) — slender, pelagic piscivores, with long well-toothed jaws. Found in the lagoon and reef flat, but most commonly seen along the reef slope where they take dussumieriids. When disturbed these fishes leap and skip across the surface at about a 45° angle with only the ventral lobe of the caudal fin in the water (Fig. 63:15).

Hemirhamphidae (Garfishes) — elongate, with a long, extended lower jaw. Surface feeding some times with the lower jaw further modified into a flat scoop. They occur in shallow water.

Exocoetidae (Flyingfish) — pelagic, feeding primarily on plankton around the reef. They are not commonly seen by divers, but are easily disturbed by boats and take flight in long aerial glides. The gliding is made possible by extension of the wing-like pectorals and the necessary speed is attained by rapid beating of the caudal fin which remains in the water during parts of the glide (Fig. 63:14).

Order Beryciformes

Monocentridae (Pineapplefishes) — small, box-like, covered with heavy plate-like scales, and the dorsal and pelvic fins with stout spines, and with bioluminescent organs under the lower jaw. Nocturnally active and inhabit caves in the reef by day.

Holocentridae (Squirrelfish, Soldierfish) — primarily nocturnal, inhabiting crevices and coral branches by day. Most commonly seen on the shallow reef slope where their usual red colour makes them conspicuous. All species have large opercular spines and very large eyes, and are difficult to distinguish from one another (Fig. 63:17).

Order Zeiformes

Caproididae (Boarfishes) — small, rhomboid-shaped, in deeper water between reefs.

Gasterosteiformes

Pegasidae (Seamoths) — broad, depressed bodies encased in bony rings, and with large pectoral fins. In deeper water between reefs.

Order Syngnathiformes

Aulostomidae (Trumpetfish) — long tube-like capable of a variety of colour changes. They are piscivorous, pipetting smaller fishes with their long snouts, often while lying motionless in vertical head-down position. Often they will accompany a larger fish in order to get closer to their prey (Fig. 63:18).

Fistulariidae (Cornetfish, Hair-tailed Flutemouths) — long, slender with a tubular snout, differing from the Aulostomidae in the long, filamentous caudal extension. Confined almost entirely to the reef slope where they are often seen in schools (Fig. 63:11).

Centriscidae (Razorfishes) — small, thin or flattened and nearly transparent. They swim in a vertical position, snout down, in small synchronized groups. Related to pipefishes and seahorses.

Solenostomidae (Ghost Pipefishes) — small, compressed with two dorsal fins, the first with long feeble spines, the second on an elevated base. Rare, they are found on deeper parts of reef slopes.

Syngnathidae (Pipefishes, Seahorses) — small, covered in bony plates, the mode of swimming is specialized relying heavily on the dorsal fin. Males carry the eggs in a ventral pouch. Common among the corals and algae of the entire reef, but due to their size, colour and benthic habits, are not often seen. Their food consists of tiny crustaceans and possibly larval fishes (Fig. 63:20).

Order Scorpaeniformes

Scorpaenidae (Scorpionfish) — small to medium-sized, well-camouflaged, benthic sluggish, preying on fishes that approach too closely. Their venomous spines make them dangerous if handled. They occur in most reef habitats, but most are observed under ledges along the reef slope (Fig. 63:21,22).

Caracanthidae (Orbicular Velvetfishes) — small oval-bodied scaleless but covered with tiny papillae. Uncommon, they occur on the outer reef slopes in shallow water.

Aploactinidae (Velvetfishes) — small, covered with fine papillae giving a velvety appearance. The dorsal fin begins far above the eyes. Rare, little known of their habits.

Triglidae (Gurnards) — medium-sized, with casque-like bony head and large pectoral fins, the lowermost pectoral rays enlarged and free. Found on soft bottoms between reefs.

Dactylopteridae (Flying Gurnards) — small, blunt, boney-headed, with enlarged pectoral fins, the inner rays of which are free. Benthic-living, uncommon and found mostly in deeper water between reefs. Juveniles are surface dwellers with similar habits to flying fishes.

Platycephalidae (Flatheads) — medium-sized, excellent eating, seldom seen on the reef, but sometimes taken on hook and line. Their camouflage and habit of lying almost covered in sand allow them to capture unsuspecting fishes that swim by (Fig. 63:23).

Order Perciformes

Centropomidae (Barramundi) — medium to large carnivores, including the well-known estuarine barramundi, and the Knightfish *(Psammaperca waigiensis)* found around inshore reefs.

Acropomatidae (Split Fins) — perch-like, with two dorsal fins and anus well forward near pelvic fin base. Occur in deeper waters between reefs.

Serranidae (Rock Cods, Groupers, Coral Trout) — small to large carnivores found in all habitats but most common on reef slopes. The larger epinephelines are solitary, sluggish by nature, capturing their prey during a short high-speed dash. Smaller anthiines occur often in large schools and are plankton feeders. The larger species are commonly caught by fishermen, and are considered excellent eating. Individuals more than 2 m long may be dangerous (Fig. 63:24–26).

Pseudochromidae (Dottybacks) — small, perch-like, mostly handsomely coloured carnivores found close to coral in which they shelter (Fig. 63:27).

Pleisiopidae (Roundheads) — small, occasionally found over the reef flats, lagoons and reef slopes (Fig. 63:28).

Acanthoclinidae (Banded Longfins) — small, perch-like occurring mostly in temperate waters. A single species, *Belonepterygium fasciolatum* is known from the Great Barrier Reef. Common on reef flats, but cryptic.

Terapontidae (Grunters) — small to medium-sized carnivores occurring in small numbers almost everywhere over a reef. They can make grunting noises (Fig. 63:29).

Kuhliidae (Flagtails) — small, silvery, with a single, deeply notched dorsal fin and a caudal fin marked with black stripes or spots, like a flag. They are nocturnal predators, feeding mainly on small crustaceans. Uncommon.

Priacanthidae (Bullseyes) — strongly compressed, reddish-coloured, with very large black eyes, they are seen sheltering between coral branches by day, but emerge to feed on small fishes at night (Fig. 63:30).

Apogonidae (Cardinalfish) — small, predominantly red, nocturnal carnivores, shelter in caverns or between coral branches by day. The males incubate the eggs and young in the mouth (Fig. 63:31).

Sillaginidae (Whiting) — small to medium-sized, excellent eating quality, relatively uncommon. They are associated with sandy areas, particularly shallow lagoons where they forage for burrowing crustaceans and worms.

Malacanthidae (Tilefishes) — moderately elongate, laterally compressed, with blunt heads and a single dorsal fin. Found around reefs, but uncommon.

Rachycentridae (Black Kingfish, Cobia) — fast-swimming carnivores feeding on fish, crabs, and squid or cuttlefish. Sometimes caught off the reef edge and prized by fishermen. Distinguished from Trevally and Jacks by a dorso-ventrally flattened head (Fig. 63:32).

Echeneidae (Suckerfish, Remoras) — Streamlined, with the first dorsal fin modified into an elaborate sucking disc by which they attach themselves, preferably, to fast-swimming fishes such as sharks in order to obtain scraps of food dropped by the host. They also attach themselves to ships, turtles, and even divers (Fig. 63:33).

Carangidae (Trevally, Jacks) — fast-swimming, pelagic, piscivores frequenting reef slopes. They are excellent eating and provide good sport for fishermen when taken on light gear (Fig. 64:34).

Coryphaenidae (Dolphinfish) — beautifully coloured, blunt-headed, fast-swimming, and powerful. They are primarily oceanic, but sometimes are taken near reefs. They are valued for their fighting and excellent flesh (Fig. 64:35).

194

34. Carangidae

35. Coryphaenidae

36. Lutjanidae

37. Caesionidae

38. Nemipteridae

39. Nemipteridae

40. Gerreidae

41a. Haemulidae

41b. Haemulidae

42. Lethrinidae

43. Sparidae

44. Mullidae

45. Pempheridae

46. Kyphosidae

47. Ephippidae

48. Chaetodontidae

49. Pomacanthidae

50. Pomacentridae

51. Mugilidae

52. Sphyraenidae

53. Labridae

54. Scaridae

55. Pinguipedidae

56. Blennidae

57. Callionymidae

58. Gobiidae

59a. Zandidae

59b. Acanthuridae

60. Siganidae

61. Scombridae

62. Bothidae

63. Soleidae

64. Balistidae

65. Ostraciidae

66. Tetraodontidae

67. Diodontidae

Fig. 64. Representative fishes of some families occurring on the Great Barrier Reef.

Lutjanidae (Sea Perch, Hussars, Snappers) — voracious carnivores preying on fishes and large crustaceans. They are found in all reef habitats, but some appear to be restricted to shallower water. Most are of excellent food quality, although some are suspected of ciguatera poisoning (Fig. 64:36).

Caesionidae (Fusiliers, Banana Fish) — small, brightly coloured, midwater plankton-feeding, found in lagoon and outer reef slope habitats (Fig. 64:37).

Gerreidae (Silver Biddies) — small, silvery, with protrusible mouths and deciduous scales, occurring almost exclusively over near-shore sandy areas where they feed on crustaceans. Often taken for bait (Fig. 64:40).

Haemulidae (Grunters, Javelinfish, Sweetlips) — medium-sized perch-like, some with conspicuous colouration. Associated with most reef habitats, near coral. They feed largely on crustaceans (Fig. 64:41a,b).

Sparidae (Silver Bream) — medium-sized, deep-bodied, preying on crustaceans and small molluscs, particularly around sandy areas. Most seen in lagoons (Fig. 64:43).

Lethrinidae (Emperors) — distinctively coloured, snapper-like, with scaleless head and cheeks. Found in all reef habitats, but most conspicuous near coral where they feed on small fish and larger crustaceans. They are excellent eating (Fig. 64:42).

Nemipteridae (Monocle Bream, Threadfin Bream) — small to moderate-sized, colourful carnivores preying on small fishes and crustaceans. Found over most of the region but commonly near the bottom (Fig. 64:38,39).

Mullidae (Goatfishes) — small, colourful, feeding on crustaceans and worms obtained by probing the bottom with well-developed chin barbels. Found over sandy or silty areas wherever they occur on reefs (Fig. 64:44).

Pempheridae (Sweepers) — small, silver or pink, sometimes forming huge schools in shallow water along reef slopes (Fig. 64:45).

Kyphosidae (Drummers) — small to medium-sized, algal feeders, inconspicuously coloured and most commonly seen in shallow lagoons, on reef flats, and over beach rock on high evening tides (Fig. 64:46).

Ephippidae (Batfishes) — deep-bodied, highly compressed with greatly extended dorsal and anal fins. They are conspicuous at moderate depths on the reef slope in the vicinity of large coral heads (Fig. 64:47).

Chaetodontidae (Coralfish, Butterflyfish) — small, brilliantly coloured, with extremely compressed bodies, feeding on coral polyps and small crustaceans using their tiny mouths as forceps. Ubiquitous and common (Fig. 64:48).

Pomacanthidae (Angelfishes) — small to medium-sized, brilliantly coloured, with elongate, sometimes highly compressed bodies, occurring wherever coral is found, but most common along the reef slope where they scrape algae and small crustaceans from rock (Fig. 64:49).

Pomacentridae (Damselfishes) — small, colourful, moving quickly among the coral branches in which they seek refuge. They are territorial and common everywhere over reefs. Most species are omnivores (Fig. 64:50).

Cirrhitidae (Hawkfishes) — small, brightly coloured, found in all reef habitats, often associated with coral.

Cheilodactylidae (Morwongs) — a small group, mainly temperate, they are restricted to the southern Great Barrier Reef where they usually occur in more exposed reef habitats.

Opistognathidae (Jawfishes) — small, robust, with large mouths, they typically inhabit holes in sand or coral rubble bottoms on outer reef slopes in shallow or deep water.

Mugilidae (Mullet) — medium-sized, edible algal feeders with a specialized gizzard-like stomach. Most common in estuaries and coastal waters, but frequenting lagoon and beach areas throughout much of the year (Fig. 64:51).

Polynemidae (Threadfins) — with bluntly rounded snout, ventral mouth, and pectoral fin with a lower section that has 3–7 free thread-like rays. Usually encountered near the coast, in river mouths and brackish mangrove areas.

Labridae (Tuskfish, Wrasses) — a large, diverse, group of small to medium-sized, brilliantly colourated elongate fishes with a variety of feeding specializations, although most are true omnivores. They occur in all reef habitats, especially near coral (Fig. 64:53).

Scaridae (Parrotfishes) — medium-sized with fused teeth resembling a parrot's beak, used to graze algae from rocky surfaces. They occur in most reef habitats, but are conspicuous over the reef crest and reef flat at low tide when their colourful tails and dorsal fins are exposed. Colour is related to sexuality and maturity in these hermaphroditic fishes (Fig. 64:54).

Champsodontidae (Sabre Gills) — small, with large pelvic fins located in front of pectoral fins, from deeper inter-reefal waters.

Uranoscopidae (Stargazers) — small to moderately-large, dorsally flattened, bottom-living, with large mouths and small eyes. Uncommon, they usually occur in deeper water between reefs.

Trichonotidae (Sand-Divers) — a small family, extremely elongate, and slender with projecting lower jaw and first few dorsal rays usually elongate in males. Usually hover over clean sandy bottoms into which they dive for shelter when disturbed.

Creediidae (Sand Eels) — small cryptic, living in the sand and feeding on microcrustacea. Similar habits to the Sand-Divers.

Pinguipedidae (Grubfishes) — small carnivores in most reef habitats but, tend to be inconspicuous because of their mottled colouration and benthic habits (Fig. 64:55).

Tripterygiidae (Triplefins) — small, blenny-like, benthic, with three dorsal fins. Found in all reef habitats.

Clinidae (Weedfishes) — small blenny-like with a single long dorsal fin, uncommon.

Blenniidae (Blennies) — small largely omnivorous, benthic, abundant, in holes and crevices in all reef habitats. Some species mimic other fishes in colour and behaviour (Fig. 64:56).

Callionymidae (Dragonets) — cylindrical, usually living buried in sand with only the eyes protruding. Rarely seen on reefs, owing to their mottled colour and benthic habits (Fig. 64:57).

Schindleriidae (Floaters) — small neotenic with mainly larval characters, occurring in plankton around reefs.

Eleotridae (Gudgeons) — goby-like, with pelvic fins separated. Rare on reefs.

Gobiidae (Gobies, Gudgeons) — a large group of small, mainly omnivorous fishes, found resting on the bottom or in coral in all reef habitats. Some very selective in the corals they inhabit (Fig. 64:58).

Microdesmidae (Wormfishes) — small, goby-like, burrowing, living in the sand.

Siganidae (Spine Feet, Happy Moments) — small to medium-sized browsing herbivores with strong spines that can inflict painful wounds. Many with intricate markings, but most are drab. Encountered most frequently on reef flats and slopes (Fig. 64:60).

Zanclidae (Moorish Idols) — a monotypic family, related to the surgeonfishes, common in shallow water over reefs (Fig. 64:59a).

Acanthuridae (Surgeonfish, Unicornfish) — medium-sized, with knife-like bony plates on the caudal peduncle. They often occur in schools, grazing on algae on reef slope and reef crest habitats. Most are drab (Fig. 64:59b).

Sphyraenidae (Barracudas, Sea Pike) — elongate, to 2.5 m long, voracious carnivores with fang-like dentition, seen predominantly in mid-water habitats along reef slopes. Larger ones are dangerous (Fig. 64:52).

Trichiuridae (Hairtails) — very elongate, tapering bodies, caudal fin small or absent, teeth large and fang-like. Rare, they are found between the reefs.

Xiphiidae (Swordfishes) — a single species, the swordfish, *Xiphias gladius*, is closely allied to the billfishes, but lacks jaw teeth and pelvic fins, and has only one keel on the side of the tail base. Uncommon, occurs only occasionally near reefs.

Istiophoridae (Billfishes) — includes the marlins and sailfish, with a long bill-like snout used to attack and stun prey fishes. They grow to a large size and are highly prized gamefishes. Occur near offshore reefs, particularly in the northern Great Barrier Reef.

Scombridae (Spanish Mackerel, Tunas) — highly-prized fast-swimming, pelagic carnivores with high food quality, occur sometimes in schools, along the reef slope, where they feed on smaller fishes by chasing them at high speeds. They may be taken on lures. Tuna are very important commercially, particularly in the waters off New Guinea (Fig. 64:61).

Order Pleuronectiformes

Bothidae (Left Handed Flounders) — small, attractively marked, strongly compressed, benthic carnivores, lying on their sides often covered in sand. They are restricted to sandy areas where they are inconspicuous (Fig. 64:62).

Soleidae (Soles) — flattened, lying on their sides in sandy areas where they easily escape notice. They differ from the Bothidae in having a more elongate body and often the caudal fused with the dorsal and anal fins (Fig. 64:63).

Cynoglossidae (Tongue Soles) — elongate, mostly tapering-bodied flatfishes occuring in deeper off-reef waters.

Order Tetraodontiformes

Triacanthidae (Tripodfishes) — like Triggerfish, with enlarged dorsal and ventral fin spines. Rare, they are found in deeper water between reefs.

Balistidae (Triggerfish) — often in pairs, they seek protection by entering holes and erecting the first dorsal spine which is locked in place by the second dorsal spine. They inflate themselves by swallowing water, but to a lesser extent than true puffers. Some are elaborately coloured. They are inquisitive, appear to be omnivores with a preference for small crustaceans and are found in all reef habitats (Fig. 64:64).

Monacanthidae (Leatherjackets) — small, often attractively marked, closely related to the balistids with an erectile first dorsal spine. They are most frequently encountered in reef flat and reef slope habitats, but sometimes occur in deep water.

Ostraciidae (Boxfishes) — body rigid, with scales modified into heavy, attractively coloured, bony plates. All movements are produced by protruding fins. Found over most coral areas, especially in shallow water (Fig. 64:65).

Tetraodontidae (Pufferfish) — small to medium-sized, able to swallow large amounts of air or water in order to inflate their bodies when threatened. Frequently seen in reef flat and reef slope habitats, but are not a conspicuous part of the fish community. They are poisonous and should not be eaten (Fig. 64:66).

Diodontidae (Porcupinefishes) — small to medium-sized with the peculiar habit of swallowing air or water in order to inflate themselves, thus extending the numerous spines embedded in their skin. Most often encountered in crevices and under tabular corals along reef slopes (Fig. 64:67).

Class Reptilia

Snakes, Turtles and Lizards

Hydrophiidae — Sea Snakes

Seven species of sea snakes have been reported from the Great Barrier Reef region. Three of these *(Aipysurus laevis, A. duboisii, Emydocephalus annulatus)* are commonly directly associated with corals, and a fourth *(Astrotia stokesii)* occurs in a variety of other habitats as well. *Aipysurus laevis* is the most abundant species and the one most often sighted by snorkelers and divers. *Emydocephalus* and *A. duboisii* are sometimes conspicuous and locally abundant, especially in the northern parts of the reef and in the Coral Sea, *Astrotia* is widely distributed but never occurs in large numbers. The other three species occur in the deeper waters between reefs and often are sighted from boats when they surface to breathe. They occasionally wander into shallower areas of coral or are washed ashore on cays. The most common of these are *Acalyptophis peronii* and *Disteira kingii*. *Pelamis platurus*, a pelagic species associated with surface slicks, sometimes occurs coincidentally in the vicinity of reefs and is the species most frequently washed ashore accidentally.

Another group of species occupy non-reefal habitats such as mangrove swamps, turbid waters, estuaries or sandy or muddy bottomed areas along the Queensland coast. They include *Aipysurus eydouxii, Disteira major, Enhydrina schistosa, Hydrophis elegans, H. ornatus,* and *Lapemis curtus*. Some of these have been reported near coral reefs, in deep channels between reefs, or as strays into coral areas but none should be considered as a typical coral reef inhabitant.

All of the hydrophiid seasnakes are venomous, and, except for those that eat only fish eggs (see below), are potentially dangerous to humans. Information on the seven species reported from the Great Barrier Reef region is set out below (see Cogger 1991).

Aipysurus laevis (Olive Seasnake) — variable in colour. On the Great Barrier Reef often almost uniform brown (males) or grey (females). In other localities lighter ventrally with light or spotted scales scattered over the dorsum to give a variegated appearance. Scales smooth and imbricate. Body stout and heavy. The females (to over 2 m) are about twice as large as males.

This species forages among crevices for a variety of fish and moulting crustaceans. Females produce 1–5 young, usually in April. It is found on the reefs of the continental shelves of Papua New Guinea and northern Australia, in the Gulf of Carpentaria, the Great Barrier Reef and reefs of the Coral Sea to, and including, New Caledonia.

A. laevis is curious and sometimes approaches and follows divers, but seldom attempts to bite unless severely provoked. Only the fangs of exceptionally large individuals can penetrate a wet suit (Fig. 65A).

Aipysurus duboisii (Dubois' Seasnake) — variable in colour and pattern, usually dark purplish brown, sometimes completely black, although in some areas it has lighter blotches on the sides. As it moves, white skin between the scales is exposed, forming a reticulated pattern outlining the scales. Scales usually smooth and imbricate, occasionally with a slight central keel or series of tubercles. The body is moderately built. Average total length 0.7 m.

Dubois' Seasnake lives in primarily shallow water on coral reefs. It feeds on fish and often eels. It occurs on reefs of northern Australia, southern Papua, the Great Barrier Reef and southern Coral Sea east to New Caledonia.

It is not pugnacious but may bite if handled. A wet suit is adequate protection against bites (Fig. 65B).

Astrotia stokesii (Stokes' Seasnake) — variably coloured, ranging from creamy white to yellow with a series of greenish, dorsal saddle-blotches, to uniformly brown, grey or even black. The young often more conspicuously patterned. Its most distinguishing feature is a double row of leaf-like scales on the ventral midline. The head is large, and the laterally flattened body is of tremendous girth. This is the bulkiest (although not the longest) species of sea snake known. It is a fish-eater.

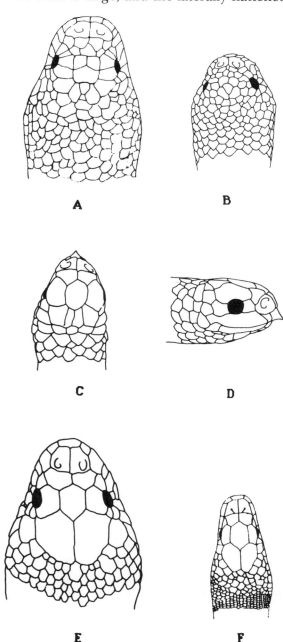

It occurs in a wide variety of habitats including sandy areas, muddy water and coral reefs. It is known from the tropical waters of Papua New Guinea and northern Australia westward to the Middle East and eastward into the Coral Sea, but does not extend to New Caledonia.

It is potentially a very dangerous snake. Although it seldom attacks unprovoked, when molested it may bite vigorously and repeatedly, delivering large doses of venom on successive bites. It has a large gape, and long fangs that can penetrate a wet suit (Fig. 65E).

Emydocephalus annulatus (The Turtle-headed Seasnake) — one of the most variable colour patterns of any seasnake, from uniform black to dark brown or dark grey through various degrees of banding to conspicuously contrasted dark and light bands, often with flecks of contrasting colour, completely circling the body. The most distinctive feature is a spine (males) and a slight, blunt point (females) on the snout. A large scale covers most of the upper lip, giving the head a "turtle-like" appearance; hence the common name. Average length 75 cm.

It inhabits shallow water on coral reefs of the tropical waters of Australia from the Timor Sea to the Coral Sea. It feeds exclusively on fish eggs and has a reduced venom gland and fangs. It is not dangerous to humans, being reluctant to bite even when provoked (Fig. 65C,D).

Fig. 65. Some common seasnakes of the Great Barrier Reef: **A**, *Aipysurus laevis*. **B**, *Aipysurus duboisii*. **C**, *Emydocephalus annulatus* (top view). **D**, *Emydocephalus annulatus* (side view). **E**, *Astrotia stokesii*. **F**, *Pelamis platurus*.

Acalyptophis peronii (Horned Seasnake) — cream, grey or pale brown with a series of darker brown blotches on the dorsum. Scales on the head rough and irregular and raised around the eye to give the animal a "horned" appearance. It is slender with a maximum length of about 1 metre. It feeds on fish, often searching holes in the sea floor for gobies. It occurs in the tropical waters of northern Australia and the Coral Sea.

It is shy and unlikely to attack humans; nothing is known about its venom.

Disteira kingii (King's Seasnake) — attractively marked, with black head and throat, the upper part of the body grey, and darker diamond-shaped blotches extending down the sides. The lower part of the body cream to pale brown with a series of spots and/or triangular blotches, and a midventral dark stripe. It is slender and delicately built, maximum length about 1.85 m.

It occurs in tropical Australia, usually in deeper water. Little is known about its habits or venom.

Pelamis platurus (Yellow-bellied Seasnake) — black to dark brown above, bright sulphur yellow below, and a yellow tail ornately marked with black spots. Body slender, average length about 70 cm. Brood size varies from one to six young.

It is a pelagic surface dweller tending to congregate in slicks — a habit unique among seasnakes. It feeds by striking small fish that come to shelter beneath it. It appears to be distasteful and has few, if any, predators. It swims backwards equally as well as forwards. It is the most widely distributed seasnake, occurring primarily in tropical and subtropical waters from the western coast of the Americas through the Pacific and Indian oceans to East Africa. It has small fangs and usually attacks only if provoked. (Fig. 65F).

Acrochordidae, Laticaudidae

In addition to the true seasnakes several other marine snakes are in the Great Barrier Reef region. The Little Filesnake (*Acrochordus granulatus*; family Acrochordidae) usually inhabits freshwater, estuaries or muddy marine habitats, but occasionally occurs on reefs. Two Sea Kraits (*Laticauda colubrina* and *L. laticaudata*; family Laticaudidae) are recorded from the Great Barrier Reef, never as breeding populations. They probably are strays from coral reefs in Papua New Guinea or other southwestern Pacific archipelagoes where they are common. They are easily recognized by their conspicuous alternation of black and blue bands.

Terrestrial Reptiles

A total of nine species of terrestrial snakes and 31 species of lizards have been recorded from the islands of the Great Barrier Reef. The list is almost certainly incomplete as many islands have not been surveyed for their herpetofauna. The list does not include the islands of Torres Strait, which have a number of species of Papuan origin.

Terrestrial snakes include a blind-snake (*Ramphotyphlops polygrammicus*; Typhlopidae), a python (*Liasis maculosus*; Boidae), three colubrids (the tree snakes *Boiga irregularis* and *Dendrelaphis punctulata* and the Slaty-grey Snake *Stegonotus cucullatus*) and four species of elapids (*Demansia psammophis*, *D. torquata*, *Furina tristis* and an undescribed *Cacophis*). The family Elapidae includes the dangerous, venomous snakes of Australia, but the four listed above are not considered a hazard to humans. There have been reports of death-adders from the Whitsunday Group.

The lizards include six species of geckos (family Gekkonidae), one legless lizard (Pygopodidae), two Goannas (Varanidae) and 22 species of skinks (Scincidae).

All of the snakes and some of the lizards are found on rocky, continental islands but not cays. They occur in habitats similar to the ones they occupy on the adjacent mainland, and as such are extensions of the mainland fauna. Other lizards characteristic of cays, or commonly reported from cays of the Great Barrier Reef, are set out below (largely from Cogger 1991).

Most of these occur only on cays of the northern and central parts of the reef. In the south, only Lady Elliot and Wilson islands have lizards and the small cays of the Swain Reefs and Coral Sea Territories lack them altogether. A further seven species (a gecko, *Heteronotia binoei*; the Rusty Goanna *Varanus semiremex*; and five skinks, *Carlia dogare*, *C. longipes*, *C. pectoralis*, *C. rhomboidalis* and *Lygisaurus laevis*) have been recorded from only a few islands or cays. The *Carlia* species in particular occupy some part of the mainland coast and occasionally reach adjacent continental islands. One subspecies (*C. pectoralis inconnexa*) is confined to a few islands in the Whitsunday Group.

Family Gekkonidae — Geckos

Gehyra dubia — nocturnal, arboreal, in dry sclerophyll forest and savannah woodlands. Above it is grey-brown or grey to almost pale cream, sometimes with obscure darker markings of various sorts and usually an irregular, narrow black stripe on the temporal region of the head, sometimes extending on to the side of the face. Below it is whitish to rich lemon-yellow. Adults about 80 mm snout to vent. It occurs in eastern Australia from the Cape York Peninsula south to central New South Wales, and on some of the Barrier Reef islands.

Hemidactylus frenatus (House Gecko) — arboreal, with toes expanded to form climbing pads (Fig. 66); often associated with humans and frequently lives in and around buildings. Pale creamy white to grey or dark brown sometimes with scattered dark spots; some white below. About 60 mm snout to vent. It occurs in Indo-Malaysia, many Pacific islands, Papua New Guinea and northern Australia (in various mainland localities and on some of the cays of the Great Barrier Reef and Torres Strait).

Lepidodactylus lugubris — mostly in the crown of palms or other low vegetation but also buildings. Pale creamy-fawn above with darker brown flecks and mottling, especially on the sides. A series of W-shaped marks down the centre of the back and tail. A narrow brown stripe bordered by a pale upper edge is along the face, through the eye to the forearm. Adults about 50 mm snout to vent. This species occurs in Indo-Malaysia, New Guinea, the islands of Oceania, and in Australia is known from various coastal localities in northeastern Queensland, and on many islands of the Torres Strait and northern Great Barrier Reef.

Nactus pelagicus (Pelagic Gecko) — nocturnal terrestrial gecko, usually in forests. Brown to blackish above, sometimes with a series of dark-edged paler blotches which tend to form transverse bands, especially on the tail. Lips whitish, lighlty barred with dark brown. Below whitish, finely peppered with brown. About 80 mm snout to vent. It occurs on Cape York Peninsula and some islands of the Great Barrier Reef and Torres Strait, as well as throughout Papua New Guinea and islands of the western Pacific Ocean.

Family Scincidae — Skinks

Cryptoblepharus litoralis — often inhabits seaside areas, where it is found in ground litter and vegetation on dunes, in mangroves and on boulders of rocky foreshores. Commonly forages for amphipods and other small marine animals at low tide in the intertidal zone. Dark grey to greenish black above, usually with a ragged-edged pale stripe narrowly edged with black on the head and neck from above the eye to the tail on each side. Pale spots and flecks on the back. Metallic whitish grey below. Undersides of the hands and feet shiny black. Adults about 55 mm snout to vent. It is found along the coasts of eastern

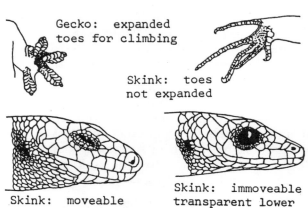

Gecko: expanded toes for climbing

Skink: toes not expanded

Skink: moveable scaly lower eyelid

Skink: immoveable transparent lower eyelid

Fig. 66. The toes and faces of two lizards from islands of the Great Barrier Reef. Left: A gecko, *Hemidactylus frenatus*. Right: a skink, *Crytoblepharus virgatus*.

Queensland and northern Northern Territory, on some islands of the Great Barrier Reef and Torres Strait and in Papua New Guinea.

Cryptoblepharus virgatus — usually arboreal, using tree trunks as lookouts for sighting prey on the ground, and often sheltering under bark. A distinct silvery stripe on each side of the back is bordered above by a medial dark area, and below by a broad dark brown lateral zone which begins as a stripe from the nostril through the eye and to the base of the tail. Underneath it is white or pale metallic blue. It is 40 mm or less snout to vent. It occurs along the eastern and southern margins of Australia and on some islands of the Great Barrier Reef and Torres Strait (Fig. 66).

Glaphyromorphus nigricaudis — slender, often found under debris, rich brown above and on the sides, sometimes with irregular small dark brown flecks or spots on the front half of the body. Lips are barred with dark brown; the underside is white to cream, sometimes with a few dark brown flecks or streaks on the throat; and the end of the tail is sometimes spotted with black. Adults are 75 mm snout to vent. This species occurs in Papua New Guinea, some islands of the Torres Strait and Great Barrier Reef and in northeastern Queensland.

Glaphyromorphus pardalis — burrowing, often found in soft soil under logs, stones or other debris; rich brown above with a dark streak across the temple and many black spots or vertical bars that sometimes form a continuous streak along the dorsolateral line. The flanks are fawn and spotted with dark brown or black, usually dark brown spots are on the rear of the head, and short, oblique, dark brown bars extend from the lips on to the lower jaw. The underside is pale and the sides of the tail are spotted or variegated with brown. This skink occurs on the Cape York Peninsula and on some of the islands of the Great Barrier Reef and Torres Strait.

Cheloniidae and Dermochelyidae — Marine Turtles

Marine turtle populations worldwide have declined dramatically in the last two centuries. The Great Barrier Reef, however, remains a refuge for some of the few remaining great breeding aggregations for four species of the family Cheloniidae, viz. flatback, *Natator depressus;* green, *Chelonia mydas;* hawksbill, *Eretmochelys imbricata*; and loggerhead, *Caretta caretta.* An additional species from the family Cheloniidae (olive ridley, *Lepidochelys olivacea*) and the sole representative of the family Dermochelyidae (leatherback, *Dermochelys coriacea*) also occur within the Great Barrier Reef but at very low density compared to the other species. The flatback turtle is indigenous to the Australian continental shelf while the other species have a worldwide distribution throughout tropical and temperate waters.

Individual turtles do not wander randomly within the oceans. Each one feeds in a specific home range within 2 500 km of its ancestral breeding area, to which it returns periodically. More than half the turtles that breed in the Great Barrier Reef migrate from feeding areas in Indonesia, Papua New Guinea, Solomon Islands, Vanuatu, New Caledonia, Fiji and northern and eastern Australia; and some that live and feed in Queensland waters migrate to breed in New Caledonia, or the Solomon Islands or beyond.

Marine turtles are long lived. Recent studies suggest that some individuals are more than 30 years old when they first breed. The adult turtle is expected to have a breeding life spanning decades. Within a breeding season the female typically lays three to six clutches of approximately 120 eggs every two weeks (depending on the species). However, the average female does not breed in successive years but at 2–8 year intervals. In the Great Barrier Reef turtles aggregate for courtship near the nesting beaches in about September to November and nesting occurs mostly from late October to March.

Turtles do no care for their eggs or young (hatchlings). Hatching success is greatest on beaches with the lowest risk of erosion and flooding, and with low densities of large terrestrial egg-eating predators. Thus, because both erosion and predators are commonly associated with development and populations of people, hatching success usually is high on remote islands. Eggs incubate in the warm sand for 7–12 weeks. The incubation period and sex of

Indo–Pacific marine turtles

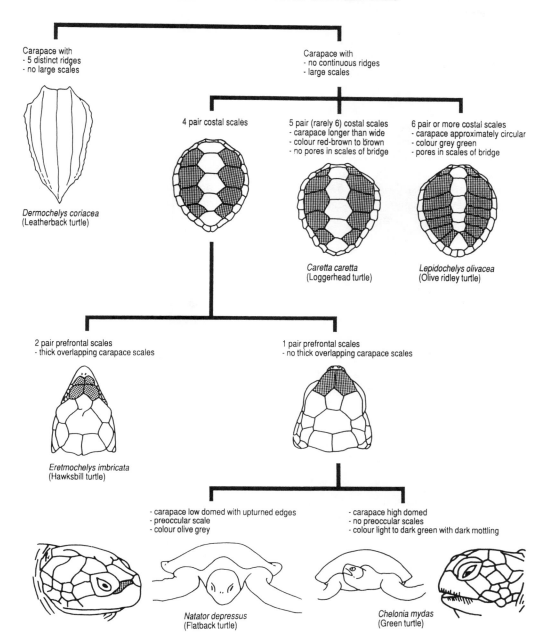

Carapace with
- 5 distinct ridges
- no large scales

Dermochelys coriacea
(Leatherback turtle)

Carapace with
- no continuous ridges
- large scales

4 pair costal scales

5 pair (rarely 6) costal scales
- carapace longer than wide
- colour red-brown to brown
- no pores in scales of bridge

Caretta caretta
(Loggerhead turtle)

6 pair or more costal scales
- carapace approximately circular
- colour grey green
- pores in scales of bridge

Lepidochelys olivacea
(Olive ridley turtle)

2 pair prefrontal scales
- thick overlapping carapace scales

Eretmochelys imbricata
(Hawksbill turtle)

1 pair prefrontal scales
- no thick overlapping carapace scales

- carapace low domed with upturned edges
- preoccular scale
- colour olive grey

Natator depressus
(Flatback turtle)

- carapace high domed
- no preoccular scales
- colour light to dark green with dark mottling

Chelonia mydas
(Green turtle)

the hatchlings are a function of the nest temperature. Cool nests produce all or mostly male hatchlings; warm nests produce all or mostly female hatchlings. The pivotal temperature that theoretically should produce a 50:50 sex ratio, varies between species and between different breeding units of the same species. The pivotal temperature of southern Great Barrier Reef flatbacks is 29.3°C, and for greens is 27.5°C.

Hatchlings emerge mostly at night from January to May. Perhaps to ensure their return to it, they are imprinted with characteristics of their natal region (chemical and directional) at some time during the incubation process or during the beach crossing. Hatchlings move to bright, low elevated areas of the horizon, and this normally leads them seaward. Once in the water, they swim perpendicularly to oncoming wave fronts as well as towards bright horizons, and under natural conditions this usually will lead them into the open ocean.

Birds and crabs on the beach cause negligible losses to the hatchling population. Apparently the greatest risk from predation is from sharks and fish in the shallow inshore area. The new born hatchling has a large yolk sac, which it internalized as it left the egg, and this can supply its nutrient needs for up to two weeks, enabling it to swim actively for several days after leaving the beach without needing to sleep or feed. This swimming frenzy carries it, with the minimum of delays, away from the inshore shallows with their high risk of predation, out into deep open waters.

Once in the open sea, the small turtle drifts with ocean currents. Loggerhead, green and hawksbill turtles appear to follow at least one full circuit of the ocean gyre. This means that small turtles of these species are virtually absent from the Great Barrier Reef. Young flatbacks maintain themselves over the continental shelf. All species feed on near-surface macroplankton during this posthatchling pelagic phase. When around the size of a very large dinner plate (possibly about 5–10 yr old) the young turtles change from a drifting to a more sedentary life style, and begin to eat benthic food. Greens are mainly herbivores, feeding mostly on algae, seagrass, and mangrove. The other species are mostly carnivores, feeding mostly on molluscs and crabs (loggerheads), small crabs (olive ridleys), sponges (hawksbills) and soft corals and other soft bodied animals (flatbacks). The leatherback turtle feeds on jellyfish.

Virtually every coral reef in the Great Barrier Reef supports a feeding group of green turtles and they are also abundant in inshore seagrass habitats. Loggerheads are most abundant in the sandy habitats of lagoonal reefs and inshore bays and estuaries. The hawksbill turtles are mostly coral reef inhabitants. Flatback and ridley turtles occur in inter-reefal soft bottom habitats, and leatherbacks live mostly outside the Reef, in oceanic waters.

For breeding, each species is usually confined to traditional areas. Green turtles nest in the Capricorn-Bunker Groups in the south and the outer barrier cays north of Princess Charlotte Bay; loggerhead turtles nest in the Capricorn-Bunker Groups, the adjacent mainland beaches south of Bustard Head and the Swain Reef cays; hawksbill turtles nest mostly on the inner shelf cays north of Princess Charlotte Bay; and flatbacks nest mostly on the inshore continental islands from Gladstone to Mackay. Small numbers of leatherback turtles breed along with the loggerheads on the mainland coast between Bundaberg and Bustard Head. There are no breeding records of olive ridley turtles from Queensland waters.

The Great Barrier Reef marine turtle populations are vulnerable to continued and extensive harvesting during their migrations to the north of Australia, and to accidental killing in fishing gear.

Birds

Seabirds

Seabirds of tropical and subtropical oceans are mainly associated with coral cays and oceanic islands where they breed. They congregate and feed in the nutrient rich waters near coral reefs and upwellings of cold currents. Oceanic birds, such as shearwaters, have a pelagic life and are not land-based outside the breeding season.

Seabirds play an important role in the development of vegetation on coral cays. Since vegetation reduces erosion, this helps to stablize and develop these cays. Firstly, they carry seeds from cay to cay and introduce some of the early colonizers to unvegetated cays. Then, by transporting essential nutrients from sea to land, via their guano and regurgitated food, they fertilize the substrates and support plant growth.

At least 23 species of seabird have been recorded as breeding on Great Barrier Reef islands: 10 species of tern, three species each of booby and fish-eating raptor, two species of frigatebird, one species each of petrel, shearwater, pelican, tropicbird and gull. Seabirds nest on about 25% of the islands, and an estimated 1.7 million breed annually there. (See Table showing numbers of breeding pairs of seabirds). In addition, there is a non-breeding population of about 425 000 birds on the Great Barrier Reef.

Three groups of breeding seabirds have a distinct latitudinal pattern of distribution.

1. The silver gull, crested tern, bridled tern and black-naped tern breed in colonies scattered along the entire length of the Great Barrier Reef;

2. The wedge-tailed shearwater, masked booby, brown booby, least frigatebird, red-tailed tropicbird, roseate tern and black noddy breed in both the northern and the southern sections; and

3. The Australian pelican, common noddy and sooty tern breed almost exclusively in the northern section.

Wedge-tailed shearwaters constitute 50% of all breeding seabirds and black noddies about 25%. Since most of them breed in the southern section, the southern section has the greatest number of breeding seabirds, whereas the northern section has the greatest diversity, within the Great Barrier Reef. For some species, the number breeding in the Great Barrier Reef may be important on a global scale. For example, between 15 and 20% of the world's roseate terns breed there.

Distribution and size of seabird colonies depend on (1) the availability of suitable nesting habitats, (2) the proximity of feeding areas, and (3) human disturbances.

Nesting and Feeding Areas

There are three types of cay or islet, each with a characteristic group of breeding species. The unvegetated cays formed of sand and shingle generally support a selection from brown booby, masked booby, black-naped tern, common noddy, crested tern and sooty tern. The cays covered with ground vegetation, but without trees, attract additional species, such as the least frigatebird, red-footed booby, red-tailed tropicbird, silver gull and wedge-tailed shearwater. Wooded cays sometimes also support the black noddy and great frigatebird. In the central section coral cays are scarce, and the few that occur are not well vegetated, limiting the number of breeding species.

Generally, for those species that can travel long distances to feeding areas, such as the wedge-tailed shearwater, sooty tern, common noddy and black noddy, the size of breeding colonies increases with the size of the nesting area available. Their colonies are not many but each may grow to tens or even hundreds of thousands of birds. On the other hand, those species that travel only short distances to feeding areas tend to breed in small, scattered colonies, irrespective of the size of the nesting areas available; and, if the food supply is not adequate in the surrounding seas, the potential nesting sites are not used by those breeding birds that forage close to their colonies.

The time of breeding depends on the internal cycle of the birds, the food supply, social factors and, in the southern section, temperature and day length. Social factors may influence the number of pairs breeding at the same time. Mortality of eggs and chicks is often caused by predation, disease, flooding of nests and exposure during poor weather. The immatures in their first year continue to suffer greater mortality than adults. Once they become adults, seabirds have long life expectancies. The crested tern, for example, lives 18–20 years and the sooty tern up to 32 years. Larger species, such as the brown booby, may live even longer.

Human Impacts

Increased human activities on the Great Barrier Reef in recent years have caused a decrease in availability and suitability of nesting areas. The ground nesting terns are most sensitive to disturbances caused by people either directly or indirectly. Frequent presence of people in nesting areas prevent the birds from nesting. For the established colony, even a brief visit to the area may drive the parents off nests and so eggs and chicks become vulnerable to predators (gulls and herons) and susceptible to heat exhaustion.

Some species appear to be more tolerant of people than others. For example, one may approach within a few metres of shearwaters without disturbing them, whereas one cannot get within 40 metres of black-naped terns or roseate terns before they fly up. **It is important to note that the birds are disturbed by the approach of people long before they take flight.** Any breeding colony is usually noisy with searching calls, greetings, squabbling and begging of birds, but if it falls silent suddenly or the noise is replaced by sharp alarm calls it is a sure sign of disturbance. If birds are swooping at you, and perhaps defaecating over you, there is never any doubt that you are the cause of the disturbance. If this happens you should move away from the colony as quickly as possible. For observation and photography of seabirds, a hide or blind is essential except for shearwaters and black noddies that have been habituated to people near buildings and camping grounds.

On large islands, you are advised to remain on the walking tracks provided. If you wander off a track, you may disturb black noddies nesting on trees or run the risk of falling into a shearwater (mutton-bird) burrow. Black noddies nesting in the undeveloped areas are far more sensitive to people than those near constant human activity. For example, on Heron Island it is possible to approach within three metres of an incubating noddy in the resort area without disturbing it, but incubating birds in the National Park will be disturbed at about eight metres. If you accidentally fall into a shearwater burrow, you should observe the collapsed burrow for 15 seconds or so for any sign of a bird under the sand and dig the bird out if the movement indicate its presence. You should be careful not to break the egg or be bitten by the shearwater. You should also check under the sand for an egg or small chick by slowly running your hand through the sand and, if you find one, dig it out carefully. In any case you should clear the tunnel so that the sitting bird, if trapped in the burrow, can leave.

Visitors to islands and cays also inadvertently cause increased predation of eggs and chicks of seabirds by attracting gulls — either directly by feeding them, or indirectly when the gulls are attracted to rubbish dumps near the breeding colonies of seabirds. As the number of gulls attracted to such food sources increases some of them start to prey on eggs and chicks. **Food scraps and rubbish should be taken away and not be fed or made available to gulls.**

Breeding Species

The distribution and abundance of the breeding seabirds of the Great Barrier Reef are tabulated below. The following accounts summarize, where possible, movements, breeding season, nesting habitat, clutch size, incubation period, fledging period, foraging grounds and diet for each species.

Herald Petrel — up to seven individuals have been recorded on Raine Island between January and August. Their breeding was confirmed in July 1982.

Wedge-tailed Shearwater (Fig. 68) — breeds along the east coast of Australia, where it arrives in October and lays in November and December. More than 80% of the breeding population occurs on the Great Barrier Reef, where the colony size varies from 100 (Fife Island, northern section) to about 400 000 pairs (North West Island, southern section). After five months of the breeding season, in which a pair raises one chick, the birds disperse northwards. Although banded birds have been recovered from New Guinea, the Philippines and central western Pacific, the exact pattern of dispersal is unknown. The nesting burrow is often over 2 m long and ends in an egg chamber. Vegetation cover, tree roots, guano or moisture in the sand support the burrow. A prolonged dry season may prevent construction of them in coral cay sand or cause burrows to collapse, trapping the occupants inside. Parents take turns to incubate the single egg for about 50 days. While one incubates, the other ventures hundreds of kilometres from the colony. They catch fish and squid from which they produce a green oil. This is regurgitated and fed to the young when they return at night after a period of 24 to 48 hours at sea. The young remain in the burrow for about 70 days, though adults leave the colony before them. Hunger forces the young to leave their nest burrows and fly off to catch their own food. At Heron Island, for example, most young leave the island during April and May, but some late season young remain on the island till June.

Australian Pelican — breeds in colonies of 10–200 birds on offshore islands in the northern section. Pelicans usually lay a clutch of two eggs (varies one to four), which they incubate for 32 to 35 days. Chicks are fed with regurgitated food for about 100 days, at first in nests

Table showing the total number of breeding pairs of 20 seabird species in the northern, central and southern sections of the Great Barrier Reef*. Numbers refer to ranges of colony sizes: (1) <10 pairs, (2) 10–<100 pairs, (3) 100–<1 000 pairs, (4) 1 000–<10 000 pairs, (5) 10 000–<100 000 pairs, (6) 100 000–<1 000 000 pairs.

Section of Great Barrier Reef	Herald Petrel	Wedge-tailed Shearwater	Australian Pelican	Great Frigatebird	Least Frigatebird	Red-footed Booby	Masked Booby	Brown Booby	Red-tailed Tropicbird	Caspian Tern	Crested Tern	Lesser Crested Tern	Bridled Tern	Sooty Tern	Black-naped Tern	Roseate Tern	Little Tern	Common Noddy	Black Noddy	Silver Gull	Source
Northern	1	4	3	2	4	3	4	5	3	2	5	4	4	5	4	4	2	5	4	3	King in press
Central	-	-	-	-	-	-	-	-	-	2	4	-	4	-	3	-	-	-	-	2	King in press
Southern	-	6	-	-	3	-	3	4	1	-	4	3	4	1	3	3	2	2	6	3	Hulsman 1984

*Northern: Far Northern and Cairns Sections of Great Barrier Reef and Marine Park; Central: Central Section and Mackay Area Islands; Southern: Swain Reefs, Capricorn and Bunker Groups of Islands.

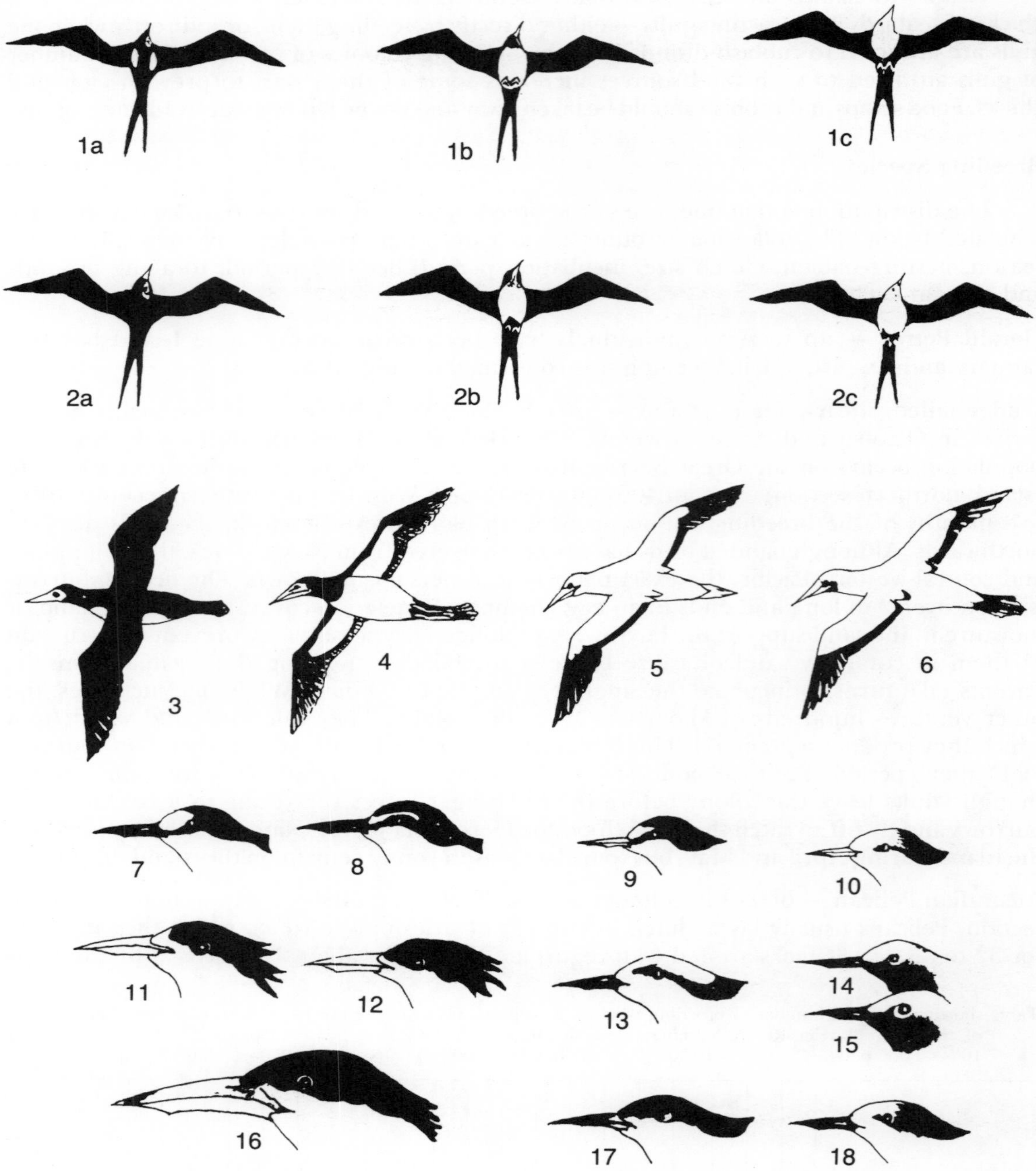

Fig. 67. 1–2, **Frigatebirds** (from below): 1, Least Frigatebird (a, male; b, female; c, juvenile). 2, Great Frigatebird (a, male; b, female; c, juvenile). 3–7, **Boobies:** 3, Brown Booby (from above). 4, Brown Booby (from below). 5, Red-footed Booby. 6, Masked Booby. **Terns in summer:** 7, Sooty Tern. 8, Bridle Tern. 9, Little Tern. 10, Little Tern (non-breeding). 11, Crested Tern. 12, Lesser Crested Tern. 13, Black-naped Tern. 14, Black Noddy. 15, Common Noddy. 16, Caspian Tern. 17, Roseate Tern. 18, Common Tern (non-breeding).

but later in a creche. They are easily disturbed at the nesting area and take a long time to return, allowing gulls to enter the colony and eat eggs and small young. They disperse long distances after breeding.

Great Frigatebird (Fig. 67:2) — pelagic, breeds at Raine and Quoin Islands (10 pairs or fewer) on the Great Barrier Reef and on cays of Coral Sea. The male has a red throat-pouch which is inflated during courtship. Nests are built on bushes or on ground by both sexes — the male collects nesting material while the female builds the nest. Single eggs are laid between April and June in most years, and are incubated for about 54 days. Both parents incubate, with shifts lasting four days or more. The chick is brooded for 45 days or so and then is left unattended for one or two days at a time. Young fledge between 140 and 168 days after hatching, but the parental care continues for up to 10 months after fledging. Age of first breeding is 5–7 years and pairs are usually permanent. If breeding is successful, they breed once every two years. Frigatebirds range over a large area in search of food. They sometimes congregate over seabird colonies and steal food from others, especially boobies. Their diet consists of flying fish, squid, turtle hatchlings, crabs, young birds and carrion. During a big storm they may be found over the continental shores and inland.

Least Frigatebird (Fig. 67:1) — a few pairs nest on the Swain Reefs and about 2 000 pairs on Raine Island where nests are found in dense colonies on several of the rockpiles and earth mounds of the central depression and in a series of discontinuous groups along the vegetated ridge. They breed biennially between May and December (laying peak in July). Breeding age and parental care are similar to those of the Great Frigatebird.

Red-footed Booby (Fig. 67:5) — colonial, nests on offshore islands and cays, but is uncommon on the Great Barrier Reef. The largest colony is located at Raine Island where up to 76 nests are found on shrubs at any time of the year. A single egg is incubated under the bird's feet for about 45 days. Flying fish and squid form the diet and parents regurgitate food for chicks.

Masked Booby (Fig. 67:6) — disperses over large distances from the breeding colonies. Its largest colony on the Great Barrier Reef is at Raine Island, where about 2 500 pairs breed between July and April. They incubate a clutch of two eggs with their webbed feet for 42–46 days. The hatchlings often sit on their parents' feet. Usually one chick from the clutch survives to fledge in about 120 days. The main diet is flying fish and squid, which the parents regurgitate to feed the young.

Brown Booby (Fig. 67:3,4) — at least 18 colonies occur on the Great Barrier Reef, including seven or so in the Swain Reefs with 10–1 000 pairs. Estimation of nesting birds includes 6 000 at Raine Island and 3 000 at Fairfax Island in recent years. They nest in a variety of terrains from flat ground and beaches to broken terrain and cliff ledges. The nest may be a scrape or a substantial structure of sticks, seaweed and other vegetation fragments. A clutch of one or two eggs (rarely three) is incubated for 43–47 days. Both sexes incubate in 12-hour shifts (rarely up to 24 hours). In one study 70% of changes in incubation occurred between dawn and 1130 hours. Like other boobies the bird covers the clutch with its webbed feet to incubate. Chicks are fed twice a day on average for about 95 days until they fledge and less often thereafter for several more months. Adults are relatively sedentary, but young are known to range over large distances, sometimes over 5 000 km, from the colony. Brown boobies are gregarious foragers, hunting flying fish and squid in deep waters and hardy-heads in shallow waters around the reef crest.

Red-tailed Tropicbird — graceful, oceanic, with a large individual range. It nests on cays of the Coral Sea, Raine Island and Lady Elliot Island on the Great Barrier Reef. At Raine Island the bird nests all the year round though the number recorded was never more than a dozen on any visit. At Lady Elliot Island a single pair nested in 1983 and 1984, and two pairs since 1985. They nest under cover and a clutch of one egg (rarely two) is incubated by both sexes with daily changeovers for about 40 days. Young are fed with squid and pelagic fish from the parent's bill inserted into the chick's mouth. They are fledged in about 40 days and leave the nesting area when 65–100 days old.

Caspian Tern (Fig. 67:16) — breeds singly or in colonies of up to 100 pairs at any time of year in northern Australia. On the Great Barrier Reef isolated pairs breed on islands off Cape York Peninsula and Creek Rock and Pelican Rock in the central section. A clutch of one or two eggs (rarely three) is incubated by both sexes, in turn, for 21 days. Hatchlings remain at the nest for a few days before parents lead them to a cover among the vegetation. Parents carry fish crosswise in their bills while flying back to feed their chicks.

Crested Tern (Fig. 67:11) — common along the Australian coast and, in the Great Barrier Reef, breeds late spring to mid-summer in colonies of almost any size up to several thousand birds (3 000 pairs in a colony at Lady Elliot Island). The nest is a scrape on sand and a clutch of one egg (rarely two) is incubated by both parents (a three-hour shift on average) for 25–30 days. Young are brooded for the first two days of hatching in the nest and then are taken away from the nesting area. They continue to be brooded and fed. They fledge in 38–40 days, but continue to be fed until they are at least four months old. Adults feed young once every one to three hours. They catch fish (mostly anchovies, flying fish, small tuna, wrasses and blennies), and sometimes squid, and carry them crosswise in their bills. Chicks may form a creche. Both adults and young leave the colony when young are about nine weeks old, though some remain around the colony throughout the year. There is a net movement northward in the post-breeding dispersal.

Lesser Crested Tern (Fig. 67:12) — mostly confined to tropical islands, and breeds in October in the northern section and in August to September in the southern section of the Great Barrier Reef. Average colony size is larger in the northern section (thousands) than in the southern section (hundreds), though yearly fluctuation of colony size is great. It nests on unvegetated banks, upper parts of beaches in the vegetation and sometimes among nesting crested terns. A clutch of one egg (occasionally two) is incubated for 25–30 days by both parents with an average shift lasting 4.75 hours. The young is brooded at the nest by a parent for the first few days of life. Away from the nest one parent remains with the chick until it is large enough to join a creche. Parents continue to feed the chick as often as once every 37 minutes until it is at least four months old. The diet is fish, mainly hardyheads, anchovies and wrasses. Outside the breeding season they disperse widely over the subtropical and tropical shores and islands.

Bridled Tern (Fig. 67:8) — nests during late spring and lays until mid-summer. Although a large number of pairs (2 500–4 000) has been estimated to nest at Eshelby Island in the central section, most colonies are small and contain fewer than 1 000 pairs. They nest under dense vegetation, on ledges and in crevices. A clutch of one egg is incubated for 28–30 days by both parents with incubation shifts averaging 5.7 hours. The chick is brooded for up to four days and fed with regurgitated fish two to four times a day. The young fledge in 52–61 days. The diet consists mainly of anchovies, flying fish and leatherjackets. Young leave the colony about three weeks after fledging, each accompanied by one or both parents. They disperse from their breeding colonies during the non-breeding season.

Sooty Tern (Fig. 67:7) — pelagic, nests at any time of year with a peak in spring. Most breeding colonies are located on offshore and oceanic islands in the northern section. The largest colony is found on Michaelmas Cay, where up to 20 000 pairs nest over the year and individuals have a subannual breeding cycle of about 9.3 months. A single egg is laid in a scrape on sand, sometimes among grass or under bushes, or on bare earth, lava or rock. Incubation is shared by both sexes and lasts 28–30 days. Young are brooded for the first few days, but thereafter both parents forage simultaneously and feed young with regurgitated food at least once a day. Chicks may form a creche and fledge in about 60 days. Sooty terns may travel long distances in search of food which consists of flying fish and squid. They catch prey by contact dipping, i.e., swooping down during flight and dipping the bill in water to catch prey at the surface. They also forage at night when squid come to the surface. After breeding they disperse over a wide area and juveniles sometimes migrate long distances.

Black-naped Tern (Fig. 67:13) — a tropical species, nests in small colonies often of fewer than 100 pairs, though some islands in the northern section support larger colonies (e.g., 250 pairs on Davie Cay). Colonies are typically located in a narrow zone just above the highwater mark and some are subject to inundation at unusually high spring tides. Nests are scrapes in the ground and mean distances between nests may vary from 0.55 m (Eagle Island) to 0.99 m (One Tree Island). A clutch of one or two eggs (rarely three) is incubated for 21–23 days by both parents with shifts averaging 1.1 hours during the day. Young are brooded for the first week of hatching, during which only one parent is available at any time to feed the chicks. Most birds (>80%) hunt within 2 km of their colonies and are often seen foraging in the surf close to the colony when they are feeding young. In one study, the mean feeding interval was about 50 minutes, but the modal frequency was four to five minutes. They eat fish, mainly anchovies, flying fish, hardyheads and sardines. Some birds remain around breeding colonies through the year, but most adults and young leave the colony about three weeks after the young fledge. Young continue to beg for another month or more.

Roseate Tern (Fig. 67:17) — a long-tailed species, is particularly vulnerable to human disturbance at the breeding ground, and only few breeding colonies are sustained in other parts of the world. On the Great Barrier Reef it nests between October and February (late spring to late summer) in colonies, varying in size from a few pairs nesting among other terns, such as the black-naped tern, to several thousand pairs. Nests are placed on high ground, usually on grass covered dunes or under dense vegetation. They are often found near a colony of black-naped terns or, occasionally, alongside crested terns. Some nests are placed under drift wood lying above the highwater mark. A clutch of one or two eggs (laid about three days apart) is incubated for 21–24 days by both parents with shifts averaging 2.5 hours. Young are brooded for about five days before they move to hide in the vegetation. They fledge in 22–30 days and wait on the shoreline while their parents forage nearby. Later they may accompany parents on fishing trips, but remain dependent on parents for food for at least two months after fledging. They forage further from the shoreline than black-naped terns, and forage singly for small fish such as anchovies and small tuna, 2–9 cm long. They leave the colony after breeding, but it is not known where most birds from the Great Barrier Reef spend the winter.

Little Tern (Fig. 67:9,10) — an inshore species, the smallest tern found in the Great Barrier Reef. Many birds with winter or juvenile plumage in summer may be migrants from the northern hemisphere. Few records of nesting by local birds exist in the northern section (Pipon Island, Stephens Island) and in the southern section (Lady Elliot Island). They breed in small colonies high up on beaches. A clutch of two or sometimes three eggs is incubated by both parents in turn for about 21 days. Young are fed with small fish, such as hardyheads and anchovies, caught in shallow waters near the colony and carried cross-wise in parents' bills. They fledge in about 19 days.

Common Noddy (Fig. 67:15) — brownish black, tern-shaped, with a white cap, breeds in colonies, mostly in the northern section (17 000 pairs at Raine Island, 6 000 pairs at Michaelmas Cay). Nests are built with sticks, seaweeds, leaves, etc., on clumps of low bushes or with little material on ground. A clutch of one egg (rarely two) is incubated by both parents in turn for 32–35 days. Young are fed with regurgitated food, mostly flying fish and squid. They fledge in about 45 days. Both young and adults disperse widely after breeding.

Black Noddy (Fig. 67:14) — also known as the white-capped noddy, is similar to the common noddy, but the body plumage is darker and the bill thinner and longer. It is typically sedentary, but may disappear completely from the colony for some weeks in winter. The nesting season extends from October to March, depending on the success of the early clutch laid in November and early December. Large colonies are found in the southern section (approximately 91 000 pairs at North West Island, 66 000 pairs at Masthead Island and 35 000 pairs at Heron Island). The nest is a platform of leaves (usually from *Pisonia*), sometimes containing seaweed, grass and twine, placed on a branch of *Pisonia* or other trees and cemented with excreta. In the northern section the species breeds all year round and nests in mangroves (4 000 pairs at Bird Island) and low shrubs as well as in *Pisonia*. A clutch of one egg is incubated for about 36 days by both parents with three-hour shifts. Eggs are often blown off the unattended nests by strong winds or knocked off by adults leaving in a hurry. Chicks have the same plumage colour as adults. They are fed once every three hours with regurgitated fish by either parent. Mortality is usually high as the chicks fallen to the ground are not fed and predation by eastern reef egrets is high in the colony. The biggest mortality occurs when the season is favourable for the seeding of *Pisonia* as the sticky seeds come down with a storm and cover both parents and chicks nesting in trees and trapping them on the ground. Fledging is completed in about 45 days. Birds usually hunt within 10 km of their colonies, but some may venture 50 km or more. They often rely on predatory fish to bring their prey to surface and hunt in flocks containing up to 3 000 birds. The diet consists of anchovies, hardyheads, squid and krill.

Silver Gull — the commonest gull around the Australian coast, is the only species of gull that breeds in the tropics. It is extremely adaptable, and frequents beaches, parks, rubbish dumps, farmland and islands. Many even commute between the mainland and the islands in the Capricornia Region of the Great Barrier Reef. Populations in this region fluctuate greatly, depending on the availability of food. They breed on many islands in colonies of 100 or more pairs. Nests are built on the ground and two or three eggs in a clutch are incubated by both parents taking turns for about 24 days. Young fledge in about four weeks when they are taken away by parents to a new place and continued to be fed for at least two more weeks before they disperse. Although it no longer breeds on Heron Island, all age classes from the begging fledglings with mottled-brown plumage, brown eyes, black bills and legs to adults with red bills and legs may be seen there. Gulls prey on the eggs and chicks of other seabirds. For instance, they eat eggs and chicks of black noddies on Heron Island and in some years their predation is the major cause of mortality of eggs and chicks of the roseate tern, black-naped tern and crested tern on islands where breeding colonies of terns are disturbed by people. Increased availability of food scraps at rubbish dumps on the coast and offshore islands is considered responsible for greater survival of first year gulls than in the past, contributing to increase in population size and, consequently, predation by gulls on eggs and chicks of other seabirds. Control of the gull population is an important part of seabird conservation.

Non-breeding Seabirds

Southern ocean birds, such as **penguins, albatrosses, giant petrels, cape petrels, prions, great skua**, may stray into the southern section of the Great Barrier Reef in winter. Of the tropical species, the **black-winged petrel** (Fig. 68) visits Capricorn and Bunker islands in some summers, while the **white-tailed tropic-bird** is a rare and irregular visitor to the entire region. Among the migratory terns the **common tern** (Fig. 67:18) and the northern race of the **little tern** visit cays in winter plumage and mix with local breeding species on roosting grounds.

Fig. 68. Wedge-tailed Shearwater. Black-winged Petrel.

Waterbirds

Breeding Waterbirds

Of the four species of cormorant that occur on the Great Barrier Reef only the **little pied cormorant** is known to nest on coral cays (Capricorn-Bunker Groups). Others visit cays but nest only on continental islands (e.g., **pied cormorant** on East Rock in the Whitsunday Passage).

Among the herons the **white-faced heron, striated heron** and **black bittern** are known to nest on continental and volcanic islands of the northern section whereas the **eastern reef egret** (Fig. 69:2) is a ubiquitous resident on all types of islands. The eastern reef egret, known as the reef heron locally, has two plumage types with the white outnumbering the grey by about three to one in the southern section. The **rufous night heron** breeds in the northern section and is associated with mangroves, except on Raine Island, where some 2 000 birds nest on low vegetation. They depend on eggs and hatchlings of the green turtle for food and migrate to Papua after breeding.

Three species of fish eating raptors breed on the Great Barrier Reef; the **osprey** and the **Brahminy kite** on continental islands, the **white-breasted sea-eagle** on coral cays as well as other islands.

Both the **pied** and the **sooty oystercatchers** (Fig. 69:1) breed on all types of island, nesting usually just above the high water mark on deserted beaches. They are sensitive to human presence and do not nest if disturbed frequently. As they are territorial the density is low on any island. The two species occupy the same niche on islands. On the other hand, the **bush thick-knee** and the **beach thick-knee**, though they both occur on continental islands, occupy different habitats and only the latter is associated with the intertidal habitat and nests near the water.

Migratory Waders

Migratory waders, or shorebirds, are found in the region between September and April, though in the northern section they are seen mostly during the migration and some individuals remain on islands through the winter (not migrating to northern breeding grounds). Common among the wintering species in southern summer are the **lesser golden plover, Mongolian plover, ruddy turnstone** (Fig. 70:1) and **grey-tailed tattler** (Fig. 70:2). The tattlers often roost on trees, but others remain on sand bars and beach rocks at high tide. Thus they are often disturbed by people walking along the beach. As the estuarine habitats are altered by human activities on the mainland, greater use will be made of island habitats by migratory waders in future.

Fig. 69. Sooty Oystercatcher. Eastern Reef Egret.

People should avoid disturbing resting waders and terns on sand bars and around the highwater mark, particularly on small islands, where the birds have no sanctuaries from beach strollers.

Land Birds

Breeding Land Birds

The distribution of land birds on continental islands reflects the bio-geographical regions of the continent. Accordingly, the islands have a fauna similar to that in comparable habitats of the adjacent mainland. It is usually attenuated depending on the size of the island. Large islands in the northern section often support the **orange-footed scrubfowl, Torresian imperial pigeon, white-rumped swiftlet, yellow-bellied sunbird, varied honeyeater** (associated with mangroves) and other tropical forest birds.

Among the coral cays only the vegetated cays provide nesting sites for a small section of coastal land birds of the

Fig. 70. Ruddy Turnstone. Grey-tailed Tattler.

mainland. Unlike the continental islands, they are limited in altitude to only a few metres above the highwater mark, their environment is simple and their resource level is low. Consequently, only the large wooded cays can support sustainable populations of land birds as a rule. The following species are found regularly on wooded cays.

Buff-banded Rail (Fig. 71:2) — strongly territorial and usually rare on uninhabited islands, but appears commonly on camping grounds and in resort areas. On Heron Island, they became abundant following the extermination of rats in 1965/66 and elimination of the feral domestic fowl in the 1970s.

Rose-crowned Fruit-dove — small, beautiful fruit-dove, is more often heard (accelerated coos) than seen in association with the strangling fig *Ficus obliqua* on large islands (e.g., North West Island).

Torresian Imperial Pigeon — a migrant from Papua to the northern section of the Great Barrier Reef, where it breeds from September to April in colonies up to 10 000 pairs or more. The large colonies

Fig. 71. Bar-shouldered Dove. Buff-banded Rail.

are established in mangroves (sometimes in rainforest) on low wooded islands close to the mainland. They may be seen flying low over the water in early morning and late afternoon as they commute to and from the adjacent mainland where they feed on fruits in lowland rainforests.

Bar-shouldered Dove (Fig. 71:1) — common, with short legs and a long tail, feeds on the ground. It has two distinct calls, one with several low frequency notes forming a melody, the other with repetitions of two notes uttered in courtship.

Sacred Kingfisher (Fig. 72:2) — the resident kingfisher of most wooded cays, nests in tree holes. It has a greenish, rather than bluish, back and buff underside. The continental islands may have, in addition, the forest kingfisher (blue back and white underside), whereas mangroves support the collared kingfisher (a larger species with greenish back and white underside).

Black-faced Cuckoo-shrike — grey with black face and throat (except young birds), is a regular winter visitor to wooded cays but some occasionally nest on large islands. It feeds in trees, and every time the bird shifts a perch it has a habit of folding its long wings again after landing.

Golden-headed Cisticola — a small fantail warbler, nests in long grass in the open. It has a territorial flight and a buzzing call. Other brownish warblers that may appear in similar habitats of the islands during migration are much larger and either unstreaked (clamorous reed-warbler) or streaked with a long graduated tail (tawny grassbird).

Silvereye (Fig. 72:1) — a small, greenish bird with a white eye-ring, grey upperback and a short, thin, pointed bill, is abundant on Heron Island (11 pairs per hectare attempt breeding each year). It may be seen foraging in *Pisonia* trees and shrubs, collecting nectar from *Cordia* flowers, eating figs and *Pipturus* fruit or scavenging on the ground. They lay eggs from September to March (peak October–December) and each pair raises one to three young per clutch (mostly two) one to five times (mostly twice) in a season. They are mated for life, and pairs often perch together and preen each other. They live up to eleven years on Heron Island. This is the only species of bird that has been differentiated into a distinct morphological race on the Great Barrier Reef. All islands of Capricorn and Bunker Groups have breeding populations of this race, which is larger (in all external measurements, particularly the bill and legs), heavier and more brightly coloured than any of the mainland races. Small mainland birds appear on islands during migration. Their numbers vary from year to year and they do not remain on the islands in the breeding season. Mainland races, however, nest on continental islands.

Low wooded islands off Cape York Peninsula and Torres Strait have another island species, the pale white-eye, which has a green back.

House Sparrow — is a recently established species on Lady Elliot Island and Heron Island.

Fig. 72. Capricorn Silvereye. Sacred Kingfisher.

White-breasted Wood-swallow — a coastal species of wood-swallow with a dark throat and white underside and rump, flies like a swallow, with broad triangular wings. It is common on continental islands but also breeds on northern wooded cays (e.g., Green Island).

Pied Currawong — a large magpie-like bird, used to breed on wooded cays of Capricorn Group, has now disappeared from most islands.

Vagrants

Casual visitors and stragglers to offshore islands and coral cays are many among coastal migrants and nomads of the mainland. Records kept of such species on Heron Island over 20 years contained, apart from straggling seabirds, two species of ibis, the **purple swamphen**, the **black swan** and 42 species of land birds.

Bird Species Reported from the Great Barrier Reef
(not including those found only on continental islands)

Spheniscidae: Little penguin *Eudyptula minor*.

Diomedeidae: Wandering albatross *Diomedea exulans*; Grey-headed albatross *Diomedea chrysostoma*; Southern giant-petrel *Macronectes giganteus*; Cape petrel *Daption capense*; Herald petrel *Pterodroma arminjoniana*; Tahiti petrel *Pterodroma rostrata*; Black-winged petrel *Pterodroma nigripennis*; Antarctic prion *Pachyptila desolata*; Fairy prion *Pachyptila turtur*; Flesh-footed shearwater *Puffinus carneipes*; Wedge-tailed shearwater *Puffinus pacificus*; Fluttering shearwater *Puffinus gavia*.

Oceanitidae: Wilson's storm-petrel *Oceanites oceanicus*; White-bellied storm-petrel *Fregetta grallaria*.

Pelecanidae: Australian pelican *Pelecanus conspicillatus*.

Sulidae: Red-footed booby *Sula sula*; Masked booby *Sula dactylatra*; Brown booby *Sula leucogaster*.

Anhingidae: Darter *Anhinga melanogaster*.

Phalacrocoracidae: Great cormorant *Phalacrocorax carbo*; Pied cormorant *Phalacrocorax varius*; Little black cormorant *Phalacrocorax sulcirostris*; Little pied cormorant *Phalacrocorax melanoleucos*.

Fregatidae: Great frigatebird *Fregata minor*; Least frigatebird *Fregata ariel*.

Phaethontidae: Red-tailed tropicbird *Phaethon rubricauda*; White-tailed tropicbird *Phaethon lepturus*.

Ardeidae: White-faced heron *Ardea novaehollandiae*; Great egret *Egretta alba*; Eastern reef egret *Egretta sacra*; Striated heron *Butorides striatus*; Rufous night heron *Nycticorax caledonicus*; Black bittern *Dupetor flavicollis*.

Plataleidae: Sacred ibis *Threskiornis aethiopica*; Straw-necked ibis *Threskiornis spinicollis*.

Anatidae: Black swan *Cygnus atratus*.

Pandionidae: Osprey *Pandion haliaetus*.

Accipitridae: Brahminy kite *Haliastur indus*; Brown goshawk *Accipiter fasciatus*; Grey goshawk *Accipiter novaehollandiae;* White-bellied sea-eagle *Haliaeetus leucogaster*.

Falconidae: Peregrine falcon *Falco peregrinus*; Brown falcon *Falco berigora*; Australian kestrel *Falco cenchroides*.

Megapodiidae: Orange-footed scrubfowl *Megapodius reinwardt;* Australian brush-turkey *Alectura lathami*.

Phasianidae: Brown quail *Coturnix australis;* Fowl *Gallus gallus* (introduced).

Carcharinus melanopterus, Black-tipped Shark.

Diagramma pictum, Grey Sweet-lips.

Labroides dimidiatus cleaning *Pomacentrus pavo*.

Forcipiger flavissimus, Long-nosed Butterfly Fish.

Pomacanthus semicirculatus, Blue Angel Fish.

The reef slope.

Pomacentrus coelestis, Damsel Fish.

Amphiprion percula, Clown Fish, amongst the tentacles of its host
anemone.

PLATE 8

Unless otherwise stated photos courtesy of
Great Barrier Reef Marine Park Authority

Cryptoblepharus litoralis. (Photo courtesy of H. G. Cogger.)

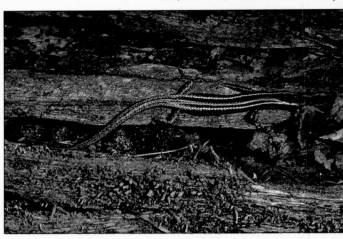

Cryptoblepharus virgatus. (Photo courtesy of H. G. Cogger.)

Turtle tracks left across a beach as a female turtle returns to the sea after laying her eggs.

Michaelmas Cay (off Cairns), ground nesting birds.

Puffinus pacificus, Wedge-tailed Shearwaters (Muttonbirds).

Anous minutus, Black Noddies nesting.

Zosterops lateralis chlorocephala, Silver-eye, island form.

Rallus philippensis, Land-rail.

Rallidae: Buff-banded rail *Rallus philippensis*; Purple swamphen *Porphyrio porphyrio*.

Gruidae: Brolga *Grus rubicundus*.

Burhinidae: Bush thick-knee *Burhinus magnirostris*; Beach thick-knee *Burhinus neglectus*.

Haematopodidae: Pied oystercatcher *Haematopus longirostris*; Sooty oystercatcher *Haematopus fuliginosus*.

Charadriidae: Masked lapwing *Vanellus miles*; Grey plover *Pluvialis squatarola*; Lesser golden plover *Pluvialis dominica;* Mongolian plover *Charadrius mongolus*; Double-banded plover *Charadrius bicinctus*; Large sand plover *Charadrius leschenaultii*; Red-capped plover *Charadrius ruficapillus.*

Scolopacidae: Ruddy turnstone *Arenaria interpres*; Eastern curlew *Numenius madagascariensis*; Whimbrel *Numenius phaeopus;* Little curlew *Numenius minutus*; Grey-tailed tattler *Tringa brevipes;* Wandering tattler *Tringa incana*; Common sandpiper *Tringa hypoleucos*; Greenshank *Tringa nebularia*; Terek sandpiper *Tringa terek*; Black-tailed godwit *Limosa limosa;* Bar-tailed godwit *Limosa lapponica*; Red knot *Calidris canutus*; Great knot *Calidris tenuirostris*; Sharp-tailed sandpiper *Calidris acuminata*; Red-necked stint *Calidris ruficollis;* Long-toed stint *Calidris subminuta;* Curlew sandpiper *Calidris ferruginea;* Sandering *Calidris alba.*

Glareolidae: Oriental pratincole *Glareola maldivarum*; Australian pratincole *Stiltia isabella.*

Stercorariidae: Great skua *Stercorarius skua.*

Laridae: Silver gull *Larus novaehollandiae*; Gull-billed tern *Gelochelidon nilotica*; Caspian tern *Hydroprogne caspia*; Common tern *Sterna hirundo*; Roseate tern *Sterna dougallii;* Black-naped tern *Sterna sumatrana;* Sooty tern *Sterna fuscata;* Bridled tern *Sterna anaethetus*; Little tern *Sterna albifrons;* Crested tern *Sterna bergii;* Lesser crested tern *Sterna bengalensis;* Common noddy *Anous stolidus*; Black noddy *Anous minutus.*

Columbidae: Superb fruit-dove *Ptilinopus superbus;* Rose-crowned fruit-dove *Ptilinopus regina;* Wompoo fruit-dove *Ptilinopus magnificus;* Torresian imperial pigeon *Ducula spilorrhoa;* Peaceful dove *Geopelia placida*; Bar-shouldered dove *Geopelia humeralis;* Emerald dove *Chalcophaps indica.*

Cacatuidae: Sulphur-crested cockatoo *Cacatua galerita.*

Loriidae: Rainbow lorikeet *Trichoglossus haematodus.*

Cuculidae: Oriental cuckoo *Cuculus saturatus;* Brush cuckoo *Cuculus variolosus;* Fan-tailed cuckoo *Cuculus pyrrhophanus;* Horsefield's bronze-cuckoo *Chrysococcyx basalis;* Shining bronze-cuckoo *Chrysococcyx lucidus;* Common koel *Eudynamis scolopacea;* Pheasant coucal *Centropus phasianinus.*

Strigidae: Southern boobook *Ninox novaeseelandiae.*

Tytonidae: Barn owl *Tyto alba.*

Apodidae: White-rumped swiftlet *Collocalia spodiopygia;* White-throated needletail *Hirundapus caudacutus.*

Alcedinidae: Azure kingfisher *Ceyx azurea*; Little kingfisher *Ceyx pusilla;* Laughing kookaburra *Dacelo novaeguineae;* Forest kingfisher *Halcyon macleayii*; Sacred kingfisher *Halcyon sancta;* Collared kingfisher *Halcyon chloris.*

Meropidae: Rainbow bee-eater *Merops ornatus.*

Coraciidae: Dollarbird *Eurystomus orientalis.*

Pittidae: Noisy pitta *Pitta versicolor.*

Hirundinidae: Welcome swallow *Hirundo neoxena*; Tree martin *Cecropis nigricans;* Fairy martin *Cecropis ariel.*

Motacilidae: Richard's pipit *Anthus novaeseelandiae;* Yellow wagtail *Motacilla flava.*

Campephagidae: Black-faced cuckoo-shrike *Coracina novaehollandiae;* White-bellied cuckoo-shrike *Coracina papuensis;* Yellow-eyed cuckoo-shrike *Coracina lineata;* Cicadabird *Coracina tenuirostris;* White-winged triller *Lalage sueurii;* Varied triller *Lalage leucomela.*

Muscicapidae: Golden whistler *Pachycephala pectoralis;* Mangrove golden whistler *Pachycephala melanura;* Rufous whistler *Pachycephala rufiventris;* Little shrike-thrush *Colluricincla megarhyncha;* Black-faced monarch *Monarcha melanopsis;* Spectacled monarch *Monarcha trivirgatus;* White-eared monarch *Monarcha leucotis;* Leaden flycatcher *Myiagra rubecula;* Satin flycatcher *Myiagra cyanoleuca;* Rufous fantail *Rhipidura rufifrons;* Grey fantail *Rhipidura fuliginosa;* Willie Wagtail *Rhipidura leucophrys.*

Sylviidae: Clamorous reed-warbler *Acrocephalus stentoreus;* Tawny grassbird *Megalurus timoriensis;* Golden-headed cisticola *Cisticola exilis.*

Meliphagidae: Noisy friarbird *Philemon corniculatus;* Little friarbird *Phlimon citreogularis;* Yellow-spotted honeyeater *Meliphaga notata;* Graceful honeyeater *Meliphaga gracilis;* Varied honeyeater *Lichenostomus versicolor;* Mangrove honeyeater *Lichenostomus fasciogularis;* Brown honeyeater *Lichmera indistincta;* Dusky honeyeater *Myzomela obscura.*

Nectariniidae: Yellow-bellied sunbird *Nectarinia jugularis.*

Dicaeidae: Mistletoebird *Dicaeum hirundinaceum.*

Pardalotidae: Striated pardalote *Pardalotus striatus.*

Zosteropidae: Pale white-eye *Zosterops citrinella;* Silvereye *Zosterops lateralis.*

Passeridae: House sparrow *Passer domesticus.*

Ploceidae: Chestnut-breasted mannikin *Lonchura castaneothorax.*

Sturnidae: Metallic starling *Aplonis metallica;* Common starling *Sturnus vulgaris.*

Oriolidae: Olive-backed oriole *Oriolus sagittatus;* Figbird *Sphecotheres viridis.*

Dicruridae: Spangled drongo *Dicrurus hottentottus.*

Grallinidae: Australian magpie-lark *Grallina cyanoleuca.*

Artamidae: White-breasted Woodswallow *Artamus leucorhynchus.*

Cracticidae: Pied currawong *Strepera graculina.*

Marine Mammals

Even frequent visitors to the reef enjoy watching dolphins as they vie for position at the bow of a boat, and even a glimpse of a dugong or a large whale is memorable (Fig. 73).

The more commonly seen species of marine mammals, and a brief outline of some characteristic features are set out below. Properly recorded observations of accurately identified marine mammals help build up our rather poor knowledge of their occurrence in reef waters.

Sightings

Research on whales and dolphins is being carried out at the Queensland Museum and University of Queensland in Brisbane, and at the Museum of Tropical Queensland and Department of Zoology, James Cook University of North Queensland in Townsville. Studies on dugongs are being carried out at the Environmental Studies Unit, James Cook University. Researchers at these institutions would welcome information on sightings, especially of whales and dolphins.

There are some very good field guides to identification. Baker (1990) is particularly useful and includes all species known from Queensland. Leatherwood, Reeves, Perrin and Evans (1988) contains many photographs of animals at sea. These illustrate important features such as the profile of the head; position, size and shape of the dorsal (back) fin; shape of the tail flukes which may be raised into the air as the animal dives; and colour, including the often subtle patterns of grey on the back and side. They also show surfacing behaviour, as well as the shape of the "spout" — the condensed breath seen particularly in the larger whales. The book covers 20 of the 25 species confirmed from Queensland waters.

Estimating the distance to the animal and its size, as well as recognizing the finer details of fin shape and colour pattern come only with experience. Initially, confident identifications may be possible only when the animal is seen close to the boat or can be observed carefully with binoculars. It may be possible to get closer to whales by patient "stalking" but it must be remembered that both Commonwealth and Queensland state legislation limit approaches by vessels to 100 metres and swimmers and divers to 30 metres.

Records of sightings should include the position, time of sighting, observer's name and a description of the animals. Even rough sketches are often useful. Photographs may allow positive identifications, even if the image of the animal is quite small. Good photographs showing colour and scar patterns may even allow individual animals to be recognized again. Such photo-identification of whales has been used for various species, both within Australia and overseas. The techniques are outlined by Lien and Katona (1990).

Strandings

The Queensland Department of Primary Industries handles strandings of marine mammals within the State and has produced a brochure with contact organizations and basic first-aid techniques for stranded animals. Mass strandings present special problems but so far

1)

2)

3)

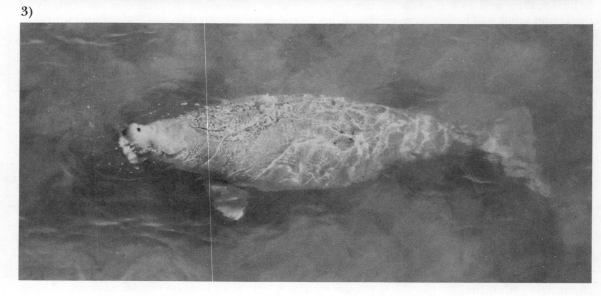

220

have not occurred within reef waters. Rescuers must keep their own safety in mind — whales and dolphins are very powerful and when in stress could injure a rescuer.

If the animal is already dead, specialists should be notified as the carcass may provide extremely important information. This can also be done through the Department of Primary Industries Fisheries and Boating Patrol or the Queensland National Parks and Wildlife Service. Any specimen of beaked whale is especially valuable.

Fisheries Officers or National Park rangers, once notified, can contact the Queensland Museum or specialists at other institutions. If nothing can be collected, then photographs should be taken. These should include a side view of the whole body and closeups of the top of the head, the throat region, dorsal fin, flukes, teeth or baleen. The exposed surface of the animal darkens very quickly and colour patterns may be more obvious on the shaded side. Thus, if it is possible to roll the animal, photographs should be taken of the shaded side, after the adhering sand has been rinsed off. Accurate notes on the location of the stranding will enable the skeletal remains to be collected later for detailed scientific examination.

Whales and Dolphins

Whales and dolphins belong to the mammalian order Cetacea. The term "whale" is applied rather loosely to larger members of the order, over 4–5 metres in length. The smaller cetaceans are generally called "dolphins" or "porpoises". Strictly speaking, the term "porpoise" is applied to six species in the family Phocoenidae, none of which has been reported from the waters around mainland Australia.

The major division in the formal classification of whales and dolphins is based not on size, but on anatomical features such as the presence either of baleen plates or teeth.

Baleen Whales

In baleen or "whalebone" whales, a series of horny baleen plates extends from the roof of the mouth along each side of the upper jaw. In all species found within Queensland waters, the throat is deeply pleated and can expand enormously to engulf a large volume of water containing the concentrated food (schooling fishes or plankton). Contraction of the throat muscles or elastic recoil of the throat forces this water out between the baleen plates. Food is trapped on a meshwork formed by the frayed inner margins of the plates. Baleen whales are the largest of the Cetacea — the blue whale *Balaenoptera musculus* reaches 31 metres in length and up to 190 tonnes in weight.

The humpback whale *(Megaptera novaeangliae)* — the baleen whale most frequently reported from reef waters. The east Australian population spends the summer months in the Antarctic, feeding on krill (a schooling, shrimp-like crustacean). It overwinters off Queensland, reaching maximum numbers in reef waters during July to September (Paterson 1991). The Great Barrier Reef region is an important breeding and nursing ground for this species. The large size (13–14 metres length) and aerial acrobatics of humpback whales makes them a favourite of whale watchers.

The southern minke whale *(Balaenoptera acutorostrata)* — apparently a similar migratory pattern to the humpback, although it is not as well documented. A dwarf form of the minke whale, with a characteristic white flipper base and shoulder patch, has been photographed by divers on the central and northern Great Barrier Reef (Fig. 73:2).

Bryde's whale *(Balaenoptera edeni)* — does not migrate south to feed in polar waters and has been called the "tropical whale". It is known from the Coral Sea and is regularly seen in southern Queensland, but appears to be rare in reef waters.

221

Fig. 73. (1) The bottlenosed dolphin, which frequently approaches boats, is the species most often seen by visitors to the Great Barrier Reef. (2) Dwarf minke wales, sighted regularly in central and northern reef waters during the winter months. (3) Much of the body of the dugong remains underwater as it surfaces to breathe. (Photographs courtesy of the Great Barrier Reef Marine Park Authority).

Toothed Whales

The second major division of cetaceans is the Odontoceti or "toothed whales". The male **sperm whale** *Physeter macrocephalus* regularly reaches 15 m length and rivals the baleen whales in size. Most toothed whales, however, are less than 10 m long.

Twenty species of toothed whale have been reported from Queensland waters (Van Dyck and Longmore 1991). Many of the small species presently recorded only from southern Queensland are oceanic and may occur just off the Great Barrier Reef in the Coral Sea. However, there are no good data. In reef waters, the casual observer is most likely to recognize only two species, the **bottlenosed dolphin** *Tursiops truncatus* (Fig. 73:1) and **spinner dolphin** *Stenella longirostris*. Both species frequently approach a boat to ride the bow wave.

The **humpback dolphin** *Sousa chinensis* and **Irrawaddy River dolphin** *Orcaella brevirostris* — found along the coast and around inshore continental islands. Irrawaddy River dolphins have been mistaken for dugongs because of their bulbous head and inconspicuous surfacing behaviour. Unlike dugongs, however, they have a dorsal (back) fin.

The **short-finned pilot whale** *(Globicephala macrorhynchus)* and **false killer whale** *(Pseudorca crassidens)* are both recorded from reef waters. They have not always been consistently identified, however, so their relative abundance along much of the coast is unknown. The same statement applies to smaller species such as the **melon-headed whale** *(Peponocephala electra)* and the **pygmy killer whale** *(Feresa attenuata)* (the last species not yet confirmed from Queensland, but to be expected).

Beaked whales are oceanic species, but there is a cluster of stranding records from Mackay to the Whitsunday Islands, well within the Great Barrier Reef. The Indo-Pacific beaked whale *Indopacetus pacificus* (Longman 1926) is known only from partial remains collected near Mackay, Queensland and Somalia, east Africa. We do not even know what it looks like!

Dugongs

Like whales and dolphins, **dugongs** *Dugong dugon* (Fig. 73:3) spend their entire lives at sea and their bodies show similar adaptations to a life of swimming and diving. A big dugong is about three metres long and weighs about 400 kg. From a distance, dugongs look rather like rotund grey-brown dolphins with their fish-like shape, whale-like tail fluke and paddle-shaped flippers. Dugongs, however, lack a dorsal fin. Their skin is very thick and smooth and is often heavily scarred. Some animals have a large white scar on their backs.

The nostrils are situated near the front of a dugong's head enabling it to breathe with most of its body beneath the surface. As a result, dugongs are often missed by casual observers, even though the Great Barrier Reef region is estimated to support some 11 000 dugongs, making it one of the most important areas for dugongs in the world.

Unlike dolphins, dugongs are not active predators. Their primary food is seagrass and dugongs are associated with seagrass beds throughout the Great Barrier Reef region. Individuals can move large distances fairly quickly. One male tagged with a satellite transmitter moved 200 kilometres between two coastal seagrass beds in two days. South of Cairns, dugongs are mainly seen along the coast or in seagrass beds associated with continental islands (although one animal was photographed at Lady Elliot Island). In the northern half of the region, dugongs are associated with large planar reefs with extensive seagrass meadows and offshore seagrass beds at depths to more than 20 metres.

The Biota
of the Islands

The Great Barrier Reef ecosystem is an intricate web with terrestrial as well as marine components, for the birds and the turtles connect the sea with the land, transferring energy in the form of food and guano from one to the other.

Most conspicuous, and indeed most necessary, are the plants. They form the habitats for colonizing animals and protect the developing cays and the older islands from erosion. The arthropods and other invertebrates are prey for birds and reptiles and for one another, some are scavengers, some detritus feeders, and some are important agents for cross-fertilization of the flora.

Continental islands have a large number of species, some probably being descendants of organisms living there when the island was separated from the mainland by rising water. Some species, however, and all of those living on coral cays (which never have been connected to the mainland) must have arrived by some form of overwater dispersal. Organisms are transported to remote islands by winds, in and on flotsam, on birds and in birds' digestive tracts, and by man — on ships, in luggage and with food brought to islands. Landfall by these means of dispersal is fortuitous. Reaching an island is just the first hurdle. Many that arrive do not survive because the environment of the island is too harsh, or does not supply their food or habitat requirements. If long-term or permanent establishment is to take place the new arrival (the animal or plant, or its seed) must live long enough to grow and reproduce. For sexual reproduction, plants must produce flowers and pollen for fertilization, and often the right insect must be present to carry the pollen to the flower. Animals can reproduce if males and females arrived together, or within a short interval of one another; or, if a female arriving on its own, it is already laden with fertile eggs or carries young. Some of these problems are avoided if the organism can clone — reproduce partheno-genetically, like some of the geckos found on islands, or vegetatively like plants grown from cuttings. However, then the island population runs the risks associated with in-breeding and lack of diversity.

In fact, given the vagaries of transport and establishment, it is surprising that so many islands have so many species. The strictly terrestrial birds and reptiles are discussed, above, with their marine representatives. Below are sections on the terrestrial invertebrates and the vascular plants of the Great Barrier Reef.

Terrestrial Invertebrates

Two studies, one in the Coral Sea (Farrow 1984) and one in the Capricorn Group (Heatwole *et al.* 1981) reflect the dynamics of the invertebrate communities of the islands in these waters. In the Capricorn Group (at One Tree Island) the invertebrates were found to include pseudoscorpions, mites, spiders, centipedes, isopods and 36 families of insects in 10 orders. Most of these were transient, or established for only short periods.

Only 26 species were permanent. In addition, there were 131 species of arthropods living below ground, mainly mites, collembolans, myriapods and insects which, unlike the species living above ground, were mostly permanent.

The study (for almost a year) on Willis Island, a small cay in the Coral Sea, resulted in a catch of 105 480 insects from 115 taxa. Sixty-seven species bred on the island and of these 45 were abundant (collectively accounting for 99.7% of the total individuals). The rest were immigrants that either did not breed or were unable to become established permanently. They arrived under the influence of wind in 13 fluxes from Queensland, a minimum distance of 450 km, and one flux probably from Papua, 600 km away. There was also substantial emigration of insects from the island.

Although few islands have been subjected to such detailed study as One Tree and Willis, the pattern of high rates of immigration and extinction, and hence species-turnover, seems to be general. An account of insects from Masthead Island based on a collection made in 1934 (Hacker 1975) contains records of 31 species. Only four of these have been recorded from nearby Heron Island. Marks (1969a) and Reeves (1969, 1971, 1972) also demonstrate variations in insular faunas on the Great Barrier Reef.

Despite the uncertainties of insular life, it is not entirely a lottery as to which species occur there. Many species are unsuited for dispersal over water or are not adapted to insular conditions. Records of them on islands are relatively rare, and they seldom persist for long. The species that travel across open expanses of sea easily and are adapted to the conditions they find once they arrive on the island constitute the truly insular fauna.

Some of these are so adapted to maritime conditions that they border between terrestrial and marine. Some small beetles, flies and spiders (see below), occur on reefs in the intertidal zone, either behind the reef rock rim or on beachrock. At high tide they are insulated from the water that covers them by a thin film of air that is retained around the body, and by pockets of air that are retained in the porous rock in which they shelter. There are mites, tardigrades and collembolans that live in the small spaces between sand grains of the beach.

Since green plants form the ultimate basis for all animal life, one might expect that islands without vegetation would also lack terrestrial animals. Such is not the case, for even sand cays that lack vegetation, usually have a terrestrial invertebrate fauna that lives on food transferred from the sea on to the islands. Marine carrion washed up on beaches is available to scavengers such as earwigs, beetles and flies. Also, the bodies of sea birds and their parasites such as ticks, lice and flies contribute carrion to the scavengers. For this reason, the pioneer fauna on small, bare cays consists mainly of bird parasites, detritus feeders and scavengers. Sometimes these are fed upon by predators such as centipedes and spiders.

The sea birds are also the main agents in the long-term transfer of energy, from the sea to the land, in the form of guano. Thus it is due to these birds that later, when an island becomes clothed in vegetation it is able to maintain populations of insects that feed on foliage, nectar and seeds, and the many species of predators that in turn eat these herbivores. Vegetated islands maintain their pioneer scavenging species on the beaches but have a much richer fauna inland associated with plants.

Isopods, millipedes, centipedes, pseudoscorpions, phalangids, mites, ticks, spiders, collembolans and 109 families in 20 orders of insects have been recorded from Great Barrier Reef Islands. However, many taxa have not been identified and there has been no systematic attempt to survey many groups. Some of the large, strong fliers such as some dragonflies and butterflies are conspicuous and often noted (see below); others such as soil mites are seldom seen.

The following notes on terrestrial arthropods have been compiled from collections made by H. Heatwole, from the islands of the Great Barrier Reef and adjacent Coral Sea.

Crustacea — the "terrestrial" crustaceans on Great Barrier Reef islands are partly marine in that they have marine immature stages, or live in the intertidal or supratidal areas. They include hermit crabs, ghost crabs, isopods and amphipods. Many are scavengers on marine carrion that washes up on the beach and serve as important transfer organisms.

Diplopoda (Millipedes) — three families of millipedes have been recorded from the Great Barrier Reef. The most common species is *Dinematocricus* sp. It occurs on a number of the continental islands but has never been taken from a coral cay.

Chilopoda (Centipedes) — occur even on some of the small, nearly bare cays. There are several species, the most conspicuous of which are the large *Scolopendra* spp. Their bite can be extremely painful as campers on certain islands have discovered.

Pseudoscorpionida (False Scorpions) — diminutive scorpion-like animals occur under bits of corals or other debris on a number of islands of the northern part of the Great Barrier Reef. There are five families represented, but by far the most common species is *Anagarypus australianus*.

Acarina (Mites and Ticks) — soil mites occur on almost all islands that have been studied. Those with stable vegetation and soils are especially rich. Eighty-nine species from 51 families are recorded from One Tree Island alone.

Ticks are important ectoparasites on sea birds. Two species are especially important and widespread, *Ornithodoros capensis* (Argasidae) and *Amblyomma locuosum* (Ixodidae). Both are found on almost all cays of the Great Barrier Reef, even those that are devoid of vegetation. They seek shelter under debris when not attached to birds and are often abundant.

Araneae (Spiders) — are abundant on many islands. Even some that lack vegetation altogether have wolf-spiders (Lycosidae) that prey on scavengers and detritus feeders. At least 33 species of 12 families are known from the Great Barrier Reef. *Diaea sticta* (Thomisidae) and *Nephila* spp. (Tetragnathidae) are among the species most commonly recorded from islands. Spiders are treated in more detail below.

Collembola (Springtails) — common soil animals on Great Barrier Reef islands, nine species from five families are known from One Tree Island alone. They are also common in the spaces between sand grains in beaches.

Dermaptera (Earwigs) — *Euborellia annulipes* (Labiduridae) is a common earwig on islands of the Great Barrier Reef. It forages on carrion.

Orthoptera (Grasshoppers, Locusts, Crickets, Katydids and their relatives) — two crickets, the Oceanic Cricket, *Teleogryllus oceanicus* (Gryllidae: Gryllinae) and *Ornebius* sp. (Gryllidae; Mogoplistinae), are common inhabitants of sand cays on the Great Barrier Reef, even those with only low vegetation. The latter has also been recorded from continental islands. *Valanga irregularis* (Acrididae; Cyrtacanthacridinae) is the largest Australian species of locust and one of the largest in the world. It feeds on the leaves of shrubs and trees in the moister tropics and subtropics, including vegetated islands, sometimes in temporary plague proportions causing extensive defoliation. A common grasshopper, *Aiolophus thalassinus tamulus* (Acrididae; Acridinae) is the most frequently encountered orthopteran on vegetated cays but has not been recorded from continental islands. In addition to these common species, 20 species from six families of Orthopterans are known from the Barrier Reef islands.

Coleoptera (Beetles) — at least 61 species from 27 families are known to occur on islands of the Great Barrier Reef. Probably there are many times more yet to be recorded. Scavenging beetles of the genus *Gonocephalum* (Tenebrionidae; Opatrinae) and the species *Dermestes ater* (Dermestidae) are found on most islands with nesting sea birds and some vegetation. They usually are found in large numbers in and under the carcasses of dead birds. Ladybirds, *Coccinella* spp., especially *C. arcuata* (Coccinellidae) also are typical of vegetated coral cays.

225

Diptera (Flies) — are common inhabitants of Barrier Reef islands accounting for at least 85 species from 35 families. The family Psychodidae characteristically has larvae that feed on decomposing organic matter and the genus *Psychoda* is able to exploit temporary sources of such food. *Psychoda alternata* is sometimes a pest of sewage treatment plants and is often seen in toilets. It also is associated with washed-up marine carrion. It is one of the most widespread insular species, a pioneer species found on small unvegetated cays as well as on the beaches of large continental islands.

Clunio pacificus (Chironomidae) occurs on intertidal rocks or corals that are only exposed at low tides. At low tide the flies can be seen hovering over exposed rocks or corals; they are not wetted by sea water, but shed it and when submerged are enclosed in a silvery film of air. It is known from Western Samoa, American Samoa, the Ryukyu Islands, Japan, the Marianas Island and probably occurs from many other locations.

Other widespread flies are *Lamprolonchaea metatarsata* (Loncheidae) on vegetated cays including those with scant low vegetation, and *Homoneura* (Lauxaniidae) on forested cays and continental islands.

Olfersia aenescens and *O. spinigera* (Hippoboscidae), ectoparasites on birds and consequently present on most islands where sea birds nest, are seldom seen away from their hosts. They scurry in a characteristic side-ways gait across the bird's plumage to disappear among the feathers.

Order Lepidoptera (Butterflies and Moths) — the moth *Utetheisa pulchelloides* (Arctiidae) is found on many of the islands of the Great Barrier Reef. Its main food plant is Octopus Bush, *Argusia argentea*, a widespread pioneer shrub. There are some islands that are inhabited by the shrub but not the moth. Usually, however, if an island has a well established population of Octopus Bush, the moth is also present. The caterpillars eat the leaves of the shrubs and the adults fed on the nectar of the flowers.

Butterflies are conspicuous amongst the insect fauna transported to islands by aerial currents and winds (Fig. 74). Most of the records are of vagrants but some transportation may be part of migratory patterns, assisted by winds. Species may become established if their food plant is also established on the island. Eighteen species of food plants are known from the islands of the Bunker Capricorn Groups, although only five species of butterfly have, so far, been found breeding there. The breeding species are those with immature stages that feed on plants close to the ground or in the layered undergrowth where they are protected from cyclonic winds.

Order Hymenoptera (Bees, Wasps, Ants and their relatives) — ants have been better collected than many other insects, 72 species from 22 genera being known from the islands of the Great Barrier Reef and Coral Sea. However, of the 29 islands from which ants are recorded only six had 10 or more species. These were the continental islands of Farmer (10 species), Palfrey (14), Restoration (15), Penrith (19) and Lizard (23) and a large, forested sand cay, Nymph (14 species). Most of the smaller, remote cays with little or no vegetation lack ants altogether and those few from which ants have been recorded (e.g., Porpoise Cay, Wreck Reef, Southwest Cay, Chilcott Reef, several cays from Swain Reefs) contain only one or two species. Some of the slightly larger cays with low vegetation (e.g., Northeast Island, Herald Cays, Chilcott Island) have 3–4 species and those with trees and shrubs may have up to six or seven species of ants (e.g., Wreck Island, Erskine Island, One Tree Island). Some continental islands are hardly more than emergent rocks (e.g., Round Island, Lighthouse Rock) and these have a single species, whereas larger, well-vegetated ones have more.

Only a few species of ants were widely distributed on islands; for example 35 species (49%) occurred on only one island and only six species (7%) occurred on five or more islands. The latter included two species of *Iridomyrmex* (*Iridiomyrmex* sp., 13 islands; *I. glaber* (6)), *Cordiocondyla nuda* (8), *Oecophylla smaragdina* (8), *Camponotus* sp. (7) and *Paratrechina longicornis* (5). Except *C. nuda* these occurred mainly on the larger continental islands or on forested sand cays. *C. nuda* can be considered a pioneer species. It was the most common species on small, nearly bare sand cays and was not reported from any continental islands.

Bees and wasps occur occasionally on the larger, heavily vegetated islands. Parasitoids of other insects and of spiders are frequent inhabitants of forested sand cays and of continental islands. Fifteen genera of the family Braconidae are known from Barrier Reef and Coral Sea islands, the most often represented being *Agathiella*, *Apanteles* and *Iphiaulax*. None has been recorded from small cays with little or no vegetation.

1. *Ocybadistes walkeri*
2. *Catopsilia pomona pomona*
3. *Eurema hecabe phoebus*
4. *Eurema smilax*
5. *Elodina parthia*
6. *Elodina padusa*
7. *Delias aganippe*
8. *Anaphaeis java teutonia*
9. *Appias paulina ega*
10. *Danaus chrysippus petilia*
11. *Danaus hamatus hamatus*
12. *Euploea core corinna*
13. *Euploea tulliolus tulliolus*
14. *Catopyrops florinda halys*
15. *Syntarucus plinius pseudocassius*
16. *Theclinesthes miskini miskini*
17. *Melanitis leda bankia*
18. *Polyura pyrrhus sempronius*
19. ♂ *Hypolimnas bolina nerina*
20. ♀
21. *Vanessa kershawi*
22. *Junonia villida calybe*
23. *Acraea andromacha andromacha*
24. *Nacaduba kurava parma*
25. *Nacaduba biocellata biocellata*
26. *Lampides boeticus*
27. *Zizina labradus labradus*
28. *Zizeeria karsandra*
29. *Candalides erinus erinus*

SCALE:
— = 1 cm for numbers 25, 29
⌐—⌐ = 1 cm for numbers 1, 14–16, 24, 26–28
⌐—⌐ = 1 cm for numbers 2–13, 17–23
*Under surface of the wing.

Fig. 74. Butterflies recorded from Heron Island.

227

Miscellaneous Insects — in addition to the orders of insects discussed above, there are a few others that are poorly represented. Odonata (Dragonflies and Damselflies) have had four species from three families recorded. These are mostly conspicuous, strong fliers that can easily fly from the mainland to islands and are merely visitors. Many islands lack the water required by odonates for breeding. Roaches (Blattodea) are represented by four species from three families, Mantodea (Mantids) by three species in two families and Neuroptera (Lace-wings) by five species from three families. These are all probably underestimates of the true numbers of taxa. Finally, Thysanura (Silverfish), Isoptera (Termites), Embioptera (Embiids), Psocoptera (Psocids), Phthiraptera (Lice), Homoptera (Aphids and their relatives), Heteroptera (Bugs) and Trichoptera (Caddis-flies) have been recorded from the Great Barrier Reef islands but specimens have not been identified beyond the higher taxonomic levels.

Spiders

The three most successful spider families on the mainland are also those best represented on the Great Barrier Reef. These are the orb-weaving spiders (Araneidae), the jumping spiders (Salticidae) and the comb-footed spiders (Theridiidae). They may have arrived naturally, by air or sea currents, or have been transported by man. Generally they reflect the fauna of the adjacent mainland and occasionally that of areas further north. Soon after hatching, young spiders are dispersed on air currents by "parachuting" on silken threads. There is great mortality at this stage but if they reach land they are good colonizers as they are all carnivorous and most eat a wide assortment of invertebrates. They are able to survive long periods without food providing they do not become desiccated.

The orb-weavers include the Large Garden Orb-Weaver, *Eriophora transmarina*, the Golden Orb-Weavers *Nephila plumipes* and *N. maculata* which spin large webs using yellow silk to make the sticky spiral thread, and many smaller spiders including the Jewel Spiders, *Gasteracantha brevispina* and *G. fornicata*, and the leaf-curlers. In damp areas *Cyclosa* spp. build small webs decorated with a vertical band of debris; the spider sits in the middle at the hub of the orb-web and is difficult to see.

Most of the jumping spiders live under bark; others are foliage or ground dwellers. Many are active during the day and their elaborate courtship, a series of signals to the female by the male with his palps and body, may be observed.

The comb-footed spiders usually build a small tangle-web with some sticky catching threads attached to the substrate. One theridiid, *Argyrodes antipodiana* is a kleptoparasite in orb-webs to which it attaches a support web which allows it to swing to safety with stolen food bundles or to escape the host if threatened (Whitehouse 1986).

The most interesting spider on the Great Barrier Reef is *Desis maxillosa* (Desidae) which is restricted to the reef flat. The spiders do not spin webs to catch prey but hunt among the littoral fauna when the tide is out. As the tide comes in the spiders retreat to crevices or holes in the coral closing the entrance with a sheet of silk, excluding the water and trapping enough air to meet the respiratory needs of the spider until the tide goes out again. A related spider, *Paratheuma australis* is found only among loose broken coral or in crevices or holes in rocks a few centimetres to about one metre above normal high-tide level.

Terrestrial Plants

At Heron Island, where terrestrial flora has been observed since 1931, the considerable change in species composition is an example of the changes that occur at other places. The island was first inhabited in the mid-1920s, and most floral changes result from human interference. Plants such as the coconut and poinciana were introduced as ornamentals, but others arrived accidentally, some perhaps in soil around intended introductions. A few may have reached the cay by natural means. Some of the introduced species have been short-lived, some are represented only by the introduced specimen, and others appear to have become a permanent part of the flora. Also, some of the losses among indigenous species probably are the result of human activity. *Ficus obliqua* var. *petiolaris* may have been lost through clearing for building sites. *Spinifex sericeus* and *Ipomoea pes-caprae* subsp. *brasiliensis,* occupying the outermost fringe of vegetation, suffer the trampling of many feet and have disappeared from the cay recently. Of a total of 67 plants recorded from Heron Island (MacGillivray and Rodway 1931; Fosberg, Thorne and Moulton 1961; Gillham 1963; Cribb 1976; Cribb and Cribb 1985; Smith and Heatwole 1985), some are currently absent, and about half are not indigenous to the cay.

Mangroves do not occur in the Bunker and Capricorn Groups, although sometimes they are present further north (Lear and Turner 1977).

Common Indigenous Flowering Plants of the Cays of the Great Barrier Reef

Abutilon albescens (Lantern Bush), a soft shrub about 1 m high. Its heart-shaped leaves have a suede-like surface texture. Attractive cupped orange-yellow flowers, about 4 cm across, usually open about noon (Fam. Malvaceae) Fig. 75:1.

Argusia argentea (Octopus Bush), with rigid, silvery-hairy leaves, is one of the commonest shrubs bordering the beach. The small white flowers, the two sexes on different plants, are on radiating branches with vaguely octopus-like coiled tips. The crooked branching pattern of older specimens is distinctive (Fam. Boraginaceae) Fig. 75:2.

Barringtonia asiatica (Box Fruit), occurs in the central and northern reef regions and is known most widely through its four-angled fruits like small squared coconuts, which are common in drift well beyond the species range. The tree bears large leaves often 30 cm or more long, broadest in the upper part, and spectacular flowers which open at dusk to reveal a mass of stamens, pink above and white below (Fam. Lecythidaceae).

Calophyllum inophyllum (Alexandrian Laurel), a notable tree on some central and northern shores, where its widely spreading branches may extend well seawards of the high water mark. The tough, shiny, elliptical leaves have closely placed, fine parallel veins from the midrib. Round green fruits, up to the size of golf balls, follow attractive flowers with white petals and masses of yellow stamens (Fam. Clusiaceae).

Caesalpinia bonduc (Nicker Nut), a scrambling shrub with large bipinnate leaves up to 70 cm long amply armed with vicious hooks, has sprays of yellow flowers followed by prickly pods about 6 cm long, each containing two blue-grey, slightly angular, marble-like seeds (Fam. Caesalpiniaceae).

Canavalia rosea (Fire Bean, Sea Bean) is a prostrate dune creeper with trifoliolate leaves and purple-pink pea flowers followed by beans which are edible after boiling (Fam. Fabaceae).

Cassytha filiformis (Dodder Laurel), a partial parasite, covers other plants with a yellow tangle of leafless stems attached to the host by numerous short parasitizing roots (Fam. Lauraceae).

Casuarina equisetifolia var. *incana* (Coastal She-oak) is often the commonest tree fringing the sandy shore. What appear to be slender leaves are characteristic weeping branchlets with whorls of reduced, scale-like leaves. The cone-like compound fruit releases winged individual fruits (Fam. Casuarinaceae) Fig. 75:3.

Celtis paniculata, a small tree, its leaves three-veined from the base, without hairs, and with smooth margins (Fam. Umaceae) Fig. 74:4.

Colubrina asiatica, a beach shrub of central and northern shores, with arching or sprawling canes to 2 m long, bearing shiny heart-shaped leaves in two ranks. Small groups of rounded, eventually black, fruit occur in the leaf axils (Fam. Rhamnaceae).

Cordia subcordata (Sea Trumpet) a shrub or small tree with ovate leaves and attractive orange trumpet-shaped flowers, about 4 cm across, has distinctive crumpled petals (Fam. Boraginaceae) Fig. 75:5.

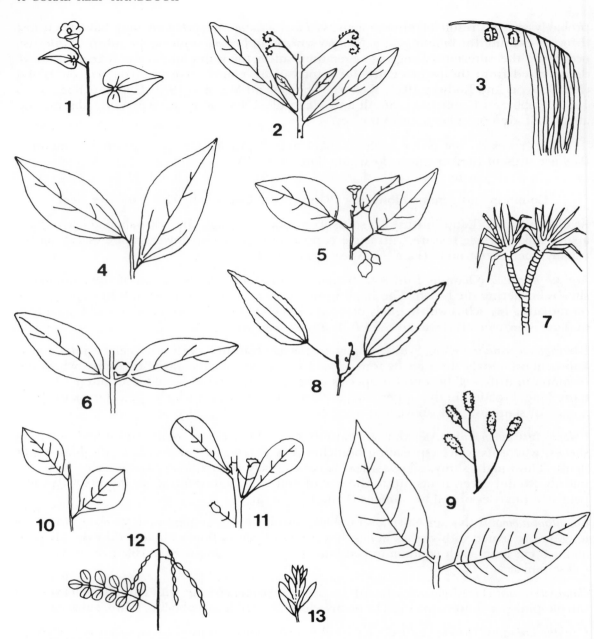

Fig. 75. Vascular Plants recorded from the Great Barrier Reef.

Crinum pedunculatum (Crinum Lily) has rosettes of sword-like soft leaves up to 1 m long. The flowering stalk bears a terminal group of up to 20 buds which open, a few at a time, into handsome white flowers each with six slender petals. Some plants have a short trunk up to 70 cm long (Fam. Amaryllidaceae).

Ficus opposita (Sandpaper Fig), a small tree, its opposite leaves with a sandpapery surface. Its round figs are palatable when black and fully ripe, when they are often eaten by birds (Fam. Moraceae) Fig. 75:6.

Guettarda speciosa, a shrub or small tree of central and northern shores. Its opposite, broadly ovate leaves, often about 15 cm long, have prominent yellowish veins. The white flowers, their petals united in a tube with 4–9 spreading lobes, are strongly perfumed at night and early morning (Fam. Rubiaceae).

Hibiscus tiliaceus (Cotton Tree), a widely spreading small tree with heart-shaped leaves finely hairy on the underside has yellow flowers with dark purple centre which do not open as widely as those of cultivated *Hibiscus. Thespesia populnea,* in the same family and superficially similar, lacks hairs on the leaf undersurface (Fam. Malvaceae).

Ipomoea pes-caprae subsp. *brasiliensis* (Goat's-foot Convolvulus), an early beach colonizer, its rapidly-growing prostrate stems often growing down to where waves at high tide deflect the growing points, is easily recognized by its showy, purple, bell-shaped flowers and the bilobed leaves which have suggested a goat's foot (Fam. Convolvulaceae).

Pandanus tectorius (Screw Pine), one of the most distinctive trees of the Reef area has branches ending in dense clusters of sword-like leaves with prickly margins and keel. Stout prop-roots descend from the lower part of the trunk. The ripe fruit is an orange, head-sized group of wedge-shaped segments (Fam. Pandanaceae) Fig. 75:7.

Pipturus argenteus (Native Mulberry), a shrub or small tree has long-stalked leaves, three-veined from the base. Female trees bear soft white palatable fruits about 6 mm across (Fam. Urticaceae) Fig. 75:8.

Pisonia grandis (Pisonia), large pale-trunked tree with soft ovate leaves is particularly characteristic of cays in the Capricorn and Bunker Groups where it often forms the main forest. In summer its clusters of elongate sticky fruits foul the feathers of birds to such an extent that many are unable to fly and eventually starve to death (Fam. Nyctaginaceae) Fig. 75:9.

Plumbago zeylanica a small, weak shrub, its stems with fine, longitudinal ridges, have leaf stalks dilated at the base to form a small ring round the stem. Flowers are blue (Fam. Plumbaginaceae) Fig. 75:10.

Scaevola sericea (Cardwell Cabbage), one of the commonest shrubs bordering the beach is easily recognized by its shiny leaves, broadest in the upper part, and its fan-shaped flowers, usually white but sometimes with a purplish tinge (Fam. Goodeniaceae) Fig. 75:11.

Sophora tomentosa (Silver Bush), a shrub with pinnate, silvery leaves, yellow pea flowers and slender pods deeply constricted between the seeds (Fam. Fabaceae) Fig. 75:12.

Spinifex sericeus (Beach Spinifex), an early colonizer of dunes, has rapidly extending fibrous, yellowish stems, usually just below the surface, producing tufts of silvery-hairy leaves. The roly-poly, spiky fruit clusters are bowled along the beach by the wind (Fam. Poaceae).

Suriana maritima, shrub with crowded leaves, linear-spatulate, finely hairy, about 2 cm long. The flowers are yellow (Fam. Surianaceae) Fig. 75:13.

Terminalia arenicola (Beach Almond), one of several species of *Terminalia* likely to be found close to the beach has mainly whorled, horizontal branches that produce a tiered effect. Its leaves, broadest in the upper part, often turn orange-red before falling. Fruits are almond-shaped with a thin, purple, fleshy outer layer (Fam. Combretaceae).

Trachymene cussoni (Beach Parsley) has deeply divided leaves forming parsley-like clumps along the beach. The clusters of small white flowers are followed by closely packed groups of flattened fruits (Fam. Apiaceae).

Thuarea involuta (Bird's-beak Grass), a distinctive grass with relatively short, softly hairy leaves, is often an early colonizer of sand, sometimes found as a ground cover beneath trees and shrubs near the beach. The flowering axis, at first erect and partly enclosed by a boat-shaped sheath, gradually bends downwards, enclosing two seeds at the base. At this stage the structure has a vague resemblance to a bird's head and is buoyant enough to be dispersed by water (Fam. Poaceae).

Vigna marina (Dune Bean), a creeping beach plant with trifoliolate leaves, yellow pea flowers and slender pods up to 6 cm long (Fam. Fabaceae).

Wedelia biflora (Beach Sunflower) often forms thickets of arching canes with opposite, harsh, aromatic leaves. A yellow flowering head, like a small sunflower, is borne terminally and followed by two more arising, one on each side of its base (Fam. Asteraceae).

Maritime Archaeology

Colonial Shipping and Shipwrecks

In the Age of Sail, vessels depended on the wind for propulsion, and were susceptible to the vicissitudes of the weather and the sea. Seafaring within confined waters was difficult at the best of times and extant accounts show that early European mariners viewed navigation in Great Barrier Reef waters with trepidation. James Cook described the myriad reefs, coral cays and islands as "labyrinthine", and Matthew Flinders referred to his course as "threading the needle". The reefs were poorly charted, and unpredictable tidal currents often drove ships off course — such deviations often not noticed until disaster was imminent.

Colonial Trade and Communication

Despite these hazards, navigation of Great Barrier Reef waters was inevitable, for the newly established colonies relied exclusively on shipping for trade contacts and communication with Asia and Europe.

Although partially charted and described by James Cook, who had traversed the coastal waters from Fraser Island to Lizard Island in *HMS Endeavour* (1770), the route (later to be known as the "inner route") between the Australian coast and the Reef was considered too dangerous, and generally was avoided by merchant ships during the late 18th and early 19th centuries. Most of the reefs were by-passed when captains chose the "outer route" to Asian ports, or they were avoided altogether when they chose the "easternmost route" (Fig. 76) (Richards 1986).

The "outer route" however, was not entirely free of hazards and dozens of vessels were wrecked on reefs in the Coral Sea, or were lost while negotiating the narrow entrances to passages which lead through the northern limits of the Great Barrier Reef to Torres Strait (Fig. 77). For instance, in 1803, the *Cato* and the *HMS Porpoise* (with Matthew Flinders on board, homewardbound after his surveys of the Australian coast) were lost at the same time on Wreck Reef in the Coral Sea while bound for England via India. Because of the dangers of the outer route a few merchant ships cautiously started using the "inner route". This seemed a less hazardous option, especially after more information became available as a result of Charles Jeffreys' successful passage to Ceylon via the "inner route" in *HMS Kangaroo* (1815). Following Jeffreys' account of his safe voyage, the merchant ship *Lady Elliot,* commanded by Joshua Abbott, made another successful passage to Ceylon in 1816. On the voyage Abbott discovered Lady Elliot Island. As more merchantmen followed Jeffreys' and

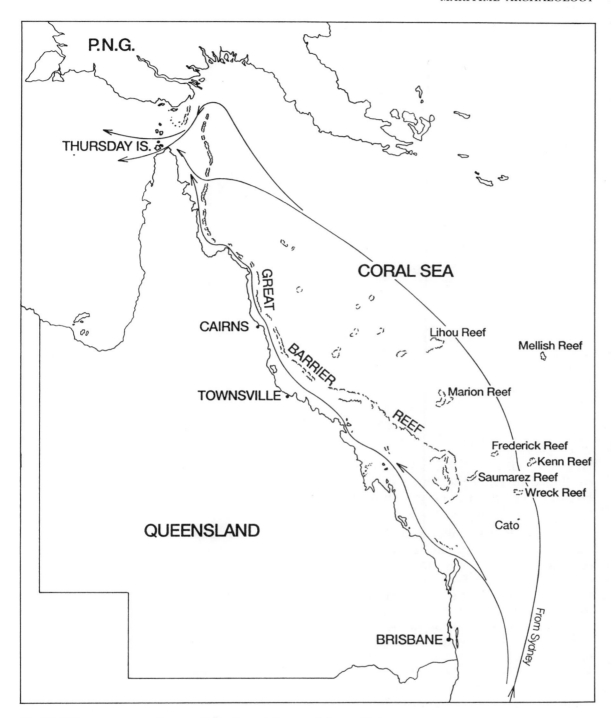

Fig. 76. 19th century routes between Australia and the rest of the world.

Abbott's examples, the government responded to the call for better charts of the "inner route". After the loss of the *Frederick* off Cape Flinders in 1818, surveys were carried out by Philip Parker King in *HMS Mermaid* (King 1827).

Throughout the 1820s, 1830s and 1840s captains debated the relative merits of the two routes. Philip Parker King was an ardent champion of the "inner" route and advised that it was by far the safest and less arduous route to South East Asia and India (*Nautical Magazine*, 1833: 433–35). It was largely a result of King's arguments that naval ships and vessels under government charter were advised to use the "inner route" after about 1830.

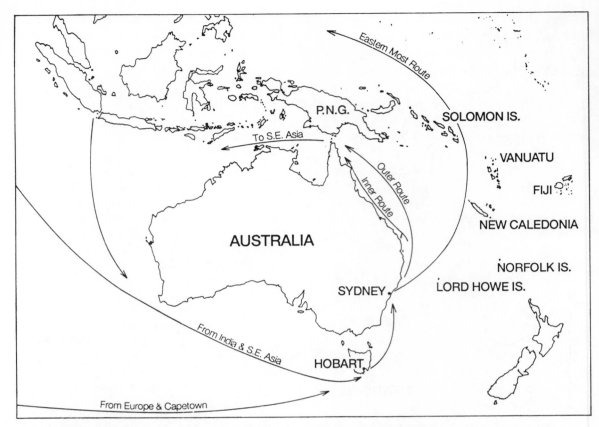

Fig. 77. The Inner and Outer Routes between Sydney and South East Asia and India.

However, King's advice was not always heeded, and the majority of merchant captains continued to avoid the "inner route". The "outer route" continued to claim victims. The *Ferguson,* bound for Madras with troops, was wrecked while attempting a passage through the northern Great Barrier Reef in 1840.

Although the "inner route" was preferred, the Colonial government continued to commission hydrographic surveys and improve navigation aids for the "outer route", especially around the northern entrances. Included in these were Francis Blackwood's and Charles Yule's surveys, of the Raine Island, Murray Islands and Great Northern Entrances during the 1840s. The permanent beacon on Raine Island stands today in silent testimony to these surveys, and to the government's efforts to improve the safety of its mariners — on whom its trade and communcation depended. Nevertheless, the "outer route" continued to take a tremendous toll on shipping. During 1854 alone more than 15 vessels were lost on Coral Sea reefs or along the narrow entrances and passages through the Great Barrier Reef. In the late 1850s and early 1860s, development of colonial settlements along the Queensland coast increased the frequency of shipping and made the use of the "inner route" inevitable. After about 1850 the Capricorn Channel came to be considered the safest entrance into Great Barrier Reef waters (MacGillivray 1852). Located approximately 80 miles to the north of Fraser Island, it came to be widely used by coastal trading vessels from Sydney and Brisbane bound for Rockhampton, Broadsound, Pioneer River (Mackay), Port Denison (Bowen), Townsville and Cairns. Northbound vessels for south Queensland ports — Maryborough, Baffle Creek, Burnett River (Bundaberg) and Port Curtis (Gladstone) — used the Curtis Channel. After about 1870, as navigation aids, ports and settlements along the Queensland coast proliferated, most ship's captains came to favour the "inner route".

In spite of easier access to safe havens and the establishment of lighthouses and beacons, more than 650 vessels had been wrecked on reefs of the Great Barrier Reef by the turn of the century. They were vessels on one or another of the standard routes to Asia; or they were vessels plying their trade between Queensland and South Pacific destinations, wrecked in and around the smaller passages between the reefs — passages that had been pioneered in the 1870s and 1880s by captains entering or leaving minor Queensland ports and settlements.

Although ships still founder on the reefs, it happens less often. Nowadays vessels are encouraged to, and usually do, avail themselves of the expert services of a member of the Torres Strait Pilot Service when negotiating passage through these waters.

Cultural Resource Inventory

Wrecksites represent many aspects of Australia's diverse maritime heritage. They reflect the history of early exploration, trade, settlement, economic and social development and resource use. Considering the vital importance of shipping to all these aspects of Australia's development during the 18th and 19th centuries, shipwrecks are part of the national heritage. Each shipwreck site has a particular cultural significance. For instance, *HMS Pandora (1791)* is an example of a ship used during the period of early European contact and exchange with the peoples of the South Pacific, and was directly associated with the infamous *HMS Bounty*. The brig *Morning Star (1814)*, wrecked off Quoin Island, may preserve material evidence of early trade between Hobart, Sydney and India. *HMS Mermaid (1829)* was the vessel which, in 1819 and 1820 under the command of Philip Parker King, was used for exploration and detailed charting of the Australian coast. The *Foam (1893)* wrecked in the Magnetic Passage off Townsville is the only known site of a schooner involved in the Queensland labour recruiting trade. Passenger steamers which maintained trade links between Queensland and other Australian ports are the *Gothenberg (1875)*, the *Yongala (1911)*, and the *Quetta (1891)*, which sailed between Queensland and Asia. The *Yongala* also has considerable contemporary economic significance as a recreational dive site. To date 18 sites off the Queensland coast have been nominated for protection under the Commonwealth *Historic Shipwrecks Act (1976)*.

The Queensland Museum is the designated authority for research of shipwrecks in Commonwealth waters off the Queensland coast and is pursuing an ongoing programme of significance assessment in which most sites are researched, surveyed and recorded with minimal disturbance to preserve the information they contain. Research is done to discover as much as possible about the wrecked vessels, their design, place of construction and country of origin — and to place them in their historical socio-economic context. A few selected sites of exceptional significance, *viz.* the *Pandora* and the *Foam*, may be excavated and their artefacts retrieved for research, conservation and display in museums and interpretation centres.

So far, assessment surveys have been conducted on shipwrecks in the Coral Sea, notably at Wreck Reef, where four sites have been located — among which are the historic wrecks of the *Porpoise* and the *Cato*. Sites on Cockburn Reef and Great Detached Reef in the north, and at Old Reef and Little Broadhurst Reef off Townsville are undergoing assessment. In work around the Capricorn-Bunker Groups at the southern end of the Reef, nine of the 23 known pre-World War I wrecksites have been located, and four of these have been gazetted as historic sites. They are the wrecks of the sailing ships *Polmaise (1873)* and *Deutschland (1883)*, which carried immigrants to Queensland and maintained direct trade links between Queensland and Europe during the 1870s and 1880s; the wreck of an as yet unidentified coastal trading schooner (ca. 1860) and the wreck of the *Tambaroora (1879)*, an early example of a small iron steamer which maintained trade links between Central Queensland and southern ports.

The research into the maritime history of the Capricorn-Bunker islands and reefs has revealed a wealth of information on the history of early European exploitation of the.guano resources on the coral cays of this area (see below).

Researching the Maritime Record: Shipping and Guano Mining in Capricornia

In spite of its reputation as a navigational hazard to vessels plying their trade on the major 19th century routes from Australia to Asia, the Great Barrier Reef was also known for its natural resources. These were attractive enough to induce a variety of 19th century entrepreneurs to risk capital on commercial maritime ventures to harvest the Reef's natural resources.

Exploitation began early. In 1803, while on a whaling voyage in the *Albion*, Eber Bunker noted that the Bunker Islands were rich with turtles, oysters and bêche-de-mer, and he later recommended their commercial exploitation. He was not the first to recommend commercial exploitation of the Reef's natural resources. In the journal of his voyage in the *Endeavour* (1768–70), Joseph Banks noted the diversity of natural resources in the waters off the coast of Hervey Bay and commented that if a pearling industry were to be established in the area, it should *"turn out to an immence advantage"* (Beaglehole 1962 vol 2: 67).

Nevertheless, there appear to be no records of widespread early 19th century pearling or bêche-de-mer fishing activities in these waters, and during the first decades of the 19th century, whaling appears to have been the only major organized, commercial exploitation of the Great Barrier Reef's natural resources. The log of the Yankee whaler *Hannah and Eliza* records a catch several miles to the east of the Bunker Islands in September 1805 (PMB Reel 377). Whaling vessels also frequently called in at the Capricorn-Bunker Islands to gather firewood for their try-pots.

Although bêche-de-mer was gathered on a large scale in the Coral Sea, and off New Caledonia and Fiji, it was only after overfishing in those waters that bêche-de-mer fishermen gradually shifted their activities to the Great Barrier Reef and Queensland coastal waters, from about 1830 onwards.

Mining of guano deposits may also have begun on a limited scale during the late 1830s and early 1840s when world prices and demand for this fertilizer reached record levels. This led to a worldwide search for deposits on remote, tropical, offshore islands and coasts known for their large populations of seabirds [Craig 1964 pp. 25–55 in *Mariner's Mirror* 50.1; Morrell 1844 in *Nautical Magazine*, vol. 13 pp. 366–74, 418–23.]

The documentation of Great Barrier Reef guano mining begins with the arrival of the ship *Margaret,* which had left Liverpool in 1850 on a lengthy trading voyage to San Francisco, Tahiti and Sydney, subsequently returning to Liverpool in 1852, via China and Bombay. Before calling in at Sydney, the *Margaret* put in at Lady Elliot Island on 12th June 1851, specifically to collect samples of guano. In the account of this visit to Lady Elliot Island a cleared area in the centre of the island is mentioned. This could have been cleared by whalers collecting firewood, or it may mean that guano miners had been there before the *Margaret's* arrival (AJCP Reel M714).

Several weeks after the *Margaret's* visit, two more vessels called at Lady Elliot Island. The *Bolton Abbey* and *Countess of Minto* had also sailed under specific orders to Lady Elliot Island for its guano deposits. After several weeks at anchor off Lady Elliot Island, during which both crews were camped on the island and engaged in the labourious mining and loading operations, the *Bolton Abbey* was driven ashore during a storm. She became a total wreck on 25th August 1851. The *Countess of Minto* narrowly missed the same fate and was blown out to sea with only two of her crew on board. They actually managed to save the vessel and eventually navigate it safely to Sydney.

The next visitor appears to have been the barque *Clarinda* which had also sailed to Lady Elliot Island with specific orders to load guano. Arriving at her destination on 12th January 1852, *Clarinda's* Captain McIlwraith landed and found *". . . the wrecks of two vessels on shore, with every appearance of the crews having recently left . . ."* (MBC 21 April 1852).

One of these wrecks is certainly the *Bolton Abbey* (whose crew, together with most of the crew from the *Countess of Minto,* was rescued by HMCS *Bramble* in October 1851). However, the identity of McIlwraith's second wreck has not been determined as no additional primary source material has yet been found. The Moreton Bay Courier article reporting McIlwraith's experiences was apparently to inform prospective guano entrepreneurs that the quality of Lady Elliot Island guano was too poor to justify the expense and risks involved (as exemplified by the two wrecks) in mining it. The article also mentions that, shortly after McIlwraith's visit, two more vessels — the *Arab* and the *Sea* had called at the island, also with specific instructions to load guano. The *Sea's* crew did not bother to mine any as the captain considered it of inferior quality and immediately sailed off to Callao in South America. However, the *Arab's* crew did take 15 tons, which was trans-shipped to Sydney and analysed but — as the article implies — the inferior quality of Lady Elliot Island guano had not been worth the considerable effort expended to extract it.

In spite of this first negative assessment of the Reef's guano, interest in Lady Elliot Island's deposits was demonstrated again in the early 1860's when several Melbourne and Tasmania based merchants applied to the colonial authorities in Brisbane for leases to mine Lady Elliot Island as well as several other islands in the Coral Sea. In 1863, the government began to regulate the industry and leases for Lady Elliot Island and Bird Islet (Coral Sea) were granted to the Anglo-Australian Guano Company, based in Hobart, Dr William Crowther being the major shareholder. Crowther owned a number of whaling vessels, and these appear to have doubled, not only as supply vessels for the island-based miners, but also as cargo vessels shipping the guano to Hobart. In his journal, J. W. Robinson, captain of one of Crowther's whaling vessels (1862–1864), and later Lady Elliot Mine Manager (1865), describes the day to day events on the island (Robinson 1865 ms). He describes a makeshift lighthouse, as well as the wreck of yet another vessel: the *Golden City*. Adding to the steadily growing tally, the *Diana* — another guano vessel — was wrecked at Fairfax Island in 1864. Mining operations at Lady Elliot Island were carried on until the island's deposits were exhausted in 1898.

Although there is substantial evidence that other Capricorn-Bunker Islands — for instance, Lady Musgrave and Fairfax Islands — were mined during the 1860s, 1870s and 1880s, these operations were not on the same scale as mining on Lady Elliot Island, and they appear to have been illicit until the mid 1890s when leases were issued for North West, Lady Musgrave, Fairfax and Tryon Islands.

By the late 1890s Great Barrier Reef guano mining was extensive, involving a workforce of between 200 to 300 mostly Indian, Malay or Chinese labourers supervised by a European staff. Other Great Barrier Reef Islands were also mined, for instance Bell Cay and Raine Island. Depending on world prices, the guano was shipped overseas to England and New Zealand or interstate to southern ports. Many of the islands, especially Lady Elliot, were devasted as a result of the industry and to this day have not recovered. In due course, as a result of over-exploitation as well as new technology which changed the fertilizer industry, guano mining ceased altogether. If it were not for maritime history, little would be known of these activities which, in the 19th century made such an impact on the islands of the Great Barrier Reef.

The Great Barrier Reef Marine Park

The Great Barrier Reef, a complex of about 2 900 reefs, is contained in the world's largest Marine Park, its eastern limits along the edge of the continental shelf, and the western limits generally along the Queensland coast (in some places at the low water mark). The Park covers an area of about 350 000 sq km, stretching for about 2 000 km along the northeastern coast of Australia.

The management authority, The Great Barrier Reef Marine Park Authority, set up by Commonwealth Government legislation in 1975, has as its long-term goal the protection, wise use and enjoyment of the Great Barrier Reef, in perpetuity, through the development of the Marine Park and its zoning for multiple acceptable uses. Thus, fishing, tourism, research and shipping are regulated, while mining is a prohibited use. The Park is not a National Park, it is a Park managed for reasonable use and ecologically sustainable development. The Authority works in co-operation with the Queensland State Government which is responsible for the islands in the region. Overall, it is a complex administrative operation. It has been estimated that reef-related activities are worth about $1,000 million a year. It is not surprising, therefore, that there often are conflicting pressures for use and conservation of its resources which the Authority must resolve.

To contribute to its effectiveness in managing this resource, and to enhance the enjoyment of visitors to the reef, the Authority undertakes educational programmes both about the Reef, and about its own activities. Visitors contemplating a visit to the reef should find out about the zoning plans in the region they intend to visit. Permits are required for collecting or any manipulative scientific work in most zones of the Park, and application for these should be made to the Queensland Department of Environment and Heritage, Brisbane 4000; or from the Great Barrier Reef Marine Park Authority, Flinders Street, Townsville 4810.

Selected References and Further Reading

GENERAL AND HISTORICAL

Bennett, I., 1988. The Great Barrier Reef. Lansdowne: Sydney.

Frankel, E., 1978. Bibliography of the Great Barrier Reef. Great Barrier Reef Marine Park Authority: Townsville.

Great Barrier Reef Expedition Reports, 1931–1968, Vols 1–7. British Museum: London.

Heatwole, H., 1976. The ecology and biogeography of coral cays. Pp. 369–87 in Biology and Geology of Coral Reef, Vol. 3 ed by O. A. Jones and R. Endean. Academic Press: New York.

Heatwole, H., 1987. A Coral Island. Collins: Sydney.

Mather, P. and Talbot, F. H., 1975. Research Facilities in the Great Barrier Reef, their history, operation and funding. Search 6(8): 335–38.

Maxwell, W. G. H., 1968. Atlas of the Great Barrier Reef. Elsevier: Amsterdam, London and New York.

Talbot, F. H. (ed), 1984. The Readers Digest Book of the Great Barrier Reef. Readers Digest: Sydney.

GEOLOGY AND GEOMORPHOLOGY

Hopley, D., 1982. Geomorphology of the Great Barrier Reef. John Wiley and Sons: New York.

Davies, P. J., Symonds, P. A., Feary, D. A. and Pigram, C. J., 1989. The evolution of the carbonate platforms of Northeast Australia. Pp. 233–58 in Controls on carbonate platform and basin development, Vol. 44 ed by P. D. Crevello et. al. Special Publication Society of Economic Paleontologists and Mineralogists.

Flood, P., 1977. Coral cays of the Capricorn and Bunker Groups, Great Barrier Reef Province, Australia. Atoll Res. Bull. 195: 1–7.

Jones, O. A. and Endean, R. (eds), 1976. Biology and Geology of Coral Reefs. Vol. 1, Geology. Academic Press: New York.

ALGAE, SEAGRASSES

Cribb, A. B., 1965. The marine and terrestrial vegetation of Wilson Island, Great Barrier Reef. Proc. R. Soc. Qd. 77: 53–62.

Cribb, A. B., 1966. The Algae of Heron Island, Great Barrier Reef, Australia. Pap. Gt. Barrier Reef Comm. Univ. Qd 1: 1–23.

Cribb, A. B., 1969. Sea sawdust. Qd Nat. 19(4–6): 115–17.

Cribb, A. B., 1969. Some marine fungi from the Great Barrier Reef area. Qd Nat. 19(4–6): 118–20.

Cribb, A. B., 1972. Vegetation of Hoskyn Island and reef. Qd Nat. 20(4–6): 92–100.

Cribb, A. B., 1973. The Algae of the Great Barrier Reefs. Pp. 47–75 in Biology and geology of coral reefs, Vol. II ed by A. O. Jones and R. Endean. Academic Press, New York.

Cribb, A. B., 1975. Algal vegetation of Masthead Island Reef. Qd Nat. 21(3–4): 79–83.

Cribb, A. B. and Cribb, J., 1985. Plant Life of the Great Barrier Reef and Adjacent Shores. University of Queensland Press: St Lucia.

Lanyon, J., 1986. Seagrasses of the Great Barrier Reef; a guide to the identification of seagrasses in the Great Barrier Reef. GBRMPA Special Publication Series No. 3, GBRMPA, Townsville. 54 pp.

Price, I. R., Larkum, A. N. D. and Bailey, A., 1976. Check List of benthic marine plants collected in Lizard Island area. Aust. J. Plant Physiol. 3: 3–8.

GENERAL INVERTEBRATES

Barnes, R. D., 1980. Invertebrate Zoology. 4th Edition. Holt, Saunders: Japan.

Higgins, R. P. and Thiel, H., 1988. Introduction to the Study of Meiofauna. Smithsonian Institution Press: Washington, 488 pp.

Hulings, N. C. and Gray, J. S., 1971. A manual for the study of Meiofauna. *Smithsonian Contributions to Zoology* **78**: 1–83.

Hutchings, P. A. and Weate, B. P., 1978. Comments on the technique of acid dissolution of coral rock to extract endo-cryptolithic fauna. *Aust. Zool.* **19**: 315–20.

Lincoln, R. J. and Sheals, J. G., 1979. Invertebrate Animals — Collection and Preservation. British Museum (NH): London.

FORAMINIFERIDA

Albani, A. D., 1968. Recent Foraminiferida of the central coast of New South Wales. *Australian Marine Sciences Association Handbook* **1**: 1–37.

Brady, H. B., 1884. Report on the Foraminifera dredged by *H.M.S. Challenger* during the years 1873–1876. *Reports of the Scientific Results of the Voyage of* H.M.S. Challenger, 9(Zool): 1–814.

Collins, A. C., 1958. Foraminifera. *Scient. Rep. Gt Barrier Reef Exped.* **6**: 335–437.

Jell, J. S., Maxwell, W. G. H. and McKellar, R. G., 1965. The significance of the larger Foraminifera in the Heron Island Reef sediments. *J. Paleont.* **39**: 273–79.

PLANKTON

Dakin, W. J. and Colefax, A. N., 1940. The plankton of the Australian coastal waters of NSW Part I. *Publications of the Univ. of Sydney, Dept. Zoology, Monograph No. 1*, Aust. Med. Publ. Co. Ltd.: Glebe, NSW

Hodgson, B. R., 1982. Seasonal variation of macro-zooplankton in coastal and reef waters at Heron Island. University of NSW: Kensington.

McWilliam, P. S., Sale, P. F. and Anderson, D. T., 1981. Seasonal changes in resident zooplankton sampled by emergence traps in One Tree Lagoon, Great Barrier Reef. *J. exp. mar. Biol. Ecol.* **52**: 185–203.

Sale, P. F., McWilliam, P. S. and Anderson, D. T., 1976. Composition of the near-reef zooplankton at Heron Reef, Great Barrier Reef. *Mar. Biol.* **34**: 59–66.

Sale, P. F., McWilliam, P. S. and Anderson, D. T., 1978. Faunal relationships among the near-reef zooplankton at three locations on Heron Reef, Great Barrier Reef, and seasonal changes in this fauna. *Mar. Biol.* **49**: 133–45.

Wickstead, J. H., 1965. An introduction to the study of tropical plankton. Hutchinson Tropical Monographs.

PORIFERA — SPONGES

Bergquist, P. R., 1969. Shallow Water Demospongiae from Heron Island. *Pap. Gt. Barrier Reef Comm. Univ. Qd* 1(4): 63–72, pls. 1–2.

Bergquist, P. R., 1978. Sponges. Hutchinson: London, pp. 1–268.

Bergquist, P. R., Ayling, A. M. and Wilkinson, C. R., 1988. Foliose Dictyoceratida of the Australian Great Barrier Reef. 1. Taxonomy and phylogenetic relationships. *Mar. Ecol.* **9**(4): 291–320.

Burton, M., 1934. Sponges. *Scient. Rep. Gt Barrier Reef Exped.* **4**(14): 513–621, pls. 1–2.

Cannon, L. R. G., Goeden, G. B. and Campbell, P., 1987. Community patterns revealed by trawling in the inter-reef regions of the Great Barrier Reef. *Mem. Qd Mus.* **25**(1): 45–70.

Fromont, J., 1989. Aspects of the reproductive biology of *Xestospongia testudinaria* (Great Barrier Reef). *Proc. 6th Internatl Coral Reef Symp., Australia, 1988* **2**: 685–91.

Fromont, J., 1991. Descriptions of species of the Petrosida (Porifera: Demospongiae) occurring in the tropical waters of the Great Barrier Reef. *The Beagle. Records of the Northern Territory Museum of Arts and Sciences* 8(1): 73–96.

Hammond, L. S. and Wilkinson, C. R., 1985. Exploitation of sponge exudates by coral reef holothuroids. *J. exp. mar. Biol. Ecol.* **94**(1–3): 1–10.

Hartman, W. D., 1982. Porifera. Pp. 640–66 *in* Synopsis and Classification of Living Organisms, Vol. 1 ed by S. P. Parker. McGraw-Hill: New York.

Hooper, J. N. A., 1991. Revision of the family Raspailiidae (Porifera: Demospongiae), with description of Australian species. *Invertebrate Taxonomy* 5(6): 1179–415.

Lang, J. C., Hartman, W. D. and Land, L. S., 1975. Sclerosponges: primary framework constructors on the Jamaican deep fore-reef. *J. mar. Res.* **33**(2): 223–31.

Levi, C., 1973. Systématique de la classe des Demospongiaria (Démosponges). Pp. 577–631 *in* Traité de Zoologie. Anatomie, Systématique, Biologie. III. Spongiaires ed by P. Brien, C. Levi, M. Sara, O. Tuzet and J. Vacelet. (Sér ed P–P. Grasse). Masson et Cie: Paris.

Levi, C., 1991. Lithistid sponges from the Norfolk Rise. Recent and Mesozoic Genera. Pp. 72–82 *in* Fossil and Recent Sponges ed by J. Reitner and H. Keupp. Springer-Verlag: Berlin, Heidelberg.

Reitner, J. and Engeser, T., 1983. Contributions to the systematics and palaeoecology of the family Acanthochaetetidae Fischer, 1970 (order Tabulospongida, class Sclerospongiae). *Geobios* **16**: 773–79.

Rigby, J. K. and Stearn, C. W., 1983. Sponges and spongiomorphs. Notes for a short course. Univeristy of Tennessee, *Dept. of Geological Sciences Studies in Geology* **7**: 1–220.

Rudman, W. B. and Avern, G. J., 1989. The genus *Rostanga* Bergh, 1879 (Nudibranchia: Dorididae) in the Indo-West Pacific. *Zool. J. Linn. Soc.* **96**: 281–338.

Rutzler, K., 1975. The role of burrowing sponges in bioerosion. *Oecologia* 19(3): 203–16.

Wiedenmayer, F., Hooper, J. N. A. and Racek, A. A., 1992. Porifera. In press *in* Zoological Catalogue of Australia ed by D. W. Walton. Australian Government Printing Service: Canberra.

Wilkinson, C. R., 1983. Net Primary Productivity in Coral Reef Sponges. *Science N.Y.* **219**: 410–12.

Wilkinson, C. R., 1988. Foliose Dictyoceratida of the Australian Great Barrier Reef. 2. Ecology and distribution of these prevalent sponges. *Mar. Ecol.* **9**(4): 321–28.

Wilkinson, C. R. and Cheshire, A. C., 1989. Patterns in the distribution of sponge populations across the central Great Barrier Reef. *Coral Reefs* **8**: 127–34.

Wood, R., 1990. Reef-building sponges. *American Scientist* **78**: 224–35.

Yamaguchi, M., 1986. Outbreaks of *Terpios* in the Ryukyus. *Coral Reef Newsletter* (16): iii, 4.

CTENOPHORA

Harbison, G. R. and Madin, L. P., 1982. Ctenophora. Pp. 707–15 *in* Synopsis and Classification of Living Organisms ed by S. P. Parker. McGraw-Hill: New York.

CNIDARIA — HYDROZOA AND SCYPHOZOA

Fenner, P. J., Williamson, J., Callinan V. I. and Audley, I., 1986. Further understanding of, and a new treatment for, "Irukandji" *(Carukia barnesi)* stings. *Med. J. Aust.* **145**: 569, 572–74.

Hartwick, R., 1987. The Box Jellyfish. Pp. 95–105 *in* Toxic Plants and Animals: A guide for Australia ed by J. Covacevich, P. Davie and J. Pearn. Queensland Museum: Brisbane.

Kramp, P. L., 1953. Hydromedusae. *Scient. Rep. Gt Barrier Reef Exped.* **6**(4): 259–322.

Kramp, P. L., 1961. Synopsis of the medusae of the World. *J. mar. Biol. Ass. UK* **40**: 1–469.

Millard, N. A. H., 1975. Monograph on the Hydroida of Southern Africa. *Ann. SA Mus.* **68**: 1–513.

Pennycuik, P. R., 1959. Faunistic Records from Queensland V. Marine and Brackish water Hydroids. *Pap. Dept. Zool. Univ. Qd Zoology* **1**: 141–210.

Totton, A. K. and Bargmann, H. E., 1965. A Synopsis of the Siphonophora. British Museum (Natural History): London.

Werner, B., 1975. Bau und Lebensgeschichte des Polypen von *Tripedalia cystophora* (Cubozoa, class nov. Carybdeidae) und seine Bedeutung fur die Evolution der Cnidaria. *Helgolaender Wiss. Meeresunters.* **27**: 461–504.

CNIDARIA — ANTHOZOA

Babcock, R. C. and Ryland, J. S., 1990. Larval development of a tropical zoanthid (*Protopalythoa* sp.). *Invert. Reprod. Develop.* **17**: 229–36.

Bayer, F. M., Grasshoff, M., Verseveldt, J., 1983. Illustrated trilingual glossary of morphological terms applied to Octocorallia. E. J. Brill/Dr W. Backhuys: Leiden.

Calgren, O., 1937. Ceriantharia and Zoantharia. *Scient. Rep. Gt Barrier Reef Exped.* **5**(5): 177–207.

Calgren, O., 1951. Corallimorpharia, Actinaria and Zoantharia from New South Wales and south Queensland. *Ark. Zool.* **1**: 131–46.

Cannon, L. R. G., Goeden, G. B. and Campbell, P., 1987. Community patterns revealed by trawling in the inter-reef regions of the Great Barrier Reef. *Mem. Qd Mus.* **25**: 45–70.

Crossland, C., 1952. Madreporia, Hydocorallinae, *Heliopora* and *Tubipora*. *Sci. Rep. Gt Barrier Reef Exped.* **3**: 85–257.

Deas, W., Domm, S., 1976. Corals of the Great Barrier Reef. Ure Smith: Sydney.

Dunn, D., 1981. The clownish anemone: Stichodactylidae (Coelenterata: Actiniaria) and other sea anemones symbiotic with pomacentrid fishes. *Trans. Amer. Phil. Soc.* **71**: 1–115.

Fadlallah, Y. H., Karlson, R. H. and Sebens, K. P., 1984. A comparative study of sexual reproduction in three species of Panamanian zoanthids (Coelenterata: Anthozoa). *Bull. Mar. Sci.* **35**(1): 80–89.

Faulkner, D. R and Chesher, R., 1979. Living Corals. Clarkson, N. Potter, Inc.: New York.

Grasshoff, M., 1981. Polypen und kolonien der blumentier (Anthozoa). 2. Die achtstrahligen korallen (Octocorallia). *Natur und Museum* **111**(2): 29–45. Frankfurt.

Grasshoff, M., 1981a. Polypen und kolonien der blumentier (Anthozoa). 3. Die Hexacorallia. *Natur und Museum* **111**(5): 134–50.

Haddon, A. C., 1895. Branched worm-tubes and *Acrozoanthus*. *Scient. Proc. R. Dubl. Soc.*, N.S., **8**: 344–46.

Haddon, A. C., 1898. The Actiniaria of Torres Straits. *Scient. Trans R. Dubl. Soc.*, Ser. 2, **6**: 393–522.

Haddon, A. C. and Shackelton, A. M., 1891. Actiniae I. Zoantheae. Reports on the zoological collections made in the Torres Straits by A. C. Haddon, 1888–1889. *Scient. Trans R. Dubl. Soc.*, Ser. 2, **4**: 673–701.

Harrison, P. L. and Wallace, C. C., 1990. Reproduction, dispersal and recruitment of scleractinian corals. *In* Coral Reefs ed by Z. Dubinsky. Elsevier: Amsterdam.

Herberts, C., 1987. Ordre des Zoanthaires. Pp. 783–810 *in* Traité de Zoologie. ed by P.–P. Grasse. Masson: Paris.

Kojis, B. L. and Quinn, N. J., 1981. Aspects of sexual reproduction and larval development in the shallow water hermatypic coral, *Goniastrea australensis* (Edwards and Haime, 1857). *Bull. Mar. Sci.* **3**: 558–73.

Kojis, B. L. and Quinn, N. J., 1982a. Reproductive strategies in four species of *Porites* (Scleractinia). *Proc. 4th Internatl Coral Reef Symp.* Manila **2**: 146–51.

Kojis, B. L. and Quinn, N. J., 1982b. Reproductive ecology of two faviid corals (Coelenterata: Scleractinia). *Mar. Ecol. Prog. Ser.* **8**: 251–55.

Kuhlmann, D. H. H., 1985. Living Coral Reefs of the World. Arco Publishing Inc.: New York.

241

Larson, K. S. and Larson, R. J., 1982. On the ecology of *Isaurus duchassaingi* (Andres) (Cnidaria: Zoanthidea) from South Water Cay, Belize. Pp. 1–539 *in* The Atlantic barrier reef ecosystem at Carrie Bow Cay, Belize, I, Vol. 12 ed by K. Rutzler and I. G. MacIntyre. *Smithson. Contr. Mar. Sci.*

Muirhead, A. and Ryland, J. S., 1985. A review of the genus *Isaurus* Gray, 1828 (Zoanthidea), including new records from Fiji. *J. nat. Hist.* **19**: 323–35.

Opresko, D. M., 1972. Redescriptions and reevaluations of the Antipatharians described by I. F. de Pourtales. *Bull. Mar. Sci.* **22**(4): 951–1017, 13 figs.

Ryland, J. S. and Babcock, R. C. Annual cycle of gametogenesis and spawning in a tropical zoanthid, *Protopalythoa* sp. *Hydrobiologia* (in press).

Saville-Kent, W., 1893. The Great Barrier Reef of Australia. W. H. Allen, London, 387 pp.

Sheppard, C. R. C., 1983. A Natural History of the Coral Reef. Blandford Press: Poole.

Stephenson, W. and Wells, J. W., 1956. The corals of Low Isles, Queensland. *Pap. Dep. Zool. Univ. Qd* **1**: 1–59.

Veron, J. E. N., 1985. Corals of Australia and the Indo-Pacific. Angus and Robertson: Sydney.

Veron, J. E. N. and Pichon, M., 1976. Scleractinia of Eastern Australia. Part 1: families Thamnasteriidae, Astrocoeniidae, Pocilloporidae. *Aust. Inst. Mar. Sci. Monograph Ser.* 86 pp.

Veron, J. E. N. and Pichon, M., 1979. Scleractinia of Eastern Australia. Part 3: families Agariciidae, Siderastreidae, Fungiidae, Oculinidae, Merulinidae, Mussidae, Pectiniidae, Caryophyllidae, Dendrophyllidae. *Aust. Inst. Mar. Sci. Monograph Ser.* 422 pp.

Veron, J. E. N. and Pichon, M., 1983. Scleractinia of Eastern Australia. Part 4: Family Poritidae. *Aust. Inst. Mar. Sci. Monograph Ser.* 159 pp.

Veron, J. E. N., Pichon, M. and Wijsman-Best, M., 1977. Scleractinia of Eastern Australia. Part 2: Family Faviidae. *Aust. Inst. Mar. Sci. Monograph Ser.* 233 pp.

Veron, J. E. N. and Wallace, C. C., 1984. Scleractinia of Eastern Australia. Part 5: Family Aroporidae. *Aust. Inst. Mar. Sci. Monograph Ser.* 485 pp.

WORMS

Berry, G. N. and Cannon, L. R. G., 1981. The life history of *Sulcascaris sulcata* (Nematoda: Ascaridoidea), a parasite of marine molluscs and turtles. *Int. J. Parasit.* **11**: 43–54.

Bruce, N. L., 1990. Redescription of the ascaridoid nematode *Hysterothylacium scomberomori* (Yamaguti) from Australian spanish mackerel *Scomberomorus commerson* (Lacepede). *Mem. Qd Mus.* **28**: 427–34.

Bruce, N. L. and Cannon, L. R. G., 1989. *Hysterothylacium, Iheringascaris* and *Maricostula* new genus, nematodes (Ascaridoidea) from Australian pelagic marine fishes. *J. nat. Hist.* **23**: 1397–441.

Cannon, L. R. G., 1986. Turbellaria of the World: a guide to families and genera. Queensland Museum, Brisbane, 136 pp.

Cannon, L. R. G., 1990a. *Anoplodium* (Rhabdocoela, Platyhelminthes) endosymbiotes of sea cucmbers from Australia and New Zealand. *Zool. Scripta* **19**: 395–402.

Cannon, L. R. G., 1990b. *Apidioplana apluda* n. sp., a turbellarian symbiote of gorgonian corals from the Great Barrier Reef, with a review of the family Apidioplanidae (Polycladida: Acotylea). *Mem. Qd Mus.* **28**: 435–42.

Cannon, L. R. G. and Lester, R. J. G., 1988. Two turbellarians parasitic in fish. *Dis. aquat. Org.* **5**: 15–22.

Decraemer, W., 1978. Morphological and taxonomic study of the genus *Tricoma* Cobb (Nematoda: Desmoscolecida), with the description of new species from the Great Barrier Reef of Australia. *Aust. J. Zool. Supp.* **55**: 1–121.

Dittman, S., 1991. Plathelminthes in tropical intertidal sediments of northeast Australia. *Hydrobiologia.* **227**: 369–74.

Kozloff, E. N., 1969. Morphology of the orthonectid *Rhopalura ophiocomae.* *J. Parasit.* **55**: 171–95.

Kristensen, R. M., 1983. Loricifera, a new phylum with aschelminthes characters from the meiobenthos. *Zeit. Zool. Syst. Evol.* **21**: 163–80.

Lester, R. J. G. and Sewell, K. B., 1989. Checklist of parasites from Heron Island, Great Barrier Reef. *Aust. J. Zool.* **37**: 101–28.

Schmidt, G. D., 1986. CRC Handbook of Tapeworm Identification. CRC Press: Boca Raton. 675 pp.

Winsor, L., 1988. A new acoel (Convolutidae) from the north Queensland coast, Australia. *Fortsch. Zool.* **36**: 391–94.

Winsor, L., 1990. Marine Turbellaria (Acoela) from north Queensland. *Mem. Qd Mus.* **28**: 785–800.

Yamaguti, S., 1961. Systema Helminthum III. The Nematodes of Vertebrates. 2 vols. John Wiley and Sons: New York, 1261 pp.

Yamaguti, S., 1963a. Systema Helminthum IV. Monogenea and Aspidocotylea. John Wiley and Sons: New York, 699 pp.

Yamaguti, S., 1963b. Systema Helminthum V. Acanthocephala. John Wiley and Sons: New York, 423 pp.

Yamaguti, S., 1971. Synopsis of Digenetic Trematodes of Vertebrates. 2 vols. Keigaku: Tokyo, 1074 pp; pls.

POLYCLAD TURBELLARIANS

Cannon, L. R. G., 1990. *Apidioplana apluda* n.sp., a turbellarian symbiote of gorgonian corals from the Great Barrier Reef, with a review of the family Apidioplanidae (Polycladida:Acotylea). *Mem. Qd Mus.* **28**: 435–42.

Prudhoe, S., 1985. A Monograph on Polyclad Turbellaria. British Museum (NH): London, 259 pp.

NEMERTEA

Gibson, R., 1978. Two new lineid heteronemerteans from Australia. *Zool. J. Linn. Soc.* **62**: 1–37.

Gibson, R., 1979a. Nemerteans of the Great Barrier Reef. 1. Anopla Palaeonemertea. *Zool. J. Linn. Soc.* **65**: 305–37.

Gibson, R., 1979b. Nemerteans of the Great Barrier Reef. 2. Anopla Heteronemertea (Baseodiscidae). *Zool. J. Linn. Soc.* **66**: 137–60.

Gibson, R., 1981a. Nemerteans of the Great Barrier Reef. 3. Anopla Heteronemertea (Lineidae). *Zool. J. Linn. Soc.* **71**: 171–235.

Gibson, R., 1981b. Nemerteans of the Great Barrier Reef. 4. Anopla Heteronemertea (Valenciniidae). *Zool. J. Linn. Soc.* **72**: 165–74.

Gibson, R., 1982. Nemerteans of the Great Barrier Reef. 5. Enopla Hoplonemertea (Monostilifera). *Zool. J. Linn. Soc.* **75**: 269–96.

Gibson, R., 1983. Nemerteans of the Great Barrier Reef. 6. Enopla Hoplonemertea (Polystilifera: Reptantia). *Zool. J. Linn. Soc.* **78**: 73–104.

Moore, J. and Gibson, R., 1981. The *Geonemertes* problem (Nemertea). *J. Zool., Lond.* **194**: 175–201.

Punnett, R. C., 1900. On some nemerteans from Torres Straits. *Proc. Zool. Soc. Lond.* 825–31.

Riser, N. W., 1988. *Arhynchonemertes axi* gen. n., sp. n. (Nemertinea) — an insight into basic acoelomate bilaterian organology. *Prog. Zool.* **36**: 367–73.

SEGMENTED WORMS

Brinkhurst, R. O., 1982. British and other marine and estuarine oligochaetes. *In* Synopses of the British Fauna (New Series) 21. Cambridge University Press: Cambridge, 127 pp.

Erséus, C., 1979–1984. Oligochaeta, Tubificidae: (Taxonomic revisions of various marine genera and descriptions of new species), *Zool. Scr.* 1979, **8**: 139–51; 1980, **9**: 97–112; 1981a, **10**: 15–31; 1981b, **10**: 111–32; 1983, **12**: 25–36; 1984, **13**: 239–72.

Erséus, C., 1982. Taxonomic revision of the marine genus *Limnodriloides* (Oligochaeta: Tubificidae). *Verh. naturwiss. Ver. Hamburg* (NF) **25**: 207–77.

Erséus, C. and Davis, D., 1989. The marine Tubificidae (Oligochaeta) of Hawaii. *Asian Mar. Biol.* **6**: 73–100.

Erséus, C. and Jamieson, B. G. M., 1981. Two new genera of marine Tubificidae (Oligochaeta) from Australia's Great Barrier Reef. *Zool. Scripta* **10**: 105–10.

Gibbs, P. E., 1969. Aspects of polychaete ecology with particular reference to commensalism. *Phil. Trans. Roy. Soc. B.* **255**: 443–58.

Grassle, J. F., 1973. Variety in coral reef communities. Pp. 247–70 *in* The Biology and Geology of Coral Reefs, Vol. 1 ed by O. A. Jones and R. Endean. Academic Press: New York and London.

Grygier, M. J., 1990. Distribution of Indo-Pacific *Myzostoma* and host specificity of comatulid-associated Myzostomida. *Bull. Mar. Sci.* **47**: 182–91.

Hutchings, P. A., 1986. Biological destruction of coral reefs. *Coral Reefs* **4**: 239–52.

Jamieson, B. G. M., 1977. Marine meiobenthic Oligochaeta from Heron and Wistari Reefs (Great Barrier Reef) of the genera *Clitellio, Limnodriloides* and *Phallodrilus* (Tubificidae) and *Grania* (Enchytraeidae). *Zool. J. Linn. Soc.* **61**: 329–49.

Westheide, W., 1988. Polychaeta. Pp. 332–44 *in* Introduction to the Study of Meiofauna ed by R. P. Higgins and H. Thiel. Smithsonian Institution Press: Washington.

SIPUNCULA AND ECHIURA

Edmonds, S. J., 1980. A revision of the systematics of Australian sipunculans (Sipuncula). *Rec. S. Aust. Mus.* **18**(1): 1–74.

Edmonds, S. J., 1987. Echiurans from Australia (Echiura). *Rec. S. Aust. Mus.* **32**(2): 119–38.

Stephens, A. C. and Edmonds, S. J., 1972. The Phyla Sipuncula and Echiura. Trustees of British Museum (NH): London.

CRUSTACEANS

General

Manton, S. M., 1977. The Arthropoda: Habits, Functional Morphology and Evolution. Oxford University Press (Clarendon): London and New York.

Cirripedia

Jones, D. S., Anderson, J. T. and Anderson, D. T., 1990. Checklist of the Australian Cirripedia. *Technical Reports of the Australian Museum* **3**: 1–38.

Phyllocarida

Dahl, E., 1985. Crustacea Leptostraca: principles of taxonomy and a revision of the European shelf species. *Sarsia* **70**: 135–65.

Kazmi, Q. B. and Tirmizi, N. M., 1989. A new species of *Nebalia* from Pakistan (Leptostraca). *Crustaceana* **56**: 293–98.

Wagele, J. W., 1983. *Nebalia marerubi,* sp. nov. aus dem Roten Meer (Crustacea: Phyllocaridea: Leptostraca). *J. nat. Hist.* **17**: 127–38.

Peracarida

Bowman, T. E. and Abele, L. G., 1982. Classification of the recent Crustacea. Pp. 1–27 *in* The Biology of the Crustacea, Vol. 1 ed by L. G. Abele. Academic Press: New York, pp. i–xx, 1–319.

Parker, S. P. (ed), 1982. Synopsis and Classification of Living Organisms, Vol. 2. McGraw-Hill: New York, pp. 1–1232.

Schram, F. R., 1986. Crustacea. Oxford University Press: Oxford, pp i–xii, 1–606.

Watling, L., 1983. Peracaridan disunity and its bearing on eumalacostracan phylogeny with a redefinition of eumalacostracan superorders. Pp. 213–28 *in* Crustacean Issues 1. Crustacean Phylogeny ed by F. R. Schram. A. A. Balkema: Rotterdam, pp. i–xi, 1–372.

Mysidacea

Mauchline, J., 1980. The biology of mysids. *Advances in Marine Biology* **18:** 1–369.

Mauchline, J. and Murano, M., 1977. World list of the Mysidacea. *J. Tokyo Univ. Fish.* **64:** 39–88.

Murano, M., 1988. Heteromysids (Crustacea: Mysidacea) from northern Australia with description of six new species. *The Beagle, Rec. NT Mus.* **5:** 27–50.

Murano, M., 1990. Three new leptomysids (Mysidacea) from northern Australia. *Crustaceana* **59:** 231–44.

Tattersall, W. M., 1936. Mysidacea and Euphausiacea. *Scient. Rep. Gt Barrier Reef Exped.* **5:** 143–76.

Cumacea

Day, J., 1980. Southern African Cumacea Part 4. Families Gynodiastylidae and Diastylidae. *Annls S. Afr. Mus.* **82:** 187–292.

Hale, H. M., 1951. Australian Cumacea. No. 17. The family Diastylidae (cont.). *Rec. Aust. Mus.* **9:** 353–70.

Jones, N. S., 1963. The marine fauna of New Zealand: crustaceans of the order Cumacea. *New Zealand Department of Scientific and Industrial Research, Bulletin* **152:** 1–80.

Watling, L., 1991a. Rediagnosis and revision of some Nannastacidae (Crustacea: Cumacea). *Proc. Biol. Soc. Washington* **104:** 751–57.

Watling, L., 1991b. Revision of the cumacean family Leuconidae. *J. Crust. Biol.* **11:** 569–82.

Tanaidacea

Boesch, D. F., 1973. Three new tanaids (Crustacea: Tanaidacea) from southern Queensland. *Pacific Science* **27:** 168–88.

Sieg, J. and Heard, R. W., 1988. Tanaidacea (Crustacea: Peracarida) of the Gulf of Mexico. The family Pseudotanaidae from less than 200 metres, with the descriptions of *Pseudotanais mexilcolpos* n. sp. and a key to the known genera and species of the world. *Proc. Biol. Soc. Washington* **101:** 39–59.

Shiino, S. M., 1963. Tanaidacea collected by the Naga Expedition in the Bay of Nha-Trang, South Viet-Nam. *Reports of the Faculty of Fisheries Prefectural University of Mie* **4:** 437–507.

Shiino, S. M., 1965. Tanaidacea from the Bismarck Archipelago. *Vidensk Meddr. dansk natuur. Foren* **128:** 177–203.

Amphipoda

Arimoto, J., 1976. Taxonomic studies of caprellids (Crustacea, Amphipoda, Caprellidae) found in the Japanese and adjacent waters. *Special Publs Seto mar. Biol. Lab.,* Series III, pp. 229.

Barnard, K. H., 1931. Amphipoda. *Scient. Rep. Gt Barrier Reef Exped.* **4:** 111–35.

Barnard, J. L., 1976. Amphipods (Crustacea) from the Indo-Pacific tropics: a review. *Micronesica* **12:** 169–81.

Barnard, J. L., 1981. Redescription of *Iphiplateia whiteleggei*, a New Guinea marine amphipod. *Proc. Biol. Soc. Washington* **94:** 1211–18.

Barnard, J. L. and Karaman, G. S., 1991. The families and genera of marine gammaridean Amphipoda (except marine gammaroids). *Rec. Aust. Mus., Supplement* **13** (parts 1 and 2): 1–866.

Berents, P. B., 1983. The Melitidae of Lizard Island and adjacent reefs, the Great Barrier Reef, Australia (Crustacea: Amphipoda). *Rec. Aust. Mus.* **35:** 101–43.

Bowman, T. E. and Gruner, H. E., 1973. The families and genera of Hyperiidea (Crustacea: Amphipoda). *Smithsonian Contributions to Zoology* **146:** i–iv, 1–64.

Lowry, J. K. and Stoddart, H. E., 1989. The Scopelocherid genus *Aroni* (Crustacea: Amphipoda: Lyssianasoidea) with notes on the association between scopelocheirid amphipods, cassid gastropods and spatangoid echinoids. *Rec. Aust. Mus.* **41:** 111–20.

Lowry, J. K. and Stoddart, H. E., 1990. The Wandinidae, a new Indo-Pacific family of Lyssianassoid Amphipoda (Crustacea). *Rec. Aust. Mus.* **42:** 159–71.

Myers, A. A., 1985. Shallow-water, coral reef and mangrove Amphipoda (Gammaridea) of Fiji. *Rec. Aust. Mus.* Supplement **5:** 1–143.

Myers, A. A., 1988. The genera *Archaeolembos*, n.gen., *Bemlos* Shoemaker, *Protolembos* Myers and *Globosolembos* Myers (Amphipoda, Aoridae, Aorinae) from Australia. *Rec. Aust. Mus.* **40:** 265–332.

Sedlack-Weinstein, E., 1991. Three new records of cyamids (Amphipoda) from Australian cetaceans. *Crustaceana* **60:** 90–104.

Stock, J. H., 1984. The first record of Bogidiellidae (Crustacea: Amphipoda) from the Pacific: *Bogidiella (Xystriogidiella)* n. subgen. *capricornae* new species from the Great Barrier Reef. *Bull. Mar. Sci.* **34:** 380–85.

Thomas, J. D. and Barnard, J. L., 1990. *Jerbarnia stocki*, a new species from the Barrier Reef. *Beaufortia* **41:** 169–76.

Zeidler, W., 1990. Pelagic amphipods, Infraorder Physosomata (Crustacea: Amphipoda: Hyperiidea) from the CSK International Zooplankton Collection (western North Pacific) with description of four new species of *Scina*. *Publs Seto mar. Biol. Lab.* **34:** 167–200.

Isopoda

Bruce, N. L., 1986. Cirolanidae (Crustacea: Isopoda) of Australia. *Rec. Aust. Mus.,* Supplement **6:** 1–239.

Bruce, N. L., 1990. The genera *Catoessa, Elthusa, Enispa, Ichthyoxenus, Idusa, Livoneca* and *Norileca* n. gen. (Isopoda: Cymothoidae), crustacean parasites of marine fishes with descriptions of eastern Australian species. *Rec. Aust. Mus.* **42:** 247–300.

Harrison, K. and Holdich, D. M., 1984. Hemibranchiate sphaeromatids (Crustacea: Isopoda) from Queensland, Australia, with a world-wide review of the genera discussed. *Zool. J. Linn. Soc.* **81**: 275–387.

Holdich, D. M. and Harrison, K., 1980. The crustacean isopod genus, *Gnathia* Leach from Queensland waters with descriptions of nine new species. *Aust. J. mar. Freshw. Res.* **31**: 215–40.

Kensley, B., 1982. *Prethura hutchingsae*, new genus, new species, an asellote isopod from the Great Barrier Reef, Australia (Crustacea: Isopoda: Pleurocopida). *J. Crustacean Biol.* **2**: 255–60.

Kensley, B. and Schotte, M., 1989. Guide to the Marine Isopod Crustaceans of the Caribbean. Smithsonian Institution: Washington D.C., pp. 308.

Poore, G. C. B., 1987. *Serolina*, a new genus for *Serolis minuta* Beddard (Crustacea: Isopoda: Serolidae) with descriptions of eight new species from eastern Australia. *Mem. Mus. Vict.* **48**: 141–89.

Poore, G. C. B. and Lew Ton, H., 1988. *Amakusanthura* and *Apanthura* (Crustacea: Isopoda: Anthuridae) with new species from tropical Australia. *Mem. Mus. Vict.* **49**: 107–47.

Poore, G. C. B. and Lew Ton, H., 1990. *Chelanthura* (Crustacea: Isopoda: Anthuridae), a new genus from Southern Australia. *Mem. Mus. Vict.* **51**: 109–19.

Stomatopoda

Manning, R. B., 1980. The superfamilies, families, and genera of recent stomatopod Crustacea, with diagnoses of six new families. *Biol. Soc. Washington* **93**(2): 362–72.

Moosa, M. K., 1991. The Stomatopoda of New Caledonia and Chesterfield Islands. Pp. 149–219 *in* Le benthos des fonds meubles des lagon de Nouvelle-Caledonie, Vol. 1 ed by B. Richer De Forges. *Études et Théses, ORSTOM, Paris*.

Penaeidea

Grey, D. L., Dall, W. and Baker, A., 1983. A Guide to the Australian Prawns. Northern Territory Government Printing Office: Darwin.

Caridea

Banner, D. M. and Banner, A. H., 1973. The alpheid shrimp of Australia. Part I: The lower genera. *Rec. Aust. Mus.* **28**(15): 291–382.

Banner, D. M. and Banner, A. H., 1975. The alpheid shrimp of Australia. Part 2: The genus *Synalpheus*. *Rec. Aust. Mus.* **29**(12): 267–389, appendix.

Banner, D. M. and Banner, A. H., 1981. The alpheid shrimp of Australia. Part III: The remaining alpheids, principally the genus *Alpheus*, and the family Ogyridae. *Rec. Aust. Mus.* **34**(1): 1–357.

Bruce, A. J., 1976. Shrimps and prawns of coral reefs. Pp. 37–94 *in* Biology and Geology of Coral Reefs, Vol. III ed by O. A. Jones and R. Endean. Academic Press: New York.

Bruce, A. J., 1983. The Pontoniine shrimp fauna of Australia. *Mem. Aust. Mus.* **18**: 195–218.

Holthuis, L. B., 1955. The recent genera of the caridean and stenopodidean shrimps (Class Crustacea, Order Decapoda, Supersection Natantia) with keys for their determination. *Zool. Verh.* **26**: 1–157.

Stenopodidea

Goy, J. W., 1992. A new species of *Stenopus* from Australia, with a redescription of *Stenopus cyanoscelis* (Crustacea: Decapoda: Stenopodidea). *J. nat. Hist.* **26**: 79–102.

Thalassinidea

Poore, G. C. B. and Griffin, D. J. G., 1979. The Thalassinidea (Crustacea: Decapoda) of Australia (1). *Rec. Aust. Mus.* **32**(6): 217–321.

Palinura

Holthuis, L. B., 1991. Marine lobsters of the world. An annotated and illustrated catalogue of species of interest to fisheries known to date. *FAO Fisheries Synopsis* No. 125, **13**: i–viii, 1–292.

Brachyura

Griffin, D. J. G., 1969. Swimming crabs (Crustacea, Decapoda, Portunidae) from One Tree Island, Capricorn group, Queensland. *Rec. Aust. Mus.* **27**(19): 349–54.

Griffin, D. J. G. and Tranter, H., 1986. The Decapoda Brachyura of the Siboga Expedition. Part VIII. Majidae. *Siboga-Expeditie. Leiden* **Monogr. XXXIX, C4 (= Livr. 148)**: 7 + 1–335.

Lucas, J. S., 1980. Spider Crabs of the Family Hymenosomatidae (Crustacea: Brachyura) with particular reference to Australian species: Systematics and Biology. *Rec. Aust. Mus.* **33**(4): 148–247, figs 1–10.

Patton, W. K., 1966. Decapod Crustacea commensal with Queensland branching corals. *Crustaceana* **10**(3): 271–95.

Sakai, T., 1976. Crabs of Japan and the Adjacent Seas. Kodansha: Tokyo, pp. i–xxix, 1–773.

Serene, R., 1984. Crustacés Décapodes Brachyoures de l'Ocean Indien Ocidental et de la Mer Rouge, Xanthoidea: Xanthidae et Trapeziidae. Avec un addendum par Crosnier, A.: Carpilliidae et Menippidae. *Faune Tropicale. Office de la Recherche Scientifique et Technique Outre-Mer. Paris* **24**: 1–400.

Stephenson, W., 1960. The Australian Portunids (Crustacea: Portunidae). IV. Remaining genera. *Aust. J. mar. Freshw. Res.* **11**(1): 73–122.

Stephenson, W., 1961. The Australian Portunids (Crustacea: Portunidae). V. Recent collections. *Aust. J. mar. Freshw. Res.* **12**(1): 92–128.

Stephenson, W. and Campbell, B., 1959. The Australian Portunids (Crustacea: Portunidae) III. The genus *Portunus*. *Aust. J. mar. Freshw. Res.* **10**(1): 84–124.

Stephenson, W. and Hudson, J., 1957. The Australian Portunids (Crustacea: Portunidae). I. The genus *Thalamita*. *Aust. J. mar. Freshw. Res.* **8**(3): 312–86.

Stephenson, W., Hudson, J. and Campbell, B., 1957. The Australian Portunids (Crustacea: Portunidae). I. the genus *Charybdis*. *Aust. J. mar. Freshw. Res.* **8**(4): 491–507.

Ward, M., 1936. Crustacea Brachyura from the coasts of Queensland. *Mem. Qd Mus.* **11**(1): 1–13.

Hermit Crabs

Bennett, I., 1987. Australian Seashores (W. J. Dakin's classic study). Angus and Robertson: Sydney.

Cutress, C. E. and Ross, D. M., 1969. The sea anemone *Calliactis tricolor* and its association with the hermit crab *Dardanus venosus*. *J. Zool., London* **158**: 225–41.

Endean, R., 1982. Australia's Great Barrier Reef. University of Queensland Press: Australia.

Grant, F. E. and McCulloch, A. R., 1906. On a collection of Crustacea from the Port Curtis District, Queensland. *Proc. Linn. Soc. NSW* **31**: 2–53.

Haig, J. and Ball, E. E., 1988. Hermit Crabs from north Australian and eastern Indonesian waters (Crustacea Decapoda: Anomura: Paguroidea) collected During the 1975 *Alpha Helix* Expedition. *Rec. Aust. Mus.* **40**: 151–96.

Morgan, G. J., 1991. A review of the Hermit Crab genus *Calcinus* Dana (Crustacea: Decapoda: Diogenidae) from Australia, with descriptions of two new species. *Invertebrate Taxonomy* **5**: 869–913.

Ross, D. M., 1970. The commensal association of *Calliactis polypus* and the hermit crab *Dardanus gemmatus* in Hawaii. *J. Zool. Canada* **48**: 351–57.

Schuhmacher, H., 1977. A Hermit Crab, Sessile on Corals, Exclusively Feeds by Feathered Antennae. *Oecologia* (Berlin) **27**: 371–74.

Stephenson, W., Endean, R. and Bennett, I., 1958. An ecological survey of the marine fauna of Low Isles, Queensland. *Aust. J. mar. Freshw. Res.* **9**: 261–318.

Talbot, F. (ed), 1984. Readers Digest Book of the Great Barrier Reef. Readers Digest: Sydney.

Ward, M., 1928. The Crustacea of the Capricorn and Bunker Groups, Queensland. *Aust. Zoologist* **5**: 241–46.

MOLLUSCS

Coleman, N., 1975. What Shell is that? Paul Hamlyn: Sydney, 308 pp.

Coleman, N., 1989. Nudibranchs of the South Pacific. Sea Australian Resource Centre: Springwood, Qld.

Lamprell, K. and Whitehead, T., 1992. Bivalves of Australia. Crawford House Press: Bathurst, NSW, 188 pp.

Lu, C. C. and Phillips, J. U., 1985. An annotated checklist of the Cephalopoda from Australian waters. *Occ. Pap. Mus. Vict.* **2**: 21–36.

Rudman, W. B., 1991a. Purpose in pattern: the evolution of colour in chromodorid nudibranchs. *J. Moll. Stud.* **57**: 5–21.

Rudman, W. B., 1991b. Further studies on the taxonomy and biology of the octocoral-feeding genus *Phyllodesmium* Ehrenberg, 1831 (Nudibranchia: Aeolidoidea). *J. Moll. Stud.* **57**: 167–203.

Short, J. W. and Potter, D. G., 1975. Shells of Queensland and the Great Barrier Reef. Robert Brown and Associates, Bathurst, NSW, 135 pp.

Sweeney, M. J., Roper, C. F. E., Mangold, K. M., Clarke M. R. and Boletzky, S. V. (eds), 1992. "Larval" and juvenile cephalopods: a manual for their identification. *Smithsonian Contributions to Zoology* **513**: 1–282.

Thompson, T. E., 1976. Biology of the opisthobranch mollusc. Ray Society: London, 206 pp.

Tucker Abbott, R. and Dance, S. P., 1983. Compendium of seashells. E. P. Dutton: New York, 410 pp.

BRYOZOA

Harmer, S. F., 1915–57. The Polyzoa of the Siboga Expedition.
1. Entoprocta. Ctenostomata and Cyclostomata (1915);
2. Cheilostomata Anasca (1926);
3. Cheilostomata Ascophora, Family Reteporidae (1934);
4. Cheilostomata Ascophora, II (1957). *Siboga Exped.* **28**: 1–1147.

Hastings, A. B., 1932. The Polyzoa, with a note on an associated hydroid. *Scient. Rep. Gt Barrier Reef Exped.* **4**: 399–458.

Ross, J. R. P., 1974. Reef associated Ectoprocta from central region, Great Barrier Reef. *Proc. 2nd Internatl Coral Reef Symp.* Brisbane 1973 **1**: 349–52.

Ryland, J. S., 1970. Bryozoans. Hutchinson: London.

Ryland, J. S., 1974. Bryozoa in the Great Barrier Reef province. *Proc. 2nd Int. Coral Reef Symp.* **1**: 341–48.

ECHINODERMATA

Arnold, P. W. and Birtles, R. A., 1989. Soft-sediment marine invertebrates of southeast Asia and Australia: a guide to identification. Australian Institute of Marine Science: Townsville, 272 pp.

Cannon, L. R. G. and Silver, H., 1986. Sea cucumbers of northern Australia. Queensland Museum: Brisbane, 60 pp.

Clark, A. M., 1975. The Swain Reefs Expedition: Crinoidea. *Rec. Aust. Mus.* **29**: 391–406.

Clark, A. M. and Rowe, F. W. E., 1971. Monograph of the shallow water Indo-west Pacific echinoderms. Bristish Museum (NH): London, 301 pp.

246

Clark, H. L., 1946. The echinoderm fauna of Australia. Its composition and origin. *Carneg. Inst. Wash. Pubn.* **566:** 1–567.

Endean, R., 1953. Queensland faunistic records. III. Echinodermata (excluding Crinoidea) *Pap. Dept. Zool. Univ. Qd* **1:** 51–60.

Endean, R., 1956. Queensland faunistic records. IV. Further Records of Echinodermata (excluding Crinoidea) *Pap. Dept. Zool. Univ. Qd* **1:** 123–40.

Endean, R., 1961. Queensland faunistic records. IV. Additional records of Echinodermata (excluding Crinoidea) *Pap. Dept. Zool. Univ. Qd* **1:** 289–98.

Wilkinson, C. R. (ed), 1990. *"Acanthaster planci"* special issue. *Coral Reefs* **9:** 93–172.

TUNICATA

Alldredge, A. L., 1978. Appendicularians. *Scient. Am.* **235:** 95–102.

Berrill, N. J., 1950. The Tunicata. *Ray Soc. Publs* **133:** 1–354.

Kott, P., 1980. Algal bearing didemnid ascidians of the Indo-west-Pacific. *Mem. Qd Mus.* **20**(1): 1–38.

Kott, P., 1981. The ascidians of the reef flats of Fiji. *Proc. Linn. Soc. NSW* **105**(3): 147–212.

Kott, P., 1982. Didemnid-algal symbioses: host species in the Western Pacific with notes on the symbiosis. *Micronesica* **18**(1): 95–127.

Kott, P., 1984. Related species of *Trididemnum* in symbiosis with Cyanophyta. *Proc. Linn. Soc. NSW* **107:** 515–20.

Kott, P., 1985. The Australian Ascidiacea, Part 1. Phlebobranchia and Stolidobranchia. *Mem. Qd Mus.* **23:** 1–438.

Kott, P., 1989. Form and Function in the Ascidiacea. *Bull. Mar. Sci.* **45**(2): 253–76.

Kott, P., 1990. The Australian Ascidiacea, Part 2. Aplousobranchia (1). *Mem. Qd Mus.* **29**(1): 1–266.

Kott, P., 1992. The Australian Ascidiacea, Part 3. Aplousobranchia (2). *Mem. Qd Mus.* **32**(2): 375–625.

Kott, P., Parry, D. and Cox, G. C., 1984. Prokaryotic symbionts with a range of ascidian hosts. *Bull. Mar. Sci.* **34:** 308–12.

Thompson, H., 1948. Pelagic Tunicates of Australia. CSIRO: Melbourne.

FISHES

Eschmeyer, W. N., 1990. Catalogue of the genera of recent fishes. California Academy of Sciences: San Francisco.

Randall, J. E., Allen, G. R. and Steene, R. C., 1990. Fishes of the Great Barrier Reef and Coral Sea. Crawford House Press: Bathurst, Australia.

REPTILIA

Bustard, H. R., 1970. Turtles, Natural History and Conservation. Collins: London and Sydney.

Bustard, H. R., 1972. Australian Sea Turtles, Their Natural History and Conservation. Collins: London and Sydney.

Bustard, H. R., 1974. Barrier Reef sea turtle populations. *Proc. 2nd Internatl Coral Reef Symp.* Brisbane 1973. **1:** 227–34. Great Barrier Reef Committee: Brisbane.

Cogger, H. G., 1951. Reptiles and amphibians of Australia. (5th edition). A. H. and A. W. Reed: Sydney.

Cogger, H. G., 1975. Sea snakes of Australia and New Guinea. Pp. 59–136 *in* The Biology of sea snakes ed by W. A. Dunson. University Park Press: Baltimore, 530 pp.

Heatwole, H., 1975. Sea snakes found on reefs in the southern Coral Sea (Saumarez, Swains, Cato Island). Chapter 8. pp. 163–71; Predation on sea snakes. Chapter 12, pp. 233–49; Attacks by sea snakes on divers. Chapter 22, pp. 503–16 *in* The biology of sea snakes ed by W. A. Dunson. University Park Press: Baltimore, 530 pp.

Heatwole, H., 1987. Seasnakes. University of New South Wales Press: Kensington.

Limpus, C. J., 1975. Coastal sea snakes of subtropical Queensland waters (23°–28°S). Pp. 173–82 *in* The biology of sea snakes ed by W. A. Dunson. University Park Press: Baltimore.

Limpus, C. J., 1980. The green turtles, *Chelonia mydas* (L.) in Eastern Australia. *James Cook Univ. North Qld Res. Monograph* **1:** 5–22.

Limpus, C. J., 1980. Observations on the hawksbill turtle (*Eretmochelys imbricata*) nesting along the Great Barrier Reef. *Herpetologica* **36**(3): 265–71.

Moorhouse, F. W., 1933. Notes on the Green Turtle (*Chelonia mydas*). *Rept. Gt Br. R. Comm.* **4:** 1–22.

Sutherland, S. K., 1983. Australian Animal Toxins. Oxford University Press: Melbourne.

BIRDS

Seabird Islands

Since 1973 the Australian Bird Study Association has published a series of articles on "Seabird Islands" to record breeding status of seabirds on the islands around the Australian coast. So far, the following islands from the Great Barrier Reef region have been included in this series. Apart from No. 15 which appeared in the old journal, *Australian Bird Bander* (ABB), the articles have been published in *Corella*. Many authors, notably B. R. King, C. J. Limpus and T. A. Walker, contributed to the following:

1976: No. 15 Heron Island *ABB* **14:** 3.

1977: No. 43 Raine Island *Corella* **1:** 45, No. 44 Masthead Island **1:** 48.

1979: No. 66 One Tree Island **3:** 37.

1983: No. 127 MacLennan Cay **7:** 69, No. 128 Pandora Cay **7:** 71, No. 129 Ashmore Banks **7:** 74, No. 130 Sandbank No. 8 **7:** 76, No. 131 Sandbank No. 7 **7:** 7, 8.

1985: No. 150 Bird Islands **9:** 73, No. 151 Quoin Island **9:** 75, No. 152 Pelican Island **9:** 78, No. 153 Stainer Island **9:** 81, No. 154 Davie Cay **9:** 83, No. 155 Tydeman Cay **9:** 85, No. 156 Sandbank No. 1, **9:** 87, No. 157 Stapleton Island **9:** 89, No. 158 Combe Island **9:** 91, No. 159 Michaelmas Cay **9:** 94.

1986: No. 43/1 Raine Island **10:** 73, No. 160 Pipon Island **10:** 78, No. 161 Eagle Island **10:** 81, No. 162 Brook Islands **10:** 84, No. 163 Eshelby Island **10:** 87, No. 164 Frigate Cay **10:** 89, No. 165 Bylund Cay **10:** 91, No. 166 Price Cay **10:** 93, No. 167 Bell Cay **10:** 95, No. 168 Gannet Cay **10:** 98.

1988: No. 180 Booby Island **12:** 69.

1989: No. 190 Cholmondeley Island **13:** 41, No. 191 Wallace Island 13, No. 192 Saunders Island **13:** 45, No. 193 Magra Island **13:** 47, No. 194 Bacchi Cay **13:** 49, No. 195 Thomas Cay **13:** 51, No. 196 Erskine Island **13:** 53, No. 197 Rocky Islets **13:** 107, No. 198 Redbill Island **13:** 110, No. 199 Holbourne Island **13:** 112, No. 200 North Reef Island **13:** 115, No. 201 Lady Elliot Island **13:** 1, 18.

1991: No. 207 Piper Islands **15:** 53, No. 208 Chapman Island **15:** 55, No. 209 Sherrard Island **15:** 57, No. 210 Fife Island **15:** 59, No. 211 Bramble Cay **15:** 109, No. 212 South Barnard Islands **15:** 112, No. 213 East Rock **15:** 115, No. 214 Distant Cay **15:** 117.

Reviews and handbooks

Draffan, R. D. W., Garnett, S. T. and Malone, G. J., 1983. Birds of the Torres Strait: annotated list and biogeographical analysis. *Emu* **83:** 207–34.

Hulsman, K., 1984. Seabirds of the Capricornia Section, Great Barrier Reef Marine Park. Pp. 53–60 *in* The Capricornia Section of the Great Barrier Reef Past, Present and Future ed by W. T. Ward and P. Saenger. Royal Society of Queensland: Brisbane.

Kikkawa, J., 1976. The birds of the Great Barrier Reef. Pp. 279–341 *in* Biology and Geology of Coral Reefs ed by O. A. Jones and R. Endean. Academic Press: New York.

King, B. R., in press. Seabirds and seabird islands of Queensland. *Corella.*

Lane, B. A., 1987. Shorebirds in Australia. Nelson Publ.: Melbourne.

Schodde, R. and Tidemann, S. C. (eds), 1986. Readers Digest Complete Book of Australian Birds. Readers Digest: Sydney.

Serventy, D. L., Serventy, V. and Warham, J., 1971. The Handbook of Australian Seabirds. A. H. and A. W. Reed: Sydney.

Selected references

Barnes, A. and Hill, G. J. E., 1989. Census and distribution of black noddy *Anous minutus* nests on Heron Island, November 1985. *Emu* **89:** 129–34.

Catterall, C. P., 1985. Winter energy deficits and the importance of fruit versus insects in a tropical island bird population. *Aust. J. Ecol.* **10:** 265–79.

Hill, G. J. E. and Barnes, A., 1989. Census and distribution of wedge-tailed shearwater *Puffinus pacificus* burrows on Heron Island, November 1985. *Emu* **89:** 135–39.

Hulsman, K., 1977. Breeding success and mortality of terns at One Tree Island, Great Barrier Reef. *Emu* **77:** 49–60.

Hulsman, K., 1988. Structure of seabird communities: an example from Australian waters. Pp. 59–91 *in* Seabirds and Other Marine Vertebrates: Commensalism, Competition and Predation ed by J. Burger. Columbia University Press: New York.

Hulsman, K., Dale, P. and Jahnke, B. R., 1984. Vegetation and nesting preferences of black noddies at Masthead Island, Great Barrier Reef. II. Patterns at the micro-scale. *Aust. J. Ecol.* **9:** 343–52.

Hulsman, K. and Langham, N. P. E., 1985. Breeding biology of the bridled tern *Sterna anaethetus. Emu* **85:** 240–49.

Kikkawa, J., 1980. Winter survival in relation to dominance classes among silvereyes *Zosterops lateralis chlorocephala* of Heron Island, Great Barrier Reef. *Ibis* **122:** 437–46.

Kikkawa, J., 1987. Social relations and fitness in silvereyes. Pp. 253–66 *in* Animal Societies: Theories and Facts ed by Y. Ito, J. L. Brown and J. Kikkawa. Japan Scientific Societies Press: Tokyo.

Kikkawa, J. and Catterall, C. P., 1991. Are winter dominance, spacing and foraging behaviours related to breeding success in silvereyes? *Acta XX Congr. Intern. Ornithol.* (Christchurch 1990), pp. 1204–13.

Kikkawa, J. and Wilson, J. M., 1983. Breeding and dominance among the Heron Island silvereyes *Zosterops lateralis chlorocephala. Emu* **83:** 181–98.

King, B. R., 1990. Distribution and status of the Torresian imperial pigeon *Ducula spilorrhoa* in northeastern Queensland: Cooktown to Cape York. *Emu* **90:** 248–53.

King, B. R. and Reimer, D. S., 1991. Breeding and behaviour of the Herald petrel *Pterodroma arminjoniana* on Raine Island, Queensland. *Emu* **91:** 122–25.

Langham, N. P. and Hulsman, K., 1986. The breeding biology of the crested tern *Sterna bergii. Emu* **86:** 23–32.

Prendergast, H. D. V., Brooks, A. and Taylor, I. M., 1985. Summer wader counts on Tryon Island, Capricorn Group. *Sunbird* **15:** 80–83.

Slater, P., Slater, P. and Slater, R., 1986. The Slater Field Guide to Australian Birds. Rigby: Dee Why.

Smith, G. C., 1990. Factors influencing egg-laying and feeding of chicks of black-naped terns (*Sterna sumatrana*). *Emu* **90:** 88–96.

Smith, G. C., 1991. The roseate tern *Sterna dougallii gracilis* breeding on the northern Great Barrier Reef. *Corella* **15:** 33–36.

Walker, T. A., 1987. Birds of Bushy Island (with a summary of the nesting status of bird species on southern Great Barrier Reef cays). *Sunbird* **17:** 52–58.

Walker, T. A., 1988. Crested terns *Sterna bergii* on southern Great Barrier Reef islands, 1985–1986. *Corella* **12:** 53–56.

Walker, T. A., 1988. Roseate terns *Sterna dougallii* on southern Great Barrier Reef islands, 1985–1986. *Corella* **12**: 56–58.

Walker, T. A., 1988. Population of the silver gull *Larus novaehollandiae* on the Capricorn and Bunker islands, Great Barrier Reef. *Corella* **12**: 113–18.

MARINE MAMMALS

Baker, A. N., 1990. Whales and dolphins of Australia and New Zealand. An identification guide, 2nd edition. Allen and Unwin Australia Pty Ltd: North Sydney. 133 pp.

Dalton, T. and Isaacs, R., 1992. The Australian Guide to Whale Watching. Weldon: Sydney.

Harrison, R. and Bryden, M. M. (eds), 1988. Whales, Dolphins and Porpoises. Weldon: Sydney.

Leatherwood, S., Reeves, R. R., Perrin, W. F. and Evans, W. E., 1988. Whales, dolphins and porpoises of the eastern north Pacific and adjacent arctic waters. A guide to their identification, 2nd edition. Dover Publ. Inc.: New York, ix + 245 pp.

Lien, J. and Katona, S., 1990. A guide to the photographic identification of individual whales based on their natural and acquired markings. American Cetacean Society: San Pedro, California, 77 pp.

Marsh, H., 1989. Dugongidae. Pp. 1030–38 *in* Fauna of Australia IB. Mammals ed by D. W. Walton and B. J. Richardson. Australian Government Publishing Service: Canberra.

Marsh, H., 1991. Our tropical sirens: *Australian Geographic* **21**: 42–57.

Paterson, R. A., 1991. The migration of humpback whales *Megaptera novaengliae* off east coast Australia. *Mem. Qd Mus.* **30**: 333–41.

Queensland Dept Primary Industries, 1991. Queensland contingency plan for dealing with stranded marine mammals. Brochure QL91012.

Tucker, M., 1989. Whales and whale watching in Australia. Australian National Parks and Wildlife Service: Canberra.

Van Dyck, S. M. and Longmore, N. W., 1991. The mammal records. Pp. 284–336 *in* An Atlas of Queensland's frogs, reptiles, birds and mammals ed by G. J. Ingram and R. J. Raven. Queensland Museum: Brisbane.

TERRESTRIAL INVERTEBRATES

Britton, E. G., 1971. New intertidal beetle (Coleoptera: Limnichidae) from the Great Barrier Reef. *J. Ent.* Ser. B. *Taxonomy* **40**(2): 83–91.

Chadwick, C. E., 1962. Some insects and terrestrial arthropods from Heron Island. *Proc. Linn. Soc. NSW* **87**(2): 196–99.

Common, I. F. B., 1973. Lepidoptera (moths and butterflies). Chapter 36. Pp. 765–866 *in* CSIRO The Insects of Australia. Melbourne University Press: Carlton.

Common, I. F. B. and Waterhouse, D. F., 1972. Butterflies of Australia. Angus and Robertson: Sydney.

Colless, D. H. and McAlpine, D. K., 1973. Diptera (flies). Chapter 34, Pp. 656–740 *in* CSIRO The Insects of Australia. Melbourne University Press: Carlton.

Farrow, R. A., 1984. Detection of transoceanic migration of insects to a remote island in the Coral Sea, Willis Island. *Aust. J. Ecol.* **9**: 253–72.

Fletcher, B. S., 1973. Observations on a movement of insects at Heron Island, Queensland. *J. Aust. Ent. Soc.* **12**: 157–60.

Hacker, H., 1975. Insects on Masthead Island, May 1934. *Qd Nat.* **21**(3–4): 65–66.

Heatwole, H., 1971. Marine-dependent terrestrial biotic communities on some cays in the Coral Sea. *Ecology* **52**(2): 363–66.

Heatwole, H., 1981. A Coral Island. Collins: Sydney.

Heatwole, H., Done, T. and Cameron, E., 1981. Community Ecology of a Coral Cay, a Study of One-Tree Island, Great Barrier Reef, Australia. *Monographiae Biologicae* **43**: 1–379.

Key, K. H. L., 1973. Orthoptera (grasshoppers, locusts, crickets). Chapter 21, Pp. 323–47 *in* CSIRO The Insects of Australia. Melbourne University Press: Carlton.

Mackerras, I., 1949. Marine insects. *Proc. R. Soc. Qd* **61**(3): 19–29.

Marks, E. N., 1969a. Mosquitoes (Culicidae) on Queensland's coral cays. *Qd Nat.* **19**(4–6): 94–98.

Marks, E. N., 1969b. Ticks at Lady Musgrave Island, Capricorn Group. *Qd Nat.* **19**(4–6): 98.

Reeves, D. M., 1969. Notes on some butterflies from North West Island, Capricorn Group. *Qd Nat.* **19**(4–6): 103–05.

Reeves, D. M., 1971. Notes on some butterflies from Erskine Island, Capricorn Group. *Qd Nat.* **20**(1–3): 54–55.

Reeves, D. M., 1972. Notes on some butterflies from Hoskyn Island, Bunker Group. *Qd Nat.* **20**(4–6): 118–20.

Smith, J. M. B. and Heatwole, H., 1985. Notes on the changing flora of Heron Island and some other coral cays of the Capricorn Group, Great Barrier Reef. *Qd Nat.* **25**(5–6): 126–33.

Stone, A. and Wirth, W. W., 1947. On the marine midges of the genus *Clunio* Haliday (Diptera, Tendipedidae). *Proc. Ent. Soc. Washington* **49**: 201–24.

Whitehouse, M. E. A., 1986. The foraging behaviours of *Argyrodes antipodeana* (Thesidiidae), a kleptoparasitic spider from New Zealand. *J. Zool. N.Z.* **13**: 151–68.

VASCULAR PLANTS

Cribb, A. B., 1965. The marine and terrestrial vegetation of Wilson Island, Great Barrier Reef. *Proc. R. Soc. Qd* **77**: 53–62.

Cribb, A. B., 1969. The vegetation of North West Island. *Qd Nat.* **19**(4–6): 85–93.

Cribb, A. B., 1969. The Pisonia. *Qd Nat.* **19**(4–6): 110–14.

Cribb, A. B., 1972. The vegetation of Hoskyn I. and reef. *Qd Nat.* **20**(4–6): 92–100.

Cribb, A. B., 1975. Some fungi from Masthead Island. *Qd Nat.* **21**(3–4): 73.

Cribb, A. B., 1975. Terrestrial vegetation of Masthead Island. *Qd Nat.* **21**(3–4): 74–78.

Cribb, A. B., 1976. Changes in the terrestrial flora of Heron Island. *Qd Nat.* **21**(5–6): 110–12.

Cribb, A. B. and Cribb, J. W., 1985. Plant Life of the Great Barrier Reef and Adjacent Shores. University of Queensland Press: St Lucia.

Fosberg, F. R. and Stoddart, D. R., 1991. Plants of the reef islands of the northern Great Barrier Reef. *Atoll Res. Bull.* **348**: 1–82.

Fosberg, F. R., Thorne, R. F. and Moulton, J. M., 1961. Heron Island, Capricorn Group, Australia. *Atoll Res. Bull.* **82**.

Gillham, Mary E., 1963. Coray cay vegetation at Heron Island, Great Barrier Reef. *Proc. R. Soc. Qd* **73**: 79–92.

Lear, R. and Turner, T., 1977. Mangroves of Australia. University of Queensland Press: St Lucia.

MacGillivary, W. D. K. and Rodway, F. A., 1931. Plants on islands of the Bunker and Capricorn Groups. *Repts Great Barrier Reef Comm.* **3**: 58–63.

Merrill, E. D., 1945. Plant Life of the Pacific World. Macmillan: New York.

Stoddart, D. R. and Fosberg, F. R., 1991. Phytogeography and vegetation of the reef islands of the northern Great Barrier Reef. *Atoll. Res. Bull.* **349**: 1–20.

Walker, T. A., 1991a. *Pisonia* islands of the Great Barrier Reef, part 1. The distribution abundance and dispersal by seabirds of *Pisonia grandis*. *Atoll Res. Bull.* **350**: 1–23.

Walker, T. A., 1991b. *Pisonia* islands of the Great Barrier Reef, part 3. Changes in the vascular flora of Lady Musgrave Island. *Atoll Res. Bull.* **350**: 24–30.

Walker, T. A., Chaloupka, M. Y. and King, B. R., 1991. *Pisonia* islands of the Great Barrier Reef, part 2. The vascular floras of Bushy and Redbill Islands. *Atoll Res. Bull.* **350**: 31–42.

White, C. J. and MacGillivary, W. D. K., 1926. The biology of North West Island, Capricorn Group. (H). Botany. *Aust. Zoologist* **4**: 251–52.

MARITIME ARCHAEOLOGY

Further Reading

Beaglehole, J. C. (ed), 1968. The Journals of Captain James Cook on his voyages of discovery, 3 volumes. Cambridge University Press. Vol. 1 — The Voyage of the Endeavour (1768–71).

Flinders, Matthew, 1814. A voyage to Terra Australis (. . .) in the years 1801–03 in *HMS Investigator*, 2 volumes. London.

Gesner, P., 1991. Pandora: an archaeological perspective. Queensland Museum: Brisbane.

Gill, J. C. H., 1988. The Missing Coast: Queensland takes shape. Queensland Museum: Brisbane.

Henderson, G., 1986. Maritime Archaeology in Australia. University of Western Australia Press: Perth.

UNESCO, 1981. Protection of the underwater heritage. No. 4 Technical handbooks for Museums series. UNESCO: Paris.

References

King, Philip Parker, 1827. A narrative of a survey of the inter-tropical and western coasts of Australia (. . .) 1818 and 1822. Murray: London.

King, Philip Parker, 1833. Australian navigation. *Nautical Magazine* **3**: 433–36.

King, Philip Parker, 1834. A description of the northeast coast of Australia. *Nautical Magazine* **4**: 132–36.

Beaglehole, J. C. (ed), 1968. The Endeavour Journals of Joseph Banks 1768–71. Angus and Roberston: Sydney.

MacGillivray, J., 1852. Narrative of the voyage of *HMS Rattlesnake* (. . .) 1846–50. London.

Pacific Manuscripts Bureau, Research School for Pacific Studies, PMB Reel 377. Australian National University: Canberra.

Australian Joint Copying Project, AJCP Reel M714. National Library: Canberra.

Craig, R., 1964. The African Guano Trade. *Mariners' Mirror* **50**(1): 25–53.

Morrell, B., 1844. Narrative of a Guano voyage. *Nautical Magazine* **13**: 357–62.

Robinson, J. W., 1865–66. Journal kept at Lady Elliot Island 1865–66. (W. L. Crowther Library, State Library of Tasmania: Hobart).

General and Taxonomic*
Index

(*genus level and above)

259